W9-BFW-282

Apocalyptic Literature

APOCALYPTIC LITERATURE

A READER

MITCHELL G. REDDISH

EDITOR

Regis College Library
15 ST. MARY STREET
TORONTO, ONTARIO, CANADA
M4Y 2R5

BS
646
A635
1995

HENDRICKSON
PUBLISHERS

APOCALYPTIC LITERATURE: A READER
Edited by Mitchell G. Reddish

© 1990 by Abingdon Press, assigned 1995 to Mitchell G. Reddish.
Assigned 1995 to Hendrickson Publishers, Inc.
All rights reserved.

Hendrickson Publishers, Inc.
P. O. Box 3473
Peabody, Massachusetts 01961-3473

ISBN 1-56563-210-9

Third printing — January 2003

Printed in the United States of America

To Barbara
and our children
Tim, Beth, and Michael

ACKNOWLEDGMENTS

Grateful acknowledgment is made for permission to use the following copyrighted material:

1 Enoch, translated by M. A. Knibb; the *Syriac Apocalypse of Baruch,* translated by R. H. Charles, revised by L. H. Brockington; the *Testament of Abraham,* translated by N. Turner; the *Testament of Levi* (which is a section of the *Testaments of the Twelve Patriarchs*), translated by M. de Jonge; the *Assumption of Moses,* translated by R. H. Charles, revised by J. P. M. Sweet; all copyright © 1984 by Oxford University Press. Reprinted from *The Apocryphal Old Testament,* edited by H. F. D. Sparks (1984).

2 Esdras, from the Revised Standard Version Bible, copyright 1946, 1952, 1971 by the Division of Christian Education of the National Council of the Churches of Christ in the USA.

The *War Rule* 1, 15–19; the *Community Rule* 3–4, and the *New Jerusalem,* from *The Dead Sea Scrolls in English* by G. Vermes (Penguin Books, 1962, 1965, 1968, 1975, 1987), copyright © G. Vermes, 1962, 1965, 1968, 1975, 1987.

The *Apocalypse of Peter,* translated by H. Duensing; the *Apocalypse of Paul,* translated by H. Deunsing; the *Apocalypse of Thomas,* translated by A. de Santos Otero; all reprinted from *New Testament Apocrypha,* volume 2, edited by Wilhelm Schneemelcher and Edgar Hennecke, English translation edited by R. McL. Wilson. Used by permission of Westminster John Knox Press. Copyright © 1964 J. C. B. Mohr (Paul Siebeck), Tübingen. English translation © 1965 Lutterworth Press.

Selections from the *Shepherd of Hermas* reprinted by permission of the publishers and the Loeb Classical Library from *The Apostolic Fathers,* volume 2, translated by Kirsopp Lake. Cambridge, Mass.: Harvard University Press, 1913.

The (*First*) *Apocalypse of James,* translated by William R. Schoedel, edited by Douglas M. Parrott; and the (*Gnostic*) *Apocalypse of Paul,* translated by George W. MacRae and William R. Murdock, edited by Douglas M. Parrott, from *The Nag Hammadi Library* by James M. Robinson, General Editor. Copyright © 1978, 1988 by E. J. Brill. Reprinted by permission of Harper & Row, Publishers, Inc. and E. J. Brill.

Sibylline Oracles 2:34–55; 149–347, translated by John J. Collins, from *The Old Testament Pseudepigrapha,* volume 1, edited by James H. Charlesworth. Copyright © 1983 by James H. Charlesworth. Reprinted by permission of Doubleday, a division of Bantam, Doubleday, Dell Publishing Group, Inc.

The *Ascension of Isaiah* 6–11, translated by M. A. Knibb, from *The Old Testament Pseudepigrapha,* volume 2, edited by James H. Charlesworth. Copyright © 1985 by James H. Charlesworth. Reprinted by permission of Doubleday, a division of Bantam, Doubleday, Dell Publishing Group, Inc.

CONTENTS

FOREWORD

Apocalyptic literature has received considerable scholarly attention in recent years, both for its inherent interest and for its importance in the formation of Christianity. Nonetheless this literature remains strange and forbidding not only to students but also to many scholars who specialize in other areas. A major reason for this has been the lack of a collection of texts that is suitable for classroom use. Mitchell Reddish's anthology is designed to fill that lack.

The virtues of Reddish's volume may be appreciated by comparison with the best collection of Jewish apocalyptic texts now available, *The Old Testament Pseudepigrapha*, volume 1, *Apocalyptic Literature and Testaments*, edited by J. H. Charlesworth. The two books are quite different in purpose. Charlesworth's volume is by far the more scholarly; its translations are annotated, and its introductions are more detailed. Reddish's anthology does not attempt to compete with it on any of these grounds. Precisely because of its scholarly virtues, however, Charlesworth's volume is often too ponderous for classroom use. Reddish's selection limits the corpus to a range that can be covered in an undergraduate course. Charlesworth's edition will remain indispensable for the scholar and specialized student, but Reddish's presentation is surely more accessible to the nonspecialist.

In addition to the practical advantage of its limitation, Reddish's anthology has three major virtues that should be emphasized.

First, it is organized in a way that brings order to a body of literature that is often perceived as chaotic. I admit to being partial to the typology

11

followed here, but the advantages of some such division of the material cannot be denied. Apocalyptic literature has too often been treated as an undifferentiated whole. The division into types allows the reader to perceive the different texts more clearly.

Second, while the collection of Jewish apocalypses is not nearly as complete as that of Charlesworth, Reddish's book has the advantage of including a sample of Qumran texts in the same volume. These texts were quite properly omitted from Charlesworth's collection of pseudepigrapha, but they are of immediate relevance for Jewish apocalypticism, and no one who teaches a course on the subject can afford to omit them.

Finally, this is the first anthology that brings together Jewish and Christian apocalypses in a single book. It is not unusual to read in textbooks that apocalyptic literature died out after the first century C.E. This common assertion is simply not true. The genre flourished in Christian circles down to the Middle Ages. Anthologies often shape our perception of a field. If Reddish's anthology makes students of apocalypticism aware of the extent and importance of the Christian apocalypses, it will have made a significant contribution to scholarship.

John J. Collins

PREFACE

This anthology arose out of the need for an affordable, one-volume reader that would contain a wide sampling of both Jewish and Christian apocalyptic texts. Several excellent collections devoted to either Jewish or Christian writings are available. Unfortunately, none of these contains both Jewish and Christian works. *Apocalyptic Literature: A Reader* is designed to make accessible to the interested student a representative sampling of Jewish and early Christian apocalyptic literature, along with brief introductions to each work that will help the reader situate the work in its historical and literary contexts and give the reader an overview of the contents of the work. This anthology is designed for the non-specialist. The introductions, therefore, avoid detailed, technical discussions and critical analyses of the texts and translations. Furthermore, the texts themselves are not, for the most part, annotated. The reader who is interested in more detailed studies of introductory issues related to the works, or who has questions about variant readings, manuscript traditions, or translation decisions related to the texts included here, is encouraged to examine the more comprehensive studies of these documents listed in the bibliography at the end of the book.

This work is not intended to be a complete collection of Jewish and early Christian apocalyptic writings. It is a representative sampling. Several other texts easily could have been included. The goal in choosing specific texts was to include the best-known, most interesting, and most influential writings. In many cases, the selection of writings was easy. No collection of Jewish apocalyptic literature could justifiably omit *1 Enoch* or 4 Ezra. Likewise, no Christian collection could justifiably omit the *Apocalypse of Peter* or the *Apocalypse of Paul.* In other cases, however, the choice was more difficult. Certainly some individuals may, for various reasons, prefer the inclusion of other texts. I believe the works included here will provide the best introduction to apocalyptic literature for the general reader.

The paradigm for the selection and arrangement of texts is that developed by the Society of Biblical Literature's Genres Project, which was published in *Semeia* 14 (1979). This model was chosen because it uses clearly defined, easy to understand criteria for identifying the apocalyptic genre and for grouping the texts into two major categories: apocalypses that contain otherworldly journeys and those that contain no otherworldly journeys. To present a balanced understanding of apocalyptic literature, this anthology contains examples of both Jewish and Christian apocalypses from each of these two major categories. The apocalypses that are included are those whose classification has substantial scholarly support.

Examples of writings that have major similarities to apocalyptic literature but cannot be categorized strictly as apocalypses are also included. These writings were included to demonstrate that apocalyptic ideas were often conveyed in a literary genre other than that of an apocalypse. Furthermore, placing such texts alongside true apocalypses will help students to understand the distinctive elements of the genre better.

This collection is limited to Jewish and early Christian noncanonical literature. The restriction of the contents to noncanonical literature was solely on the basis of space limitations. It would have been helpful to have included at least Daniel from the Hebrew Bible and Revelation from the New Testament as examples of apocalypses, as well as Mark 13 and other passages as examples of related texts. They are readily accessible elsewhere, however. Limiting the volume to Jewish and early Christian literature is due again to space considerations. For this reason, Greco-Roman and Persian apocalypses and related texts are not included.

For most of the selections included here, translators' footnotes have been omitted. In a few cases, however, footnotes have been included when it was felt that the information contained in them was necessary for a proper reading of the texts. In all cases, the annotations are those of the translators. Where appropriate, textual signs have been added to the texts to correspond to the information in the footnotes.

By making these apocalyptic writings more accessible to the general reader, it is hoped that more people will gain an appreciation for the contributions these writings have made in the history of Judaism and Christianity and will understand better the continuing influence of their ideas on modern society. Even more important, it is hoped that the reader will come to appreciate these writings on their own merits, as expressions of individuals and groups who struggled to find meaning and hope in an often confusing world.

Sincere thanks are due several people who helped make this work possible: Rex Matthews, Senior Academic Editor at Abingdon Press, who patiently guided and encouraged the production of this book; Professor John J. Collins, who graciously read the manuscript and made several insightful suggestions; my colleagues in the Department of Religion at Stetson University, who continually provide emotional and intellectual support and encouragement and who have endured my fascination with apocalypticism; Clyde Fant, in particular, also one of my colleagues in the Department of Religion, who read all the introductions to the texts and helped hone my writing skills and whose irreverent and humorous marginal glosses enlivened the production of this project; Stetson University, for providing special funds for research and typing; Savilla Beasley, who carefully typed the texts; and most of all my family, to whom this work is dedicated, who patiently allowed me to devote time that belonged to them to the completion of this project.

TEXTUAL SIGNS

In translating ancient documents, scholars sometimes are faced with passages that are difficult to translate because the text has been damaged, is in fragments, or has been altered. In those situations, translators must attempt to reconstruct the original wording of a text. The signs below have been devised to indicate to the reader when there are problems in a text underlying a particular translation, or when words have been added to make a text more understandable in translation. (Texts included in this anthology that used other signs have been modified to conform to the signs given here.)

[ ]   indicates letters or words that have been restored to the text on the basis of the translator's or editor's conjecture of what was originally in the text.

⟨ ⟩   indicates a translator's or editor's correction of an apparently erroneous text.

{ }   indicates material that the translator or editor believes is erroneous or superfluous and should be omitted.

( )   indicates material that has been added by the translator or editor in order to clarify the meaning of a text or to make the text read more smoothly.

(?)   indicates that the translation or meaning is uncertain due to a fragmentary or corrupt text.

. . .   indicates that a portion of the text is missing.

17

INTRODUCTION

The terms *apocalypse* and *apocalyptic* have become standard parts of the vocabulary of modern society. Politicians warn of a nuclear apocalypse. Ecologists describe the apocalyptic effects of pollution, acid rain, and abuse of the environment. *Apocalypse Now* was the title of a movie that depicted the chaos and insanity of the Vietnam War. So commonplace have the terms become that when strong winds fanned a brush fire into a raging inferno in a Los Angeles suburb, one observer described the scene as "just like hell, like an apocalypse." Although apocalyptic terminology has become widely used, most people are unfamiliar with the literature from which the terms and the ideas originated. The best way to understand the meaning of apocalyptic terms, ideas, and motifs is to study apocalyptic literature itself.

What Is Apocalyptic Literature?

The term *apocalyptic* has been used to describe a broad range of ideas, motifs, and literature that have varying degrees of similarity. In an attempt to bring about precision and clarity, scholars often distinguish among apocalyptic eschatology, apocalypse, and apocalypticism. The words *apocalypse, apocalyptic,* and *apocalypticism* are all derived from the Greek word *apokalypsis,* which means "revelation." Apocalyptic eschatology refers to a particular view of God's activity in the future. The term *eschatology* literally means "teachings about the last things"—that is, beliefs about how God will bring about God's ultimate purpose for the universe.

19

Eschatological beliefs can be found in the prophetic writings of the Hebrew Bible, but their eschatology is not apocalyptic. Prophetic eschatology envisioned God accomplishing divine plans within the context of human history and by means of human agents. God acted within political events and through world leaders. The prophets proclaimed that one day God would establish Jerusalem as a world center with a Davidic king on the throne of Israel. Israel's enemies would be defeated, the faithful would be rewarded, and the wicked would be punished. All of these events would occur on earth, within the normal bounds of history, brought about by God through human means.

Prophetic eschatology began to give way to apocalyptic eschatology, however, as the people of Israel began to lose confidence in such events occurring within history. Hope was shifted from this world and this age to another world and another age. God would not employ ordinary means but supernatural forces to bring about the divine plan. Apocalyptic eschatology, then, finds hope primarily in the future. This hope may take the form of God's bringing an end to this wicked world. A new world is created (or the present one is transformed); a new age begins. On the other hand, at times apocalyptic eschatology may not be concerned with destruction of the world but retribution after death. The righteous are rewarded and the wicked punished in the next life. In both types of apocalyptic eschatology, however, hope and retribution occur outside the bounds of normal human experience. In Judaism, the shift from prophetic to apocalyptic eschatology was a gradual process. The historical and social conditions of the post-exilic period of Israel's history seem to have been important factors in the development of their apocalyptic eschatology.

The term *apocalypse* refers to a particular literary genre. Although all scholars do not agree on the precise characteristics of an apocalypse, a useful definition has been proposed by John J. Collins and other members of the Apocalypse Group of the Society of Biblical Literature's Genres Project. Their definition of an apocalypse states:

> "Apocalypse" is a genre of revelatory literature with a narrative framework, in which a revelation is mediated by an otherworldly being to a human recipient, disclosing a transcendent reality which is both temporal, insofar as it envisages eschatological salvation, and spatial insofar as it involves another, supernatural world.[1]

Since this definition has been adopted in this anthology and has provided the criteria for the selection and arrangement of the included texts, several elements of this definition should be elaborated. First, an apocalypse is revelatory literature—that is, the author claims to have received a divine revelation. This revelation is usually in the form of a dream or vision and is mediated by or interpreted by an angel.

Second, the human recipient of the revelation is normally presented as a famous hero of the past (Abraham, Enoch, Daniel, Ezra, Adam, Elijah). In actuality, the author is a much later individual who writes pseudonymously—that is, in the name of some venerable figure from the past. The technique of pseudonymity was used to lend authority to the writing, to suggest that the work was not of recent origin but came from a respected figure of ancient time.

Third, the content of apocalypses involves both horizontal and vertical (or temporal and spatial) dimensions. The horizontal dimension is the interest in salvation beyond human history. This usually involves divine judgment in the afterlife, followed by rewards or punishments. The vertical, or spatial, dimension is seen in the descriptions of otherworldly beings and otherworldly places: angels and demons, places of eternal reward and punishment (for example, heaven and hell), and the abode of God.

Apocalypses also can be divided into two major categories: those that contain an otherworldly journey and those that contain no otherworldly journey. In the first category, the author describes an experience of being taken on a tour of otherworldly regions—heaven, hell, Sheol, the outer boundaries of the earth. Vivid descriptions are given of what the author has seen. Of particular interest to these writers are descriptions of the abode of the dead, the places of eternal reward and punishment, the pain and torture inflicted upon the wicked, the dwelling place of God, and the locations of the stars, planets, and other heavenly bodies. Some of these apocalypses focus on the heavenly ascent of the author, describing in detail the ascent through the various levels of the heavens and the contents of each heavenly realm. This interest in the fixed series of heavens, and the concern over the order and regularity of the heavenly bodies found in some texts, served a practical purpose. The order and stability of the universe was a sign that God had all things under control. In spite of how events might appear to those on earth, who were living in the midst of chaos, destruction, and confusion, the universe was not out of control. God had predetermined the nature of the universe and the course of world history. At the appropriate time—which was very soon—God would bring history to a climax, and the rewards and punishments seen by the writer would become reality.

Apocalypses of the second type contain no journeys to otherworldly regions. Instead, revelation is given to the apocalyptist in a dream or vision or is disclosed by means of an angel who appears and converses with the recipient of the revelation. Even in those cases in which revelation comes by means of a dream or vision, an angelic figure usually appears to serve as an interpreter of the revelation. Apocalypses that contain no otherworldly journeys normally stress the temporal elements more than the spatial, and therefore a major concern is eschatological predictions. Especially important are signs of the endtime that are revealed to the author. Individuals who are observant of these signs are able to detect that the end is near and that the present course of the world, in which history is dominated by evil, is drawing to a close. Signs of the dying of this age can be seen in events in nature (earthquakes; famines; disturbances among the sun, moon, and stars; unnatural births; destruction by fires) and among humanity (wars, rampant evil, violence).

Another frequent type of eschatological prediction involves descriptions of the final judgment. The last judgment is the great day of reckoning, the time when all will be judged according to their deeds—individuals, nations, angels, and demons. The wrongs of the world will be corrected, evil will be punished, and righteousness will be rewarded. This eschatological judgment will be God's final act of retribution and justice. The true nature of reality will then become evident. Whereas throughout world history evil and wickedness might have appeared dominant and superior, now that is seen as only false appearance. In reality, God and God's ways of justice and righteousness ultimately prevail, and the last judgment is proof of that reality. Descriptions of eternal rewards and punishments frequently accompany scenes of the last judgment.

A characteristic of many of these apocalypses without an otherworldly journey is an interest in the events of history. Major events of the past are recounted. Often this takes the form of *ex eventu* prophecy, or prophecy "after the fact." This technique coincides with the literary device of pseudonymous authorship, in which the author claims to be some renowned figure from the past. Appearing to write from the perspective of the ancient past (although actually writing from a much later time), the apocalyptist "predicts" major events of world history, particularly events involving the Jewish people. The writers sometime describe history as being divided into predetermined periods. The present age is usually located in one of the final periods of history, and the history of the world is about to draw to a close. Along with or instead of this periodization of history, some of the *ex eventu* prophecies "foretell" the emergence and downfall of various kings and kingdoms of the world.

The use of *ex eventu* prophecy served at least two purposes for the apocalyptic writer. First, the use of these fulfilled "prophecies" enhanced the credibility and authority of the writer: If the venerable figure from the past had been correct in all these "predictions," readers reasoned that the person must be correct when foretelling events yet to come. Second, *ex eventu* prophecies engendered hope and assurance for persecuted and oppressed individuals. By describing what was to come, the apocalyptist reinforced the idea of history as being determined and ordered. The apocalyptist was able to describe these events only because God had determined them in advance. History, therefore, like individuals, must ultimately bow to God's designs. Furthermore, showing that the present period of world history is one of the last periods affirmed that the end was imminent. Suffering and oppression would not have to be endured much longer. The faithful must persist only a short while more, then God would intervene and eschatological salvation would ensue.

All writings that contain apocalyptic ideas should not be classified as apocalypses, however. An apocalypse is a particular literary genre, exhibiting the characteristics discussed above. A writer may choose to convey apocalyptic notions (divine intervention, eschatological judgment, otherworldly conflicts), but opt to do so using some other literary form—oracles, testaments, letters, parables. The parables of Jesus are a good example of writings that contain apocalyptic ideas, but are not apocalypses. Their literary form is the parable. Their contents are often apocalyptic, but their form is not. In this anthology, several examples of texts that are not apocalypses but are related to them have been included.

The final term that needs to be defined is *apocalypticism*. Apocalypticism is a pattern of thought or a world view dominated by the kinds of ideas and motifs found in apocalypses—emphasis on other worlds (heaven, hell, the abode of the dead) and otherworldly beings (God, Satan, angels, demons), supernatural intervention in world events, apocalyptic eschatology, and divine retribution beyond death. Certain historical movements can be designated as apocalyptic movements when apocalypticism provides the means by which their adherents view reality. Apocalypticism is usually very dualistic—earthly realities versus heavenly realities, this age versus the age to come, God versus Satan (or whatever name is given to the leader of the forces of evil), angels versus demons, righteous individuals versus wicked individuals. The entire universe is caught up in a conflict between good and evil. Events in heaven are mirrored on earth, and earthly struggles are manifestations of the battle between God and evil throughout the cosmos. The righteous understand their present difficulties in terms of this cosmic conflict—that is, they are not fighting human evil only, but are locked in a battle with evil that has cosmic proportions. Adherents to apocalypticism see the world in opposing terms: One belongs either to the righteous or to the wicked; there is no room for compromise.

The group of Jewish individuals who lived at Qumran and produced the Dead Sea Scrolls are usually considered apocalyptic because their writings demonstrate that their "symbolic universe"—that is, their way of understanding how the world functions—was built upon the ideas prevalent in apocalyptic literature. In the Qumran writings, history is seen as a battle between the Sons of Light and the Sons of Darkness. A final eschatological battle will occur when God will intervene through the angel Michael, the Prince of Light, and will defeat the forces of evil led by Belial, the Angel of Darkness. Through this supernatural intervention, God would deliver the righteous.

The Purpose of Apocalyptic Literature

Apocalyptic literature is crisis literature. These writings were produced during a time of perceived crisis to offer hope to oppressed and beleaguered individuals by giving them an alternative picture of reality. The crises faced by the people varied. In some instances, the crisis was military or political oppression (Daniel, Revelation); in other instances, it was a theological crisis (4 Ezra); in still other cases, the crisis was a sense of alienation brought about when one group felt cut off from the rest of society (the Qumran writings). The historical and sociological context of several of the apocalypses can no longer be determined. In many cases, however, apocalyptic writings do seem to be responses to some kind of crisis, either real or perceived. In reality, a crisis may not have existed. From the perspective of the apocalyptic writer, however, a crisis did exist. The reality of the crisis is not as important as the perception, because the authors wrote on the basis of their perception of the situation.

Critical studies of the book of Revelation have struggled with the

24

question of imperial persecution of the church during the latter years of the first century. Virtually no evidence exists in contemporary sources to support the idea of official persecution of the church. Yet, the author of the book of Revelation is greatly concerned about persecution, martyrdom, and steadfast witnesses. The resolution of this dilemma lies not so much in the reality of a massive persecution, but in the author's perception that such was the case. John of Patmos knew of at least a few instances of persecution and martyrdom. These provided the basis for his understanding of the situation. Whereas, objectively speaking, very little persecution may have existed, from the perspective of John and those who were feeling oppressed and threatened, imperial persecution seemed to be a reality. On the basis of this perception, John wrote to provide his readers a different way of viewing the situation, an alternative symbolic universe. The worldly reality seemed to be that God had lost control; Satan and Satan's forces had the upper hand. The Roman emperor as Satan's representative held all power. What John did through his apocalypse was to give his readers a different way of understanding their situation, an eschatological view of current events. Beyond the appearance was the reality that God was bringing order out of the chaos of the universe. Satan and his cohorts, especially the Roman emperor, would be defeated by the heavenly armies. God would be victorious. This divine victory extended to God's people, too. Those who remained faithful would share in God's new kingdom.

One of the functions of many apocalypses, such as Revelation, was to offer hope and comfort to the faithful by means of an alternative vision. They were encouraged to endure their situations, being assured that ultimately God would triumph. The current social or political situations were relativized because they were shown to be only temporary. God would soon bring about a change, another world in which the righteous are not the alienated ones but the rewarded ones.

Apocalyptic literature also functioned as a form of protest against society. It was resistance literature, whether the "enemy" was political, military, social, or theological. Protest and resistance can take many forms. Passive resistance involves a refusal to comply with the demands of the ruling authorities in a non-confrontational manner. One resists quietly and unobtrusively, attempting to avoid detection and confrontation. Active resistance could take either of two forms. Resistance may be violent, armed resistance, as is the case in violent revolutions and class conflicts. Apocalyptic writings do not seem to be intended to foster this kind of resistance. The outlook of apocalyptic writers generally is that the course of world events has already been determined by God and will be brought to completion by God. Human efforts to change God's designs are futile. A second form of active resistance is nonviolent in nature. One openly confronts the ruling forces and challenges their authority and their world view. Martyrdom is the extreme example of this kind of protest. Martyrs refuse to accept the world view of their oppressors. They claim allegiance to a higher authority. Their valiant actions are a challenge to the understanding of reality presented by their persecutors. The apocalyptists serve as another example of this kind of protest. They, too, challenge the dominant society's understanding of reality. They present another view of the world by telling their readers that true power and authority in the world belong to God. All human institutions and rulers are flawed; God alone is the ruling power. Through their visions of another world and a higher reality, apocalyptists challenge and confront the present systems. They resist the claims of tyrannical rulers, unjust systems, and inadequate world views. Through their writings, they challenge others to resist also.

Apocalyptic thought has at times been criticized for its "pie-in-the-sky-by-and-by" attitude. Critics have accused apocalyptic writers of encouraging people to focus only on the world to come with the result that the present world, with its social and political ills, is ignored. Apocalyptic ideas, they claim, lull people into accepting life as it is now by offering them hope for the afterlife. This is an unfair critique of apocalyptic writings, however. Properly understood, these writings are a challenge to the established order of things, not an endorsement or even an acceptance of them. Apocalyptic literature calls upon its readers to resist the charms and delusions of the present world, to look beyond them and see a better world, to realize the ultimate authority in the world. The vision of the world as God intends it should serve as a catalyst for resistance and change, not a sedative to encourage hopeless acceptance of the current situation.

Apocalyptic literature is dangerous for the established order. Rather than being understood as fostering an escapist mentality, apocalyptic literature should be understood as protest literature. The apocalyptic writers spoke out against a world of evil, violence, oppression, and injustice. They provided visions of a better world, a world of peace and justice. They called for allegiance to a higher authority, not to human institutions, but to God. True, the idea held by the apocalyptists that history was in God's hands and that human effort could do little to change it prevented them from sounding calls for political and social revolt. Yet, their writings were still a form of protest, of refusing to accept the present social and historical reality. The transcendent future that had been revealed to them would not allow them to settle for the status quo, but beckoned them to a new world. Through their literary works, they challenged others to follow that vision also.

Apocalyptic literature functions, then, not only to offer comfort and consolation, but also to register a strong word of protest. Both aspects are important and should not be separated. If only comfort and hope are emphasized, there is the danger that apocalyptic literature will be misused to encourage individuals to ignore their social and political responsibilities by living only for the future. On the other hand, if only the protest element is stressed, the risk is great that the transcendent perspective of apocalyptic literature will be lost. The new world of the apocalyptists is not a human construct brought into being solely through human efforts. Most important, it is God's new world, God's new creation, brought into reality through divine means.

Apocalyptic literature should function in this dual capacity—by consoling and challenging, by offering comfort and demanding protest. Through the centuries, it has largely functioned in that way. The book of Daniel provided hope and protest during the second century B.C.E., when Antiochus Epiphanes persecuted the Jews of Palestine. The *Testament of Abraham* did not challenge a human enemy, but the fear of death. It offered its readers comfort and hope in the face of death, the enemy of all humanity. The apocalyptic writings from Qumran provided a different understanding of the religious and social order of Palestine for those sectarian Jews who opposed the current practices of the high priest and Temple worship. The book of Revelation, with its protests against the beast of the Roman Empire and its visions of a new world, gave meaning to the struggles of the faithful and held out hope for a different reality.

The Prevalence of Apocalyptic Literature

The Hebrew Bible contains only one apocalypse: the book of Daniel. Other apocalypses were produced within Judaism, but none of these writings was eventually accepted as canonical. The book of Daniel exhibits the apocalyptic characteristics of pseudonymity and *ex eventu* prophecy. Although the story is set during the time of the Babylonian exile of the people of Judah (sixth century B.C.E.), the work was actually written around 165 B.C.E. when Antiochus Epiphanes, king of Syria and

27

ruler of Palestine, was persecuting the Jewish people. The book is composed of two sections: chapters 1–6 and chapters 7–12.

The first section consists of several tales about Daniel and his friends, who are in exile in Babylon. Persecuted because of their faith, the young men remain true to God, who helps them in their times of distress. These stories, which were likely ancient tales of heroic faithfulness, were used by the author of Daniel to foster hope and encouragement among his readers, who were faced with a similar threat to their faith, the threat of Antiochus Epiphanes.

The second section of Daniel, chapters 7–12, is the apocalyptic section of the work. This section contains four visions that Daniel receives. Cast in the form of *ex eventu* prophecies, these visions reveal the course of world history, culminating in the defeat of Antiochus Epiphanes and the establishment of God's eschatological kingdom. Through these visions, the author of Daniel was reminding the Jewish people that even someone as wicked as Antiochus would eventually be defeated by God. Therefore, they were not to give up hope, but were to remain faithful to God.

Among non-biblical Jewish writings, fourteen works qualify as apocalypses. These writings were produced from the third century B.C.E. to the second century C.E. Some arose in Palestine, others from Diaspora Judaism. The dates given below are, in many cases, only approximate. Other ancient Jewish writings contain the word *apocalypse* in their titles, but do not qualify as apocalypses according to the definition of that term cited above.

Jewish Apocalypses[2]

1. The "Book of the Watchers" (*1 Enoch* 1–36)—3rd century B.C.E.
2. The "Book of the Heavenly Luminaries" (*1 Enoch* 73–82)—3rd century B.C.E.
3. The "Animal Apocalypse" (*1 Enoch* 85–90)—2nd century B.C.E.
4. The "Apocalypse of Weeks" (*1 Enoch* 93:1-10; 91:11-17)—2nd century B.C.E.
5. *Jubilees* 23—2nd century B.C.E.
6. The *Testament of Levi* 2–5—2nd century B.C.E.
7. The *Testament of Abraham*—1st century B.C.E.—2nd century C.E.
8. The *Apocalypse of Zephaniah*—1st century B.C.E.-1st century C.E.
9. The "Similitudes of Enoch" (*1 Enoch* 37–71)—1st century C.E.
10. *2 Enoch*—1st century C.E.
11. 4 Ezra—1st century C.E.
12. *2 Baruch*—1st century C.E.

13. The *Apocalypse of Abraham*—1st–2nd century c.e.
14. *3 Baruch*—1st–2nd century c.e.

In addition to these writings, which fit the formal definition of an apocalypse given above, several other writings contain major apocalyptic elements. In the Hebrew Bible, certain passages have been noted for their apocalyptic or "proto-apocalyptic" nature. Chapters 40–48 of Ezekiel exhibit a kinship to later apocalypses in their extensive use of visions in which an angelic figure serves as a guide and interpreter for Ezekiel. Zechariah 1–6 also uses this visionary form. Additionally, these visions in Zechariah are highly symbolic, also a characteristic of later apocalypses.

Other passages in the Hebrew Bible, while not presented as apocalyptic visions, exhibit a movement from prophetic eschatology to apocalyptic eschatology. Zechariah 9–14 speaks of the defeat of Israel's enemies and the coming of a new king. The descriptions of the coming of the final battle and God's universal reign have more in common with the visions of the apocalyptists than with the pronouncements of the prophets. In a similar way, chapters 38–39 of Ezekiel describe a cataclysmic conflict between Israel and Gog of Magog. In the book of Joel, the almost exclusive orientation to the future, and particularly the listing of the signs that will precede the day of the Lord, are major concerns of later apocalyptists. Strictly speaking, Isaiah 24–27, often called the Apocalypse of Isaiah, is not an apocalypse. It lacks the visionary form and angelic mediators common to the genre. The contents of these chapters, however, are similar to the eschatological pronouncements of Jewish apocalypses in that they contain ideas of universal judgment, an eschatological banquet, and destruction of God's enemies. These passages (as well as others that have been noted by various scholars) probably should be seen as reflecting the beginning stages of apocalyptic literature in Israel. They provide the bridge between prophetic and apocalyptic thought.

Just as apocalypses are not limited to the Hebrew canon, so also related writings that contain apocalyptic elements can be found outside the Hebrew Bible. Examples of such related writings are certain texts from the collection of materials discovered at Qumran near the Dead Sea (for example, the *War Scroll*, the *Rule of the Community*, the *New Jerusalem*, some of the *Thanksgiving Hymns*, the *Testament of Moses*, the *Testament of the Twelve Patriarchs*, the *Testament of Job*, and some of the *Sibylline Oracles*).

29

Turning to early Christianity, one finds only one apocalypse in the New Testament: the book of Revelation. The book of Revelation opens with the Greek word *apokalypsis,* meaning "revelation." Some scholars have questioned the classification of Revelation as an apocalypse since the work also claims to be a prophecy (1:3; 22:19) and in some ways adheres to the form of a letter (see 1:4-9, 22:21). Furthermore, the work does not adopt the common apocalyptic technique of pseudonymity. "John" is apparently the real name of the author. Nevertheless the work does fit the definition of an apocalypse. The major focus of the work is revelation, which occurs through visionary experiences. The content of the revelation includes both personal and cosmic eschatology and exhibits considerable interest in otherworldly beings and places. Written during the last decade of the first century c.e., the book of Revelation issues a challenge to its readers to resist the claims of emperor worship (see chap. 13) and to remain faithful witnesses for God, even if the price of such faithfulness is martyrdom. By describing the eventual destruction of Rome and the other forces of evil and by assuring the readers of eschatological rewards for the faithful, the author offered hope and encouragement to Christians who were being persecuted (or at least perceived the possibility of persecution). Warnings against false teachings and exhortations to ethical living are also concerns of the work, particularly in the letters to the seven churches in chapters 2 and 3.

Although Revelation is the only apocalypse in the New Testament, the apocalyptic world view is pervasive in the New Testament writings. The resurrection of Jesus is understood as an apocalyptic event. The title "Son of man" that is applied to Jesus in the Gospels is an apocalyptic phrase. Jesus' parables are mostly about the kingdom of God, again an apocalyptic notion. Eschatological judgment, resurrection, future rewards and punishments, destruction of the forces of evil, conflict between good and evil forces, angels and demons—all of these ideas in the New Testament are derived from an apocalyptic understanding of reality.

Several passages in the New Testament show strong apocalyptic influence. Mark 13 (and its parallels, Luke 21 and Matt. 24–25) is the best known example from the Gospels. This passage, sometimes called the "Little Apocalypse," contains several characteristics of apocalyptic thought: signs of the endtime; the intervention of an otherworldly, eschatological figure; ingathering of the elect; and a cataclysmic end of history. Much debate has raged among scholars concerning the historicity, source, and interpretation of this passage. Regardless of the answers to these questions, the passage certainly is apocalyptic in orientation. It falls short, however, of being an apocalypse because it lacks an otherworldly mediator of its revelation. Jesus of Nazareth, prior to his resurrection, is presented in the Gospels as an earthly, human figure.

Two passages from Paul's letters indicate his apocalyptic outlook also. In 1 Thessalonians 4:13–5:11, Paul deals with the Thessalonians' concern that fellow believers who have already died will not participate in the new kingdom. Paul presents an apocalyptic scenario in which Christ will descend to earth from heaven, deceased believers will be resurrected, and all Christians will then live forever in the new kingdom with Christ. Furthermore, he tells them that this coming of Christ will be sudden and unannounced. They are to live in anticipation and readiness for that eschatological event. Concerns about resurrection and the nature of the afterlife are also topics of discussion in 1 Corinthians. Some members of the church in Corinth were espousing inaccurate views of the resurrection. To correct these false teachings, Paul discusses the significance of Jesus' resurrection, the issue of bodily resurrection, and even presents a brief order of events of the endtime (1 Cor. 15).

In 2 Thessalonians 2:1-12, which is possibly pseudonymous and not actually from Paul, the author answers concerns that the end is near or has already begun by giving his readers an apocalyptic timetable of eschatological events. The end is not yet because all these events have not yet occurred. A final example from the New Testament is 2 Peter 3:1-13. The writer of this letter must deal with problems created by the delay of Christ's return. Scoffers were ridiculing the belief in his return, while the hope of believers was apparently diminishing. The writer reaffirms the coming of Christ, accompanied by a massive conflagration that will destroy the heavens and the earth as a prerequisite for new heavens and a new earth. Apocalyptic influences in the New Testament are by no means limited to these few passages. Apocalyptic eschatology and imagery permeate the entire corpus of the New Testament.

Noncanonical works provide further evidence of the influence of apocalyptic ideas on the early church. Several apocalypses were produced in the early centuries of the church. Some of these, while eventually being considered noncanonical, did exert tremendous influence over certain groups within Christianity. Some of the works listed below were originally Jewish writings, but were later extensively revised by Christian writers. In their present form, then, they are

Christian documents. The dates given are the approximate dates for the Christian versions of the works. These works are noncanonical apocalypses, likely produced in, or containing elements from, the early centuries of the common era. Many of these works were revised on several occasions. Because they often contain no internal clues, dating the works is extremely difficult. In many cases, the dates given are tentative. Gnostic Christian works are not included in this list.

Christian Apocalypses[3]

1. The *Shepherd of Hermas*—1st or 2nd century
2. The *Book of Elchasai*—2nd century
3. The *Ascension of Isaiah* 6–11—1st or 2nd century
4. The *Apocalypse of Peter*—2nd century
5. 5 Ezra 2:42-48—2nd century
6. *Jacob's Ladder*—2nd century?
7. The *Testament of the Lord* 1:1-14—3rd century?
8. The *Questions of Bartholomew*—3rd century?
9. The *Apocalypse of Sedrach*—2nd–4th century?
10. The *Apocalypse of Paul*—4th century
11. The *Testament of Isaac* 2–3a—1st–5th century?
12. The *Testament of Isaac* 5–6—1st–5th century?
13. The *Testament of Jacob* 1–3a—2nd–5th century?
14. The *Testament of Jacob* 2–5—2nd–5th century?
15. The *Story of Zosimus*—3rd–5th century
16. The *Apocalypse of St. John the Theologian*—2nd–9th century?
17. The *Book of the Resurrection of Jesus Christ by Bartholomew the Apostle* 8b–14a—3rd–6th century?
18. The *Book of the Resurrection of Jesus Christ by Bartholomew the Apostle* 17b–19b—3rd–6th century?
19. The *Apocalypse of the Virgin Mary*—4th–9th century?
20. The *Apocalypse of Esdras*—5th–9th century?
21. The *Apocalypse of the Holy Mother of God Concerning the Punishments*—4th–11th century?
22. The *Apocalypse of James, the Brother of the Lord*—pre-11th century
23. The *Mysteries of St. John the Apostle and Holy Virgin*—pre-11th century

Related works from early Christian writers that have been heavily influenced by apocalyptic ideas would include some of the *Sibylline Oracles* that were authored or expanded by Christian writers (books 1–2, 7, 8), the *Apocalypse of Elijah*, the *Apocalypse of Thomas*, 6 Ezra (2 Esdras 15–16), the *Testament of Adam*, the *Penitence of Adam*, Didache 16, the *Ascension of Isaiah* 3:13–4:18, and the *Apocalypse of John the Theologian Attributed to John Chrysostom*.

The Sources of Apocalyptic Thought

Apocalypticism is a complex phenomenon, yielding no easy answer to the question of its origins. Competent scholars have argued for various traditions as primary factors leading to the production of Jewish apocalyptic literature. Some have argued that Hebrew prophecy gave birth to apocalyptic thought. Others have suggested Israelite wisdom traditions as the major influence on the apocalyptists. Babylonian divination writings, Near Eastern (particularly Canaanite) mythology, and Egyptian literature have also been posited as major sources for Jewish apocalyptic thought. Another widely held view has explained apocalypses as borrowing heavily from the Persian religion of Zoroastrianism. Resurrection, dualism, periodization of history, and eschatological judgment followed by rewards and punishments can all be found in Zoroastrian writings. Nevertheless a major problem in viewing Jewish apocalyptic thought as depending on Persian religion is the uncertainty of dating the Persian material. Much of the Zoroastrian literature that presents the clearest similarities to Jewish apocalyptic thought comes from several centuries after the Jewish writings. Embedded within this late Persian literature, however, are earlier traditions, some of which likely predate Jewish apocalypticism and thus could have influenced it.

The best answer to the question of the origin of Jewish apocalyptic thought is to recognize that apocalypticism grew out of post-exilic prophecy within Israel, but was enriched by ideas and imagery borrowed, either directly or indirectly, from several traditions in the Hellenistic world. Persian, Babylonian, Egyptian, Greek, Roman, and Canaanite influences affected Jewish apocalypticism. In addition, other strands of Hebrew thought, such as wisdom traditions, contributed to the complex phenomenon that came to be known as Jewish apocalypticism. Later, Jewish apocalyptic thought itself was modified when Christianity, born out of a Judaism heavily enriched with apocalyptic ideas, adapted the form and the content of Jewish apocalyptic literature for the presentation of its own beliefs.

The Continuing Importance of Apocalyptic Literature

Through the years, apocalyptic literature has suffered in two ways. First, it has often been ignored because it is viewed as being irrelevant for modern society, is considered too difficult to understand, or is seen as the arena for religious fanatics or extremists. Among people who

33

have strong faith commitments to the books of the Bible, the books of Daniel and Revelation are seldom read. They are the outcasts among biblical literature, known for their bizarre imagery and enigmatic symbolism. Some enterprising individuals who decide to tackle these works in order that their biblical knowledge will be more complete often end up having their suspicions of these writings confirmed. They come away from their study more confused and more convinced that, indeed, these works should be ignored. This conviction is unfortunate, for as will be shown below, Daniel and Revelation are vital parts of the canon. These works, when properly understood, continue to offer words of hope and comfort in a chaotic world.

Even among theologians, apocalyptic literature has in the past been ignored. It was seen as an anomaly, a perversion, and was not thought to represent mainstream Jewish or Christian thought. The influence of apocalyptic thought on Judaism and Christianity was said to be minimal and, therefore, could be safely ignored, or at least given little attention. Fortunately, apocalypticism has been "rediscovered" in recent years. Its importance for an adequate understanding of the development of Judaism and Christianity is now an accepted position among scholars. The famous statement of Ernst Käsemann that apocalyptic was "the mother of Christian theology," (*New Testament Questions of Today*, trans. W. J. Montague [London: SCM Press, 1969]) although perhaps an exaggeration, underscores the importance of studying apocalyptic literature for those who seek a better understanding of Judaism and Christianity.

The second way that apocalyptic literature has suffered, in addition to being ignored, is that it has been abused by overzealous and misguided interpreters who misuse apocalyptic writings to support their erroneous viewpoints. The most flagrant examples of such abuse occur among those who turn the poetic visions of apocalyptic writers into literal blueprints of endtime events, often complete with timetables and charts, indicating in detail all that is to happen before the world comes to an end. This approach is certainly not new. History is strewn with examples of individuals who have been guilty of this kind of distortion of apocalyptic writings, from the twelfth-century mystic Joachim of Fiore to the nineteenth-century founder of Adventism, William Miller, to the twentieth-century popular writer of sensationalist "prophecies," Hal Lindsey (author of *The Late Great Planet Earth* and subsequent works).

Unfortunately, the approach taken by Hal Lindsey and others like him is often the only interpretation of apocalyptic literature known to the general public. Lindsey's premillennial dispensationalist theology (a complex belief system that originated with John Darby in the early 1800s and was popularized by the *Scofield Reference Bible*) expects a literal return of Jesus to earth to initiate a thousand-year earthly reign. At the conclusion of this messianic kingdom, God's final kingdom will be ushered in. Lindsey provides all the details about endtime events, describing the various cosmic and human catastrophes that will occur as well as the final judgments, punishments, and rewards. Comparing the situation of the modern world with apocalyptic descriptions in the Bible, Lindsey assures his readers that they are living in the last days. Present conditions are proof that the end is near. Faithful Christians need not worry, however, according to Lindsey. Before the "Great Tribulation" occurs, which will be a time of unfathomable terror on the wicked, the righteous will be snatched from the earth and carried to heaven during the "Rapture."

The fallacies of Lindsey's approach (and others of that nature) are too numerous to detail here. In general, however, two major problems exist with this approach to apocalyptic literature. First, this approach ignores the historical and social matrix out of which apocalyptic literature arose. Apocalyptic writers addressed the situation of their own time, attempting to offer hope and encouragement to their readers who were in distress. Lindsey's interpretation of apocalyptic writings, in which the works offer scenarios of the end that are unfolding in the modern world, turns them into cryptic writings that would have been incomprehensible, and thus meaningless, for their original audience. This misuse of apocalyptic writings, in addition to rendering them irrelevant for their original readers, is also extremely egotistical. All writings, according to this view, must have been specifically written for the modern reader.

A second problem with this approach is that it evidences no awareness of the nature and purpose of the apocalyptic genre. Lindsey reads apocalyptic literature the way one would read a front-page story in a newspaper. Apocalyptic literature, however, is not factual reporting. It is a special kind of literary work, filled with symbolism, figurative imagery, and ancient myths. It is more closely akin to poetry than to prose, more like an abstract painting than a photograph. These works need to be taken seriously, but not literally. In fact, to read them as literal, historical accounts is to distort rather than to elucidate their messages. All interpreters of the canonical books of Daniel and Revelation, including Hal Lindsey, would do well to familiarize themselves with other Jewish and early Christian apocalyptic writings.

By so doing, they would be less likely to misinterpret the canonical apocalypses.

If, as argued above, apocalyptic literature is occasional literature—that is, addressed to a particular situation in a particular time—does that mean that apocalyptic writings have no value for the modern reader? Certainly not. Apocalyptic literature is still important literature. From a nonreligious viewpoint, apocalyptic ideas and themes have been extremely influential throughout history. Their importance for an adequate understanding of first-century Judaism and early, as well as contemporary, Christianity is firmly established. In addition, artists, poets, novelists, and musicians have all borrowed images and motifs from apocalyptic literature. Pieter Bruegel, Hieronymous Bosch, Michelangelo, and Albrect Dürer are only a few of the many artists who have depicted apocalyptic scenes. Dante, John Milton, William Blake, T. S. Eliot, and the modern novelist Walker Percy are all indebted to apocalyptic thought. Olivier Messiaen's *Quartet for the End of Time*, Handel's *Messiah*, and even modern rock music utilize material drawn from apocalypticism. The titles of recent movies, such as *Apocalypse Now*, *Pale Rider*, and *The Seventh Sign* betray their indebtedness to apocalyptic thought. Since apocalyptic thought is such a significant part of Western culture, the more familiar one is with apocalyptic literature, the better equipped one will be to understand and critique that culture.

The reason why apocalyptic literature has had such a pervasive influence on society is that in spite of its ancient origin it has not lost its ability to communicate. Particularly for those people who value the religious dimension of apocalyptic literature, these writings continue to challenge and comfort. The eschatological visions of the apocalypses often serve as catalysts, motivating the people of God to work to make those visions of freedom, peace, justice, and reconciliation a reality. They serve as forceful reminders that the world as it is now is not the way it should be. Furthermore, apocalyptic literature challenges the people of God to confront the "beasts" of modern society, whatever form they may assume—political, economic, social, or religious. Any individual or institution that dehumanizes and oppresses the people of the world has taken on the role of the apocalyptic beasts.

Apocalyptic writings continue to offer hope also to people who feel overwhelmed by the world. The problems confronting the modern world are certainly enormous—overpopulation, environmental pollution and deterioration, threat of nuclear annihilation, global conflicts, crime, poverty, hunger. The apocalyptic writers invite their modern readers to look beyond the problems to the God who is still sovereign over the universe. They affirm that ultimately God will prevail.

In this way, apocalyptic literature is timeless. Rooted in the ancient past and addressed to ancient problems, it continues to speak to new generations with its message of hope and comfort and its challenge to remain faithful. No one situation ever exhausts the full meaning of apocalyptic images. They continue to be reapplied in new situations whenever the forces of evil seem overwhelming and hope recedes into the distance.

An example of the continuing vitality of apocalypticism is seen in a recent book by Allan A. Boesak, a South African minister and eloquent opponent of apartheid. In *Comfort and Protest*,[4] a commentary on the book of Revelation, Boesak demonstrates how the struggles and fears of John of Patmos have become a reality for blacks in South Africa today. They know what it is like to be alienated and persecuted, he says, and for some, even to suffer martyrdom. The beasts of the Apocalypse may have taken on new forms and new methods, but for Boesak the same beasts that John saw in Asia Minor have appeared now in South Africa. Boesak convincingly argues that John's apocalyptic vision is as appropriate for the twentieth-century South African as it was for the first-century resident of Asia Minor. Revelation offers hope by giving the oppressed a vision of another world, another day, when peace, love, and justice will dominate. Yet, Revelation speaks a word of protest also. John's vision proclaims that ultimate power and authority rest with God—not with Rome or Pretoria, not with the emperor or the president. To God alone belongs total allegiance. The people of God are called to resist governments that claim power that is not theirs, to resist economic and social systems that dehumanize and imprison people, to resist and challenge religious institutions that become the mouthpieces for propaganda rather than proclaimers of the total message of God. In this way, apocalyptic literature continues to function as an instrument of hope and protest.

The texts included in this anthology bear witness to the vitality and appeal of apocalyptic literature in the ancient world. Although none of these texts is considered canonical within Judaism or Christianity today, their influence has not vanished. The continued use of motifs, images, and ideas derived from them attests to the continuing power of apocalyptic thought to inspire, challenge, and encourage.

NOTES

1. John J. Collins, ed., *Apocalypse: The Morphology of a Genre, Semeia* 14 (1979): 9.
2. This list was compiled from the works classified as apocalypses in John J. Collins, "The Jewish Apocalypses" in Collins, *Apocalypse,* pp. 21-49.
3. This list was compiled from the works classified as apocalypses in Adela Yarbro Collins, "The Early Christian Apocalypses," in Collins, *Apocalypse,* pp. 61-105.
4. Allan A. Boesak, *Comfort and Protest: Reflections on the Apocalypse of John of Patmos* (Philadelphia: Westminster, 1987).

PART ONE

Jewish Apocalyptic Literature

CHAPTER ONE

APOCALYPSES THAT CONTAIN NO OTHERWORLDLY JOURNEYS

THE ANIMAL APOCALYPSE (1 ENOCH 85–90)

Commentary

The "Animal Apocalypse" is part of a larger work known as *1 Enoch* or *Ethiopian Enoch*. Several ancient writings were attributed to Enoch, who, according to Genesis 5, was the seventh descendant of Adam and the father of Methuselah. The description of Enoch in Genesis 5:24 ("Enoch walked with God; and he was not, for God took him") led to Enoch's being viewed as a mysterious and intriguing figure. Enoch was remembered in later tradition as an exceptionally righteous man to whom, after being taken up by God, various heavenly and cosmological secrets were revealed. In addition to *1 Enoch*, other writings attributed to Enoch include *2 Enoch* (or *Slavonic Enoch*) and *3 Enoch*.

First Enoch is composed of at least five separate works: (1) the "Book of the Watchers" (chaps. 1–36); (2) the "Similitudes of Enoch," or the "Parables of Enoch" (chaps. 37–71); (3) the "Astronomical Book," or the "Book of the Luminaries" (chaps. 72–82); (4) the "Dream Visions" (chaps. 83–90); and (5) the "Epistle of Enoch" (chaps. 91–108).

These writings derive from various authors and time periods. This collection of writings is known as *Ethiopic Enoch* because the only existing copy of the complete text is found in an Ethiopic version. Large portions of the text also exist in Greek versions, along with some small fragments in Latin and Syriac. Manuscripts containing at least a portion from each of these works, except the "Similitudes," have been discovered among the Dead Sea manuscripts at Qumran. The Dead Sea manuscripts, written in Aramaic, provide us with the earliest known copies of any of *1 Enoch*. The original language of *1 Enoch* was probably Aramaic or Hebrew, or it may have been like the book of Daniel, a combination of the two.

The dates for the composition of the individual sections of 1 Enoch are generally estimated to be from the third century B.C.E. to the first century C.E. The date for the collection of the five sections into one complete work as it now exists is uncertain. Proposals by scholars have ranged from the first century C.E. to the fourth century C.E.

The section of *1 Enoch* referred to as the "Dream Visions" (chaps. 83–90) is composed of two visions that Enoch purportedly recounted to his son Methuselah. In the first vision (chaps. 83–84), Enoch sees the coming destruction of the earth on account of humanity's sinfulness. The second vision (chaps. 85–90), unrelated to the first, is an allegory of biblical history from the creation of Adam to the coming of the messianic kingdom. This work is known as the "Animal Apocalypse" because various animals represent people (for example, Adam is a bull, Eve is a heifer, Noah is a white bull who becomes a man, the Israelites are sheep, and the Gentiles are wild animals). The heavenly beings who have sexual intercourse with earthly women (described in Gen. 6:1-4 and elaborated on in *1 Enoch* 6–36) are portrayed as fallen stars, whose offspring are giants in the form of elephants, camels, and asses.

In the preview of history that Enoch is shown, most of the major figures in Israel's history are depicted: Abraham, Jacob, Joseph, Moses, Saul, David, Solomon, and Elijah. Following the fall of Jerusalem to the Babylonians, the "Lord of the sheep" appoints seventy shepherds, representing angelic guardians or overseers, who are responsible for the safety and leadership of the sheep. These angelic shepherds all fail as caretakers and at the final judgment are thrown into the abyss of fire. The deliverance of the sheep from the wild animals begins with the appearance of a sheep with a big horn (90:9), who successfully fights against the wild beasts. (This conquering sheep is perhaps paralleled in the triumphant, warring lamb of the book of Revelation. See especially Revelation 5 and 14). The preview of history ends as the "Lord of the sheep" appears in order to execute judgment and punishment on the wicked. A new era begins, an era characterized by peace and centered around a "new house" (perhaps Jerusalem) that the Lord of the sheep sets up. All the animals reside within this house, with the birds and wild animals worshiping the sheep. "And all those which had been destroyed and scattered" (90:33) were gathered together, apparently implying resurrection. A white bull with big horns—perhaps symbolizing the Messiah—is born and is revered by all the animals. Finally, the animals are transformed into white bulls, the same kind of animals as were Adam and the patriarchs at the beginning of history. The new age, then, is a return to the beginning.

In the "Animal Apocalypse" Enoch receives his revelation by means of a vision in which angels serve as mediators, but not interpreters, of the revelation. In the vision, Enoch is taken up by angels to a high place from which he views the course of history, but he does not go on any otherworldly journeys. The technique of *ex eventu* prophecy is used by the author to present a review of history.

The composition of the "Animal Apocalypse" can be dated to the time of the Maccabean revolt on the basis of the description of the ram with a great horn (90:9-16), which is widely recognized as a reference to Judas Maccabeus. Since this is the last historical reference in the work, it was likely composed in Judea between 164 B.C.E. and 161 B.C.E. as a response to the crisis brought about by Antiochus Epiphanes. The author gives hope to the readers by pointing to the ultimate fate of the wicked and God's establishment of a "new house" for the righteous. Furthermore, the preview of history not only serves to give confidence in the prediction of events yet to occur but also shows that the course of the world is predetermined. All of history is under the control of God.

The text of the "Animal Apocalypse" given here is the translation by M. A. Knibb, contained in *The Apocryphal Old Testament*. Knibb's work is a translation of primarily one Ethiopic manuscript (Ryl. Eth. MS 23), corrected by other texts only in places where this manuscript does not appear to make sense.

1 Enoch 85–90

85. And after this I saw another dream, and I will show it all to you, my son. ²And Enoch raised (his voice) and said to his son Methuselah, To you I speak, my son. Hear my words, and incline your ear to the dream-vision of your father. ³Before I took your mother Edna, I saw in a vision on my bed, and behold a bull came out of the earth, and that bull was white; and after it a heifer came out, and with the heifer came two bullocks, and one of them was black, and the other red. [4]And that black bullock struck the red one, and pursued it over the earth, and from then on I could not see that red bullock. [5]But that black bullock grew, and a heifer went with it; and I saw that many bulls came out from it which were like it and followed behind it. [6]And that cow, that first one, came from the presence of that first bull, seeking that red bullock, but did not find it; and thereupon it moaned bitterly, and continued to seek it. [7]And I looked until that first bull came to it and calmed it, and from that time it did not cry out. [8]And after this she bore another white bull, and after it she bore many black bulls and cows. [9]And I saw in my sleep that white bull, how it likewise grew and became a large white bull, and from it came many white bulls, and they were like it. [10]And they began to beget many white bulls which were like them, one following another.

86. And again I looked with my eyes as I was sleeping, and I saw heaven above, and behold a star fell from heaven, and it arose and ate and pastured amongst those bulls. [2]And after this I saw the large and the black bulls, and behold all of them changed their pens and their pastures and their heifers, and they began to moan, one after another. [3]And again I saw in the vision and looked at heaven, and behold I saw many stars, how they came down and were thrown down from heaven to that first star, and amongst those heifers and bulls; they were with them, pasturing amongst them. [4]And I looked at them and saw, and behold all of them let out their private parts like horses and began to mount the cows of the bulls, and they all became pregnant and bore elephants and camels and asses. [5]And all the bulls were afraid of them and were terrified before them, and they began to bite with their teeth, and to devour, and to gore with their horns. [6]And so they began to devour those bulls, and behold all the children of the earth began to tremble and shake before them, and to flee.

87. And again I saw them, how they began to gore one another and to devour one another, and the earth began to cry out. [2]And I raised my eyes again to heaven and saw in the vision, and behold there came from heaven beings who were like white men; and four came from that place, and three (others) with them. [3]And those three who came out last took hold of me by my hand, and raised me from the generations of the earth, and lifted me onto a high place, and showed me a tower high above the earth, and all the hills were lower. [4]And one said to me, Remain here until you have seen everything which is coming upon these elephants and camels and asses, and upon the stars, and upon all the bulls.

88. And I saw one of those four who had come out first, how he took hold of that first star which had fallen from heaven, and bound it by its hands and its feet, and threw it into an abyss; and that abyss was narrow, and deep, and horrible and dark. ²And one of them drew his sword and gave (it) to those elephants and camels and asses, and they began to strike one another, and the whole earth shook because of them. ³And as I looked in the vision, behold one of those four who had come out cast from heaven and gathered and took all the large stars whose private parts (were) like the private parts of horses, and bound them all by their hands and their feet, and threw them into a chasm of the earth.

89. And one of those four went to a white bull and taught him a mystery, trembling as he was. He was born a bull, but became a man, and built for himself a large vessel and dwelt on it, and three bulls dwelt with him in that vessel, and they were covered over. ²And I again raised my eyes to heaven and saw a high roof, with seven water-channels on it, and those channels discharged much water into an enclosure. ³And I looked again, and behold springs opened on the floor of that large enclosure, and water began to bubble up and to rise above the floor; and I looked at that enclosure until its whole floor was covered by water. ⁴And water and darkness and mist increased on it; and I looked at the height of that water, and that water had risen above that enclosure and was pouring out over the enclosure, and it remained on the earth. ⁵And all the bulls of that enclosure were gathered together until I saw how they sank and were swallowed up and destroyed in that water. ⁶And that vessel floated on the water, but all the bulls and elephants and camels and asses sank to the bottom, together with all the animals, so that I could not see them. And they were unable to get out, but were destroyed and sank into the depths. ⁷And again I looked in the vision until those water-channels were removed from that high roof, and the chasms of the earth were made level, and other abysses were opened. ⁸And the water began to run down into them until the earth became visible, and that vessel settled on the earth; and the darkness departed, and light appeared. ⁹And that white bull who became a man went out from that vessel, and the three bulls with him. And one of the three bulls was white, like that bull, and one of them (was) red as blood, and one (was) black; and that white bull passed away from them. ¹⁰And they began to beget wild-animals and birds, so that there arose from them every kind of species: lions, tigers, wolves, dogs, hyenas, wild-boars, foxes, badgers, pigs, falcons, vultures, kites, eagles and ravens. But amongst them was born a white bull. 11And they began to bite one another; but that white bull which was born amongst them begat a wild ass and a white bull with it, and the wild asses increased. 12But that bull which was born from it begat a black wild-boar and a white sheep; and that wild-boar begat many boars, and that sheep begat twelve sheep. 13And when those twelve sheep had grown, they handed one of their number over to the asses, and those asses in turn handed that sheep over to the wolves; and that sheep grew up amongst the wolves. 14And the Lord brought the eleven sheep to dwell with it and to pasture with it amongst the wolves, and they increased and became many flocks of sheep. 15And the wolves began to make them afraid, and they oppressed them until they made away with their young, and they threw their young into a river with much water; but those sheep began to cry out because of their young, and to complain to their Lord. 16But a sheep which had been saved from the wolves fled and escaped to the wild asses. And I saw the sheep moaning and crying out, and petitioning their Lord with all their power, until that Lord of the sheep came down at the call of the sheep from a high room, and came to them, and looked at them. 17And he called that sheep which had fled from the wolves, and spoke to it about the wolves that it should warn them that they should not touch the sheep. 18And the sheep went to the wolves in accordance with the word of the Lord, and another sheep met that sheep and went with it; and the two of them together entered the assembly of those wolves, and spoke to them, and warned them that from then on they should not touch the sheep. 19And after this I saw the wolves, how they acted even more harshly towards the sheep with all their power, and the sheep cried out. 20And their Lord came to the sheep, and began to beat those wolves; and the wolves began to moan, but the sheep became silent, and from then on they did not cry out. 21And I looked at the sheep until they escaped from the wolves; but the eyes of the wolves were blinded, and those wolves went out in pursuit of the sheep with all their forces. 22And the Lord of the sheep went with them as he led them, and all his sheep followed him; and his face (was) glorious, and his appearance terrible and magnificent. 23But the wolves began to pursue those sheep until they met them by a stretch of water. 24And that stretch of water was divided, and the water stood on one side and on the other before them; and their Lord, as he led them, stood between them and the wolves. 25And while those wolves had not yet seen the sheep, they went into the middle of that stretch of water; but the wolves pursued the sheep, and those wolves ran after them into that stretch of water. 26But when they saw the Lord of the sheep, they turned to flee before him; but that stretch of water flowed together again and suddenly resumed its natural form, and the water swelled up and rose until it covered those wolves. 27And I looked until all the wolves which had pursued those sheep were destroyed and drowned. 28But the sheep escaped from that water and went to a desert where there was neither water nor grass; and they began to open their eyes and to see; and I saw the Lord of the sheep pasturing them and giving them water and grass, and that sheep going and leading them. 29And that sheep went up to the summit of a high rock, and the Lord of the sheep sent it to them. 30And after this I saw the Lord of the sheep standing before them, and his appearance (was) terrible and majestic, and all those sheep saw him and were afraid of him. 31And all of them were afraid and trembled before him; and they cried out after that sheep with them which was in their midst, We cannot stand before our Lord, nor look at him. 32And that sheep which led them again went up to the summit of that rock; and the sheep began to be blinded and to go astray from the path which it had shown to them, but that sheep did not know. 33And the Lord of the sheep was extremely angry with them, and that sheep knew, and went down from the summit of the rock, and came to the sheep, and found the majority of them with their eyes blinded and going astray from his path. 34And when they saw it, they were afraid and trembled before it, and wished that they could return to their enclosure. 35And that sheep took some other sheep with it, and went to those sheep which had gone astray, and then began to kill them; and the sheep were afraid of it. And that sheep brought back those sheep which had gone astray, and they returned to their enclosures. 36And I looked there at the vision until that sheep became a man, and built a house for the Lord of the sheep, and made all the sheep stand in that house. 37And I looked until that sheep which had met that sheep which led the sheep fell asleep; and I looked until all the large sheep were destroyed and small ones rose up in their place, and they came to a pasture, and drew near to a river of water. 38And that sheep which led them, which had become a man, separated from them and fell asleep; and all the sheep sought it and cried out very bitterly over it. 39And I looked until they left off crying for that sheep and crossed that river of water; and there arose all the sheep which led them in place of those which had fallen asleep, and they led them. 40And I looked until the sheep came to a good place and a pleasant and glorious land, and I looked until those sheep were satisfied; and that house (was) in the middle of them in the pleasant land. [41]And sometimes their eyes were opened, and sometimes blinded, until another sheep rose up and led them, and brought them all back, and their eyes were opened. [42]And the dogs and the foxes and the wild-boars began to devour those sheep until the Lord of the sheep raised up a ram from among them which led them. [43]And that ram began to butt those dogs and foxes and wild-boars, on one side and on the other, until it had destroyed them all. [44]And the eyes of that sheep were opened, and it saw that ram in the middle of the sheep, how it renounced its glory and began to butt those sheep, and (how) it trampled on them and behaved unbecomingly. [45]And the Lord of the sheep sent the sheep to another sheep and raised it up to be a ram, and to lead the sheep in place of that sheep which had renounced its glory. [46]And it went to it, and spoke with it alone, and raised up that ram, and made it the prince and leader of the sheep; and during all this those dogs oppressed the sheep. [47]And the first ram pursued that second ram, and that second ram rose and fled before it. And I looked until those dogs made the first ram fall. [48]And that second ram rose up and led the small sheep, and that ram begat many sheep and fell asleep; and a small sheep became ram in place of it, and became the prince and leader of those sheep. [49]And those sheep grew and increased; but all the dogs and foxes and wild-boars were afraid and fled from it, and that ram butted and killed all the animals, and those animals did not again prevail amongst the sheep and did not seize anything further from them. [50]And that house became large and broad, and for those sheep a high tower was built on that house for the Lord of the sheep; and that house was low, but the tower was raised up and high; and the Lord of the sheep stood on that tower, and they spread a full table before him. [51]And I saw those sheep again, how they went astray, and walked in many ways, and left that house of theirs; and the Lord of the sheep called some of the sheep and sent them to the sheep, but the sheep began to kill them. [52]But one of them was saved and was not killed, and it sprang away and cried out against the sheep, and they wished to kill it; but the Lord of the sheep saved it from the hands of the sheep, and brought it up to me, and made it remain (there). [53]And he sent many other sheep to those sheep to testify (to them) and to lament over them. [54]And after this I saw how when they left the house of the Lord of the sheep and his tower, they went astray in everything, and their eyes were blinded; and I saw how the Lord of the sheep wrought much slaughter among them in their pastures until those sheep (themselves) invited that slaughter and

48

betrayed his place. ⁵⁵And he gave them into the hands of the lions and the tigers and the wolves and the hyenas, and into the hands of the foxes, and to all the animals; and those wild animals began to tear those sheep in pieces. ⁵⁶And I saw how he left that house of theirs and their tower and gave them all into the hands of the lions, that they might tear them in pieces and devour them, into the hands of all the animals. ⁵⁷And I began to cry out with all my power, and to call the Lord of the sheep, and to represent to him with regard to the sheep that they were being devoured by all the wild animals. ⁵⁸But he remained still, although he saw (it), and rejoiced that they were devoured and swallowed up and carried off, and he gave them into the hands of all the animals for food. ⁵⁹And he called seventy shepherds and cast off those sheep that they might pasture them; and he said to the shepherds and to their companions, Each one of you from now on is to pasture the sheep, and do whatever I command you. ⁶⁰And I will hand (them) over to you duly numbered and will tell you which of them are to be destroyed, and destroy them. And he handed those sheep over to them. ⁶¹And he called another and said to him, Observe and see everything that the shepherds do against these sheep, for they will destroy from among them more than I have commanded them. ⁶²And write down all the excess and destruction which is wrought by the shepherds, how many they destroy at my command, and how many they destroy of their own volition; write down against each shepherd individually all that he destroys. ⁶³And read out before me exactly how many they destroy of their own volition, and how many are handed over to them for destruction, that this may be a testimony for me against them, that I may know all the deeds of the shepherds, in order to hand them over (for destruction), and may see what they do, whether they abide by my command which I have commanded them, or not. ⁶⁴But they must not know (this), and you must not show (this) to them, nor reprove them, but (only) write down against each individual in his time all that the shepherds destroy and bring it all up to me. ⁶⁵And I looked until those shepherds pastured at their time, and they began to kill and to destroy more than they were commanded, and they gave those sheep into the hands of the lions. ⁶⁶And the lions and the tigers devoured and swallowed up the majority of those sheep, and the wild-boars devoured with them; and they burnt down that tower and demolished that house. ⁶⁷And I was extremely sad about the tower, because that house of the sheep had been demolished; and after that I was unable to see whether those sheep went into that house. ⁶⁸And the shepherds and their companions handed those sheep over to all the

49

animals that they might devour them; each one of them at his time received an exact number, and (of) each one of them after the other there was written in a book how many of them he destroyed. . . . [69]And each one killed and destroyed more than was prescribed, and I began to weep and to moan very much because of those sheep. [70]And likewise in the vision I saw that one who wrote, how every day he wrote down each one which was destroyed by those shepherds, and (how) he brought up and presented and showed the whole book to the Lord of the sheep, everything that they had done, and all that each one of them had made away with, and all that they had handed over to destruction. [71]And the book was read out before the Lord of the sheep, and he took the book in his hand, and read it, and sealed it, and put it down. [72]And after this I saw how the shepherds pastured for twelve hours, and behold, three of those sheep returned and arrived and came and began to build up all that had fallen down from that house; but the wild-boars hindered them so that they could not. [73]And they began again to build, as before, and they raised up that tower, and it was called the high tower; and they began again to place a table before the tower, but all the bread on it (was) unclean and was not pure. [74]And besides all (this) the eyes of these sheep were blinded so that they could not see, and their shepherds likewise; and they handed yet more of them over to their shepherds for destruction, and they trampled upon the sheep with their feet and devoured them. [75]But the Lord of the sheep remained still until all the sheep were scattered abroad and had mixed with them, and they did not save them from the hand of the animals. [76]And that one who wrote the book brought it up, and showed it, and read (it) out in the dwelling of the Lord of the sheep; and he entreated him on behalf of them, and petitioned him as he showed him all the deeds of their shepherds, and testified before him against all the shepherds. [77]And he took the book, and put it down by him, and went out.

90. And I looked until the time that {thirty-seven}[a] shepherds had pastured (the sheep) in the same way, and, each individually, they all completed their time like the first ones; and others received them into their hands to pasture them at their time, each shepherd at his own time. [2]And after this I saw in the vision all the birds of heaven coming; the eagles, and the vultures, and the kites, and the ravens; but the eagles led all the birds; and they began to devour those sheep, and to peck out their

---

[a]A mistake for "thirty-five."

eyes, and to devour their flesh. ³And the sheep cried out because their flesh was devoured by the birds, and I cried out and lamented in my sleep on account of that shepherd who pastured the sheep. ⁴And I looked until those sheep were devoured by the dogs and by the eagles and by the kites, and they left on them neither flesh nor skin nor sinew until only their bones remained; and their bones fell upon the ground, and the sheep became few. ⁵And I looked until the time that twenty three shepherds had pastured (the sheep); and they completed, each in his time, fifty-eight times. ⁶And small lambs were born from those white sheep, and they began to open their eyes, and to see, and to cry to the sheep. ⁷But the sheep did not cry to them and did not listen to what they said to them, but were extremely deaf, and their eyes were extremely and excessively blinded. ⁸And I saw in the vision how the ravens flew upon those lambs, and took one of those lambs, and dashed the sheep in pieces and devoured them. ⁹And I looked until horns came up on those lambs, but the ravens cast their horns down; and I looked until a big horn grew on one of those sheep, and their eyes were opened. ¹⁰And it looked at them, and their eyes were opened, and it cried to the sheep, and the rams saw it, and they all ran to it. ¹¹And besides all this those eagles and vultures and ravens and kites were still continually tearing the sheep in pieces and flying upon them and devouring them; and the sheep were silent, but the rams lamented and cried out. ¹²And those ravens battled and fought with it, and wished to make away with its horn, but they did not prevail against it. ¹³And I looked at them until the shepherds and the eagles and those vultures and kites came and cried to the ravens that they should dash the horn of that ram in pieces; and they fought and battled with it, and it fought with them and cried out that its help might come to it. ¹⁴And I looked until that man who wrote down the names of the shepherds and brought (them) up before the Lord of the sheep came, and he helped that ram and showed it everything, (namely that) its help was coming down. ¹⁵And I looked until that Lord of the sheep came to them in anger, and all those who saw him fled, and they all fell into the shadow before him. ¹⁶All the eagles and vultures and ravens and kites gathered together and brought with them all the wild sheep, and they all came together and helped one another in order to dash that horn of the ram in pieces. ¹⁷And I looked at that man who wrote the book at the command of the Lord until he opened that book of the destruction which those twelve last shepherds had wrought, and he showed before the Lord of the sheep that they had destroyed even more than (those) before them. ¹⁸And I looked until the Lord of the sheep came to them and took in his hand the staff of his anger and struck the earth; and the earth was split, and all the animals and the birds of heaven fell from those sheep and sank in the earth, and it closed over them. ¹⁹And I looked until a big sword was given to the sheep, and the sheep went out against all the wild animals to kill them, and all the animals and the birds of heaven fled before them. ²⁰And I looked until a throne was set up in the pleasant land, and the Lord of the sheep sat on it; and they took all the sealed books and opened those books before the Lord of the sheep. ²¹And the Lord called those men, the seven first white ones, and commanded (them) to bring before him the first star which went before those stars whose private parts (were) like the private parts of horses . . . and they brought them all before him. ²²And he said to that man who wrote before him, who was one of the seven white ones—he said to him, Take those seventy shepherds to whom I handed over the sheep, and who, on their own authority, took and killed more than I commanded them. ²³And behold I saw them all bound, and they all stood before him. ²⁴And the judgement was held first on the stars, and they were judged and found guilty; and they went to the place of damnation, and were thrown into a deep (place), full of fire, burning and full of pillars of fire. ²⁵And those seventy shepherds were judged and found guilty, and they also were thrown into that abyss of fire. ²⁶And I saw at that time how a similar abyss was opened in the middle of the earth which was full of fire, and they brought those blind sheep, and they were all judged and found guilty and thrown into that abyss of fire, and they burned; and that abyss was on the south of that house. ²⁷And I saw those sheep burning, and their bones were burning. ²⁸And I stood up to look until he folded up that old house, and they removed all the pillars, and all the beams and ornaments of that house were folded up with it; and they removed it and put it in a place in the south of the land. ²⁹And I looked until the Lord of the sheep brought a new house, larger and higher than that first one, and he set it up on the site of the first one which had been folded up; and all its pillars (were) new, and its ornaments (were) new and larger than (those of) the first one, the old one which he had removed. And the Lord of the sheep (was) in the middle of it. ³⁰And I saw all the sheep which were left, and all the animals on the earth and all the birds of heaven falling down and worshipping those sheep, and entreating them and obeying them in every command. ³¹And after this those three who were dressed in white and had taken hold of me by my hand, the ones who had brought me up at first—they, with the hand of that ram also holding me, took me up and put me down in the middle of those sheep before the judgement was held. ³²And those sheep were all white, and their wool thick and pure. ³³And all those which had been destroyed and scattered and all the wild animals and all the birds of heaven gathered together in that house, and the Lord of the sheep rejoiced very much because they were all good and had returned to his house. ³⁴And I looked until they had laid down that sword which had been given to the sheep, and they brought it back into his house, and it was sealed before the Lord; and all the sheep were enclosed in that house, but it did not hold them. ³⁵And the eyes of all of them were opened, and they saw well, and there was not one among them that did not see. ³⁶And I saw that that house was large and broad and exceptionally full. ³⁷And I saw how a white bull was born, and its horns (were) big, and all the wild animals and all the birds of heaven were afraid of it and entreated it continually. ³⁸And I looked until all their species were transformed, and they all became white bulls; and the first one among them was a ⟨wild-ox⟩, and that ⟨wild-ox⟩ was a large animal and had big black horns on its head. And the Lord of the sheep rejoiced over them and over all the bulls. ³⁹And I was asleep in the middle of them; and I woke up and saw everything. ⁴⁰And this is the vision which I saw while I was asleep, and I woke up and blessed the Lord of righteousness and ascribed glory to him. ⁴¹But after this I wept bitterly, and my tears did not stop until I could not endure it: when I looked, they ran down on account of that which I saw, for everything will come to pass and be fulfilled; and all the deeds of men in their order were shown to me. ⁴²That night I remembered my first dream, and because of it I wept and was disturbed, because I had seen that vision.

THE APOCALYPSE OF WEEKS (1 Enoch 93:1-10; 91:11-17)

Commentary

The "Apocalypse of Weeks" is a short apocalyptic writing contained in *1 Enoch* 93:1-10 and 91:11-17. In its present form, the work is a part of the "Epistle of Enoch," one of the five major divisions of *1 Enoch* (see the discussion of *1 Enoch* in the introduction to the "Animal Apocalypse"). The "Epistle of Enoch" went through several stages of editing, which included various additions to and rearrangements of the text. Rearrangement of materials is most obvious with the "Apocalypse of Weeks." In the Ethiopic version, the first seven "weeks" of world history are described in 93:1-10; the last three weeks are found in 91:11-17. That the Ethiopic arrangement represents a dislocation of the material is supported by the discovery of the Dead Sea manuscripts found at Qumran. In one of the Qumran fragments, the material in 91:11-17 immediately follows the material in 93:1-10. The "Apocalypse of Weeks," therefore, probably originally consisted of *1 Enoch* 93:1-10 followed by *1 Enoch* 91:11-17. Scholars disagree over whether the work ever circulated independently as a separate unit.

The "Apocalypse of Weeks" gives no explicit clues that would date the composition of the work. Its discovery among the Dead Sea manuscripts limits the date of composition to no later than the first half of the first century B.C.E., since the manuscript fragment that contains this material is usually dated around 50 B.C.E. Attempts to date the writing earlier, even to pre-Maccabean times (prior to 166 B.C.E.), have focused on two issues. First, there is no mention in the writing of the persecution and crisis brought about by Antiochus Epiphanes in 167 B.C.E. Second, the author of the pseudepigraphical book of *Jubilees* seems to have been familiar with the "Epistle of Enoch," including the "Apocalypse of Weeks." Although scholarly opinion differs on the date of *Jubilees*, current scholarship generally dates *Jubilees* during the second century B.C.E., usually around 160 B.C.E. If *Jubilees* does in fact allude to the "Apocalypse of Weeks," then the "Apocalypse of Weeks" should be dated no later than the beginning decades of the second century B.C.E.

In the "Apocalypse of Weeks," Enoch claims to have received this revelation in three ways: by means of a heavenly vision; through the words of angels; and from the "tablets of heaven" (93:2). Although the angels mediate the revelation to Enoch, they do not interpret it. The revelation that Enoch receives, presented in the form of *ex eventu* prophecy, is an overview of the history of the world. History is divided into ten "weeks." The first seven weeks describe the course of human history up to the time of the author, who views the contemporary world as being an "apostate generation" (93:9). The current situation will not last long, however; the eschatological crisis is at hand. At the end of the seventh week, the "chosen righteous from the eternal plant of righteousness will be chosen" (93:10) and the wicked will be destroyed. The eighth and ninth weeks will be periods when righteousness prevails and judgment and destruction come upon the wicked. In the tenth week, the evil Watcher angels (see *1 Enoch* 6–36) will suffer judgment and "the great eternal heaven" will appear. This begins an endless era characterized by goodness and righteousness in which "all the powers of heaven will shine for ever" (91:16).

This division of history into distinct periods supports the author's attempt to bring hope and encouragement to the readers. The events of the world are not arbitrary or haphazard. Rather, world history is predetermined and is under the control of God. Through the revelation given to "Enoch" the future course of world history is now made known. The righteous who are suffering at the hands of the wicked can be comforted by knowing that ultimately righteousness and justice will prevail. Furthermore, the location of the author and his readers in the seventh week, the week of the eschatological crisis, is not accidental. The placement of the readers near the end of world history assures them that wickedness will not prevail much longer. God's judgment will occur shortly. The lack of historical clues in the "Apocalypse of Weeks" makes it impossible to know what crisis precipitated the writing of this apocalypse. This lack of specificity, however, made the work appropriate for any time or situation in which the "righteous" felt oppressed by the "wicked."

The text of the "Apocalypse of Weeks" given here is the translation by M. A. Knibb, contained in *The Apocryphal Old Testament.* Knibb's work is a translation of primarily one Ethiopic manuscript (Ryl. Eth. MS 23), corrected by other texts only in places where this manuscript does not appear to make sense.

1 Enoch 93:1-10; 91:11-17

93. And after this Enoch began to speak from the books. ²And Enoch said, Concerning the sons of righteousness and concerning the chosen of the world and concerning the plant of righteousness and uprightness I will speak these things to you and make (them) known to you, my children, I Enoch, according to that which appeared to me in the heavenly vision, and (which) I know from the words of the holy angels and understand from the tablets of heaven. ³And Enoch then began to speak from the books and said, I was born the seventh in the first week, while justice and righteousness still lasted. ⁴And after me in the second week great wickedness will arise, and deceit will have sprung up; and in it there will be the first end, and in it a man will be saved. And after it has ended, iniquity will grow, and he will make a law for the sinners. ⁵And after this in the third week, at its end, a man will be chosen as the plant of righteous judgement; and after him will come the plant of righteousness for ever. ⁶And after this in the fourth week, at its end, visions of the holy and righteous will be seen, and a law for all generations and an enclosure will be made for them. ⁷And after this in the fifth week, at its end, a house of glory and of sovereignty will be built for ever. ⁸And after this in the sixth week all those who live in it (will be) blinded, and the hearts of all, lacking wisdom, will sink into impiety. And in it a man will ascend; and at its end the house of sovereignty will be burnt with fire, and in it the whole race of the chosen root will be scattered. ⁹And after this in the seventh week an apostate generation will arise, and many (will be) its deeds, but all its deeds (will be) apostasy. ¹⁰And at its end the chosen righteous from the eternal plant of righteousness will be chosen, to whom will be given sevenfold teaching concerning his whole creation.

91. ¹¹And after this the roots of iniquity will be cut off, and the sinners will be destroyed by the sword; from the blasphemers they will be cut off in every place, and those who plan wrongdoing and those who commit blasphemy will be destroyed by the sword. ¹²And after this there will be another week, the eighth, that of righteousness, and a sword will be given to it that the righteous judgement may be executed on those who do wrong, and the sinners will be handed over into the hands of the righteous. ¹³And at its end they will acquire houses because of their righteousness, and a house will be built for the great king in glory for ever. ¹⁴And after this in the ninth week the righteous judgement will be revealed to the whole world, and all the deeds of the impious will vanish from the whole earth; and the world will be written down for destruction, and all men will look to the path of uprightness. ¹⁵And after this in the tenth week, in the seventh part, there will be the eternal judgement which will be executed on the Watchers, and the great eternal heaven which will spring from the midst of the angels. ¹⁶And the first heaven will vanish and pass away, and a new heaven will appear, and all the powers of heaven will shine for ever (with) sevenfold light. [17]And after this there will be many weeks without number for ever in goodness and in righteousness, and from then on sin will never again be mentioned.

4 EZRA (2 Esdras 3–14)

Commentary

The names given to literature associated with the Jewish prophet Ezra are varied and confusing; the Septuagint, the Latin versions, and various English versions of the Bible differ. The writing presented here, often called 4 Ezra, is the same as chapters 3–14 of a composite work frequently referred to as 2 Esdras. This material from a Jewish writer was later supplemented by two additional sections, chapters 1–2 (5 Ezra) and chapters 15–16 (6 Ezra), which come from Christian authors.

The setting of 4 Ezra is supposedly the city of Babylon "in the thirtieth year after the destruction of our city"—that is, Jerusalem around 556 B.C.E. Its reputed author is Ezra, the scribe who brought the Jewish Law back to Jerusalem and led in the restoration of Judaism after the exile. Actually, 556 B.C.E. is several decades too early for the time of Ezra the scribe, and, like most apocalypses, 4 Ezra was written pseudonymously. Most scholars are convinced that it was written around 100 C.E. by a Palestinian Jew, approximately thirty years after the Roman destruction of Jerusalem (70 C.E.). The author bemoans the Babylonian destruction of the city, although his real concern is with its very recent destruction at the hands of the Romans. The eagle vision in chapters 11–12, referring to the Roman Empire, supports this dating.

This destruction of Jerusalem was a catastrophe in Jewish history. The nation was thrown into political, social, and religious turmoil. The Temple was destroyed; the sacrificial system and priesthood were gone. Serious questions arose among the Jewish people. Why did God allow such things to happen? Did God no longer care for the people of Israel? Why did the wicked prosper while the righteous suffered?

Four Jewish apocalypses wrestle with these issues: 4 Ezra, *2 Baruch,* the *Apocalypse of Abraham,* and *3 Baruch.* The writer of 4 Ezra arrives at two answers to the perplexing questions about theodicy—that is, the problem of how a good and powerful God can allow righteous people to suffer. The first answer is similar to the one Job received in the canonical book of Job—no answer. God's ways are above human understanding. The second answer, however, moves the discussion from theodicy to eschatology. God does not explain why suffering and inequities exist, but points beyond the problem to the ultimate solutions in the next world, where final retribution will be achieved at the last judgment, followed by rewards for the righteous and punishments for the wicked.

Fourth Ezra is composed of seven sections. The first three sections (3:1-5:20; 5:21-6:34; 6:35-9:25) are dialogues between Ezra and the angel Uriel, concerning the justice of God. Ezra experiences extreme anguish as he struggles with human sinfulness and the plight of the people of Israel. He cannot understand how God could allow the enemies of God to prosper and take Israel captive. Surely Israel has not sinned more than the other nations have. Overwhelmed by this injustice, Ezra complains: "It would be better for us not to be here than to come here and live in ungodliness, and to suffer and not understand why" (4:12). Ezra can accept the fact of Israel's sinfulness; what he cannot fathom is why God uses wicked nations as instruments of divine punishment. He tells God: "If thou dost really hate thy people, they should be punished at thy own hands" (5:30). Throughout the dialogues, Ezra sees himself as one of the sinners and, therefore, destined for punishment. One of the most moving passages in the book occurs after the angel has described for Ezra the rewards and punishments in the afterlife. In despair over the coming judgment and the punishment that will follow, Ezra cries:

> O Adam, what have you done? For though it was you who sinned, the fall was not yours alone, but ours also who are your descendants. For what good is it to us, if an eternal age has been promised to us, but we have done deeds that bring death? And what good is it that an everlasting hope has been promised us, but we have miserably failed? (7:[118-120]).

The fourth section (9:26–10:59) contains Ezra's vision of Zion, first as a woman, then as a city. This vision is a turning point in the book. As the result of Ezra's consoling of the grieving woman, he is able to find consolation for his own grief and encouragement for the future. In the fifth section (11:1–12:51), which is a reinterpretation of the fourth beast in Daniel 7, Ezra sees a vision of a great eagle, symbolizing the Roman Empire. The eagle dominates the world, ruling with violence, terror, and deceit. Another creature appears in the vision, however: a lion, representing God's Messiah, who will destroy the wicked and save the righteous.

The sixth section (13:1-58), another dream vision, presents an individual described as "something like the figure of a man," who arises from the sea (13:3) and is identified by God as "my Son" (13:32). God has been keeping this individual for many ages until the time should arrive for him to be revealed. This figure is a modification of the "one like a son of man" in Daniel 7:13-14, to whom is given eternal dominion over all humanity. Although inspired by the Danielic figure, the individual in 4 Ezra differs considerably. The figure in Daniel exercises a royal role, ruling over the eschatological kingdom. The figure in 4 Ezra plays primarily a military role, destroying the enemies of God. Furthermore, in Daniel the "son of man" seems to represent a heavenly figure (perhaps the archangel Michael) and at the same time is a collective representation of "the people of the saints of the Most High" (Dan. 7:27). In 4 Ezra, the figure is definitely an individual. In neither work are these enigmatic figures identified as the Messiah. In fact, in Daniel, the "one like a son of man" seems not to be the Messiah. In 4 Ezra, on the other hand, the role and characteristics of the Son are so similar to the role and characteristics of the Messiah described in chapter 12 that the Son must surely be understood as the Messiah.

The development of the "one like a son of man" idea from Daniel can be seen in other works besides 4 Ezra. In the "Similitudes of Enoch" (*1 Enoch* 37–71) the Son of man is a pre-existent figure who serves as eschatological judge and destroyer of God's enemies and is enthroned at the right hand of God. Furthermore, he is explicitly identified as the Messiah. In the New Testament, the Gospel writers portray Jesus as using the title Son of man as his favorite self-designation. For them, Son of man is definitely a title for the Messiah who will come at the end of the ages with the angels in the role of eschatological judge. (How Jesus used and understood the phrase "Son of man" is debatable.)

In the seventh and final part of the book (14:1-48) Ezra is commanded to dictate the contents of ninety-four books that are revealed to him. Twenty-four of these (the books of the Hebrew Bible) he is to make public; seventy additional books are reserved for the wise alone.

The eschatological teachings of 4 Ezra are particularly noteworthy. In several places (5:1-13; 6:17-28; 8:63–9:13), the writer describes the signs of the end of the age, the eschatological woes that will bring this world to an end. In response to his questions about these events, Ezra is told that the end will be soon; this age is rapidly drawing to a close (4:26-27, 44-50; 5:50-55). A detailed eschatological scenario is revealed in chapter 7. Those who survive the destruction of the eschatological woes will serve with God's "son the Messiah" during a four-hundred-year messianic reign. At the conclusion of this four-hundred-year period, the Messiah and his followers will die, and a resurrection of all people for judgment will follow. The unrighteous will be consigned to the "furnace of Gehenna," while the righteous will enjoy the "paradise of delight." The intermediate state of the dead (7:[75-101]) is also discussed in this chapter. The souls of the dead will be granted seven days after leaving their bodies to view the secrets of the afterlife. After that time, they will go to their assigned places, the wicked to torment and the righteous to their dwelling places. There they will await the final judgment at the end of time. The visions of chapters 11–13, however, present different eschatological events. In these visions, the major focus is not on judgment, rewards, and punishments in the afterlife but on the final battles between the Messiah and the wicked.

Most scholars are convinced that 4 Ezra was originally written in Hebrew or Aramaic and that a later Greek translation became the basis for the various Latin and oriental versions. (Only a fragment of a Greek manuscript, containing a few verses of chapter 15, still exists.) The oldest known copy of 4 Ezra, a ninth-century Latin manuscript, does not contain verses [36-105] of chapter 7. The majority of existing Latin manuscripts were apparently derived from either this ninth-century manuscript or related ones because they also lack these verses. Early English translations, including the King James Version, followed the Latin manuscripts and did not include these verses in their editions. The discovery in the nineteenth century of a ninth-century Latin manuscript containing the missing verses supported their presence in several oriental versions and led scholars and later translators to include them in subsequent editions of 4 Ezra. (These verses are indicated in the text given here by brackets around the verse numbers.) Their absence from the oldest remaining copy of 4 Ezra is explained as an intentional excision for theological reasons: these verses explicitly deny the validity of prayers for the dead, a practice that arose early in the life of the church.

The text used here is taken from the Revised Standard Version of the Bible.

4 Ezra 3–14

3. In the thirtieth year after the destruction of our city, I Salathiel, who am also called Ezra, was in Babylon. I was troubled as I lay on my bed, and my thoughts welled up in my heart, ²because I saw the desolation of Zion and the wealth of those who lived in Babylon. ³My spirit was greatly agitated, and I began to speak anxious words to the Most High, and said, ⁴"O sovereign Lord, didst thou not speak at the beginning when thou didst form the earth—and that without help—and didst command the dust ⁵and it gave thee Adam, a lifeless body? Yet he was the workmanship of thy hands, and thou didst breathe into him the breath of life, and he was made alive in thy presence. [6]And thou didst lead him into the garden which thy right hand had planted before the earth appeared. [7]And thou didst lay upon him one commandment of thine; but he transgressed it, and immediately thou didst appoint death for him and for his descendants. From him there sprang nations and tribes, peoples and clans, without number. [8]And every nation walked after its own will and did ungodly things before thee and scorned thee, and thou didst not hinder them. [9]But again, in its time thou didst bring the flood upon the inhabitants of the world and destroy them. [10]And the same fate befell them: as death came upon Adam, so the flood upon them. [11]But thou didst leave one of them, Noah with his household, and all the righteous who have descended from him.

[12]"When those who dwelt on earth began to multiply, they produced children and peoples and many nations, and again they began to be more ungodly than were their ancestors. [13]And when they were committing iniquity before thee, thou didst choose for thyself one of them, whose name was Abraham; [14]and thou didst love him, and to him only didst thou reveal the end of the times, secretly by night. [15]Thou didst make with him an everlasting covenant, and promise him that thou wouldst never forsake his descendants; and thou gavest to him Isaac, and to Isaac thou gavest Jacob and Esau. [16]And thou didst set apart Jacob for thyself, but Esau thou didst reject; and Jacob became a great multitude. [17]And when thou didst lead his descendants out of Egypt, thou didst bring them to Mount Sinai. [18]Thou didst bend down the heavens and shake the earth, and move the world, and make the depths to tremble, and trouble the times. [19]And thy glory passed through the four gates of fire and earthquake and wind and ice, to give the law to the descendants of Jacob, and thy commandment to the posterity of Israel.

[20]"Yet thou didst not take away from them their evil heart, so that thy law might bring forth fruit in them. [21]For the first Adam, burdened with an evil heart, transgressed and was overcome, as were also all who were descended from him. [22]Thus the disease became permanent; the law was in the people's heart along with the evil root, but what was good departed, and the evil remained. [23]So the times passed and the years were completed, and thou didst raise up for thyself a servant, named David. [24]And thou didst command him to build a city for thy name, and in it to offer thee oblations from what is thine. [25]This was done for many years; but the inhabitants of the city transgressed,[26]in everything doing as Adam and all his descendants had done, for they also had the evil heart. [27]So thou didst deliver the city into the hands of thy enemies.

28"Then I said in my heart, Are the deeds of those who inhabit Babylon any better? Is that why she has gained dominion over Zion? 29For when I came here I saw ungodly deeds without number, and my soul has seen many sinners during these thirty years. And my heart failed me, 30for I have seen how thou dost endure those who sin, and hast spared those who act wickedly, and hast destroyed thy people, and hast preserved thy enemies, 31and hast not shown to any one how thy way may be comprehended. Are the deeds of Babylon better than those of Zion? 32Or has another nation known thee besides Israel? Or what tribes have so believed thy covenants as these tribes of Jacob? 33Yet their reward has not appeared and their labor has borne no fruit. For I have traveled widely among the nations and have seen that they abound in wealth, though they are unmindful of thy commandments. 34Now therefore weigh in a balance our iniquities and those of the inhabitants of the world; and so it will be found which way the turn of the scale will incline. 35When have the inhabitants of the earth not sinned in thy sight? Or what nation has kept thy commandments so well? 36Thou mayest indeed find individual men who have kept thy commandments, but nations thou wilt not find."

4. Then the angel that had been sent to me, whose name was Uriel, answered 2and said to me, "Your understanding has utterly failed regarding this world, and do you think you can comprehend the way of the Most High?" 3Then I said, "Yes, my lord." And he replied to me, "I have been sent to show you three ways, and to put before you three problems. 4If you can solve one of them for me, I also will show you the way you desire to see, and will teach you why the heart is evil."

5I said, "Speak on, my lord."

And he said to me, "Go, weigh for me the weight of fire, or measure for me a measure of wind, or call back for me the day that is past."

6I answered and said, "Who of those that have been born can do this, that you ask me concerning these things?"

7And he said to me, "If I had asked you, 'How many dwellings are in the heart of the sea, or how many streams are at the source of the deep, or how many streams are above the firmament, or which are the exits of hell, or which are the entrances of paradise?' 8perhaps you would have said to me, 'I never went down into the deep, nor as yet into hell, neither did I ever ascend into heaven.' 9But now I have asked you only about fire and wind and the day, things through which you have passed and without which you cannot exist, and you have given me no answer about

63

them!" 10And he said to me, "You cannot understand the things with which you have grown up; 11how then can your mind comprehend the way of the Most High? And how can one who is already worn out by the corrupt world understand incorruption?" When I heard this, I fell on my face 12and said to him, "It would be better for us not to be here than to come here and live in ungodliness, and to suffer and not understand why."

13He answered me and said, "I went into a forest of trees of the plain, and they made a plan 14and said, 'Come, let us go and make war against the sea, that it may recede before us, and that we may make for ourselves more forests.' 15And in like manner the waves of the sea also made a plan and said, 'Come, let us go up and subdue the forest of the plain so that there also we may gain more territory for ourselves.' 16But the plan of the forest was in vain, for the fire came and consumed it; 17likewise also the plan of the waves of the sea, for the sand stood firm and stopped them. 18If now you were a judge between them, which would you undertake to justify, and which to condemn?"

19I answered and said, "Each has made a foolish plan, for the land is assigned to the forest, and to the sea is assigned a place to carry its waves."

20He answered me and said, "You have judged rightly, but why have you not judged so in your own case? 21For as the land is assigned to the forest and the sea to its waves, so also those who dwell upon earth can understand only what is on the earth, and he who is above the heavens can understand what is above the height of the heavens."

22Then I answered and said, "I beseech you, my lord, why have I been endowed with the power of understanding? 23For I did not wish to inquire about the ways above, but about those things which we daily experience: why Israel has been given over to the Gentiles as a reproach; why the people whom you loved has been given over to godless tribes, and the law of our fathers has been made of no effect and the written covenants no longer exist; 24and why we pass from the world like locusts, and our life is like a mist, and we are not worthy to obtain mercy. 25But what will he do for his name, by which we are called? It is about these things that I have asked."

26He answered me and said, "If you are alive, you will see, and if you live long, you will often marvel, because the age is hastening swiftly to its end. 27For it will not be able to bring the things that have been promised to the righteous in their appointed times, because this age is full of sadness and infirmities. 28For the evil about which you ask me has been sown, but the harvest of it has not yet come. ²⁹If therefore that which has been sown is not reaped, and if the place where the evil has been sown does not pass away, the field where the good has been sown will not come. ³⁰For a grain of evil seed was sown in Adam's heart from the beginning, and how much ungodliness it has produced until now, and will produce until the time of threshing comes! ³¹Consider now for yourself how much fruit of ungodliness a grain of evil seed has produced. ³²When heads of grain without number are sown, how great a threshing floor they will fill!"

³³Then I answered and said, "How long and when will these things be? Why are our years few and evil?" ³⁴He answered me and said, "You do not hasten faster than the Most High, for your haste is for yourself, but the Highest hastens on behalf of many. ³⁵Did not the souls of the righteous in their chambers ask about these matters, saying, 'How long are we to remain here? And when will come the harvest of our reward?' ³⁶And Jeremiel the archangel answered them and said, 'When the number of those like yourselves is completed; for he has weighed the age in the balance, ³⁷and measured the times by measure, and numbered the times by number; and he will not move or arouse them until that measure is fulfilled.' "

³⁸Then I answered and said, "O sovereign Lord, but all of us also are full of ungodliness. ³⁹And it is perhaps on account of us that the time of threshing is delayed for the righteous—on account of the sins of those who dwell on earth."

⁴⁰He answered me and said, "Go and ask a woman who is with child if, when her nine months have been completed, her womb can keep the child within her any longer."

⁴¹And I said, "No, lord, it cannot."

And he said to me, "In Hades the chambers of the souls are like the womb. ⁴²For just as a woman who is in travail makes haste to escape the pangs of birth, so also do these places hasten to give back those things that were committed to them from the beginning. ⁴³Then the things that you desire to see will be disclosed to you."

⁴⁴I answered and said, "If I have found favor in your sight, and if it is possible, and if I am worthy, ⁴⁵show me this also: whether more time is to come than has passed, or whether for us the greater part has gone by. ⁴⁶For I know what has gone by, but I do not know what is to come."

⁴⁷And he said to me, "Stand at my right side, and I will show you the interpretation of a parable."

⁴⁸So I stood and looked, and behold, a flaming furnace passed by

before me, and when the flame had gone by I looked, and behold, the smoke remained. [49]And after this a cloud full of water passed before me and poured down a heavy and violent rain, and when the rainstorm had passed, drops remained in the cloud.

[50]And he said to me, "Consider it for yourself; for as the rain is more than the drops, and the fire is greater than the smoke, so the quantity that passed was far greater; but drops and smoke remained."

[51]Then I prayed and said, "Do you think that I shall live until those days? Or who will be alive in those days?"

[52]He answered me and said, "Concerning the signs about which you ask me, I can tell you in part; but I was not sent to tell you concerning your life, for I do not know.

5. "Now concerning the signs: behold, the days are coming when those who dwell on earth shall be seized with great terror, and the way of truth shall be hidden, and the land shall be barren of faith. [2]And unrighteousness shall be increased beyond what you yourself see, and beyond what you heard of formerly. [3]And the land which you now see ruling shall be waste and untrodden, and men shall see it desolate. [4]But if the Most High grants that you live, you shall see it thrown into confusion after the third period;

> and the sun shall suddenly shine
>   forth at night,
> and the moon during the day,
> [5] Blood shall drip from wood,
>   and the stone shall utter its voice;
> the peoples shall be troubled,
>   and the stars shall fall.

[6]And one shall reign whom those who dwell on earth do not expect, and the birds shall fly away together; [7]and the sea of Sodom shall cast up fish; and one whom the many do not know shall make his voice heard by night, and all shall hear his voice. [8]There shall be chaos also in many places, and fire shall often break out, and the wild beasts shall roam beyond their haunts, and menstruous women shall bring forth monsters. [9]And salt waters shall be found in the sweet, and all friends shall conquer one another; then shall reason hide itself, and wisdom shall withdraw into its chamber, [10]and it shall be sought by many but

shall not be found, and unrighteousness and unrestraint shall increase on earth. [11]And one country shall ask its neighbor, 'Has righteousness, or any one who does right, passed through you?' And it will answer, 'No.' [12]And at that time men shall hope but not obtain; they shall labor but their ways shall not prosper. [13]These are the signs which I am permitted to tell you, and if you pray again, and weep as you do now, and fast for seven days, you shall hear yet greater things than these."

[14]Then I awoke, and my body shuddered violently, and my soul was so troubled that it fainted. [15]But the angel who had come and talked with me held me and strengthened me and set me on my feet.

[16]Now on the second night Phaltiel, a chief of the people, came to me and said, "Where have you been? And why is your face sad? [17]Or do you not know that Israel has been entrusted to you in the land of their exile? [18]Rise therefore and eat some bread, so that you may not forsake us, like a shepherd who leaves his flock in the power of cruel wolves."

[19]Then I said to him, "Depart from me and do not come near me for seven days, and then you may come to me."

He heard what I said and left me. [20]So I fasted seven days, mourning and weeping, as Uriel the angel had commanded me.

[21]And after seven days the thoughts of my heart were very grievous to me again. [22]Then my soul recovered the spirit of understanding, and I began once more to speak words in the presence of the Most High. [23]And I said, "O sovereign Lord, from every forest of the earth and from all its trees thou hast chosen one vine, [24]and from all the lands of the world thou hast chosen for thyself one region, and from all the flowers of the world thou hast chosen for thyself one lily, [25]and from all the depths of the sea thou hast filled for thyself one river, and from all the cities that have been built thou hast consecrated Zion for thyself, [26]and from all the birds that have been created thou hast named for thyself one dove, and from all the flocks that have been made thou hast provided for thyself one sheep, [27]and from all the multitude of peoples thou hast gotten for thyself one people; and to this people, whom thou hast loved, thou hast given the law which is approved by all. [28]And now, O Lord, why hast thou given over the one to the many, and dishonored the one root beyond the others, and scattered thine only one among the many? [29]And those who opposed thy promises have trodden down those who believed thy covenants. [30]If thou dost really hate thy people, they should be punished at thy own hands."

[31]When I had spoken these words, the angel who had come to me on a previous night was sent to me, [32]and he said to me, "Listen to me, and I

will instruct you; pay attention to me, and I will tell you more."

³³And I said, "Speak, my lord." And he said to me, "Are you greatly disturbed in mind over Israel? Or do you love him more than his Maker does?"

³⁴And I said, "No, my lord, but because of my grief I have spoken; for every hour I suffer agonies of heart, while I strive to understand the way of the Most High and to search out part of his judgment."

³⁵And he said to me, "You cannot." And I said, "Why not, my lord? Why then was I born? Or why did not my mother's womb become my grave, that I might not see the travail of Jacob and the exhaustion of the people of Israel?"

³⁶He said to me, "Count up for me those who have not yet come, and gather for me the scattered raindrops, and make the withered flowers bloom again for me; ³⁷open for me the closed chambers, and bring forth for me the winds shut up in them, or show me the picture of a voice; and then I will explain to you the travail that you ask to understand."

³⁸And I said, "O sovereign Lord, who is able to know these things except he whose dwelling is not with men? ³⁹As for me, I am without wisdom, and how can I speak concerning the things which thou hast asked me?"

⁴⁰He said to me, "Just as you cannot do one of the things that were mentioned, so you cannot discover my judgment, or the goal of the love that I have promised my people."

⁴¹And I said, "Yet behold, O Lord, thou dost have charge of those who are alive at the end, but what will those do who were before us, or we, or those who come after us?"

⁴²He said to me, "I shall liken my judgment to a circle; just as for those who are last there is no slowness, so for those who are first there is no haste."

⁴³Then I answered and said, "Couldst thou not have created at one time those who have been and those who are and those who will be, that thou mightest show thy judgment the sooner?"

⁴⁴He replied to me and said, "The creation cannot make more haste than the Creator, neither can the world hold at one time those who have been created in it."

⁴⁵And I said, "How hast thou said to thy servant that thou wilt certainly give life at one time to thy creation? If therefore all creatures will live at one time and the creation will sustain them, it might even now be able to support all of them present at one time."

⁴⁶He said to me, "Ask a woman's womb, and say to it, 'If you bear ten

children, why one after another?' Request it therefore to produce ten at one time."

⁴⁷I said, "Of course it cannot, but only each in its own time."

⁴⁸He said to me, "Even so have I given the womb of the earth to those who from time to time are sown in it. ⁴⁹For as an infant does not bring forth, and a woman who has become old does not bring forth any longer, so have I organized the world which I created."

⁵⁰Then I inquired and said, "Since thou hast now given me the opportunity, let me speak before thee. Is our mother, of whom thou hast told me, still young? Or is she now approaching old age?"

⁵¹He replied to me, "Ask a woman who bears children, and she will tell you. ⁵²Say to her, 'Why are those whom you have borne recently not like those whom you bore before, but smaller in stature?' ⁵³And she herself will answer you, 'Those born in the strength of youth are different from those born during the time of old age, when the womb is failing.' ⁵⁴Therefore you also should consider that you and your contemporaries are smaller in stature than those who were before you, ⁵⁵and those who come after you will be smaller than you, as born of a creation which already is aging and passing the strength of youth."

⁵⁶And I said, "O Lord, I beseech thee, if I have found favor in thy sight, show thy servant through whom thou dost visit thy creation."

6. And he said to me, "At the beginning of the circle of the earth, before the portals of the world were in place, and before the assembled winds blew, ²and before the rumblings of thunder sounded, and before the flashes of lightning shone, and before the foundations of paradise were laid, ³and before the beautiful flowers were seen, and before the powers of movement were established, and before the innumerable hosts of angels were gathered together, ⁴and before the heights of the air were lifted up, and before the measures of the firmaments were named, and before the footstool of Zion was established, ⁵and before the present years were reckoned; and before the imaginations of those who now sin were estranged, and before those who stored up treasures of faith were sealed—⁶then I planned these things, and they were made through me and not through another, just as the end shall come through me and not through another."

⁷And I answered and said, "What will be the dividing of the times? Or when will be the end of the first age and the beginning of the age that follows?"

⁸He said to me, "From Abraham to Isaac, because from him were born Jacob and Esau, for Jacob's hand held Esau's heel from the beginning. ⁹For Esau is the end of this age, and Jacob is the beginning of the age that follows. ¹⁰For the beginning of a man is his hand, and the end of a man is his heel; between the heel and the hand seek for nothing else, Ezra!"

¹¹I answered and said, "O sovereign Lord, if I have found favor in thy sight, ¹²show thy servant the end of thy signs which thou didst show me in part on a previous night."

¹³He answered and said to me, "Rise to your feet and you will hear a full, resounding voice. ¹⁴And if the place where you are standing is greatly shaken ¹⁵while the voice is speaking, do not be terrified; because the word concerns the end, and the foundations of the earth will understand ¹⁶that the speech concerns them. They will tremble and be shaken, for they know that their end must be changed."

¹⁷When I heard this, I rose to my feet and listened, and behold, a voice was speaking, and its sound was like the sound of many waters. ¹⁸And it said, "Behold, the days are coming, and it shall be that when I draw near to visit the inhabitants of the earth, ¹⁹and when I require from the doers of iniquity the penalty of their iniquity, and when the humiliation of Zion is complete, ²⁰and when the seal is placed upon the age which is about to pass away, then I will show these signs: the books shall be opened before the firmament, and all shall see it together. ²¹Infants a year old shall speak with their voices, and women with child shall give birth to premature children at three or four months, and these shall live and dance. ²²Sown places shall suddenly appear unsown, and full storehouses shall suddenly be found to be empty; ²³and the trumpet shall sound aloud, and when all hear it, they shall suddenly be terrified. ²⁴At that time friends shall make war on friends like enemies, and the earth and those who inhabit it shall be terrified, and the springs of the fountains shall stand still, so that for three hours they shall not flow.

²⁵"And it shall be that whoever remains after all that I have foretold to you shall himself be saved and shall see my salvation and the end of my world. ²⁶And they shall see the men who were taken up, who from their birth have not tasted death; and the heart of the earth's inhabitants shall be changed and converted to a different spirit. ²⁷For evil shall be blotted out, and deceit shall be quenched; ²⁸faithfulness shall flourish, and corruption shall be overcome, and the truth, which has been so long without fruit, shall be revealed."

²⁹While he spoke to me, behold, little by little the place where I was standing began to rock to and fro. ³⁰And he said to me, "I have come to

show you these things this night. ³¹If therefore you will pray again and fast again for seven days, I will again declare to you greater things than these, ³²because your voice has surely been heard before the Most High; for the Mighty One has seen your uprightness and has also observed the purity which you have maintained from your youth. ³³Therefore he sent me to show you all these things, and to say to you: 'Believe and do not be afraid! ³⁴Do not be quick to think vain thoughts concerning the former times, lest you be hasty concerning the last times.' "

³⁵Now after this I wept again and fasted seven days as before, in order to complete the three weeks as I had been told. ³⁶And on the eighth night my heart was troubled within me again, and I began to speak in the presence of the Most High. ³⁷For my spirit was greatly aroused, and my soul was in distress.

³⁸I said, "O Lord, thou didst speak at the beginning of creation, and didst say on the first day, 'Let heaven and earth be made,' and thy word accomplished the work. ³⁹And then the Spirit was hovering, and darkness and silence embraced everything; the sound of man's voice was not yet there. ⁴⁰Then thou didst command that a ray of light be brought forth from thy treasuries, so that thy works might then appear.

⁴¹"Again, on the second day, thou didst create the spirit of the firmament, and didst command him to divide and separate the waters, that one part might move upward and the other part remain beneath.

⁴²"On the third day thou didst command the waters to be gathered together in the seventh part of the earth; six parts thou didst dry up and keep so that some of them might be planted and cultivated and be of service before thee. ⁴³For thy word went forth, and at once the work was done. ⁴⁴For immediately fruit came forth in endless abundance and of varied appeal to the taste; and flowers of inimitable color; and odors of inexpressible fragrance. These were made on the third day.

⁴⁵"On the fourth day thou didst command the brightness of the sun, the light of the moon, and the arrangement of the stars to come into being; ⁴⁶and thou didst command them to serve man, who was about to be formed.

⁴⁷"On the fifth day thou didst command the seventh part, where the water had been gathered together, to bring forth living creatures, birds, and fishes; and so it was done. ⁴⁸The dumb and lifeless water produced living creatures, as it was commanded, that therefore the nations might declare thy wondrous works.

⁴⁹"Then thou didst keep in existence two living creatures; the name of one thou didst call Behemoth and the name of the other Leviathan.

⁵⁰And thou didst separate one from the other, for the seventh part where the water had been gathered together could not hold them both. ⁵¹And thou didst give Behemoth one of the parts which had been dried up on the third day, to live in it, where there are a thousand mountains; ⁵²but to Leviathan thou didst give the seventh part, the watery part; and thou hast kept them to be eaten by whom thou wilt, and when thou wilt.

⁵³"On the sixth day thou didst command the earth to bring forth before thee cattle, beasts, and creeping things; ⁵⁴and over these thou didst place Adam, as ruler over all the works which thou hadst made; and from him we have all come, the people whom thou hast chosen.

⁵⁵"All this I have spoken before thee, O Lord, because thou hast said that it was for us that thou didst create this world. ⁵⁶As for the other nations which have descended from Adam, thou hast said that they are nothing, and that they are like spittle, and thou hast compared their abundance to a drop from a bucket. ⁵⁷And now, O Lord, behold, these nations, which are reputed as nothing, domineer over us and devour us. ⁵⁸But we thy people, whom thou hast called thy first-born, only begotten, zealous for thee, and most dear, have been given into their hands. ⁵⁹If the world has indeed been created for us, why do we not possess our world as an inheritance? How long will this be so?"

7. When I had finished speaking these words, the angel who had been sent to me on the former nights was sent to me again, ²and he said to me, "Rise, Ezra, and listen to the words that I have come to speak to you."

³I said, "Speak, my lord." And he said to me, "There is a sea set in a wide expanse so that it is broad and vast, ⁴but it has an entrance set in a narrow place, so that it is like a river. ⁵If any one, then, wishes to reach the sea, to look at it or to navigate it, how can he come to the broad part unless he passes through the narrow part? ⁶Another example: There is a city built and set on a plain, and it is full of all good things; ⁷but the entrance to it is narrow and set in a precipitous place, so that there is fire on the right hand and deep water on the left; ⁸and there is only one path lying between them, that is, between the fire and the water, so that only one man can walk upon that path. ⁹If now that city is given to a man for an inheritance, how will the heir receive his inheritance unless he passes through the danger set before him?"

¹⁰I said, "He cannot, lord." And he said to me, "So also is Israel's portion. ¹¹For I made the world for their sake, and when Adam transgressed my statutes, what had been made was judged. ¹²And so the entrances of this world were made narrow and sorrowful and toilsome;

72

they are few and evil, full of dangers and involved in great hardships. [13]But the entrances of the greater world are broad and safe, and really yield the fruit of immortality. [14]Therefore unless the living pass through the difficult and vain experiences, they can never receive those things that have been reserved for them. [15]But now why are you disturbed, seeing that you are to perish? And why are you moved, seeing that you are mortal? [16]And why have you not considered in your mind what is to come, rather than what is now present?"

[17]Then I answered and said, "O sovereign Lord, behold, thou hast ordained in thy law that the righteous shall inherit these things, but that the ungodly shall perish. [18]The righteous therefore can endure difficult circumstances while hoping for easier ones; but those who have done wickedly have suffered the difficult circumstances and will not see the easier ones."

[19]And he said to me, "You are not a better judge than God, or wiser than the Most High! [20]Let many perish who are now living, rather than that the law of God which is set before them be disregarded! [21]For God strictly commanded those who came into the world, when they came, what they should do to live, and what they should observe to avoid punishment. [22]Nevertheless they were not obedient, and spoke against him;

> they devised for themselves vain
>   thoughts,
> [23] and proposed to themselves
>   wicked frauds;
> they even declared that the Most
>   High does not exist,
> and they ignored his ways!
>
> [24] They scorned his law,
>   and denied his covenants;
> they have been unfaithful to his
>   statutes,
> and have not performed his works.

[25]"Therefore, Ezra, empty things are for the empty, and full things are for the full. [26]For behold, the time will come, when the signs which I have foretold to you will come to pass, that the city which now is not seen shall appear, and the land which now is hidden shall be disclosed. [27]And

every one who has been delivered from the evils that I have foretold shall see my wonders. 28For my son the Messiah shall be revealed with those who are with him, and those who remain shall rejoice four hundred years. 29And after these years my son the Messiah shall die, and all who draw human breath. 30And the world shall be turned back to primeval silence for seven days, as it was at the first beginnings; so that no one shall be left. 31And after seven days the world, which is not yet awake, shall be roused, and that which is corruptible shall perish. 32And the earth shall give up those who are asleep in it, and the dust those who dwell silently in it; and the chambers shall give up the souls which have been committed to them. 33And the Most High shall be revealed upon the seat of judgment, and compassion shall pass away, and patience shall be withdrawn; 34but only judgment shall remain, truth shall stand, and faithfulness shall grow strong. 35And recompense shall follow, and the reward shall be manifested; righteous deeds shall awake, and unrighteous deeds shall not sleep. [36]Then the pit of torment shall appear, and opposite it shall be the place of rest; and the furnace of hell shall be disclosed, and opposite it the paradise of delight. [37]Then the Most High will say to the nations that have been raised from the dead, 'Look now, and understand whom you have denied, whom you have not served, whose commandments you have despised! [38]Look on this side and on that; here are delight and rest, and there are fire and torments!' Thus he will speak to them on the day of judgment— [39]a day that has no sun or moon or stars, [40]or cloud or thunder or lightning or wind or water or air, or darkness or evening or morning, [41]or summer or spring or heat or winter or frost or cold or hail or rain or dew, [42]or noon or night, or dawn or shining or brightness or light, but only the splendor of the glory of the Most High, by which all shall see what has been determined for them. [43]For it will last for about a week of years. [44]This is my judgment and its prescribed order; and to you alone have I shown these things."

[45]I answered and said, "O sovereign Lord, I said then and I say now: Blessed are those who are alive and keep thy commandments! [46]But what of those for whom I prayed? For who among the living is there that has not sinned, or who among men that has not transgressed thy covenant? [47]And now I see that the world to come will bring delight to few, but torments to many. [48]For an evil heart has grown up in us, which has alienated us from God, and has brought us into corruption and the ways of death, and has shown us the paths of perdition and removed us far from life—and that not just a few of us but almost all who have been created!"

74

[49]He answered me and said, "Listen to me, Ezra, and I will instruct you, and will admonish you yet again. [50]For this reason the Most High has made not one world but two. [51]For whereas you have said that the righteous are not many but few, while the ungodly abound, hear the explanation for this.

[52]"If you have just a few precious stones, will you add to them lead and clay?"

[53]I said, "Lord, how could that be?"

[54]And he said to me, "Not only that, but ask the earth and she will tell you; defer to her, and she will declare it to you. [55]Say to her, 'You produce gold and silver and brass, and also iron and lead and clay; [56]but silver is more abundant than gold, and brass than silver, and iron than brass, and lead than iron, and clay than lead.' [57]Judge therefore which things are precious and desirable, those that are abundant or those that are rare?

[58]I said, "O sovereign Lord, what is plentiful is of less worth, for what is more rare is more precious."

[59]He answered me and said, "Weigh within yourself what you have thought, for he who has what is hard to get rejoices more than he who has what is plentiful. [60]So also will be the judgment which I have promised; for I will rejoice over the few who shall be saved, because it is they who have made my glory to prevail now, and through them my name has now been honored. [61]And I will not grieve over the multitude of those who perish; for it is they who are now like a mist, and are similar to a flame and smoke—they are set on fire and burn hotly, and are extinguished."

[62]I replied and said, "O earth, what have you brought forth, if the mind is made out of the dust like the other created things! [63]For it would have been better if the dust itself had not been born, so that the mind might not have been made from it. [64]But now the mind grows with us, and therefore we are tormented, because we perish and know it. [65]Let the human race lament, but let the beasts of the field be glad; let all who have been born lament, but let the four-footed beasts and the flocks rejoice! [66]For it is much better with them than with us; for they do not look for a judgment, nor do they know of any torment or salvation promised to them after death. [67]For what does it profit us that we shall be preserved alive but cruelly tormented? [68]For all who have been born are involved in iniquities, and are full of sins and burdened with transgressions. [69]And if we were not to come into judgment after death, perhaps it would have been better for us."

[70]He answered me and said, "When the Most High made the world and Adam and all who have come from him, he first prepared the judgment and the things that pertain to the judgment. [71]And now understand from your own words, for you have said that the mind grows with us. [72]For this reason, therefore, those who dwell on earth shall be tormented, because though they had understanding they committed iniquity, and though they received the commandments they did not keep them, and though they obtained the law they dealt unfaithfully with what they received. [73]What, then, will they have to say in the judgment, or how will they answer in the last times? [74]For how long the time is that the Most High has been patient with those who inhabit the world, and not for their sake, but because of the times which he has foreordained!"

[75]I answered and said, "If I have found favor in thy sight, O Lord, show this also to thy servant: whether after death, as soon as everyone of us yields up his soul, we shall be kept in rest until those times come when thou wilt renew the creation, or whether we shall be tormented at once?"

[76]He answered me and said, "I will show you that also, but do not be associated with those who have shown scorn, nor number yourself among those who are tormented. [77]For you have a treasure of works laid up with the Most High; but it will not be shown to you until the last times. [78]Now, concerning death, the teaching is: When the decisive decree has gone forth from the Most High that a man shall die, as the spirit leaves the body to return again to him who gave it, first of all it adores the glory of the Most High. [79]And if it is one of those who have shown scorn and have not kept the way of the Most High, and who have despised his law, and who have hated those who fear God— [80]such spirits shall not enter into habitations, but shall immediately wander about in torments, ever grieving and sad, in seven ways. [81]The first way, because they have scorned the law of the Most High. [82]The second way, because they cannot now make a good repentance that they may live. [83]The third way, they shall see the reward laid up for those who have trusted the covenants of the Most High. [84]The fourth way, they shall consider the torment laid up for themselves in the last days. [85]The fifth way, they shall see how the habitations of the others are guarded by angels in profound quiet. [86]The sixth way, they shall see how some of them will pass over into torments. [87]The seventh way, which is worse than all the ways that have been mentioned, because they shall utterly waste away in confusion and be consumed with shame, and shall wither with fear at seeing the glory of the Most High before whom they sinned

while they were alive, and before whom they are to be judged in the last times.

[88]"Now this is the order of those who have kept the ways of the Most High, when they shall be separated from their mortal body. [89]During the time that they lived in it, they laboriously served the Most High, and withstood danger every hour, that they might keep the law of the Lawgiver perfectly. [90]Therefore this is the teaching concerning them: [91]First of all, they shall see with great joy the glory of him who receives them, for they shall have rest in seven orders. [92]The first order, because they have striven with great effort to overcome the evil thought which was formed with them, that it might not lead them astray from life into death. [93]The second order, because they see the perplexity in which the souls of the ungodly wander, and the punishment that awaits them. [94]The third order, they see the witness which he who formed them bears concerning them, that while they were alive they kept the law which was given them in trust. [95]The fourth order, they understand the rest which they now enjoy, being gathered into their chambers and guarded by angels in profound quiet, and the glory which awaits them in the last days. [96]The fifth order, they rejoice that they have now escaped what is corruptible, and shall inherit what is to come; and besides they see the straits and toil from which they have been delivered, and the spacious liberty which they are to receive and enjoy in immortality. [97]The sixth order, when it is shown to them how their face is to shine like the sun, and how they are to be made like the light of the stars, being incorruptible from then on. [98]The seventh order, which is greater than all that have been mentioned, because they shall rejoice with boldness, and shall be confident without confusion, and shall be glad without fear, for they hasten to behold the face of him whom they served in life and from whom they are to receive their reward when glorified. [99]This is the order of the souls of the righteous, as henceforth is announced; and the aforesaid are the ways of torment which those who would not give heed shall suffer hereafter."

[100]I answered and said, "Will time therefore be given to the souls, after they have been separated from the bodies, to see what you have described to me?"

[101]He said to me, "They shall have freedom for seven days, so that during these seven days they may see the things of which you have been told, and afterwards they shall be gathered in their habitations."

[102]I answered and said, "If I have found favor in thy sight, show further to me, thy servant, whether on the day of judgment the

righteous will be able to intercede for the ungodly or to entreat the Most High for them, [103]fathers for sons or sons for parents, brothers for brothers, relatives for their kinsmen, or friends for those who are most dear."

[104]He answered me and said, "Since you have found favor in my sight, I will show you this also. The day of judgment is decisive and displays to all the seal of truth. Just as now a father does not send his son, or a son his father, or a master his servant, or a friend his dearest friend, to be ill or sleep or eat or be healed in his stead, [105]so no one shall ever pray for another on that day, neither shall any one lay a burden on another; for then every one shall bear his own righteousness or unrighteousness."

36[106]I answered and said, "How then do we find that first Abraham prayed for the people of Sodom, and Moses for our fathers who sinned in the desert, 37[107]and Joshua after him for Israel in the days of Achan, 38[108]and Samuel in the days of Saul, and David for the plague, and Solomon for those in the sanctuary, 39[109]and Elijah for those who received the rain, and for the one who was dead, that he might live, 40[110]and Hezekiah for the people in the days of Sennacherib, and many others prayed for many? 41[111]If therefore the righteous have prayed for the ungodly now, when corruption has increased and unrighteousness has multiplied, why will it not be so then as well?"

42[112]He answered me and said, "This present world is not the end; the full glory does not abide in it; therefore those who were strong prayed for the weak. 43[113]But the day of judgment will be the end of this age and the beginning of the immortal age to come, in which corruption has passed away, 44[114]sinful indulgence has come to an end, unbelief has been cut off, and righteousness has increased and truth has appeared. 45[115]Therefore no one will then be able to have mercy on him who has been condemned in the judgment, or to harm him who is victorious."

46[116]I answered and said, "This is my first and last word, that it would have been better if the earth had not produced Adam, or else, when it had produced him, had restrained him from sinning. 47[117]For what good is it to all that they live in sorrow now and expect punishment after death? 48[118]O Adam, what have you done? For though it was you who sinned, the fall was not yours alone, but ours also who are your descendants. 49[119]For what good is it to us, if an eternal age has been promised to us, but we have done deeds that bring death? 50[120]And what good is it that an everlasting hope has been promised us, but we have miserably failed? 51[121]Or that safe and healthful habitations have been reserved for us, but we have lived wickedly? 52[122]Or that the glory of the Most High will defend those who have led a pure life, but we have walked in the most wicked ways? 53[123]Or that a paradise shall be revealed, whose fruit remains unspoiled and in which are abundance and healing, but we shall not enter it, 54[124]because we have lived in unseemly places? 55[125]Or that the faces of those who practiced self-control shall shine more than the stars, but our faces shall be blacker than darkness? 56[126]For while we lived and committed iniquity we did not consider what we should suffer after death."

57[127]He answered and said, "This is the meaning of the contest which every man who is born on earth shall wage, 58[128]that if he is defeated he shall suffer what you have said, but if he is victorious he shall receive what I have said. 59[129]For this is the way of which Moses, while he was alive, spoke to the people, saying, 'Choose for yourself life, that you may live!' 60[130]But they did not believe him, or the prophets after him, or even myself who have spoken to them. 61[131]Therefore there shall not be grief at their destruction, so much as joy over those to whom salvation is assured."

62[132]I answered and said, "I know, O Lord, that the Most High is now called merciful, because he has mercy on those who have not yet come into the world; 63[133]and gracious, because he is gracious to those who turn in repentance to his law; 64[134]and patient, because he shows patience toward those who have sinned, since they are his own works; 65[135]and bountiful, because he would rather give than take away; 66[136]and abundant in compassion, because he makes his compassions abound more and more to those now living and to those who are gone and to those yet to come, 67[137]for if he did not make them abound, the world with those who inhabit it would not have life; 68[138]and he is called giver, because if he did not give out of his goodness so that those who have committed iniquities might be relieved of them, not one ten-thousandth of mankind could have life; 69[139]and judge, because if he did not pardon those who were created by his word and blot out the multitude of their sins, 70[140]there would probably be left only very few of the innumerable multitude."

8. He answered me and said, "The Most High made this world for the sake of many, but the world to come for the sake of few. 2But I will tell you a parable, Ezra. Just as, when you ask the earth, it will tell you that it provides very much clay from which earthenware is made, but only a little dust from which gold comes; so is the course of the present world. [3]Many have been created, but few shall be saved."

[4]I answered and said, "Then drink your fill of understanding, O my soul, and drink wisdom, O my heart! [5]For not of your own will did you come into the world, and against your will you depart, for you have been given only a short time to live. [6]O Lord who art over us, grant to thy servant that we may pray before thee, and give us seed for our heart and cultivation of our understanding so that fruit may be produced, by which every mortal who bears the likeness of a human being may be able to live. [7]For thou alone dost exist, and we are a work of thy hands, as thou hast declared. [8]And because thou dost give life to the body which is now fashioned in the womb, and dost furnish it with members, what thou hast created is preserved in fire and water, and for nine months the womb which thou hast formed endures thy creation which has been created in it. [9]But that which keeps and that which is kept shall both be kept by thy keeping. And when the womb gives up again what has been created in it, [10]thou hast commanded that from the members themselves (that is, from the breasts) milk should be supplied which is the fruit of the breasts, [11]so that what has been fashioned may be nourished for a time; and afterwards thou wilt guide him in thy mercy. [12]Thou hast brought him up in thy righteousness, and instructed him in thy law, and reproved him in thy wisdom. [13]Thou wilt take away his life, for he is thy creation; and thou wilt make him live, for he is thy work. [14]If then thou wilt suddenly and quickly destroy him who with so great labor was fashioned by thy command, to what purpose was he made? [15]And now I will speak out: About all mankind thou knowest best; but I will speak about thy people, for whom I am grieved, [16]and about thy inheritance, for whom I lament, and about Israel, for whom I am sad, and about the seed of Jacob, for whom I am troubled. [17]Therefore I will pray before thee for myself and for them, for I see the failings of us who dwell in the land, [18]and I have heard of the swiftness of the judgment that is to come. [19]Therefore hear my voice, and understand my words, and I will speak before thee."

The beginning of the words of Ezra's prayer, before he was taken up. He said: [20]"O Lord who inhabitest eternity, whose eyes are exalted and whose upper chambers are in the air, [21]whose throne is beyond measure and whose glory is beyond comprehension, before whom the hosts of angels stand trembling [22]and at whose command they are changed to wind and fire, whose word is sure and whose utterances are certain, whose ordinance is strong and whose command is terrible, [23]whose look dries up the depths and whose indignation makes the mountains melt away, and whose truth is established for ever—24hear, O Lord, the prayer of thy servant, and give ear to the petition of thy creature; attend to my words. 25For as long as I live I will speak, and as long as I have understanding I will answer. 26O look not upon the sins of thy people, but at those who have served thee in truth. 27Regard not the endeavors of those who act wickedly, but the endeavors of those who have kept thy covenants amid afflictions. 28Think not on those who have lived wickedly in thy sight; but remember those who have willingly acknowledged that thou art to be feared. 29Let it not be thy will to destroy those who have had the ways of cattle; but regard those who have gloriously taught thy law. 30Be not angry with those who are deemed worse than beasts; but love those who have always put their trust in thy glory. 31For we and our fathers have passed our lives in ways that bring death; but thou, because of us sinners, art called merciful. 32For if thou hast desired to have pity on us, who have no works of righteousness, then thou wilt be called merciful. 33For the righteous, who have many works laid up with thee, shall receive their reward in consequence of their own deeds. 34But what is man, that thou art angry with him; or what is a corruptible race, that thou art so bitter against it? 35For in truth there is no one among those who have been born who has not acted wickedly, and among those who have existed there is no one who has not transgressed. 36For in this, O Lord, thy righteousness and goodness will be declared, when thou art merciful to those who have no store of good works."

37He answered me and said, "Some things you have spoken rightly, and it will come to pass according to your words. 38For indeed I will not concern myself about the fashioning of those who have sinned, or about their death, their judgment, or their destruction; 39but I will rejoice over the creation of the righteous, over their pilgrimage also, and their salvation, and their receiving their reward. 40As I have spoken, therefore, so it shall be.

41"For just as the farmer sows many seeds upon the ground and plants a multitude of seedlings, and yet not all that have been sown will come up in due season, and not all that were planted will take root; so also those who have been sown in the world will not all be saved."

42I answered and said, "If I have found favor before thee, let me speak. 43For if the farmer's seed does not come up, because it has not received thy rain in due season, or if it has been ruined by too much rain, it perishes. 44But man, who has been formed by thy hands and is called

81

thy own image because he is made like thee, and for whose sake thou hast formed all things—hast thou also made him like the farmer's seed? [45]No, O Lord who art over us! But spare thy people and have mercy on thy inheritance, for thou hast mercy on thy own creation."

[46]He answered me and said, "Things that are present are for those who live now, and things that are future are for those who will live hereafter. [47]For you come far short of being able to love my creation more than I love it. But you have often compared yourself to the unrighteous. Never do so! [48]But even in this respect you will be praiseworthy before the Most High, [49]because you have humbled yourself, as is becoming for you, and have not deemed yourself to be among the righteous in order to receive the greatest glory. [50]For many miseries will affect those who inhabit the world in the last times, because they have walked in great pride. [51]But think of your own case, and inquire concerning the glory of those who are like yourself, [52]because it is for you that paradise is opened, the tree of life is planted, the age to come is prepared, plenty is provided, a city is built, rest is appointed, goodness is established and wisdom perfected beforehand. [53]The root of evil is sealed up from you, illness is banished from you, and death is hidden; hell has fled and corruption has been forgotten; [54]sorrows have passed away, and in the end the treasure of immortality is made manifest. [55]Therefore do not ask any more questions about the multitude of those who perish. [56]For they also received freedom, but they despised the Most High, and were contemptuous of his law, and forsook his ways. [57]Moreover they have even trampled upon his righteous ones, [58]and said in their hearts that there is no God—though knowing full well that they must die. [59]For just as the things which I have predicted await you, so the thirst and torment which are prepared await them. For the Most High did not intend that men should be destroyed; [60]but they themselves who were created have defiled the name of him who made them, and have been ungrateful to him who prepared life for them. [61]Therefore my judgment is now drawing near;[62]I have not shown this to all men, but only to you and a few like you."

Then I answered and said, [63]"Behold, O Lord, thou hast now shown me a multitude of the signs which thou wilt do in the last times, but thou hast not shown me when thou wilt do them."

9. He answered me and said, "Measure carefully in your mind, and when you see that a certain part of the predicted signs are past, [2]then you will know that it is the very time when the Most High is about to visit the world which he has made. [3]So when there shall appear in the world earthquakes, tumult of peoples, intrigues of nations, wavering of leaders, confusion of princes, [4]then you will know that it was of these that the Most High spoke from the days that were of old, from the beginning. [5]For just as with everything that has occurred in the world, the beginning is evident, and the end manifest; [6]so also are the times of the Most High: the beginnings are manifest in wonders and mighty works, and the end in requital and in signs. [7]And it shall be that every one who will be saved and will be able to escape on account of his works, or on account of the faith by which he has believed, [8]will survive the dangers that have been predicted, and will see my salvation in my land and within my borders, which I have sanctified for myself from the beginning. [9]Then those who have now abused my ways shall be amazed, and those who have rejected them with contempt shall dwell in torments. [10]For as many as did not acknowledge me in their lifetime, although they received my benefits, [11]and as many as scorned my law while they still had freedom, and did not understand but despised it while an opportunity of repentance was still open to them, [12]these must in torment acknowledge it after death. [13]Therefore, do not continue to be curious as to how the ungodly will be punished; but inquire how the righteous will be saved, those to whom the age belongs and for whose sake the age was made.

[14]I answered and said, [15]"I said before, and I say now, and will say it again: there are more who perish than those who will be saved, [16]as a wave is greater than a drop of water."

[17]He answered me and said, "As is the field, so is the seed; and as are the flowers, so are the colors; and as is the work, so is the product; and as is the farmer, so is the threshing floor. [18]For there was a time in this age when I was preparing for those who now exist, before the world was made for them to dwell in, and no one opposed me then, for no one existed; [19]but now those who have been created in this world which is supplied both with an unfailing table and an inexhaustible pasture, have become corrupt in their ways. [20]So I considered my world, and behold, it was lost, and my earth, and behold, it was in peril because of the devices of those who had come into it. [21]And I saw and spared some with great difficulty, and saved for myself one grape out of a cluster, and one plant out of a great forest. [22]So let the multitude perish which has been born in vain, but let my grape and my plant be saved, because with much labor I have perfected them. [23]But if you will let seven days more pass—do not fast during them, however; [24]but go into a field of flowers where no

house has been built, and eat only of the flowers of the field, and taste no meat and drink no wine, but eat only flowers, 25and pray to the Most High continually—then I will come and talk with you."

26So I went, as he directed me, into the field which is called Ardat; and there I sat among the flowers and ate of the plants of the field, and the nourishment they afforded satisfied me. 27And after seven days, as I lay on the grass, my heart was troubled again as it was before. 28And my mouth was opened, and I began to speak before the Most High, and said, 29"O Lord, thou didst show thyself among us, to our fathers in the wilderness when they came out from Egypt and when they came into the untrodden and unfruitful wilderness; 30and thou didst say, 'Hear me, O Israel, and give heed to my words, O descendants of Jacob. 31For behold, I sow my law in you, and it shall bring forth fruit in you, and you shall be glorified through it for ever.' 32But though our fathers received the law, they did not keep it, and did not observe the statutes; yet the fruit of the law did not perish—for it could not, because it was thine. 33Yet those who received it perished, because they did not keep what had been sown in them. 34And behold, it is the rule that, when the ground has received seed, or the sea a ship, or any dish food or drink, and when it happens that what was sown or what was launched or what was put in is destroyed, 35they are destroyed, but the things that held them remain; yet with us it has not been so. 36For we who have received the law and sinned will perish, as well as our heart which received it; 37the law, however, does not perish but remains in its glory."

38When I said these things in my heart, I lifted up my eyes and saw a woman on my right, and behold, she was mourning and weeping with a loud voice, and was deeply grieved at heart, and her clothes were rent, and there were ashes on her head. 39Then I dismissed the thoughts with which I had been engaged, and turned to her 40and said to her, "Why are you weeping, and why are you grieved at heart?"

41And she said to me, "Let me alone, my lord, that I may weep for myself and continue to mourn, for I am greatly embittered in spirit and deeply afflicted."

42And I said to her, "What has happened to you? Tell me."

43And she said to me, "Your servant was barren and had no child, though I lived with my husband thirty years. 44And every hour and every day during those thirty years I besought the Most High, night and day. 45And after thirty years God heard your handmaid, and looked upon my low estate, and considered my distress, and gave me a son. And I rejoiced greatly over him, I and my husband and all my neighbors; and we gave great glory to the Mighty One. ⁴⁶And I brought him up with much care. ⁴⁷So when he grew up and I came to take a wife for him, I set a day for the marriage feast.

10. "But it happened that when my son entered his wedding chamber, he fell down and died. ²Then we all put out the lamps, and all my neighbors attempted to console me; and I remained quiet until evening of the second day. ³But when they all had stopped consoling me, that I might be quiet, I got up in the night and fled, and came to this field, as you see. ⁴And now I intend not to return to the city, but to stay here, and I will neither eat nor drink, but without ceasing mourn and fast until I die."

⁵Then I broke off the reflections with which I was still engaged, and answered her in anger and said, ⁶"You most foolish of women, do you not see our mourning, and what has happened to us? ⁷For Zion, the mother of us all, is in deep grief and great affliction. ⁸It is most appropriate to mourn now, because we are all mourning, and to be sorrowful, because we are all sorrowing; you are sorrowing for one son, but we, the whole world, for our mother. ⁹Now ask the earth, and she will tell you that it is she who ought to mourn over so many who have come into being upon her. ¹⁰And from the beginning all have been born of her, and others will come; and behold, almost all go to perdition, and a multitude of them are destined for destruction. ¹¹Who then ought to mourn the more, she who lost so great a multitude, or you who are grieving for one? ¹²But if you say to me, 'My lamentation is not like the earth's, for I have lost the fruit of my womb, which I brought forth in pain and bore in sorrow; ¹³but it is with the earth according to the way of the earth—the multitude that is now in it goes as it came'; ¹⁴then I say to you, 'As you brought forth in sorrow, so the earth also has from the beginning given her fruit, that is, man, to him who made her.' ¹⁵Now, therefore, keep your sorrow to yourself, and bear bravely the troubles that have come upon you. ¹⁶For if you acknowledge the decree of God to be just, you will receive your son back in due time, and will be praised among women. ¹⁷Therefore go into the city to your husband."

¹⁸She said to me, "I will not do so; I will not go into the city, but I will die here."

¹⁹So I spoke again to her, and said, ²⁰"Do not say that, but let yourself be persuaded because of the troubles of Zion, and be consoled because of the sorrow of Jerusalem. ²¹For you see that our sanctuary has been laid waste, our altar thrown down, our temple destroyed; ²²our harp has

been laid low, our song has been silenced, and our rejoicing has been ended; the light of our lampstand has been put out, the ark of our covenant has been plundered, our holy things have been polluted, and the name by which we are called has been profaned; our free men have suffered abuse, our priests have been burned to death, our Levites have gone into captivity, our virgins have been defiled, and our wives have been ravished; our righteous men have been carried off, our little ones have been cast out, our young men have been enslaved and our strong men made powerless. 23And, what is more than all, the seal of Zion—for she has now lost the seal of her glory, and has been given over into the hands of those that hate us. 24Therefore shake off your great sadness and lay aside your many sorrows, so that the Mighty One may be merciful to you again, and the Most High may give you rest, a relief from your troubles."

25While I was talking to her, behold, her face suddenly shone exceedingly, and her countenance flashed like lightning, so that I was too frightened to approach her, and my heart was terrified. While I was wondering what this meant, 26behold, she suddenly uttered a loud and fearful cry, so that the earth shook at the sound. 27And I looked, and behold, the woman was no longer visible to me, but there was an established city, and a place of huge foundations showed itself. Then I was afraid, and cried with a loud voice and said, 28"Where is the angel Uriel, who came to me at first? For it was he who brought me into this overpowering bewilderment; my end has become corruption, and my prayer a reproach."

29As I was speaking these words, behold, the angel who had come to me at first came to me, and he looked upon me; 30and behold, I lay there like a corpse and I was deprived of my understanding. Then he grasped my right hand and strengthened me and set me on my feet, and said to me, 31"What is the matter with you? And why are you troubled? And why are your understanding and the thoughts of your mind troubled?"

32I said, "Because you have forsaken me! I did as you directed, and went out into the field, and behold, I saw, and still see, what I am unable to explain."

33He said to me, "Stand up like a man, and I will instruct you."

34I said, "Speak, my lord; only do not forsake me, lest I die before my time. 35For I have seen what I did not know, and I have heard what I do not understand. 36Or is my mind deceived, and my soul dreaming? 37Now therefore I entreat you to give your servant an explanation of this bewildering vision."

³⁸He answered me and said, "Listen to me and I will inform you, and tell you about the things which you fear, for the Most High has revealed many secrets to you. ³⁹For he has seen your righteous conduct, that you have sorrowed continually for your people, and mourned greatly over Zion. ⁴⁰This therefore is the meaning of the vision. ⁴¹The woman who appeared to you a little while ago, whom you saw mourning and began to console—⁴²but you do not now see the form of a woman, but an established city has appeared to you—⁴³and as for her telling you about the misfortune of her son, this is the interpretation: ⁴⁴This woman whom you saw, whom you now behold as an established city, is Zion. ⁴⁵And as for her telling you that she was barren for thirty years, it is because there were three thousand years in the world before any offering was offered in it. ⁴⁶And after three thousand years Solomon built the city, and offered offerings; then it was that the barren woman bore a son. ⁴⁷And as for her telling you that she brought him up with much care, that was the period of residence in Jerusalem. ⁴⁸And as for her saying to you, 'When my son entered his wedding chamber he died,' and that misfortune had overtaken her, that was the destruction which befell Jerusalem. ⁴⁹And behold, you saw her likeness, how she mourned for her son, and you began to console her for what had happened. ⁵⁰For now the Most High, seeing that you are sincerely grieved and profoundly distressed for her, has shown you the brilliance of her glory, and the loveliness of her beauty. ⁵¹Therefore I told you to remain in the field where no house had been built, ⁵²for I knew that the Most High would reveal these things to you. ⁵³Therefore I told you to go into the field where there was no foundation of any building, ⁵⁴for no work of man's building could endure in a place where the city of the Most High was to be revealed.

⁵⁵"Therefore do not be afraid, and do not let your heart be terrified; but go in and see the splendor and vastness of the building, as far as it is possible for your eyes to see it, ⁵⁶and afterward you will hear as much as your ears can hear. ⁵⁷For you are more blessed than many, and you have been called before the Most High, as but few have been. ⁵⁸But tomorrow night you shall remain here, ⁵⁹and the Most High will show you in those dream visions what the Most High will do to those who dwell on earth in the last days."

So I slept that night and the following one, as he had commanded me.

11. On the second night I had a dream, and behold, there came up from the sea an eagle that had twelve feathered wings and three heads.

²And I looked, and behold, he spread his wings over all the earth, and all the winds of heaven blew upon him, and the clouds were gathered about him. ³And I looked, and out of his wings there grew opposing wings; but they became little, puny wings. ⁴But his heads were at rest; the middle head was larger than the other heads, but it also was at rest with them. ⁵And I looked, and behold, the eagle flew with his wings, to reign over the earth and over those who dwell in it. ⁶And I saw how all things under heaven were subjected to him, and no one spoke against him, not even one creature that was on the earth. ⁷And I looked, and behold, the eagle rose upon his talons, and uttered a cry to his wings, saying, ⁸"Do not all watch at the same time; let each sleep in his own place, and watch in his turn; ⁹but let the heads be reserved for the last."

¹⁰And I looked, and behold, the voice did not come from his heads, but from the midst of his body. ¹¹And I counted his opposing wings, and behold, there were eight of them. ¹²And I looked, and behold, on the right side one wing arose, and it reigned over all the earth. ¹³And while it was reigning it came to its end and disappeared, so that its place was not seen. Then the next wing arose and reigned, and it continued to reign a long time. ¹⁴And while it was reigning its end came also, so that it disappeared like the first. ¹⁵And behold, a voice sounded, saying to it, ¹⁶"Hear me, you who have ruled the earth all this time; I announce this to you before you disappear. ¹⁷After you no one shall rule as long as you, or even half as long."

¹⁸Then the third wing raised itself up, and held the rule like the former ones, and it also disappeared. ¹⁹And so it went with all the wings; they wielded power one after another and then were never seen again. ²⁰And I looked, and behold, in due course the wings that followed also rose up on the right side, in order to rule. There were some of them that ruled, yet disappeared suddenly; ²¹and others of them rose up, but did not hold the rule.

²²And after this I looked, and behold, the twelve wings and the two little wings disappeared; ²³and nothing remained on the eagle's body except the three heads that were at rest and six little wings. ²⁴And I looked, and behold, two little wings separated from the six and remained under the head that was on the right side; but four remained in their place. ²⁵And I looked, and behold, these little wings planned to set themselves up and hold the rule. ²⁶And I looked, and behold, one was set up, but suddenly disappeared; ²⁷a second also, and this disappeared more quickly than the first. ²⁸And I looked, and behold, the two that remained were planning between themselves to reign together;

29and while they were planning, behold, one of the heads that were at rest (the one which was in the middle) awoke; for it was greater than the other two heads. 30And I saw how it allied the two heads with itself, 31and behold, the head turned with those that were with it, and it devoured the two little wings which were planning to reign. 32Moreover this head gained control of the whole earth, and with much oppression dominated its inhabitants; and it had greater power over the world than all the wings that had gone before.

33And after this I looked, and behold, the middle head also suddenly disappeared, just as the wings had done. 34But the two heads remained, which also ruled over the earth and its inhabitants. 35And I looked, and behold, the head on the right side devoured the one on the left.

36Then I heard a voice saying to me, "Look before you and consider what you see." 37And I looked, and behold, a creature like a lion was aroused out of the forest, roaring; and I heard how he uttered a man's voice to the eagle, and spoke, saying, 38"Listen and I will speak to you. The Most High says to you, 39'Are you not the one that remains of the four beasts which I had made to reign in my world, so that the end of my times might come through them? 40You, the fourth that has come, have conquered all the beasts that have gone before; and you have held sway over the world with much terror, and over all the earth with grievous oppression; and for so long you have dwelt on the earth with deceit. 41And you have judged the earth, but not with truth; 42for you have afflicted the meek and injured the peaceable; you have hated those who tell the truth, and have loved liars; you have destroyed the dwellings of those who brought forth fruit, and have laid low the walls of those who did you no harm. 43And so your insolence has come up before the Most High, and your pride to the Mighty One. 44And the Most High has looked upon his times, and behold, they are ended, and his ages are completed! 45Therefore you will surely disappear, you eagle, and your terrifying wings, and your most evil little wings, and your malicious heads, and your most evil talons, and your whole worthless body, 46so that the whole earth, freed from your violence, may be refreshed and relieved, and may hope for the judgment and mercy of him who made it.' "

12. While the lion was saying these words to the eagle, I looked, 2and behold, the remaining head disappeared. And the two wings that had gone over to it arose and set themselves up to reign, and their reign was brief and full of tumult. 3And I looked, and behold, they also disappeared, and the whole body of the eagle was burned, and the earth was exceedingly terrified.

Then I awoke in great perplexity of mind and great fear, and I said to my spirit, 4"Behold, you have brought this upon me, because you search out the ways of the Most High. 5Behold, I am still weary in mind and very weak in my spirit, and not even a little strength is left in me, because of the great fear with which I have been terrified this night. 6Therefore I will now beseech the Most High that he may strengthen me to the end."

7And I said, "O sovereign Lord, if I have found favor in thy sight, and if I have been accounted righteous before thee beyond many others, and if my prayer has indeed come up before thy face, 8strengthen me and show me, thy servant, the interpretation and meaning of this terrifying vision, that thou mayest fully comfort my soul. 9For thou hast judged me worthy to be shown the end of the times and the last events of the times."

10He said to me, "This is the interpretation of this vision which you have seen: 11The eagle which you saw coming up from the sea is the fourth kingdom which appeared in a vision to your brother Daniel. 12But it was not explained to him as I now explain or have explained it to you. 13Behold, the days are coming when a kingdom shall arise on earth, and it shall be more terrifying than all the kingdoms that have been before it. 14And twelve kings shall reign in it, one after another. 15But the second that is to reign shall hold sway for a longer time than any other of the twelve. 16This is the interpretation of the twelve wings which you saw. 17As for your hearing a voice that spoke, coming not from the eagle's heads but from the midst of his body, this is the interpretation: 18In the midst of the time of that kingdom great struggles shall arise, and it shall be in danger of falling; nevertheless it shall not fall then, but shall regain its former power. 19As for your seeing eight little wings clinging to his wings, this is the interpretation: 20Eight kings shall arise in it, whose times shall be short and their years swift; 21and two of them shall perish when the middle of its time draws near; and four shall be kept for the time when its end approaches; but two shall be kept until the end. 22As for your seeing three heads at rest, this is the interpretation: 23In its last days the Most High will raise up three kings, and they shall renew many things in it, and shall rule the earth 24and its inhabitants more oppressively than all who were before them; therefore they are called the heads of the eagle. 25For it is they who shall sum up his wickedness and perform his last actions. 26As for your seeing that the large head disappeared, one of the kings shall die in his bed, but in agonies. 27But as for the two who remained, the sword shall devour them. 28For the sword of one shall devour him who was with him; but he also shall fall by the sword in the last days. ²⁹As for your seeing two little wings passing over to the head which was on the right side, ³⁰this is the interpretation: It is these whom the Most High has kept for the eagle's end; this was the reign which was brief and full of tumult, as you have seen.

³¹"And as for the lion whom you saw rousing up out of the forest and roaring and speaking to the eagle and reproving him for his unrighteousness, and as for all his words that you have heard, ³²this is the Messiah whom the Most High has kept until the end of days, who will arise from the posterity of David, and will come and speak to them; he will denounce them for their ungodliness and for their wickedness, and will cast up before them their contemptuous dealings. ³³For first he will set them living before his judgment seat, and when he has reproved them, then he will destroy them. ³⁴But he will deliver in mercy the remnant of my people, those who have been saved throughout my borders, and he will make them joyful until the end comes, the day of judgment, of which I spoke to you at the beginning. ³⁵This is the dream that you saw, and this is its interpretation. ³⁶And you alone were worthy to learn this secret of the Most High. ³⁷Therefore write all these things that you have seen in a book, and put it in a hidden place; ³⁸and you shall teach them to the wise among your people, whose hearts you know are able to comprehend and keep these secrets. ³⁹But wait here seven days more, so that you may be shown whatever it pleases the Most High to show you." Then he left me.

⁴⁰When all the people heard that the seven days were past and I had not returned to the city, they all gathered together, from the least to the greatest, and came to me and spoke to me, saying, ⁴¹"How have we offended you, and what harm have we done you, that you have forsaken us and sit in this place? ⁴²For of all the prophets you alone are left to us, like a cluster of grapes from the vintage, and like a lamp in a dark place, and like a haven for a ship saved from a storm. ⁴³Are not the evils which have befallen us sufficient? ⁴⁴Therefore if you forsake us, how much better it would have been for us if we also had been consumed in the burning of Zion! ⁴⁵For we are no better than those who died there." And they wept with a loud voice.

Then I answered them and said, ⁴⁶"Take courage, O Israel; and do not be sorrowful, O house of Jacob; ⁴⁷for the Most High has you in remembrance, and the Mighty One has not forgotten you in your struggle. ⁴⁸As for me, I have neither forsaken you nor withdrawn from you; but I have come to this place to pray on account of the desolation of

Zion, and to seek mercy on account of the humiliation of our sanctuary. [49]Now go, every one of you to his house, and after these days I will come to you." [50]So the people went into the city, as I told them to do. [51]But I sat in the field seven days, as the angel had commanded me; and I ate only of the flowers of the field, and my food was of plants during those days.

13. After seven days I dreamed a dream in the night; [2]and behold, a wind arose from the sea and stirred up all its waves. [3]And I looked, and behold, this wind made something like the figure of a man come up out of the heart of the sea. And I looked, and behold, that man flew with the clouds of heaven; and wherever he turned his face to look, everything under his gaze trembled, [4]and whenever his voice issued from his mouth, all who heard his voice melted as wax melts when it feels the fire.

[5]After this I looked, and behold, an innumerable multitude of men were gathered together from the four winds of heaven to make war against the man who came up out of the sea. [6]And I looked, and behold, he carved out for himself a great mountain, and flew up upon it. [7]And I tried to see the region or place from which the mountain was carved, but I could not.

[8]After this I looked, and behold, all who had gathered together against him, to wage war with him, were much afraid, yet dared to fight. [9]And behold, when he saw the onrush of the approaching multitude, he neither lifted his hand nor held a spear or any weapon of war; [10]but I saw only how he sent forth from his mouth as it were a stream of fire, and from his lips a flaming breath, and from his tongue he shot forth a storm of sparks. [11]All these were mingled together, the stream of fire and the flaming breath and the great storm, and fell on the onrushing multitude which was prepared to fight, and burned them all up, so that suddenly nothing was seen of the innumerable multitude but only the dust of ashes and the smell of smoke. When I saw it, I was amazed.

[12]After this I saw the same man come down from the mountain and call to him another multitude which was peaceable. [13]Then many people came to him, some of whom were joyful and some sorrowful; some of them were bound, and some were bringing others as offerings.

Then in great fear I awoke; and I besought the Most High, and said, [14]"From the beginning thou hast shown thy servant these wonders, and hast deemed me worthy to have my prayer heard by thee; [15]now show me also the interpretation of this dream. [16]For as I consider it in my mind, alas for those who will be left in those days! And still more, alas for those who are not left! [17]For those who are not left will be sad, [18]because they understand what is reserved for the last days, but cannot attain it. [19]But alas for those also who are left, and for that very reason! For they shall see great dangers and much distress, as these dreams show. [20]Yet it is better to come into these things, though incurring peril, than to pass from the world like a cloud, and not to see what shall happen in the last days."

He answered me and said, [21]"I will tell you the interpretation of the vision, and I will also explain to you the things which you have mentioned. [22]As for what you said about those who are left, this is the interpretation: [23]He who brings the peril at that time will himself protect those who fall into peril, who have works and have faith in the Almighty. [24]Understand therefore that those who are left are more blessed than those who have died. [25]This is the interpretation of the vision: As for your seeing a man come up from the heart of the sea, [26]this is he whom the Most High has been keeping for many ages, who will himself deliver his creation; and he will direct those who are left. [27]And as for your seeing wind and fire and a storm coming out of his mouth, [28]and as for his not holding a spear or weapon of war, yet destroying the onrushing multitude which came to conquer him, this is the interpretation: [29]Behold, the days are coming when the Most High will deliver those who are on the earth. [30]And bewilderment of mind shall come over those who dwell on the earth. [31]And they shall plan to make war against one another, city against city, place against place, people against people, and kingdom against kingdom. [32]And when these things come to pass and the signs occur which I showed you before, then my Son will be revealed, whom you saw as a man coming up from the sea. [33]And when all the nations hear his voice, every man shall leave his own land and the warfare that they have against one another; [34]and an innumerable multitude shall be gathered together, as you saw, desiring to come and conquer him. [35]But he will stand on the top of Mount Zion. [36]And Zion will come and be made manifest to all people, prepared and built, as you saw the mountain carved out without hands. [37]And he, my Son, will reprove the assembled nations for their ungodliness (this was symbolized by the storm), [38]and will reproach them to their face with their evil thoughts and the torments with which they are to be tortured (which were symbolized by the flames), and will destroy them without effort by the law (which was symbolized by the fire). [39]And as for your seeing him gather to himself another multitude that was peaceable, [40]these are the ten tribes which were led away from their own land into captivity in the days of King Hoshea, whom Shalmaneser the king of the

Assyrians led captive; he took them across the river, and they were taken into another land. 41But they formed this plan for themselves, that they would leave the multitude of the nations and go to a more distant region, where mankind had never lived, 42that there at least they might keep their statutes which they had not kept in their own land. 43And they went in by the narrow passages of the Euphrates river. 44For at that time the Most High performed signs for them, and stopped the channels of the river until they had passed over. 45Through that region there was a long way to go, a journey of a year and a half; and that country is called Arzareth.

46"Then they dwelt there until the last times; and now, when they are about to come again, 47the Most High will stop the channels of the river again, so that they may be able to pass over. Therefore you saw the multitude gathered together in peace. 48But those who are left of your people, who are found within my holy borders, shall be saved. 49Therefore when he destroys the multitude of the nations that are gathered together, he will defend the people who remain. 50And then he will show them very many wonders."

51I said, "O sovereign Lord, explain this to me: Why did I see the man coming up from the heart of the sea?"

52He said to me, "Just as no one can explore or know what is in the depths of the sea, so no one on earth can see my Son or those who are with him, except in the time of his day. 53This is the interpretation of the dream which you saw. And you alone have been enlightened about this, 54because you have forsaken your own ways and have applied yourself to mine, and have searched out my law; 55for you have devoted your life to wisdom, and called understanding your mother. 56Therefore I have shown you this, for there is a reward laid up with the Most High. And after three more days I will tell you other things, and explain weighty and wondrous matters to you."

57Then I arose and walked in the field, giving great glory and praise to the Most High because of his wonders, which he did from time to time, 58and because he governs the times and whatever things come to pass in their seasons. And I stayed there three days.

14. On the third day, while I was sitting under an oak, behold, a voice came out of a bush opposite me and said, "Ezra, Ezra." 2And I said, "Here I am, Lord," and I rose to my feet. 3Then he said to me, "I revealed myself in a bush and spoke to Moses, when my people were in bondage in Egypt; 4and I sent him and led my people out of Egypt; and I led him up on Mount Sinai, where I kept him with me many days; 5and I told him many wondrous things, and showed him the secrets of the times and declared to him the end of the times. Then I commanded him, saying, 6'These words you shall publish openly, and these you shall keep secret.' 7And now I say to you: 8Lay up in your heart the signs that I have shown you, the dreams that you have seen, and the interpretations that you have heard; 9for you shall be taken up from among men, and henceforth you shall live with my Son and with those who are like you, until the times are ended. 10For the age has lost its youth and the times begin to grow old. 11For the age is divided into twelve parts, and nine of its parts have already passed, 12as well as half of the tenth part; so two of its parts remain, besides half of the tenth part. 13Now therefore, set your house in order, and reprove your people; comfort the lowly among them, and instruct those that are wise. And now renounce the life that is corruptible, 14and put away from you mortal thoughts; cast away from you the burdens of man, and divest yourself now of your weak nature, 15and lay to one side the thoughts that are most grievous to you, and hasten to escape from these times. 16For evils worse than those which you have now seen happen shall be done hereafter. 17For the weaker the world becomes through old age, the more shall evils be multiplied among its inhabitants. 18For truth shall go farther away, and falsehood shall come near. For the eagle which you saw in the vision is already hastening to come."

19Then I answered and said, "Let me speak in thy presence, Lord. 20For behold, I will go, as thou hast commanded me, and I will reprove the people who are now living; but who will warn those who will be born hereafter? For the world lies in darkness, and its inhabitants are without light. 21For thy law has been burned, and so no one knows the things which have been done or will be done by thee. 22If then I have found favor before thee, send the Holy Spirit into me, and I will write everything that has happened in the world from the beginning, the things which were written in thy law, that men may be able to find the path, and that those who wish to live in the last days may live."

23He answered me and said, "Go and gather the people, and tell them not to seek you for forty days. 24But prepare for yourself many writing tablets, and take with you Sarea, Dabria, Selemia, Ethanus, and Asiel—these five, because they are trained to write rapidly; 25and you shall come here, and I will light in your heart the lamp of understanding, which shall not be put out until what you are about to write is finished. 26And when you have finished, some things you shall make public, and some you shall deliver in secret to the wise; tomorrow at this hour you shall begin to write."

27Then I went as he commanded me, and I gathered all the people together, and said, 28"Hear these words, O Israel. 29At first our fathers dwelt as aliens in Egypt, and they were delivered from there, 30and received the law of life, which they did not keep, which you also have transgressed after them. 31Then land was given to you for a possession in the land of Zion; but you and your fathers committed iniquity and did not keep the ways which the Most High commanded you. 32And because he is a righteous judge, in due time he took from you what he had given. 33And now you are here, and your brethren are farther in the interior. 34If you, then, will rule over your minds and discipline your hearts, you shall be kept alive, and after death you shall obtain mercy. 35For after death the judgment will come, when we shall live again; and then the names of the righteous will become manifest, and the deeds of the ungodly will be disclosed. 36But let no one come to me now, and let no one seek me for forty days."

37So I took the five men, as he commanded me, and we proceeded to the field, and remained there. 38And on the next day, behold, a voice called me, saying, "Ezra, open your mouth and drink what I give you to drink." 39Then I opened my mouth, and behold, a full cup was offered to me; it was full of something like water, but its color was like fire. 40And I took it and drank; and when I had drunk it, my heart poured forth understanding, and wisdom increased in my breast, for my spirit retained its memory; 41and my mouth was opened, and was no longer closed. 42And the Most High gave understanding to the five men, and by turns they wrote what was dictated, in characters which they did not know. They sat forty days, and wrote during the daytime and ate their bread at night. 43As for me, I spoke in the daytime and was not silent at night. 44So during the forty days ninety-four books were written. 45And when the forty days were ended, the Most High spoke to me, saying, "Make public the twenty-four books that you wrote first and let the worthy and the unworthy read them; 46but keep the seventy that were written last, in order to give them to the wise among your people. 47For in them is the spring of understanding, the fountain of wisdom, and the river of knowledge." 48And I did so.

2 BARUCH

Commentary

The *Syriac Apocalypse of Baruch,* also known as *2 Baruch,* is one of several pseudonymous writings attributed to Baruch, the scribe of the sixth-century B.C.E. prophet Jeremiah. The work is thoroughly Jewish, showing little, if any, sign of Christian interpolation. Writing after the fall of Jerusalem to the Romans in 70 C.E., the author uses the fall of Jerusalem to the Babylonians in 586 B.C.E. as the setting for his work. The similarities to 4 Ezra in structure, themes, and purpose point to the time of composition as being close to that of 4 Ezra. Thus a date around the end of the first century is usually accepted for *2 Baruch.* Its close relationship to 4 Ezra and the likelihood that it was originally composed in Hebrew strongly suggest Palestine as the location in which the work was written.

Like 4 Ezra, *2 Baruch* is concerned with the destruction of Jerusalem by the Romans and the resulting theological problems for the Jewish people. The fictional setting for the work is prior to the fall of Jerusalem, but its imminent destruction is revealed to Baruch by God. Disaster will strike Jerusalem and the Jewish people, Baruch is told, because of their sinfulness. Baruch is comforted upon learning that the sacred articles in the Temple will not fall into the hands of the Babylonians, but will be carried away by an angel and deposited for safe keeping in the earth. Furthermore, the purpose of this calamity, he is told, is to chastise the Jewish people and to lead them to repentance. The wicked, on the other hand, including the Babylonians, will ultimately be punished.

Divine disclosures about the future are the major sources of hope and optimism in the writing. They accomplish this assurance not only by providing information about what is to come, but also by asserting that God is in control—that is, the course of the world is already determined. In one eschatological scenario, Baruch is told that after a time of various calamities and sufferings the Messiah will appear. The messianic period will be a time of plenty, when the hungry will rejoice at the bounty of food. When the time of the Messiah is ended, he will return to the heavens, the righteous will be resurrected, and the souls of the wicked will be tormented (chaps. 22–30). A somewhat different scenario, elaborating on the nature of the resurrection, is given in chapters 48–52.

Historical reviews containing *ex eventu* prophecy are present in *2 Baruch* in the vision of the forest, the vine, and the cedar (chaps. 36–40), which is interpreted as an allegory of four successive kingdoms (compare with Dan. 7); and in the vision of the cloud that dispensed twelve alternating showers of black and white water (chaps. 53–74). One of the major functions of these visions is to assure the people that God is still in control. Even Rome (the mighty cedar and the black eleventh water) must answer to God and will eventually be destroyed. The mediator of the revelations to Baruch, and in some cases the interpreter of the revelations, is God. The angel Ramiel, however, is sent to interpret the cloud and water vision.

A strong note of individual responsibility is sounded in *2 Baruch*. Even though Adam introduced sin into the world, he is not responsible for the sinful condition of the world because humanity has persistently repeated Adam's sin of disobedience. Ultimately each person will be judged on the basis of his or her response to the will of God as revealed in the Torah. Even Gentiles who follow the Law will find eschatological salvation. The apostate Jew, on the other hand, will suffer eternal punishment. Herein lies Baruch's primary understanding of the cause of the destruction of Jerusalem and the plight of the Jewish people. They are not innocent sufferers. Rather, they are guilty of violating the Torah. This realization points toward the remedy for the situation of Baruch and his contemporaries. They are to live in obedience to the Torah, for such obedience will give meaning to the present and will guarantee salvation for the future. God will have mercy on those who obey the Law.

Whereas it is generally asserted that *2 Baruch*, like 4 Ezra, is structured according to a sevenfold division, there is no consensus among scholars regarding the exact boundaries of those divisions. Several different divisions of the text have been proposed, none of which is entirely satisfactory. The relationship between 4 Ezra and *2 Baruch* has also been a matter of much debate among scholars. The similarities between the two works have led some scholars to argue that one work borrowed from the other. (Priority is sometimes argued for 4 Ezra, sometimes for *2 Baruch*.) Other scholars, however, have argued equally forcefully that the similarities can be explained on the basis of the authors' drawing from a common milieu, and not on the basis of dependence. Until compelling arguments to the contrary are advanced, the latter position seems to be the most tenable.

Although direct dependence cannot be proven, parallels exist between several passages in *2 Baruch* and passages in the New Testament. Some examples of parallel passages with apocalyptic ideas are *2 Baruch* 23:4-5 and Revelation 6:11; *2 Baruch* 24:1 and Revelation 20:12; *2 Baruch* 49:1–50:4 and 1 Corinthians 15:35-53; and 2 Baruch 73:1 and 1 Corinthians 15:24.

The only complete text of *2 Baruch* that has been found is contained within a sixth-century Syriac manuscript of the Bible. This is why the work is also known as the *Syriac Apocalypse of Baruch*. The title in the Syriac manuscript states that the work had been translated from Greek into Syriac. Many scholars believe that *2 Baruch* was originally written in Hebrew. Chapters 78–86 of *2 Baruch,* which contain Baruch's supposed letter to the Israelite tribes that were taken captive into Assyria, circulated independently and has been preserved in several Syriac manuscripts.

The translation included here is a revision of the translation of R. H. Charles, made by L. H. Brockington in *The Apocryphal Old Testament.*

The Book of the Revelation of Baruch, the Son of Neriah: Translated from the Greek into Syriac

1. And it came to pass in the twenty-fifth year of Jeconiah, king of Judah, that the word of the Lord came to Baruch, the son of Neriah, and said to him, ² Have you seen all that this people are doing to me, that the evils which these two tribes that remained have done are greater than (those of) the ten tribes that were carried away as captives? ³For the former tribes were forced by their kings to commit sin, but these two (tribes) have of themselves been forcing and compelling their kings to commit sin. ⁴For this reason I am about to bring ruin on this city and on its inhabitants, and for a time it shall be taken away out of my sight; and I will scatter this people among the Gentiles, that they may do good to the Gentiles. ⁵And my people shall be chastened; but the time will come when they will seek prosperity once more.

2. I have told you this so that you may tell Jeremiah, and all those that are like you, to leave this city. ²For your deeds are like a solid pillar to this city, and your prayers like an impregnable wall.

3. And I said, O Lord, my lord, have I come into the world for no other purpose than to see the evils of my mother? Surely not, my lord. ²If I have won your favour, take my life away first, so that I may join my fathers and not witness my mother's destruction. ³I am caught in a dilemma: I cannot resist thee; and yet I cannot bear to watch the ruin of

99

my mother. [4]But one thing I will ask of thee, O Lord. [5]What is to happen after this? For if thou destroyest thy city and dost deliver up thy land to those that hate us, how will the name of Israel again be remembered? [6]How will anyone proclaim thy praises? To whom will what is in thy law be explained? [7]Is the ⟨universe⟩ to return to its original state and the world to revert to primeval silence? [8]Is the human race to be ⟨destroyed⟩ and mankind to be blotted out? [9]And what is to become of all thou didst say to Moses about us?

4. And the Lord said to me, This city shall be given up for a time, and for a time the people shall be chastened; yet the world will not be consigned to oblivion. [2]Do you think that this is the city about which I said, On the palms of my hands have I engraved you? [3]This building, which now stands in your midst, is not the one that is to be revealed, (that is) with me (now), that was prepared beforehand here at the time when I determined to make Paradise, and showed it to Adam before he sinned—though when he disobeyed (my) commandment it was taken away from him, as was also Paradise. [4]And after this I showed it to my servant Abraham by night among the divided pieces of the victims. [5]And again I showed it also to Moses on mount Sinai when I showed him the pattern of the tabernacle and all its vessels. [6]And now it is preserved with me, as is also Paradise. [7]Go, then, and do as I command you.

5. And I answered and said,

> So, then, I am to be held responsible for Zion,
> For thine enemies will come to this place,
> And they will pollute thy sanctuary,
> And they will lead thine inheritance into captivity
> And make themselves masters of those whom thou hast loved;
> And they will depart again to the place of their idols,
> And they will boast before them.
> And what wilt thou do for thy great name?

[2]And the Lord said to me,

> My name and my glory are to all eternity;
> And my judgement will maintain its right in its own time.
> And you will see with your eyes

100

3 That the enemy will not overthrow Zion,
   Nor shall they burn Jerusalem,
   But they shall be the ministers of the Judge for a time.

4But go and do what I have told you to.
5And I went and took Jeremiah, and Iddo, and Seriah, and Jabish, and
Gedaliah, and all the nobles of the people, and I led them out to the
Kidron valley; and I repeated to them everything that had been told me.
6And they cried out aloud, and all of them wept. 7And we sat there and
fasted until the evening.

6. And on the next day the Chaldaean army surrounded the city; and
when evening came, I, Baruch, left the people, and I went and stood by
the oak. 2And I was grieving over Zion and lamenting over the captivity
that had come upon the people. 3And suddenly a powerful spirit lifted
me up and carried me over the wall of Jerusalem. 4And I saw four angels
standing at the four corners of the city, each of them holding a fiery
torch in his hands. 5And another angel began to descend from heaven;
and he said to them, Keep hold of your lamps, and do not light them till
I tell you. 6For I am sent first to speak a word to the earth and to put in it
what the Lord, the Most High, has commanded me. 7And I saw him
descend into the Holy of Holies, and take from it the veil, and the holy
⟨ark⟩, and (its) cover, and the two tablets, and the holy vestments of the
priests, and the altar of incense, and the forty-eight precious stones with
which the priest was adorned, and all the vessels of the tabernacle. 8And
he cried to the earth in a loud voice,

   Earth, earth, earth, hear the word of the mighty God,
   And receive what I commit to you.
   And guard them until the last times,
   So that, when you are ordered, you may restore them,
   And strangers may not get possession of them.
   9 For the time has come when Jerusalem also will be delivered
      for a time,
   Until it is said that it shall be restored again for ever.

10And the earth opened its mouth and swallowed them up.

7. And after this I heard that angel saying to the angels that held the lamps,

> Destroy and throw down the wall to its foundations,
> So that the enemy cannot boast and say,
> We have thrown down the wall of Zion,
> And we have burnt the place of the mighty God.

²⟨And the spirit restored me to⟩ the place where I had been standing before.

8. Then the angels did as he had commanded them; and when they had broken up the corners of the walls, a voice was heard from the interior of the temple, after the wall had fallen, saying,

> ² Enter, you enemies (of Jerusalem),
> And let (her) adversaries come in;
> For he who kept the house has abandoned it.

³And I, Baruch, went away. ⁴And after this the Chaldaean army entered and took possession of the house and all that was round about it. ⁵And they carried the people off as captives: some of them they killed; and they put Zedekiah the king in fetters and sent him to the king of Babylon.

9. And I, Baruch, came, together with Jeremiah, whose heart was found pure from sins, (and) who had not been captured when the city was taken. ²And we rent our clothes and wept, and we mourned and fasted seven days.

10. And after seven days the word of God came to me and said to me, ²Tell Jeremiah to go to Babylon and support the people in their captivity (there). ³But you must remain here to share in Zion's desolation; ⁴and I will show you afterwards what is to happen at the end of days. And I passed on to Jeremiah the Lord's commands. ⁵And he went away with the people; but I, Baruch, returned and sat in front of the gates of the temple and made this lament over Zion and said,

> ⁶ Happy the man who was never born,
> Or the child who died at birth.

7 But as for us who are alive, woe to us,
  Because we see the afflictions of Zion,
  And what has happened to Jerusalem.
8 I will summon the sirens from the sea, (and say),
  Come you night-demons from the desert,
  And you, demons and jackals from the forests:
  Awake and prepare yourselves for mourning,
  And take up with me the dirges,
  And make lamentation with me.
9 Sow not again, you farmers;
  And why, earth, should you yield your crops at harvest?
  Keep to yourself your goodly fruits.
10 And why any longer, vine, should you produce your wine?
  For no offering of it will again be made in Zion,
  Nor again will they offer first-fruits from it.
11 And you, heavens, withhold your dew,
  And open not the treasuries of rain.
  And you, sun, withhold the brightness of your rays,
12 And you, moon, conceal the brilliance of your light;
  For why should any light again be seen
  Where the light of Zion is darkened?
13 And you, bridegrooms, go not into (the bridal chamber),
  And let not the ⟨brides⟩ adorn themselves with garlands;
  And let not the (married) women pray for children,
14 For the barren shall rejoice above all,
  And those who have no sons will be glad,
  And those who do have sons will be in anguish.
15 For why should they bear (children) in pain,
  Only to bury (them) in grief?
16 Or why, again, should men have sons,
  Or why any more should a human infant be given a name,
  Where this mother is desolate
  And her sons are carried away as captives?
17 Speak not henceforth of beauty,
  Nor talk of comeliness.
18 And you, priests, take the keys of the sanctuary,
  And throw them (up) to the heaven above,
  And give them to the Lord and say,
  Guard thy house thyself,
  For we have been found false stewards.

¹⁹ And you, virgins, who weave fine linen
And silk with the gold of Ophir,
Take quickly all (these) things and throw (them) into the fire,
That it may bear them up to him who made them,
And the flame carry them to him who created them,
Lest the enemy get possession of them.

11. And I, Baruch, say this against you, Babylon,

If you had prospered
And Zion had dwelt in her glory,
Great would have been our grief
That you should be equal to Zion.
² But now (our) grief is infinite
And (our) lamentation measureless;
For lo, you are prosperous
And Zion desolate.
³ Who will be the judge concerning these things?
Or to whom shall we complain about what has befallen us?
O Lord, how hast thou borne (it)?
⁴ Our fathers went to (their) rest without suffering,
And the righteous sleep in the earth in peace;
⁵ For they did not know of this present distress,
And had heard nothing about what has befallen us.
⁶ Would that you had ears, o earth,
And that you had a heart, o dust,
So that you could go and announce in Sheol,
And say to the dead,
⁷ You are happier than we who are alive!

12. But I will tell you what is in my mind,

And I will speak against you, prosperous land.
² The noonday does not always burn,
Nor do the sun's rays constantly give light:
³ Do not expect and hope that you will be always prosperous
   and joyful;
And be not proud and domineering.

4 For without doubt in its own good time
  The (divine) wrath will awake against you,
  Which now is restrained by patience
  As if by reins.
5 And when I had so said, I fasted seven days.

13. And after this, I, Baruch, was standing on mount Zion, and lo, a voice came from on high and said to me, 2Stand up, Baruch, and hear the word of the mighty God. 3Because you have been dismayed at what has happened to Zion you shall be kept safe and preserved until the consummation of the times. 4And you shall serve as witness, so that if ever those prosperous cities say, Why has the mighty God brought this retribution on us?, 5you can say to them—you and those like you who have seen this evil—[This is the evil] and retribution which has come on you and on your people in its (appointed) time, so that the nations may be thoroughly chastened. 6And they will be waiting for (the end of it). 7And if they say at that time, When (will the end of it be)?, 8you shall say to them,

You who have drunk the wine that has been strained,
  Drink also of its dregs,
  (This is) the judgement of the Exalted One,
  Who has no favourites.
9 For this very reason he once had no mercy on his own sons,
  But afflicted them as if they were his enemies,
  Because they sinned:
10 Thus were they chastened then,
  That they might be sanctified.
11 But now, you peoples and nations, you are guilty,
  Because you have always trodden down the earth,
  And treated the creation shamefully;
12 For I have always showered my gifts upon you,
  And you have always been ungrateful for them.

14. And I answered and said, Lo, thou hast shown me the course of the times and what is to be after these things; and thou hast explained to me that retribution, which thou hast described to me, shall come upon the nations. 2And now I know that there have been many sinners, and they have lived in prosperity and departed from the world; but there will be few nations left in those times, to whom what thou hast said can be repeated. ³What advantage is there in this? What worse (evils) than those we have seen come upon us are we to expect to see?

⁴Once again will I speak in thy presence. ⁵How have they profited, who were men of understanding in thy sight, and did not pursue paths that led nowhere like the rest of the nations, and never said to dead (idols), Give us life, but always feared thee and followed thy ways? ⁶Lo! They have been carried off; nor because of them hast thou had mercy on Zion. ⁷Even if others did evil, was it not due to Zion that she should be forgiven because of the good things that they did, instead of being overwhelmed because of the evil things the others did? ⁸But who, O Lord, my Lord, can comprehend (the workings of) thy judgement? Or who can search out the depths of thy way? Or who can trace the profundity of thy path? ⁹Or who can describe thy unfathomable counsel? Or what man that has ever been born has ever discovered either the beginning or the end of thy wisdom? ¹⁰For we all have been made like a breath. ¹¹For as (our) breath comes up from inside (us), and does not return, but disappears, so it is with men: they do not depart (this life) as and when they would, nor do they know what will happen to them in the end. ¹²The righteous quite rightly look forward to (their) end, and they leave their dwelling here without fear, because they have a store of (good) works laid up in thy treasuries. ¹³So they leave this world without fear, and trust that they will attain the world which thou hast promised them. ¹⁴But as for us, our lot is hard: we suffer injury and insult now, and we can only look forward to (further) evils. ¹⁵But thou knowest truly what thou hast done on behalf of thy servants; for we cannot understand what is good as thou, our creator, canst.

¹⁶And yet again I will speak in thy presence, O Lord, my lord. ¹⁷When of old there was no world, and no one to inhabit it, thou didst make thy plan, and thou didst utter thy word, and immediately the works of creation stood before thee. ¹⁸And thou didst say that thou wouldest make man for thy world to be the administrator of thy works, so that it might be known that he was not made because of the world, but the world because of him. ¹⁹And now it would seem that the world which was made because of us remains, but we, for whom it was made, disappear.

15. And the Lord answered and said to me, You are quite rightly perplexed about the disappearance of man, but you are wrong in what you think about the evils that come upon sinners. ²When you said, The righteous are carried off, and the wicked are prospered; ³and again, when you said, Man cannot comprehend (the workings of) thy

106

judgement—4listen, and I will tell you: pay attention, and I will explain to you. 5Man would have had excuse for not understanding my judgement, if he had not been given the law, and I had not instructed him in understanding. 6But now, because he has transgressed with his eyes open, on this ground alone—that he knew—he must be punished. 7And as regards what you said about the righteous, that it was because of them that this world came into being, so also ⟨shall⟩ that which is to come ⟨come into being⟩ because of them. 8For this world is for them a (place of) strife, and weariness, and much trouble; but that which is to come (will be) a crown with great glory.

16. And I answered and said, O Lord, my lord, our years here are few and evil, and who is able in so brief a ⟨time⟩ to acquire what cannot be measured.

17. And the Lord answered and said to me, With the Most High it does not matter whether a man's life be long or short. 2For what profit was it to Adam that he lived nine hundred and thirty years, and yet transgressed the command that had been given him. 3The length of time that he lived did not profit him, but brought death and shortened the lives of his descendants. 4Or in what way was Moses the loser in that he lived only a hundred and twenty years, and yet, inasmuch as he obeyed his creator, brought the law to the sons of Jacob and lit a lamp for the nation of Israel?

18. And I answered and said, He that lit (the lamp) took (advantage) of (its) light; but there are few who have done as he did. 2Many of those to whom he has given light have preferred Adam's darkness and have not rejoiced in the light of the lamp.

19. And he answered and said to me, That is why he established a covenant for them at that time and said, Behold I have set before you life and death; and he summoned heaven and earth to witness against them. 2For he knew that his time was short, but that heaven and earth would endure for ever. 3Yet after his death they sinned and transgressed, though they knew that they had the law against (them), and the light which nothing could deceive, and the (celestial) spheres to add their testimony, and also me. 4Now so far as the present state of things is concerned, it is for me to pass judgement, so do not worry about them nor distress yourself because of what has happened. 5For it is now the end of time that should be considered—whether (it is a matter) of business, or of prosperity, or of misfortune—and not the beginning of it. 6Because though a man may have been prosperous when he was young, if misfortune comes upon him in his old age, he will forget all his former prosperity. 7Conversely, though a man may have been the victim of misfortune when he was young, if at the end of his life he becomes prosperous, he will not remember his former misfortunes. 8Furthermore, even if, from the day on which death was decreed against transgressors, every single man had been prosperous all through his life, and in the end had been destroyed, it would all have been in vain.

20. Behold, the time is coming when the days will speed on more swiftly than of old, and the seasons will succeed one another more rapidly than in the past, and the years will pass by more quickly than they do now. 2That is why I have now taken Zion away, so that I may the more speedily punish the world at its appointed time. 3So now hold fast in your heart everything that I command you and seal it in the recesses of your mind. 4And then will I show you the judgement of my might, and my ways that are unfathomable. 5Go, therefore, and purify yourself for seven days: eat no bread, drink no water, and speak to no one. 6And afterwards come to this place, and I will reveal myself to you, and tell you hidden truths, and give you instruction about the course of the times; for they are coming, and there will be no delay.

21. And I went away and sat in a cave in the hillside in the Kidron valley, and I purified myself there, and though I ate no bread I was not hungry, and though I drank no water I was not thirsty; and I was there till the seventh day, as he had commanded me. 2And afterwards I came to the place where he had spoken with me. 3And at sunset my mind was beset by many thoughts, and I began to speak in the presence of the Mighty One. 4And I said, O thou who hast made the earth, hear me, thou who hast fixed the vault of heaven ⟨by thy word⟩ and hast made fast the height of it by thy spirit, thou who hast called (into being) from the beginning of the world things which did not previously exist, and they obey thee. 5Thou who hast commanded the air by thy nod, and hast seen the things which are to be as the things which ⟨have been already⟩. 6Thou who rulest in (thy) great design the hosts that stand before thee, (and) dost control, as with a rod of iron, the countless holy beings whom thou didst make from the beginning, of flame and fire, which stand around thy throne. 7To thee only does it belong to do at once whatever thou dost wish. 8Thou makest the rain to fall drop by drop upon the earth, and thou alone knowest the end of the times before they come: have respect unto my prayer. 9For thou alone art able to sustain all who are, and those who ⟨have passed away⟩, and those who are to be, those who sin, and those who ⟨are righteous⟩. 10For thou alone dost live, immortal and past finding out, and thou knowest the number of mankind. 11And if in the course of time many have sinned, yet others, not a few in number, have been righteous.

12Thou knowest (the place) which thou hast reserved for the end of those who have sinned, and the destiny of the others who have been righteous. 13For if there were this life only, which belongs to all men, nothing could be more bitter than this. 14For what gain is strength that turns to weakness, or plenty that turns to famine, or beauty that turns to ugliness? 15For the nature of man is always changing. 16For what we once were, now we no longer are, and what we now are, we shall not long remain. 17For if a term had not been set for all, their beginning would have been in vain. 18But do thou inform me about everything that comes from thee, and enlighten me about everything I ask thee.

19For how long will what is corruptible endure, and for how long will mortals thrive on earth, and the transgressors in the world continue in their pollutions and corruptions? 20In thy mercy issue thy command and bring to pass everything thou saidst thou wouldst, that it may be made known to those who think thy patience is but weakness. 21And show to those who do not know ⟨that⟩ everything that has happened to us and to our city up till now ⟨has been⟩ in accordance with the patience of thy power, because for thy name's sake thou hast called us a beloved people. 22⟨So bring mortality to an end now.⟩ 23Restrain the angel of death, and let thy glory appear and the might of thy beauty be known: let Sheol be sealed so that from now onwards it may not receive the dead; and let the treasuries of souls restore those that are held fast in them. 24For there have been many years of desolation since the days of Abraham and Isaac and Jacob, and of all those like them who sleep in the earth, on whose account thou didst say thou didst create the world. 25And now show thy glory quickly, and do not put off what thou hast promised.

26And when I had finished this prayer I was completely exhausted.

22. And after this, behold, the heavens opened, and I saw (a vision), and strength was given me, and a voice was heard from on high, and it said to me, 2Baruch, Baruch, why are you troubled? 3What comfort is there for a man if he sets off on a journey by road and never reaches his journey's end, or if he goes by sea and never arrives at the port he was making for? 4Or if he promises to give someone else a present and never does, is it not (equivalent) to robbery? 5Or if he sows seed in the earth, but does not reap the fruit from it in its season, does he not suffer a total loss? 6Or if he plants a plant, can he expect any fruit from it before the regular time for fruit? 7Or if a pregnant woman bears a still-born child, is she not the (unwitting) cause of her infant's death? 8Or if a man builds a house and does not finish it by putting a roof on it, can it (properly) be called a house? Tell me that first.

23. And I answered and said, Indeed, no, O Lord, my lord. 2And he answered and said to me, Why then are you troubled about what you do not know, and upset by things you do not understand. 3For just as you have not forgotten the people who now are, and those who have passed away, so I remember those who are to come. 4Because when Adam sinned and death was decreed against those who were to be born (from him), then the number of those to be born was fixed, and for that number a place was prepared where the living might live out their lives and the dead might be kept in security. 5Thus, until that number is reached, no creature will live again—since my spirit is the creator of life—and Sheol will receive the dead. 6And again, you are to be privileged to hear what is to come after these times. 7For my redemption is near and is not as far away as once it was.

24. For behold, the time is coming when the books will be opened in which are written the sins of all who have sinned, and also the treasuries in which are stored (the records of) the righteous deeds of all created beings who have been righteous. 2And then you will appreciate—and many with you—the patience of the Most High in every generation; for he has been ever patient with all men, both with those who sin and with those who are righteous. 3And I answered and said, But behold, Lord, no one knows how many are the things that are already past, nor how many there are that are yet to come. 4For I know only too well what has happened to us, but what will happen to our enemies I do not know; nor do I know when thou wilt visit thy works.

25. And he answered and said to me, You too will be preserved till the time of (the coming of) the sign which the Most High will provide for those on earth at the end of days. 2And this shall be the sign—3when a stupor seizes those on earth and they are assailed by all kinds of misfortune and adverse circumstances. ⁴And when they say as a result of their sufferings, The Mighty One has no longer any interest in the earth, then, when they have given up hope, the time will come.

26. And I answered and said, Will the period of suffering that is to be continue for long, and will the ordeal last many years?

27. And he answered and said to me, That time will be divided into twelve separate periods, and each one of them will have its own special characteristics. ²The first period will see the beginning of the troubles. ³In the second period will occur assassinations of the great ones (of the earth). ⁴In the third period the annihilation of many by death. ⁵In the fourth period destruction by the sword. ⁶In the fifth period famine and lack of rain. ⁷In the sixth period earthquakes and terrors ⁸ . . . ⁹In the eighth period (the appearance of) many spectres and attacks by demons. ¹⁰In the ninth period the falling of fire (from heaven). ¹¹In the tenth period every kind of havoc and oppression. ¹²In the eleventh period (much) wickedness and impurity. ¹³And in the twelfth period chaos resulting from the mixing together of all these things. ¹⁴For (although) each of the periods of that time will be marked off from the rest by its special characteristics, they will (ultimately all) be mixed together and reinforce one another. ¹⁵For some will ⟨fall short⟩ in the calamities they bring and have their deficiency made up by others, while some will supply their full tale themselves and also make up for what is lacking in others, so that those on earth in those days may not understand that this is the final consummation.

28. Nevertheless, whoever is wise then will understand. ²For the measure and reckoning of that time are two parts—weeks of seven weeks. ³And I answered and said, It is good for a man to come to that time and see (what happens then): yet it is surely better that he should not come in case he fails. ⁴{But I will ask this also. ⁵Will the Incorruptible despise what is corruptible and (not care about) what happens to the corruptible, and concern himself only with what is not corruptible?} ⁶But if, Lord, what thou hast foretold to me will assuredly come to pass, reveal this also to me, if I have indeed found favour with thee. ⁷Will these things happen in one place or in (just) one area of the earth, or will the whole earth experience them?

29. And he answered and said to me, Whatever happens then will

111

happen to the whole earth; so that all who are alive will experience (it). [2]For at that time I will protect only those who are found in those days in this land. [3]And it shall be that when all is accomplished that was to come to pass in the (twelve) periods (before the end), the Messiah shall then begin to be revealed. [4]And Behemoth shall appear from his place and Leviathan shall ascend from the sea—those two great monsters I created on the fifth day of creation and have kept until then; and then they shall serve as food for all that survive. [5]The earth also shall yield its fruit ten thousandfold; and on each vine there shall be a thousand branches, and each branch shall produce a thousand clusters, and each cluster produce a thousand grapes, and each grape produce a cor of wine. [6]And those who have been hungry will rejoice; and, also, they shall see marvels every day. [7]For winds shall go forth from me bearing the scent of aromatic fruits every morning, and, at the close of day, clouds distilling a health-giving dew. [8]And at that time the storehouse of manna shall descend from on high again; and they shall eat of it in those years, because it is they who have come to the final consummation.

30. And it shall come to pass after this, when the time of the presence of the Messiah (on earth) has run its course, that he will return in glory (to the heavens): then all who have died and have set their hopes on him will rise again. [2]And it shall come to pass at that time that the treasuries will be opened in which is preserved the number of the souls of the righteous, and they will come out, and the multitude of souls will appear together in one single assembly; and those who are first will rejoice, and those who are last will not be cast down. [3]For each one of them will know that the predetermined end of the times has come. [4]But the souls of the wicked, when they see all this, will be the more discomforted. [5]For they will know that their torment is upon them and that their perdition has arrived.

31. And after this I went to the people and said to them, Summon all your elders to me, and I will speak to them. [2]And they all assembled in the Kidron valley. [3]And I answered and said to them,

> Hear, O Israel, and I will speak to you,
> And give ear, you sons of Jacob, and I will instruct you.
> [4] Forget not Zion,
> But keep in remembrance the anguish of Jerusalem.

⁵ For behold, the time is coming,
   When everything that is shall become the prey of corruption,
   And be as though it had never been.

32. But as for you, if you prepare your hearts, and sow in them the fruits of the law, it will be a protection to you when the Mighty One shakes the whole creation. ²For after a little while the building of Zion will be shaken so that it may be built again. ³But that building will not endure, but will after a time be razed to the ground, and it will remain desolate until the (appointed) time. ⁴And afterwards it must be renewed in glory and be made perfect for evermore. ⁵We should not, therefore, ⟨be distressed⟩ so much over the evil which has come now as over what is still to be. ⁶For there will be a greater trial than either of these two tribulations when the Mighty One renews his creation. ⁷And now, do not come near me for a few days, and do not seek me out until I come to you. ⁸And when I had said all this to them, I, Baruch, went my way; and when the people saw me going they cried out in dismay, saying, ⁹Where are you going, Baruch, are you going to desert us, as a father might desert his children, and leave them orphans?

33. Are these the orders your companion, the prophet Jeremiah, gave you when he said to you, ²Look after this people while I go and support the rest of (our) brothers in Babylon, who have been sentenced to be held as captives there? ³If now you are going to desert us too, it were better for all of us to die while you are still with us, and that only then should you go away.

34. And I answered and said to the people, God forbid that I should desert you or leave you. I am only going to the Holy of Holies to inquire of the Mighty One about you and about Zion, in the hope that I may get some further understanding. After this I will come back to you.

35. And I, Baruch, went to the holy place and sat down amid the ruins, and I wept and said,

² Would that mine eyes were springs (of water),
   And mine eyelids a fountain of tears;
³ For how shall I lament for Zion,
   And how shall I mourn for Jerusalem?

113

4 Because in the very place where I now lie prostrate,
 The high priest of old offered holy sacrifices,
 And burned incense of fragrant odours.
5 But now our pride has turned to dust,
 And our hearts' desire to ashes.

36. And when I had said this I fell asleep there; and I saw a vision in the night. 2And lo, a forest of trees planted on a plain, with high mountains and steep cliffs all round it; and the forest covered most of the plain. 3And lo, alongside it there grew up a vine, and from underneath it issued a softly-flowing stream. 4And when the stream reached the forest it became a raging torrent, and its waves submerged the forest and in a moment uprooted nearly all (the trees that were in) the forest and undermined the mountains that were round about it. 5And the topmost branches of the forest were laid low, and the peaks of the mountains crumbled; and (the waters from) the stream increased more and more, so that nothing was left of that great forest but a single cedar. 6And when they had beaten down and destroyed and uprooted all the other (trees that were in) the forest, so that nothing was left of it, nor could the place where once it had been be recognized, then the vine came with the stream, very quietly and unobtrusively, to a place not far from where the cedar was (lying); and the stricken cedar found itself close to the vine. 7And I looked, and lo, the vine opened its mouth and spoke and said to the cedar, Are you not the cedar that was left of the forest of wickedness, by whose means wickedness persisted and flourished all those years, and goodness never? 8You kept conquering what was not yours, and you showed no pity towards what was not yours: you kept extending your power over those who were far distant from you, and those who were near you, you held fast in the toils of your wickedness; and always you carried yourself proudly as if you could never be uprooted. 9But now your time has gone by and your hour is come. 10So, cedar, go the way of the forest, which has gone before you, and be reduced to dust like it, and let all your ashes be mingled together. 11Recline now in anguish and take your ease in torment till your last hour comes, when you will come back again and be tormented even more.

37. And after this I saw the cedar burning, and the vine flourishing; and all around it the plain was full of unfading flowers. And I awoke and got up.

38. And I prayed and said, O Lord, my lord, thou dost always enlighten those whose guide is understanding. ²Thy law is life and thy wisdom the true guide. ³Explain to me, therefore, what this vision means. ⁴For thou knowest that I have always followed the path of thy law, and from my earliest days I have never turned away from thy wisdom.

39. And he answered and said to me, Baruch, this is the interpretation of the vision you have seen. ²You saw the great forest with high and rugged mountains round it—the meaning is this: ³Behold, the time is coming when this kingdom, which once destroyed Zion, will itself be destroyed, and it will be made subject by another that will come after it. ⁴And then, after a time, that (kingdom) also will be destroyed, and yet another, a third, will arise; and that also will have the sovereignty for its time, and (then) it will be destroyed. ⁵And after this a fourth kingdom will arise, which will prove far more tyrannical and savage than any of those that went before it; and it will extend its rule like the forests on the plain, and it will hold sway for many years and exalt itself even more than the cedars of Lebanon. ⁶Truth will be hidden by it, and all those who are polluted by iniquity will take refuge in it, just as evil beasts take refuge and creep into the forest. ⁷And when the time for its end has come, and its fall is imminent, then will be revealed my Messiah's ⟨kingdom⟩, which is like the stream and the vine; and when that is revealed, it will destroy the hosts that are gathered round it. ⁸And as for the lofty cedar that you saw, the sole survivor of the forest, and what you heard the vine saying to it, the meaning is this:

40. The last leader of that time will be left alive after the rest of his hosts have been destroyed, and he will be put in fetters and taken up to mount Zion; and my Messiah will charge him with all his iniquities, and will enumerate all the evils his hosts have perpetrated, and will confront him with them. ²And afterwards he will put him to death; and he will preserve the remnant of my people, gathered in the place that I have chosen. ³And his ⟨kingdom⟩ shall stand for ever, until this world of corruption comes to an end and the times appointed are fulfilled. ⁴This is your vision, and this is what it means.

41. And I answered and said, Who will take part in this, and how many of them will there be? And who will be judged worthy of a place in that world? ²For I will declare to thee my thoughts and ask about what is in my mind. ³For I see many of thy people who have rejected thy covenant and thrown off the yoke of thy law. ⁴But again, I have seen others who have abandoned their vanities and fled for refuge beneath thy wings. ⁵What is to happen to them, and what will be their lot at the end? ⁶Can it be that everything they have done throughout their lives will be weighed, and they will be judged as the balance tips?

42. And he answered and said to me, I will explain these things to you as well. ²You asked, Who will take part in this, and how many of them will there be? Believers will receive the good things they have been promised and scoffers the reverse. ³And you asked about those who have embraced the covenant and those who have abandoned it. The answer is this. ⁴Those who were at one time subject (to the covenant), and afterwards went off and mingled with foreigners of mixed descent—their former manner of life will count for nothing. ⁵And those who started in ignorance but afterwards found the secret of life, and joined the ⟨people⟩ set apart from other peoples—their former manner of life will count for nothing either. ⁶And time will succeed to time, and season to season, and one will receive from another; and then, at the end, everything will be compared according to the measure of the times and the hours of the seasons. ⁷For corruption will claim those who belong to it, and life those who belong to it. ⁸And the dust will be summoned and told, Give up what is not yours, and surrender everything you have guarded until its (appointed) time.

43. But you, Baruch, must apply your mind to what has been said to you, and understand (the visions) that have been shown you; for many eternal consolations await you. ²For you will depart from here, and leave behind you the scenes now so familiar to you; and you will forget these corruptible things and have no recollection of what happens among mortals. ³So go and give your people their orders, and come back to this place; and afterwards fast seven days, and then I will come to you and speak to you.

44. And I, Baruch, went and came to my people; and I called my eldest son and ⟨Gedaliah, my friend⟩, and seven of the elders of the people, and I said to them

² Behold, I go to my fathers,
And tread the way of all the earth.

3 Do not forsake the way of the law,
  But guard and guide the people that are left,
  Lest they forsake the commandments of the Mighty One.
4 For you can see that he whom we serve is just,
  And that our creator has no favourites.
5 Look at what has befallen Zion,
  And what has happened to Jerusalem.
6 For the judgement of the Mighty One will be made known
    (thereby),
  And his ways, which though unfathomable, are right.
7 For if you endure and persevere in the fear of him,
  And do not forget his law,
  The times will change for your good,
  And you will see the consolation of Zion.
8 Because whatever is now, is nothing,
  But what is to be will be very great.
9 For everything corruptible will pass away,
  And everything mortal will disappear:
  No memory of it will endure,
  For it is defiled with evils.
10 What makes good progress now will end in vanity,
  And what prospers now will shortly fall
  And be reduced to dust.
11 What is to be will become the object of desire,
  And on what is to come will we set our hopes,
  For it is a time that does not pass away.
12 The age is coming, which abides for ever,
  And the new world which does not turn to corruption
  Those who own its sway:
  It has no pity for those on the road to torment,
  And leads not to perdition those who live in it.
13 For these are they who will inherit the time that has been
    spoken of,
  And theirs is the inheritance of the time that has been promised.
14 These are they who have won for themselves treasuries of wisdom,
  And with whom are found stores of understanding,
  And have not turned their backs on mercy,
  And have held fast to the truth of the law.

15 To them will be given the world to come;
But the dwelling-place of the rest—and there are many of them—
Will be in the (abyss of) fire.

45. So instruct the people as best you can: that is our task. 2For if you teach them, you may preserve them.

46. And my son and the elders of the people answered and said to me, Does the Mighty One wish to chasten us so much that he is prepared to take you from us so soon? 2Then we shall really be in darkness, and there will be no light (at all) for the people who are left. 3For where again shall we look for (instruction in) the law, or who will show us the difference between death and life? 4And I said to them, I cannot resist the will of the Mighty One: nevertheless, Israel shall never want a wise man, nor the race of Jacob a son of the law. 5Only make up your minds to obey the law; and be subject to those who, in fear, are wise and understanding, and determine that you will never depart from them. 6For if you do this, the good things I told you about before will come to you; and you will escape the punishment, about which I warned you. 7But I said nothing about my being taken up, either to them or to my son.

47. And I dismissed them and went away, and I said to them as I went, I am going to Hebron, for the Mighty One has sent me there. 2And I came to the place where I had been told to go; and I sat there, and I fasted seven days.

48. And after the seventh day I prayed before the Mighty One and said,

2 O my Lord, thou dost summon the times to come (to thee),
And they stand before thee:
Thou dost cause the power of the ages to pass away,
And they do not resist thee:
Thou dost arrange the course of the seasons,
And they obey thee.
3 Thou alone knowest for how long the generations will endure,
And thou revealest not thy mysteries to many.
4 Thou makest known the might of fire,
And thou weighest the lightness of the wind.

5 Thou dost explore the limit of the heights,
  And scrutinize the depths of darkness.
6 Thou dost decree the number (of those) who pass away and (of)
  those who are preserved,
  And thou preparest an abode for those who are to be.
7 Thou dost remember the beginning thou hast made,
  And forgettest not the destruction that is to be.
8 With frightening and formidable signs thou dost command the
  flames,
  And they change into spirits.
  And with a word thou dost quicken that which was not,
  And with (thy) mighty power thou holdest back that which not yet
  has come.
9 Thou dost instruct created things by thy understanding,
  And thou teachest the spheres to minister in their orders.
10 Armies innumerable stand before thee,
  And minister in their orders quietly at thy nod.
11 Hear thy servant,
  And give ear to my petition.
12 For we are born to live only for a little while,
  And very soon we go away.
13 But with thee hours are like an age,
  And days as generations.
14 Be not therefore angry with man, for he is nothing,
  And take no account of our deeds, for what are we?
15 For lo, it is by thy gift that we come into the world,
  And we do not leave it by our own decision.
16 For we said not to our parents, Give us birth,
  Nor did we send to Sheol and say, Receive us.
17 How then can our strength withstand thy wrath,
  Or how can we endure thy judgement?
18 Protect us in thy compassion,
  And in thy mercy help us.
19 Behold the little ones that are subject to thee,
  And save all those that draw near to thee;
  And destroy not the hope of our people
  And cut not short the times of our aid.
20 For this is ⟨the nation⟩ thou hast chosen,
  And these are the people without equal in thine eyes.

21 But I now will speak before thee,
  And tell thee what is in my mind.
22 In thee do we trust, for lo, thy law is with us,
  And we know we shall not fall so long as we keep thy statutes.
23 For all time are we blessed in this at least,
  That we have not mingled with the Gentiles.
24 For we are all one famous people,
  Who have received one law from the only One;
  And the law which is with us will help us,
  And the matchless wisdom which is in our midst will sustain us.

25 And after I had prayed and said these things I was much exhausted.
26 And he answered and said to me,

  Your prayer has been plain enough, Baruch,
  And all your words have been heard.
27 But my judgement claims what is due to it,
  And my law exacts its rights.
28 In accordance with your own words will I answer you,
  And in accordance with your prayer will I speak to you.

29For the truth is, he that has become corrupt is not at all: he has done evil so far as he could do anything; and he has neither pondered my goodness nor understood my patience. 30But you will indeed be taken up, as I have (already) told you. 31And that time I have (also) told you about will come, and the time of distress begin: it will come and pass by with a sudden fury, creating havoc through the vehemence of its onset. 32And in those days all the inhabitants of the earth will lean upon one another, because they are unaware that my judgement has come upon them.

33 For there will not be found many wise at that time,
  And the prudent will be but few
  And even those possessed of knowledge will keep silent.
34 And there will be many rumours and numerous idle tales,
  And uncanny things will be seen to happen,
  And not a few predictions will pass from mouth to mouth:
  Some of them (will prove) unfounded,
  And some (will be) confirmed.

35 And honour will be turned to shame,
  And strength fall into disrepute:
  Confidence will disappear,
  And beauty will become an object of contempt.
36 And many will say to others at that time,
  Where has discretion hidden itself,
  And where has wisdom fled for refuge?
37 And while they are meditating on these things,
  Those who had thought nothing of themselves will be seized by
    envy,
  And the even-tempered man will become a prey to passion:
  Many will be stirred up by anger to their mutual hurt,
  And they will raise up armies to shed (each others') blood,
  And in the end they will perish all together.
38 And it will come to pass at that very time,
  That it will be apparent to all that the times are changing,
  Because in all those times they polluted themselves
  And oppressed (the poor);
  And each one of them went his own way,
  And remembered not the law of the Mighty One.
39 Therefore a fire shall consume their thoughts,
  And in the flame shall the plans they have made be tested;
  For the Judge will come and will not delay.
40 Each one of the earth's inhabitants knew when he was sinning,
  But because of their pride they would not recognize my law.
41 But many will then weep bitterly
  Over the living more than over the dead.

42 And I answered and said, O Adam, What was it that you did to all your posterity? And what should be said to Eve who first listened to the serpent? 43 For all this multitude is going to corruption: innumerable are those whom the fire will devour.

44 Yet again I will speak in thy presence. 45 Thou, O Lord, my Lord, knowest what is in thy creature. 46 For thou didst of old command the dust to produce Adam; and thou knowest the number of those who have been born from him, and how much they have sinned before thee—those who have been born and have not confessed thee as their creator. 47 And, so far as all these are concerned, their end will convict them, and thy law, which they have transgressed, will requite them on thy day.

121

⁴⁸But now let us leave aside the wicked and inquire about the righteous. ⁴⁹And I will recount their blessedness and proclaim the glory that is reserved for them. ⁵⁰For without question, just as in this transitory world in which you live, you have for a little while endured much toil, so in that world, to which there is no end, you will receive great light.

49. But I will again ask of thee, O Mighty One, and beg mercy from him who made all things. ²In what form will those live who live in thy day, and what will they look like afterwards? ³Will they then resume their present form and put on these entrammelling members, which are now involved in evils and are the instruments of evils; or wilt thou perhaps transform what has been in the world, as also the world itself?

50. And he answered and said to me, Listen, Baruch, to what I say, and keep a record in your mind of everything you learn. ²For the earth will certainly then restore the dead it now receives so as to preserve them: it will make no change in their form, but as it has received them, so it will restore them, and as I delivered them to it, so also will it raise them. ³For those who are then alive must be shown that the dead have come to life again, and that those who had departed have returned. ⁴And when they have recognized those they know now, then the judgement will begin, and what you have been told already will come to pass.

51. And after the appointed day is over, the ⟨appearance⟩ of those who have been condemned will be changed, as will also be the glory of those who have been justified. ²For the appearance of the evil-doers will go from bad to worse, as they suffer torment. ³Again, the glory of those who have now been justified through (their obedience to) my law, who have had understanding in their life, and who have planted in their heart the root of wisdom—their faces will shine even more brightly and their features will assume a luminous beauty, so that they may be able to attain and enter the world which does not die, which has been promised to them then. ⁴For over this, more than over anything else, will the (others) who come then lament that they rejected my law, and stopped up their ears, so that they might not hear wisdom or receive understanding. ⁵For they will see those who are now their inferiors in a far better and more glorious state than they are—for these will be transformed so that they look like angels, while they can only contemplate in horror the decaying shadows of their former selves. ⁶For they will see (all this) first; and afterwards they will depart to their torment.

⁷ But those who have been saved by their works,
  Whose hope has been in the law,
  Who have put their trust in understanding,
  And their confidence in wisdom,
  Shall see marvels in their time.
⁸ For they shall behold the world which is now invisible to them,
  And realms now hidden from them,
⁹ And time shall no longer age them.
¹⁰ For in the heights of that world shall they dwell,
  And they shall be made like the angels,
  And be made equal to the stars;
  And they shall be changed into whatever form they will,
  From beauty into loveliness,
  And from light into the splendour of glory.

¹¹For the extent of Paradise will be spread before them, and they will be shown the majestic beauty of the living creatures that are beneath the throne, and all the armies of the angels, who are now kept back by my word lest they should reveal themselves, and are restrained by (my) command, so that they may keep their places until (the moment of) their advent comes. ¹²Then shall the splendour of the righteous exceed even the splendour of the angels. ¹³For the first shall receive the last, those whom they were expecting, and the last those of whom they had heard that they had passed away.

¹⁴ For they will then have been delivered from this world of misery
  And laid down the burden of sorrow.
¹⁵ For what then have men lost their life,
  And for what have those who were on earth exchanged their soul?
¹⁶ For then they chose for themselves this time,
  Which cannot pass without sorrow:
  They chose for themselves this time,
  Whose issues are full of lamentations and evils,
  And they denied the world which ages not those who come to it,
  And rejected that time and the glory (of it),
  So that they cannot share in the triumphs about which I have told
    you.

123

52. And I answered and said, How can ⟨we⟩ forget those whose future is punishment? ²And why, again, do we mourn for those who die, and weep for those who depart to Sheol? ³Far better, (surely), keep (our) lamentations for the beginning of that torment which is to be, and reserve (our) tears for (the) destruction when it comes. ⁴But on the other hand—⁵the righteous: what should they do now? I would say, ⁶Rejoice in the suffering you now endure: why concern yourselves about the downfall of your enemies? ⁷Make yourselves ready for what is reserved for you, and prepare yourselves for the reward laid up for you.

53. And when I said this I fell asleep there, and I saw a vision; and lo, a very great cloud was coming up out of the sea. And I kept looking at it. And lo, it was full of waters, white and black; and there were many colours in those waters, and what looked like flashes of lightning appeared at the top of it. ²And I watched the cloud as it moved, and it quickly covered all the earth. ³And after this, the cloud began to pour the waters that were in it on the earth. ⁴And I saw that the waters that descended from it were not all the same. ⁵For at first, for a time, they were all black; but afterwards I saw that the waters became bright—though there were fewer of them; and after this again I saw black (waters), and then again bright; and again black, and again bright. ⁶This happened twelve times; but there were always more black waters than bright. ⁷And when the end of the cloud came, lo, it rained black waters, darker than all that had been before, with fire mixed with them; and where those waters descended they left a trail of devastation and destruction. ⁸And after this I saw the lightning I had seen at the top of the cloud take hold of it and hurl it to the earth. ⁹And the lightning shone so brilliantly that it lit up the whole earth, and it restored those regions where the last waters had descended and left such devastation. ¹⁰And it took hold of the whole earth and subjected it to its control. ¹¹And after this I looked and I saw twelve rivers coming up out of the sea; and they began to surround the lightning and become subject to it. ¹²And I woke up in terror.

The Prayer of Baruch

54. And I besought the Mighty One and said,

Thou alone, O Lord, knowest beforehand the secrets of the world,
And what happens in its time thou dost bring about by thy word;

And in the light of what is done by those on earth
Thou wilt speed up the beginnings of the times,
And the end of the ages thou alone knowest.
2 For thee nothing is too hard,
Thou doest everything easily by a nod.
3 To thee the depths come as the heights,
And the beginnings of the ages are obedient to thy word.
4 Thou revealest to those who fear ⟨thee⟩ what is
    prepared for them,
And so dost thou comfort them.
5 Thou showest wonders to the ignorant:
Thou dost break down the dividing wall for those who do not
    know;
And thou dost light up what is dark
And reveal what is hidden to the pure,
Who in faith have submitted to thee and to thy law.
6 Thou hast shown thy servant this vision:
Reveal to me also its interpretation.
7 For I know that when I have besought thee, thou hast answered me,
And when I have made request, thou hast made response to me.
Thou didst reveal to me with what language I should praise thee,
And with which of my members I should offer (my) praises and
    hallelujahs to thee.
8 For if (all) my members were mouths, and the hairs of my head
    voices,
Even then I could not praise or magnify thee as I should,
Nor could I recount thy praise nor tell the glory of thy beauty.
9 For what am I among men,
And why am I reckoned among those of far more worth than I,
That I should have heard all these marvellous things from the Most
    High,
And numberless promises from him who created me?
10 Happy my mother among those that bear children,
And worthy of praise among women is she who gave me birth!
11 For I will not cease to praise the Mighty One,
And with a thankful voice I will recount his wonders.
12 For who can do wonders like thine, O God,
Or who can understand thy purpose in creation?
13 For with thy counsel thou dost govern all the creatures
Which thy right hand has created,

And thou hast establihed every source of light beside thee,
And the treasuries of wisdom thou hast prepared beneath thy throne.
14 Justly do they perish who have not loved thy law:
The torment of judgement awaits those who have not submitted to thy power.

15 For though Adam first sinned and brought untimely death upon all men, yet each one of those who were born from him has either prepared for his own soul (its) future torment or chosen for himself the glories that are to be—16 for without doubt he who believes will receive his reward. 17 But now, as for you, you wicked that now are, prepare to meet destruction: your punishment will come quickly, because you have rejected the understanding of the Most High. 18 For what he has done has not taught you, nor has the craftsmanship revealed perpetually in his creation persuaded you. 19 Thus Adam was responsible for himself only: each one of us is his own Adam. 20 But do thou, O Lord, explain to me the things thou hast revealed to me, and give me an answer to the questions that I asked. 21 For at the consummation retribution will fall on those who have done evil for the evil they have done, and thou wilt make glorious the faithful for their faithfulness. 22 For those who are among thine own thou rulest, and those who sin thou dost root out from among thine own.

55. And when I had finished this prayer, I sat down there under a tree, to rest in the shade of (its) branches. 2 And as I considered it, I was astonished and amazed at the immensity of the goodness that sinners on earth have rejected, and the scale of the torment they have despised, although they were very well aware that they would be tormented for their sins. 3 And while I was pondering these and similar things, lo, the angel Ramiel, who presides over genuine visions, was sent to me; and he said to me, 4 Why are you so distraught, Baruch, and why so troubled in mind? 5 For if you are so moved [when] you have only heard about the judgement, what (are you going to be like) when you see it happening before your eyes? 6 And if you are so overwrought at the prospect of the coming of the day of the Mighty One, what (will you be like) when it actually arrives? 7 And if you are so upset by what you have been told about the torment of the evil-doers, how much more (so will you be) when the complex details are disclosed? 8 And if you are distressed about what you have heard is to happen then—things both good and bad—how (will it be with you) when you see what the (Mighty One in his) majesty will reveal, when he convicts some and gives others cause for rejoicing?

56. However, you have asked the Most High to reveal to you the interpretation of the vision you have seen, and I have been sent to tell you. ²For the Mighty One has indeed made known to you the sequence of the times that have passed and of those that are yet to be in the world, from the beginning of its creation right up to its consummation—times of falsehood and times of truth. ³You saw a great cloud coming up out of the sea that went on and covered the earth: this (cloud) is the duration of the age of the world, which the Mighty One determined when he decided to make the world. ⁴And so it was that when the world had gone out from his presence, the duration of the world came into being, something of small account, established according to the richness of the understanding of him who sent it. ⁵And you saw at the top of the cloud black waters descending first upon the earth—this is the transgression of the first man, Adam. ⁶For when he transgressed untimely death appeared: sorrow came to be, and suffering was produced and pain created, and toil became the rule: pride reared its head: Sheol insisted on being renewed by blood: the conception of children was brought about and the passion of parents roused: man's whole status received a blow; and goodness languished. ⁷What could be blacker or darker than all this? ⁸This is the beginning of the black waters that you saw. ⁹And from these black waters again (other) black (waters) were derived, and even greater darkness was produced. ¹⁰For the man who was a danger to himself became a danger even to the angels. ¹¹For at the time he was created they enjoyed freedom. ¹²And some of them came down (to earth) and had intercourse with women. ¹³And those who did so then were tormented in chains. ¹⁴But the rest of the ⟨in⟩numerable host of angels restrained themselves. ¹⁵And those who lived on earth perished all together through the waters of the flood. ¹⁶These are the first black waters.

57. And after these you saw bright waters: these (represent) the fount of Abraham and his family, and the coming of his son and of his grandson, and of those like them. ²For at that time the unwritten law was observed by them and the provisions of the commandments were then fulfilled: then originated belief in the coming judgement: hope for a world to be renewed was then established; and the promise of a life to come hereafter was implanted (in men's hearts). ³These are the bright waters that you saw.

58. And the black third waters that you saw—these (represent) the mixture of all the sins of the nations that followed the death of those righteous men, and the wickedness of the land of Egypt in subjecting their sons to such cruel servitude. ²However, these in their turn had their day.

59. And the bright fourth waters that you saw (represent) the coming of Moses and Aaron and Miriam and Joshua, the son of Nun, and Caleb and all those like them. ²For at that time the lamp of the eternal law shone on all those in darkness, giving to believers the promise of their reward, and warning unbelievers about the torment of fire reserved for them. ³At that time, too, the heavens shook, and what was beneath the throne of the Mighty One trembled, when he was taking Moses to himself. ⁴For he showed him many other things together with the ordinances of the ⟨law⟩—the consummation of the ⟨times⟩—just as he has also shown you—and similarly the pattern of Zion and its dimensions, as it was to be constructed, ⟨and⟩ the pattern of the sanctuary, as it now is. ⁵Then he showed him also the dimensions of the fire, the depths of the abyss, the weight of the winds, and the number of the drops of rain; ⁶and the mastery of anger, the dignity of patience, and the truth of judgement; ⁷and the root of wisdom, the riches of understanding, and the fount of knowledge; ⁸and the height of the air, the extent of Paradise, the consummation of the ages, and the beginning of the day of judgement; ⁹and the number of the offerings, and the countries which were as yet unknown; ¹⁰and the mouth of Gehenna, the abode of vengeance, the home of faith, and the dwelling-place of hope; ¹¹and the vision of the future torment, the throng of innumerable angels, the flaming hosts, the splendour of the lightning, the sound of the thunder, the orders of the ⟨archangels⟩, the treasuries of light, the changes of the seasons, and the careful study of the law. ¹²These are the bright fourth waters that you saw.

60. And the black fifth waters you saw coming down as rain are what the Amorites did, their spells and incantations, the evils of their mysteries, and the contaminating effect of their pollutions. ²For even

Israel was then polluted and went astray in the days of the judges, although they witnessed many signs given them by their creator.

61. And the bright sixth waters that you saw—this is the time when David and Solomon were born. ²And at that time Zion was built, and the sanctuary dedicated; and much blood of the nations that had sinned then was shed, and many offerings were offered at the dedication of the sanctuary. ³And peace and tranquillity reigned at that time. ⁴(The voice of) wisdom was heard in the assembly, and the riches of understanding were prized in the congregations. ⁵And the holy festivals were celebrated enthusiastically and with much joy. ⁶The rulers' judgements were then seen to be unbiased, and the justice of the precepts of the Mighty One was maintained in truth. ⁷And because the land enjoyed (God's) favour at that time, and because those who lived there did not sin, it was made more glorious than any other land; and the city of Zion became the ruler of all lands and countries. ⁸These are the bright waters that you saw.

62. And the black seventh waters that you saw (represent) the perversion (brought about) by Jeroboam's plan to make two golden calves; ²and all the iniquities of the kings after him; and the curse of Jezebel, ³and the idol-worship that Israel practised at that time; ⁴and the withholding of the rain, and the famines that followed until women even ate their own children, ⁵and the captivity that overtook the nine and a half tribes because of their many sins—⁶for Shalmaneser, king of Assyria, came and carried them off as captives. ⁷And so far as the Gentiles are concerned, there is no need to stress how they always did what was sinful and wicked, and never what was righteous. ⁸These are the black seventh waters that you saw.

63. And the bright eighth waters that you saw—these are the integrity and honesty of Hezekiah, king of Judah, and the grace that was accorded him. ²For when Sennacherib was stirred up to destroy himself, and his anger maddened him into leading to their destruction also the motley collection of peoples that were with him: ³when, moreover, king Hezekiah heard what the king of Assyria was plotting, to come and destroy his people—the two and a half tribes that were left—and he wanted to lay waste Zion too: then Hezekiah, in trust and reliance on his righteousness, spoke with the Mighty One and said, ⁴Behold, Sennacherib is ready to destroy us; and he will boast when he has laid

129

Zion waste and take credit to himself. 5And the Mighty One heard him, for Hezekiah was wise, and he listened to his prayer, because he was righteous. 6And the Mighty One then gave instructions to his angel Ramiel—(the angel) who is speaking to you (now). 7And I went and destroyed the whole host of them—the number of the officers alone was a hundred and eighty-five thousand, and each one of them had an equal number (under his command). 8And on this occasion I burned their bodies inside, but their outer clothing and their armour I preserved intact, so that what the Mighty One had done might seem still more wonderful, and that as a result his name might be spoken of throughout the entire earth. 9Thus Zion was saved and Jerusalem delivered: Israel too was freed from (its) distress. 10And all those who were in the holy land rejoiced, and the name of the Mighty One was glorified so that it was spoken of (everywhere). 11These are the bright waters that you saw.

64. And the black ninth waters that you saw—these (represent) all the wickedness that was in the days of Manasseh, Hezekiah's son. 2For he did very many wicked things: he killed the righteous: he perverted judgement: he shed the blood of the innocent: he violated and polluted married women; and he demolished the altars and destroyed their offerings, and drove out the priests so that they could not minister in the sanctuary. 3And he made an image with five faces, four of them looked to the four winds, and the fifth at the top of the image (was there) to provoke the jealousy of the Mighty One. 4At that time (a sentence of) wrath went out from the presence of the Mighty One that Zion should be rooted up—and it has happened in your days. 5And also against the two and a half tribes there went out a decree that they too should be carried off as captives—as you have now seen. 6And to such lengths did the impiety of Manasseh go that the glory of the Most High departed from the sanctuary. 7For this reason Manasseh was even in his own day called 'The Impious', and his final lodging was in the fire. 8For though the Most High at last heard his prayer when he was shut up in the bronze horse, and the horse was melting, and a sign was given to him then, 9his life was far from perfect, and all he deserved was to know by whom he would be tormented in the end. 10For he who is able to do good is also able to punish.

65. Thus Manasseh did many wicked things, and he thought that in his time the Mighty One would not inquire into them. 2These are the black ninth waters that you saw.

66. And the bright tenth waters that you saw—these are the faithfulness of the generation of Josiah, king of Judah, who was the only one at the time who submitted himself to the Mighty One with all his heart and soul. ²And he purged the land of idols, and hallowed all the vessels that had been polluted, and restored the offerings to the altar, and lifted up the heads of the holy, and exalted the righteous, and honoured men of wisdom and understanding, and brought back the priests to their ministry, and destroyed and removed the magicians and soothsayers and necromancers from the land. ³And not only did he kill the impious that were still alive, but he also had the bones of the dead taken from their graves and burnt. ⁴And the festivals and the sabbaths he restored with their proper rites: he burned those who were polluted: he burned also the lying prophets that had deceived the people; and the people that had listened to them he threw alive into the brook Kidron, and raised a heap of stones over them. ⁵And he devoted himself heart and soul to the Mighty One; and he was remarkable in his day for his strict observance of the law, so that during his life-time no one that was uncircumcised was left anywhere in the land, nor any evil-doer. ⁶He will indeed receive an eternal reward, and he will be more honoured by the Mighty One than many at the last time. ⁷For it was because of him, and those like him, that the honours and the glories you were told about before were created and prepared. ⁸These are the bright waters that you saw.

67. And the black eleventh waters that you saw—these are the calamity that has now overtaken Zion. ²Do you imagine that the angels in the presence of the Mighty One experience no pain that Zion should be so delivered up, and when they see the Gentiles boasting in their hearts, and crowds before their idols saying,

> She is now trodden down, she who so often trod (others) down,
> And she has been reduced to servitude, she who reduced (others)?

³Do you imagine the Most High rejoices at this, or that his name is thereby glorified? ⁴How will it serve towards his righteous judgement? ⁵Yet after this, great troubles will afflict those who are dispersed among the Gentiles, and wherever they may be living they will be humiliated. ⁶So long as Zion is delivered up and Jerusalem laid waste, idols will prosper in the Gentile cities; and (while) the sweet smoke of the incense of the righteousness which is according to the law no longer ascends in

Zion, it will be replaced everywhere in Zion's neighbourhood by the smoke of godlessness. [7] And the king of Babylon, who has now destroyed Zion, will exalt himself, and he will make great claims in the Most High's presence. [8] But he also will come to grief at last. [9] These are the black waters.

68. And the bright twelfth waters that you saw—this is the meaning (of them). [2] After all this, a time will come when your people will be in such a sorry state that there is a risk of their perishing altogether. [3] Even so, they will be saved, and their enemies will fall before them. [4] And for a time they will have much joy. [5] And then, after a short interval, Zion will be rebuilt, and its offerings will be restored again, and the priests will return to their ministry, and the Gentiles also will come and acclaim it. [6] However, things will not be as they were in former times. [7] And after this, disaster will strike many nations. [8] These are the bright waters that you saw.

69. The last waters that you saw, darker than all that had been before them—those (waters) that came after the gathering together of the twelve other waters concern the whole world. [2] For the Most High made a separation at the beginning, because he alone knows what will happen. [3] As for the enormities and impious deeds that would be committed before him, he foresaw six kinds of them. [4] And as for the good deeds of the righteous to be done before him, he foresaw six kinds of them (also), apart from what he himself would do at the consummation of the age. [5] That is why there were not black waters (mixed) with black, nor bright with bright; for it is the consummation.

70. Hear then the interpretation of the last black waters which are to come after the (other) black (waters): this is the meaning. [2] Behold, the days are coming, and when the time of the age has ripened, and the harvest of its evil and its good seeds has come, the Mighty One will bring upon the earth and its inhabitants, and upon its rulers, trepidation of spirit and consternation of mind. [3] And they will hate one another, and provoke one another to fight; and obscure men will have dominion over men of reputation, and the lowly born will be exalted above the nobles. [4] And the many will be delivered into the hands of the few, and those who were nothing will rule over the strong, and the poor will have much more than the rich, and the impious will set themselves up against the brave. [5] And the wise will be silent, and (only) fools will speak: neither the designs of (ordinary) men, nor the plans of the powerful, will come to anything, nor will any hopes for the future prove well-founded. ⁶And when what has been predicted has happened, then will confusion descend upon all men: some of them will fall in battle: some of them will perish in anguish, and some of them will be ⟨destroyed⟩ by their own people. ⁷Then will the Most High reveal those peoples whom he has prepared beforehand, and they will come and make war with the leaders that then are left. ⁸And whoever escapes in the war will die by earthquake, and whoever escapes the earthquake will be burned by fire, and whoever escapes the fire will be ⟨destroyed⟩ by famine. ⁹And whoever, whether of the victors or the vanquished, escapes all these things, and comes safely through them, will be delivered into the hands of my servant, the Messiah. ¹⁰For the whole earth will devour those who live on it.

71. But the holy land will have mercy on its own, and will protect those who are living there at that time. ²This is the vision that you saw, and this is the interpretation of it. ³And I have come to tell you this because your prayer has been heard by the Most High.

72. Listen now also (to what I have to tell you) about the bright waters that are to come at the consummation after these black (waters): this is the meaning (of them). ²After the signs have appeared, which you were told about before, when the nations are in confusion, and the time of my Messiah is come, he will call all the nations together, and some of them he will spare, and some of them he will destroy. ³This is what will happen to the nations spared by him. ⁴Every nation that has not ⟨exploited⟩ Israel and has not trampled the race of Jacob underfoot will be spared. ⁵And this will be because some out of all the nations will become subject to your people. ⁶But all those who have had dominion over you, or have ⟨exploited⟩ you, will be given over to the sword.

73. And when he has brought low everything that is in the world, and has sat down in peace for ever on the throne of his kingdom,

> Then shall joy be revealed,
> And rest made manifest.
> ² And then shall healing descend as dew,
> And disease shall disappear;
> And anxiety and anguish and lamentation shall pass from men,

And gladness spread through all the earth.
3 And never again shall anyone die before his time,
Nor shall any adversity suddenly befall.
4 And law suits and accusations and contentions and revenges,
And murder and passions and envy and hatred,
And all things like these shall be done away
And go to their condemnation.
5 For it is these things that have filled this world with evils,
And it is because of these that the life of man has been so troubled.
6 And wild beasts shall come from the forest
And minister to men,
And asps and dragons shall come out of their holes
To submit themselves to a little child.
7 And women shall no longer have pain when they bear (children),
Nor shall they suffer agony when they yield the fruit of the womb.

74. And in those days the reapers shall not grow weary,
Nor those that build be toilworn;
For both works and workers together
Will prosper in complete accord.
2 For that time marks the end of what is corruptible
And the beginning of what is incorruptible.
3 Thus, what was predicted will be fulfilled in it:
It is beyond the grasp of evil men,
Accessible only to those who will not die.

4These are the bright waters that came after the last dark waters.

75. And I answered and said,

Who can be compared with thee, O Lord, in thy goodness?
For it is beyond us altogether.
2 Or who can search out thine infinite compassion?
3 Or who can comprehend thine understanding?
4 Or who is able to describe the workings of thy mind?
5 Who among mortals can hope to come near (doing any of) these
things,
Unless he is one of those to whom thou art merciful and gracious?
6 For if thou didst not have compassion upon man,
Those who are under thy right hand

Could not achieve these things—
Only those who are called to be among the number thou hast
   determined.
7 But if we, who are alive, know for what reason we have come,
And submit ourselves to him who brought us out of Egypt,
We shall come again and remember what is past,
And rejoice in what has been.
8 But if we do not know for what reason we have come
And do not recognize the sovereignty of him who brought us out of
   Egypt,
We shall come again and regret what has been now,
And grieve over what is past.

76. And he answered and said to me, Since the interpretation of this vision has been given you as you asked, Listen to what the Most High has to say, so that you may know what is to happen to you after this. 2 For you must certainly leave this world, yet you will not die, but you will be preserved until the consummation of the times. 3 So go up to the top of that mountain, and you will get a view of the entire land and be able to distinguish its various features—the tops of the mountains, the bottoms of the valleys, the depths of the seas, and the many rivers, so that you can see what you are leaving behind and where you are going. 4 This shall be in forty days time from now. 5 But now go and spend these days teaching the people as best you can, so that they may understand what will lead to death and what to life in the last times.

77. And I, Baruch, went away; and I came to the people, and I called them together, high and low alike. 2 And I said to them, Listen, you sons of Israel: see how many there are of you who have survived, out of the twelve tribes of Israel. 3 For (it was) to you and to your fathers (that) the Lord gave the law, and not to all peoples. 4 And because your brothers disobeyed the Most High's commandments he brought retribution both on you and on them: he did not spare the one, and he caused the others to be led away as captives and left none of them behind. 5 But you are here with me. 6 If, then, you direct your ways aright, you will not go as your brothers went; but they will come to you. 7 For he whom you worship is merciful, and he in whom you hope is gracious; and he can be relied on to do good and not evil. 8 You have seen, have you not, what happened to Zion? 9 Do you think, perhaps, that it was the place that sinned, and that it was because of this that it was overthrown? Or (again), that the land had committed some outrage, and that was why it was delivered up? [10]Are you not aware that it was because of you, who had sinned, that (the city), which had not sinned, was overthrown, and that it was because of (you) evil-doers that (the land), which had done no evil, was delivered up (to its) enemies? [11]And the whole people answered and said to me, So far as we can recall the good things the Mighty One has done for us, we do recall them; and what we do not remember, he in his mercy knows. [12]But do this for us, your people: write to our brothers in Babylon a letter on a scroll, (a letter) of instruction and encouragement, to reassure them also before you leave us.

[13] For the shepherds of Israel have perished,
   And the lamps that gave light have gone out,
   And the fountains have held back their streams,
   From which we used to drink.
[14] And we are left in darkness,
   Amid the trees of the forest, and in the thirst of the wilderness.

[15]And I answered and said to them,

   Shepherds and lamps and fountains come from the law;
   And though we depart, yet the law remains.
[16] If, then, you respect the law and turn your hearts to wisdom,
   A lamp will not be wanting and a ⟨shepherd⟩ will not fail,
   And no fountain will dry up.

[17]But, as you asked me, I will write (a letter) to your brothers in Babylon, and I will send it by the hands of men; and I will write also (a) similar (letter) to the nine and a half tribes, and send it by means of a bird. [18]And on the twenty-first day of the eighth month, I, Baruch, came and sat down under the oak in the shade of its branches, and no one was with me—I was alone. [19]And I wrote two letters: one I sent by an eagle to the nine and a half tribes; and the other I sent to those that were in Babylon by the hands of three men. [20]And I called the eagle and said to it, [21]The Most High created you to be the king of all the birds. [22]Go now: stop nowhere (on your journey): neither look for any roosting-place, nor settle on any tree, till you have crossed the broad waters of the river Euphrates, and come to the people that dwell there, and laid this letter at their feet. [23]Remember how, at the time of the flood, a dove brought Noah back an olive, when he had sent it out from the ark. [24]Ravens, too,

waited on Elijah, and brought him food, as they had been commanded. [25]Solomon also, when he was king, whenever he wanted to send a message or find out anything, would give instructions to a bird, and it obeyed his instructions. [26]And now, never mind how tired you are: do not stray from your course, either to right or left, but fly straight there; and carry out the instructions of the Mighty One, as I have explained them to you.

The Letter of Baruch, the son of Neriah, which he wrote to the Nine and a Half Tribes.

78. This is the letter that Baruch, the son of Neriah, sent to the nine and a half tribes, which were across the river Euphrates, in which these things were written.

[2]Baruch, the son of Neriah, to his brothers in captivity, Mercy and peace (to you). [3]I can never forget, my brothers, the love of him who created us, who loved us from the beginning and never hated us, but rather subjected us to discipline. [4]Nor can I forget that all we of the twelve tribes are united by a common bond, inasmuch as we are descended from a single father. [5]Hence my concern to leave you in this letter, before I die, some words of comfort amid the evils that have come upon you, (in the hope) that you may also be moved to share in your brothers' grief at the evil that has befallen them, and again, that you may accept as just the sentence (the Most High) passed upon you, namely, that you should be carried off as captives—even though what you have suffered is scarcely in proportion to what you did—in order that in the last times you may be found worthy of your fathers. [6]For if you realize that what you now suffer is for your good, so that you may not in the end be condemned and tormented, then you will receive eternal hope—if, that is, you have purged your minds of the vanities and errors that were the cause of your being taken away. [7]For if you do this, he will remember you continually, he who always promised on our behalf to those who were far superior to ourselves, that he will never forget us or forsake us, but in the greatness of his mercy will gather together again those who have been dispersed.

79. Now, my brothers, hear first what happened to Zion, how Nebuchadnezzar, king of Babylon, made an attack on us. [2]For we had sinned against him who created us and had not kept the commandments he gave us, although he did not chasten us as we deserved. [3]And so we

137

feel far greater sympathy for you since what happened to you happened also to us.

80. And now, my brothers, I tell you that when the enemy had surrounded the city, the angels of the Most High were sent, and (it was) they (who) threw down the fortifications of the strong wall and destroyed the firm iron corners, which could not be dislodged. ²But they hid ⟨all⟩ the vessels of the sanctuary, so that they should not be polluted by the enemy. ³And when they had done this, they surrendered to the enemy the wall that had been thrown down, the plundered house, the burnt temple, and the people who were overcome because they had been surrendered, so that the enemy could not boast and say, By our prowess in battle have we been able to lay waste even the house of the Most High. ⁴Your brothers, too, were put in chains and taken away to Babylon and made to live there. ⁵But we have been left here; and there are very few of us. ⁶This is the wretched situation I am writing to you about. ⁷For I know full well what a consolation it was for you when Zion was inhabited: the knowledge that it prospered was a major consolation for the suffering you endured in being exiled from it.

81. But as to consolation, I should tell you this. ²I was mourning for Zion, and I prayed the Most High for mercy, and I said,

³ Will things continue for us as they are to the end?
   And will these evils come upon us always?
⁴ And the Mighty One responded in the fullness of his mercy,
   And he spoke to me by way of revelation,
   So that I might receive consolation;
   And he showed me visions,
   So that I should suffer no more anguish;
   And he made known to me the mystery of the ages,
   And the advent of the times he showed me.

82. And so, my brothers, I am writing to you, so that you may find consolation in the midst of your many troubles. ²Do not doubt that our creator will avenge us on all our enemies, in accordance with what each one of them has done to us: above all, (have no doubt) that the consummation which the Most High has appointed is very near, and his mercy that is coming; and the consummation of his judgement is not far off.

3 For lo, we see now the Gentiles in great prosperity,
   Though their deeds are impious;
   But they shall be like a breath of wind (that dies away).
4 And we behold the extent of their power,
   Though what they do is wicked;
   But they shall become like a drop (from a bucket).
5 And we see the strength of their might,
   Though they resist the Mighty One every hour;
   But they shall be treated like spittle
6 And we consider their glory and grandeur,
   Though they do not observe the Most High's statutes,
   But they shall disappear like smoke.
7 And we reflect on their beauty and their gracefulness,
   Though they are soaked in pollutions;
   But as grass that withers shall they fade away.
8 And we consider their brutality and cruelty,
   Though they give no thought to (their) end;
   But as a passing wave shall they be broken.
9 And we remark the boastings of their might,
   Though they deny the beneficence of the God who gave (it) them;
   But as a passing cloud shall they pass away.

83. For the Most High will assuredly speed up his times,
   And he will assuredly bring on his seasons.
2 And he will assuredly judge those who are in his world,
   And will truly punish all men,
   In accordance with their hidden works.
3 And he will assuredly examine (their) secret thoughts,
   And what is stored away in the innermost recesses of their being,
   And he will expose and censure (them) openly.

4Do not, then, worry yourselves about these present things, but rather look to the future, because what has been promised to us will come. 5And let us not now fix our attention upon the delights the Gentiles enjoy in the present (age) but let us remember what has been promised to us in the end. 6For set times and seasons, and all that goes with them, will assuredly pass away. [7]And then the consummation of the age will reveal the great might of its ruler, when all things come to judgement. [8]So prepare yourselves for (the coming of) what you have believed in in the past, so that you do not find yourselves the losers in both worlds, by having been carried off as captives here, and being tormented there. [9]For in what is now, or in what has been, or in what is to come, in all these things, the evil is not entirely evil, nor, again, is the good entirely good.

[10] For all the health that now is is turning into disease.
[11] And all the strength that now is is turning into weakness,
   And all the might that now is is turning into impotence.
[12] And all the energy of youth is turning into old age and
      dissolution,
   And all the beauty and gracefulness that now are are turning
      into decay and ugliness.
[13] And all the proud dominion that now is is turning into
      humiliation and shame.
[14] And all praise of the splendour that now is is turning into the
      shame of speechlessness,
   And all the luxury and pomp that now are are turning into silent
      ruin.
[15] And all the delight and joy that now are are turning into worms
      and corruption.
[16] And all acclaim of the pride that now is is turning into dust
      and stillness.
[17] And all heaping-up of riches that now is is turning only into
      Sheol.
[18] And all the spoils of passion that now are are turning into
      inexorable death,
   And all passion of the lusts that now is is turning into a
      judgement of torment.
[19] And all artifice and craftiness that now are are turning into a
      proof of truth.
[20] And all sweet-smelling ointments that now are are turning
      into judgement and condemnation.
[21] And all love of falsehood is turning into well-earned degradation.

[22] Since, then, all these things are happening now, can anyone believe that vengeance is far off? [23] The consummation of all things will result in truth.

84. Behold, I have informed you about these things while I am still alive, and I am telling you (about them) so that you may understand what is worth pursuing; for the Mighty One has commissioned me to instruct you, and I will, (therefore), remind you of some of the precepts he has given us before I die. ²Remember how Moses at one time summoned heaven and earth to witness against you and said, If you transgress the law you will be scattered, but if you keep it you will be firmly planted (in your land). ³And other things, too, he told you when you, the twelve tribes, were together in the wilderness. ⁴But after his death you rejected them; and so there came upon you what had been predicted. ⁵Moses told you beforehand, so that it might not happen to you; and it happened to you, because you forsook the law. ⁶And now I also tell you, after you have suffered, that if you take note of what you have been told, you will receive from the Mighty One whatever has been appointed and reserved for you. ⁷Furthermore, may this letter stand as a witness (between us)—between you and me—so that you may remember the commandments of the Mighty One, and that I also may have a defence before him who sent me. ⁸Remember the law and Zion, the holy land and your brothers, and the covenant of your fathers; and do not forget the festivals and the sabbaths. ⁹And hand on this letter and the traditions of the law to your sons after you, just as your fathers handed (them) on to you. ¹⁰Be always regular in your prayers, and pray diligently with all your heart that the Mighty One may restore you to his favour, and that he may not take account of your many sins, but remember the faithfulness of your fathers. ¹¹For if he is not to judge us in the fullness of his mercy, woe to all of us poor mortals!

85. Consider, too, that in days gone by and in the generations of old our fathers had to help them righteous men and holy prophets. ²Moreover, we were in our own land; and they helped us when we sinned, and, relying on their merits, interceded for us with our creator, and the Mighty One heard their prayer and forgave us. ³But now the righteous have been gathered (to their fathers), and the prophets have fallen asleep, and we also have been exiled from (our) land: Zion has been taken from us, and nothing is left us now save the Mighty One and his law. ⁴But if we direct and dispose our hearts (aright), we shall retrieve everything that we have lost, and (gain) many more and much better things than we have lost. ⁵For what we have lost was subject to corruption, but what we shall receive is incorruptible. ⁶And I am writing also to our brothers in Babylon in the same terms, to assure them about

141

these things. ⁷Keep everything you have been told constantly in mind, because so long as the breath is in our bodies we are still free to choose. ⁸Once again, the Most High is patient with us here: he has shown us what is to be and has not hidden from us what is to happen in the end. ⁹Before, then, the judgement demands its own, and the truth what is its due, let us prepare ourselves to take possession, and not be taken possession of, to hope and not be put to shame, and to have rest with our fathers and not be in torment with our enemies. ¹⁰For the youth of the world is past, and the strength of the creation already exhausted: the times have run their course and the end is very near: the pitcher is near the cistern, the ship to port, the traveller to the city, and life to (its) consummation. ¹¹And yet again, prepare yourselves, so that when you have finished your journey and leave the ship, you may find rest and may not be condemned when you go away. ¹²For when the Most High brings all these things to pass, there will be there no further opportunity for repentance, no set times nor appointed seasons, no (possible) change in ways (of life), no place for prayer nor offering of petitions, no acquiring of knowledge nor giving of love, no place of repentance for the soul nor supplication for offences, no intercession by the fathers nor prayer by the prophets nor help from the righteous. ¹³But there will be there the sentence of destruction, the way of fire and the path that leads to Gehenna. ¹⁴That is why there is one law, (given) by one (man), one world and an end for all who are in it. ¹⁵Then will (the Mighty One) preserve those he can forgive, and at the same time destroy those who are polluted by (their) sins.

86. So when you receive this letter that I have written, see that you read it in your congregations. ²And think about it, especially on your fast-days. ³And may this letter serve as a means of your remembering me, as I also have remembered you in (writing) it, and always (do remember you).

87. And when I had finished this letter, and had written it carefully to the very end, I folded it, and sealed it as a safeguard, and tied it to the eagle's neck, and despatched it and sent it off.

Here ends the Book of Baruch, the son of Neriah.

CHAPTER TWO

APOCALYPSES THAT CONTAIN OTHERWORLDLY JOURNEYS

THE BOOK OF THE WATCHERS (1 ENOCH 1-36)

Commentary

The material in chapters 1–36 of *1 Enoch* is commonly known as the "Book of the Watchers" because of the episode of the "Watcher" angels that it contains (see the discussion of *1 Enoch* in the introduction to the "Animal Apocalypse"). The "Book of the Watchers" is a composite work that can be divided into at least three sections (some scholars divide it into even more sections): chapters 1–5, which serve as an introduction; chapters 6–16, in which the primary story of the Watchers is found; and chapters 17–36, which describe Enoch's journeys to the outer boundaries of the earth.

In the present arrangement of the text, chapters 1–5 serve as an introduction to all of *1 Enoch,* although originally they may have introduced only chapters 6–36 or perhaps only a portion of this material. In chapter 1, Enoch claims to have seen "a holy vision in the heavens which the angels showed to me." Enoch's vision deals with the future status of the righteous and the sinners. God will appear on Mt. Sinai to execute judgment upon the earth. The righteous will receive mercy and will prosper, but the impious will be destroyed. The material in 2:1–5:3 describes the orderliness of creation: All of nature is obedient to God and does not rebel. Humanity, on the other hand, has broken the laws of God and as a result will be punished. This punishment of the wicked, along with the rewards for the righteous, is described in 5:4-9. The righteous will inherit the earth and will experience light and joy and peace (5:7).

The story of the Watcher angels, told in chapters 6–16, is an elaboration of the tradition mentioned in Genesis 6:1-4. According to the Genesis account, "the sons of God" had sexual intercourse with "the daughters of men." Their offspring were the Nephilim, the "mighty men" or giants. In *1 Enoch* the "sons of God" are called angels or Watchers. Two versions of the story of the Watchers have been intertwined. In one account, the leader of the Watchers is named Semyaza, and the major sin of which the angels are guilty is sexual intercourse with women. In the other account, the leader is Azazel, and their sin is the revelation of heavenly secrets to humanity. Because of the wickedness that is rampant on the earth due to the Watchers and their offspring, the giants, God pronounces judgment against the earth in the form of the flood. All wickedness will be wiped out; Noah and his family will be the only earthly survivors. The evil Watchers will be bound until the day of judgment, at which time they will be destroyed and the earth will be cleansed of all wrong. The endtime is described as a paradise existence: righteousness, truth, and peace will abound; corruption and sin will be nonexistent; the earth will produce bountiful crops, and people will be extremely fertile.

In chapters 12–16 the evil Watchers ask Enoch to intercede for them with God. Subsequently Enoch has a vision in which he is taken up to heaven to the throne room of God. There God instructs Enoch to go to the Watchers and pronounce judgment against them for their disobedience.

The final section of the Book of the Watchers, chapters 17–36, describes Enoch's cosmic journeys. Led by angel guides, Enoch is given a tour of the outermost parts of the earth, where he sees such cosmological secrets as the storehouses of the winds, the foundations of the earth, the prison for the disobedient stars and angels, the gates of heaven, and even the Garden of Eden. A strong eschatological interest is evident in chapters 21–27. In chapter 21, Enoch describes his vision of the place of punishment for the evil angels. Chapter 22 contains the description of the place where the souls of the dead are kept until the day of judgment. Three (or four) separate compartments for the souls of the righteous and the wicked are described. Enoch also sees the mountain-throne where God will reign when God comes to dwell on earth (chaps. 24–25) and the place of eternal punishment for the wicked (chaps. 26–27).

Even though Enoch's journeys take place on the earth, they still should be considered otherworldly because he visits places at the outer limits of the earth where humans cannot go. The spatial dimension of this apocalypse is evident also in the emphasis on otherworldly beings, specifically the good and bad angels. Angels serve Enoch as both mediators and interpreters of revelation, in addition to being guides for his cosmic journeys.

The "Book of the Watchers" was likely written in response to a crisis. Unfortunately, the work gives no clues that indicate clearly what that crisis was. One plausible suggestion is that the evil angels who teach people forbidden secrets, including the secrets of war and weaponry, and who wreak destruction upon the earth are veiled references to the generals of Alexander the Great. These men, known as the Diadochi, fought bitter struggles for control of Alexander's empire. Like the evil Watchers, the Diadochi brought about warfare and destruction, claimed supernatural status for themselves, and imposed themselves as foreigners upon the people. By using the myth of the Watcher angels, the author of the "Book of the Watchers" sets these Hellenistic princes and their claims into perspective. They are not divine, but evil in origin. Even though they may triumph momentarily, eventually they will be punished.

The visions and heavenly journeys of Enoch serve several purposes. First, they serve to give authority to his statements. Enoch speaks as one who has been in the very presence of God and who has seen the secrets of the universe. Second, the scenes of punishment and reward offer hope by showing the ultimate outcome for the wicked and the righteous. Third, the order and regularity of the universe, along with the places of punishment and reward that are already prepared, bolster confidence that God is in control.

The evil of the Watcher angels, God's punishment of the earth, and the salvation through Noah become a typology of the writer's situation. Just as God executed judgment against the evildoers and rewarded the righteous of the past, so also God will act for the author and his readers. The apparent additions and alterations to the story of the Watcher angels suggest that the myth of the Watchers continued to function in new settings and in different crises.

Aramaic fragments discovered at Qumran, dating from the first half of the second century B.C.E., contain portions of *1 Enoch* 1–12. If chapters 1–5 were originally composed as an introduction to the rest of the "Book of the Watchers" (chaps. 6–36), then the entire work must be dated no later than the first part of the second century B.C.E. This dating is supported by the apparent familiarity with this material by the author of *Jubilees* (ca. 160 B.C.E.) and the author of *1 Enoch* 85–90 (beginning decades of the second century B.C.E.). The "Book of the Watchers" in its present form, then, probably should be dated to the early second century or even the third century B.C.E. If the historical referent for the crisis of the Watcher angels is correctly identified as the Diadochan wars and the threat of Hellenistic culture, then the story of the Watcher angels (chaps. 6–11 at least) must be dated to the third century B.C.E.

Several passages from the "Book of the Watchers" influenced the writers of the New Testament. The most obvious example is in Jude 14-15, which is a quotation of *1 Enoch* 1:9. The story of the Watcher angels and their punishment is the background for Jude 6 and 2 Peter 2:4 (see also the punishment of Satan and his cohorts in Rev. 20:1-3, 10, and 14). Many other elements in the "Book of the Watchers" are similar to elements found in New Testament writings, including Enoch's throne vision (*1 Enoch* 14; compare with Rev. 4–5) and the Tree of Life (*1 Enoch* 24–25; compare with Rev. 2:7; 22:2, 14, and 19).

The text of the "Book of the Watchers" given here is the translation by M. A. Knibb, contained in *The Apocryphal Old Testament*. Knibb's work is a translation of primarily one Ethiopic manuscript (Ryl. Eth. MS 23), corrected by other texts only in places where this manuscript does not appear to make sense.

1 Enoch 1–36

1. The words of the blessing of Enoch according to which he blessed the chosen and righteous who must be present on the day of distress (which is appointed) for the removal of all the wicked and impious. ²And Enoch answered and said, (There was) a righteous man whose eyes were opened by the Lord, and he saw a holy vision in the heavens which the angels showed to me. And I heard everything from them, and I understood what I saw, but not for this generation, but for a distant generation which will come. ³Concerning the chosen I spoke, and I uttered a parable concerning them, The Holy and Great One will come out from his dwelling, ⁴and the Eternal God will tread from there upon mount Sinai, and he will appear with his host, and will appear in the strength of his power from heaven. ⁵And all will be afraid, and the

Watchers will shake, and fear and great trembling will seize them unto the ends of the earth. 6And the high mountains will be shaken, and the high hills will be made low, and will melt like wax before the flame. 7And the earth will sink and everything that is on the earth will be destroyed, and there will be judgement upon all, and upon all the righteous. 8But for the righteous he will make peace, and he will keep safe the chosen, and mercy will be upon them. They will all belong to God, and will prosper and be blessed, and the light of God will shine upon them. 9 And behold! He comes with ten thousand holy ones to execute judgement upon them, and to destroy the impious, and to contend with all flesh concerning everything which the sinners and the impious have done and wrought against him.

2. Contemplate all the events in heaven, how the lights in heaven do not change their courses, how each rises and sets in order, each at its proper time, and they do not transgress their law. 2Consider the earth, and understand from the work which is done upon it, from the beginning to the end, that no work of God changes as it becomes manifest. 3Consider the summer and the winter, how the whole earth is full of water, and clouds and dew and rain rest upon it.

3. Contemplate and see how all the trees appear withered, and (how) all their leaves are stripped, with the exception of fourteen trees which are not stripped, which remain with the old (foliage) until the new comes after two or three years.

4. And again, contemplate the days of summer, how at its beginning the sun is above it. You seek shelter and shade because of the heat of the sun, and the earth burns with a scorching heat, and you cannot tread upon the earth, or upon a rock, because of its heat.

5. Contemplate how the trees are covered with green leaves, and bear fruit. And understand in respect of everything and perceive how he who lives for ever made all these things for you; 2and (how) his words (are) before him in each succeeding year, and all his works serve him and do not change, but as God has decreed, so everything is done. 3And consider how the seas and rivers together complete their tasks. 4But you have not persevered, nor observed the law of the Lord. But you have transgressed, and have spoken proud and hard words with your unclean mouth against his majesty. You hard of heart! You will not have peace!

147

[5]And because of this you will curse your days, and the years of your life you will destroy. And the eternal curse will increase, and you will not receive mercy. [6]In those days you will transform your name into an eternal curse to all the righteous, and they will curse you sinners for ever—you together with the sinners. [7]For the chosen there will be light and joy and peace, and they will inherit the earth. But for you, the impious, there will be a curse. [8]When wisdom is given to the chosen, they will all live, and will not again do wrong, either through forgetfulness, or through pride. But those who possess wisdom will be humble. [9]They will not again do wrong, and they will not be judged all the days of their life, and they will not die of (the divine) wrath or anger. But they will complete the number of the days of their life, and their life will grow in peace, and the years of their joy will increase in gladness and in eternal peace all the days of their life.

6. And it came to pass, when the sons of men had increased, that in those days there were born to them fair and beautiful daughters. [2]And the angels, the sons of heaven, saw them and desired them. And they said to one another, Come, let us choose for ourselves wives from the children of men, and let us beget for ourselves children. [3]And Semyaza, who was their leader, said to them, I fear that you may not wish this deed to be done, and (that) I alone will pay for this great sin. [4]And they all answered him and said, Let us all swear an oath, and bind one another with curses not to alter this plan, but to carry out this plan effectively. [5]Then they all swore together and all bound one another with curses to it. [6]And they were in all two hundred, and they came down on Ardis which is the summit of Mount Hermon. And they called the mountain Hermon, because on it they swore and bound one another with curses. [7]And these (are) the names of their leaders: Semyaza, who was their leader, Urakiba, Ramiel, Kokabiel, Tamiel, Ramiel, Daniel, Ezeqiel, Baraqiel, Asael, Armaros, Batriel, Ananel, Zaqiel, Samsiel, Sartael, . . . , Turiel, Yomiel, Araziel. [8]These are the leaders of the two hundred angels, and of all the others with them.

7. And they took wives for themselves, and everyone chose for himself one each. And they began to go in to them and were promiscuous with them. And they taught them charms and spells, and showed to them the cutting of roots and trees. [2]And they became pregnant and bore large giants, and their height (was) three thousand cubits. [3]These devoured all the toil of men, until men were unable to sustain them. [4]And the giants turned against them in order to devour men. [5]And they began to sin against birds, and against animals, and against reptiles and against fish, and they devoured one another's flesh and drank the blood from it. [6]Then the earth complained about the lawless ones.

8. And Azazel taught men to make swords, and daggers, and shields and breastplates. And he showed them the things after these, and the art of making them: bracelets, and ornaments, and the art of making up the eyes and of beautifying the eyelids, and the most precious and choice stones, and all (kinds of) coloured dyes. And the world was changed. [2]And there was great impiety and much fornication, and they went astray, and all their ways became corrupt. [3]Amezarak taught all those who cast spells and cut roots, Armaros the release of spells, and Baraqiel astrologers, and Kokabel portents, and Tamiel taught astrology, and {Asradel}[a] taught the path of the moon. [4]And at the destruction of men they cried out, and their voices reached heaven.

9. And then Michael, Gabriel, Suriel and Uriel looked down from heaven and saw the mass of blood that was being shed on the earth and all the iniquity that was being done on the earth. [2]And they said to one another, Let the devastated earth cry out with the sound of their cries unto the gate of heaven. [3]And now, to you O holy ones of heaven, the souls of men complain, saying, Bring our suit before the Most High. [4]And they said to their Lord, the King, Lord of Lords, God of Gods, King of Kings! Your glorious throne (endures) for all the generations of the world, and your name (is) holy and praised for all the generations of the world and blessed and praised! [5]You have made everything, and power over everything is yours. And everything is uncovered and open before you, and you see everything, and there is nothing which can be hidden from you. [6]See then what Azazel has done, how he has taught all iniquity on the earth and revealed the eternal secrets which were made in heaven. [7]And Semyaza has made known spells, (he) to whom you gave authority to rule over those who are with him. [8]And they went in to the daughters of men together, and lay with those women, and became unclean, and revealed to them these sins. [9]And the women bore giants, and thereby the whole earth has been filled with blood and iniquity. [10]And now behold the souls which have died cry out and complain unto

---

[a]Corrupt; the name originally was "Sahriel" ("Moon of God").

the gate of heaven, and their lament has ascended, and they cannot go out in the face of the iniquity which is being committed on the earth. ¹¹And you know everything before it happens, and you know this and what concerns each of them. But you say nothing to us. What ought we to do with them about this?

10. And then the Most High, the Great and Holy One, spoke and sent Arsyalalyur to the son of Lamech, and said to him, ²Say to him in my name, Hide yourself, and reveal to him the end which is coming, for the whole earth will be destroyed, and a deluge is about to come on all the earth, and what is in it will be destroyed. ³And now teach him that he may escape, and (that) his offspring may survive for the whole earth. ⁴And further the Lord said to Raphael, Bind Azazel by his hands and his feet, and throw him into the darkness. And split open the desert which is in Dudael, and throw him there. ⁵And throw on him jagged and sharp stones, and cover him with darkness; and let him stay there for ever, and cover his face, that he may not see light, ⁶and that on the great day of judgement he may be hurled into the fire. ⁷And restore the earth which the angels have ruined, and announce the restoration of the earth, for I shall restore the earth, so that not all the sons of men shall be destroyed through the mystery of everything which the Watchers ⟨made known⟩ and taught to their sons. ⁸And the whole earth has been ruined by the teaching of the works of Azazel, and against him write down all sin. ⁹And the Lord said to Gabriel, Proceed against the bastards and the reprobates and against the sons of the fornicators, and destroy the sons of the fornicators and the sons of the Watchers from amongst men. And send them out, and send them against one another, and let them destroy themselves in battle, for they will not have length of days. ¹⁰And they will all petition you, but their fathers will gain nothing in respect of them, for they hope for eternal life, and that each of them will live life for five hundred years. ¹¹And the Lord said to Michael, Go, inform Semyaza and the others with him who have associated with the women to corrupt themselves with them in all their uncleanness. ¹²When all their sons kill each other, and when they see the destruction of their beloved ones, bind them for seventy generations under the hills of the earth until the day of their judgement and of their consummation, until the judgement which is for all eternity is accomplished. ¹³And in those days they will lead them to the abyss of fire; in torment and in prison they will be shut up for all eternity. ¹⁴And then he will be burnt and from then on destroyed with them; together they will be bound until the end of all generations. [15]And destroy all the souls of lust and the sons of the Watchers, for they have wronged men. [16]Destroy all wrong from the face of the earth, and every evil work will cease. And let the plant of righteousness and truth appear, and the deed will become a blessing; righteousness and truth will they plant in joy for ever. [17]And now all the righteous will be humble, and will live until they beget thousands; and all the days of their youth {and their sabbaths}[b] they will fulfil in peace. [18]And in those days the whole earth will be tilled in righteousness, and all of it will be planted with trees, and it will be filled with blessing. [19]And all pleasant trees they will plant on it, and they will plant on it vines, and the vine which is planted on it will produce fruit in abundance; and every seed which is sown on it, each measure will produce a thousand, and each measure of olives will produce ten baths of oil. [20]And you, cleanse the earth from all wrong, and from all iniquity, and from all sin, and from all impiety, and from all the uncleanness which is brought about on the earth; remove them from the earth. [21]And all the sons of men shall be righteous, and all the nations shall serve and bless me, and all shall worship me. [22]And the earth will be cleansed from all corruption, and from all sin, and from all wrath, and from all torment; and I will not again send a flood upon it for all generations for ever.

11. And in those days I will open the storehouses of blessing which (are) in heaven that I may send them down upon the earth, upon the work and upon the toil of the sons of men. [2]Peace and truth will be united for all the days of eternity and for all the generations of eternity.

12. And before everything Enoch had been hidden, and none of the sons of men knew where he was hidden, or where he was, or what had happened. [2]And all his doings (were) with the Holy Ones and with the Watchers in his days. [3]And I Enoch was blessing the Great Lord and the King of Eternity, and behold the Watchers called to me, Enoch the scribe, and said to me, [4]Enoch, scribe of righteousness, go, inform the Watchers of heaven who have left the high heaven and the holy eternal place, and have corrupted themselves with the women, and have done as the sons of men do, and have taken wives for themselves, and have become completely corrupt on the earth. [5]They will have on earth neither peace nor forgiveness of sin, [6]for they will not rejoice in their sons. The slaughter of their beloved ones they will see, and over the

---

[b]Long recognized to be a mistranslation of an Aramaic phrase meaning "and their old age."

destruction of their sons they will lament and petition for ever. But they will have neither mercy nor peace.

13. And Enoch went and said to Azazel, You will not have peace. A severe sentence has come out against you that you should be bound. ²And you will have neither rest, nor mercy, nor (the granting of any) petition, because of the wrong which you have taught, and because of all the works of blasphemy and wrong and sin which you have shown to the sons of men. ³Then I went and spoke to them all together, and they were all afraid; fear and trembling seized them. ⁴And they asked me to write out for them the record of a petition that they might receive forgiveness, and to take the record of their petition up to the Lord in heaven. ⁵For they (themselves) were not able from then on to speak, and they did not raise their eyes to heaven out of shame for the sins for which they had been condemned. ⁶And then I wrote out the record of their petition and their supplication in regard to their spirits and the deeds of each one of them, and in regard to what they asked, (namely) that they should obtain absolution and forbearance. ⁷And I went and sat down by the waters of Dan in Dan which is southwest of Hermon; and I read out the record of their petition until I fell asleep. ⁸And behold a dream came to me, and visions fell upon me, and I saw a vision of wrath, (namely) that I should speak to the sons of heaven and reprove them. ⁹And I woke up and went to them, and they were all sitting gathered together as they mourned in Ubelseyael, which is between Lebanon and Senir, with their faces covered. ¹⁰And I spoke before them all the visions which I had seen in my sleep, and I began to speak these words of righteousness and to reprove the Watchers of heaven.

14. This book (is) the word of righteousness and of reproof for the Watchers who (are) from eternity, as the Holy and Great One commanded in that vision. ²I saw in my sleep what I will now tell with the tongue of flesh and with my breath which the Great One has given to men in the mouth, that they might speak with it and understand with the heart. ³As he has created and appointed men to understand the word of knowledge, so he created and appointed me to reprove the Watchers, the sons of heaven. ⁴And I wrote out your petition, but in my vision thus it appeared, that your petition will not be (granted) to you for all the days of eternity; and complete judgement (has been decreed) against you, and you will not have peace. ⁵And from now on you will not ascend into heaven for all eternity, and it has been decreed that you are to be bound

152

in the earth for all the days of eternity. 6And before this you will have
seen the destruction of your beloved sons, and you will not be able to
enjoy them, but they will fall before you by the sword. 7And your
petition will not be (granted) in respect of them, nor in respect of
yourselves. And while you weep and supplicate, you do not speak a
single word from the writing which I have written. 8And the vision
appeared to me as follows: Behold clouds called me in the vision, and
mist called me, and the path of the stars and flashes of lightning
hastened me and drove me, and in the vision winds caused me to fly and
hastened me and lifted me up into heaven. 9And I proceeded until I
came near to a wall which was built of hail stones, and a tongue of fire
surrounded it, and it began to make me afraid. 10And I went into the
tongue of fire and came near to a large house which was built of hail
stones, and the wall of that house (was) like a mosaic (made) of hail
stones, and its floor (was) snow. 11Its roof (was) like the path of the stars
and flashes of lightning, and among them (were) fiery Cherubim, and
their heaven (was like) water. 12And (there was) a fire burning around its
wall, and its door was ablaze with fire. 13And I went into that house, and
(it was) hot as fire and cold as snow, and there was neither pleasure nor
life in it. Fear covered me and trembling took hold of me. 14And as I was
shaking and trembling, I fell on my face. And I saw in the vision, 15and
behold, another house, which was larger than the former, and all its
doors (were) open before me, and (it was) built of a tongue of fire. 16And
in everything it so excelled in glory and splendour and size that I am
unable to describe to you its glory and its size. 17And its floor (was) fire,
and above (were) lightning and the path of the stars, and its roof also
(was) a burning fire. 18And I looked and I saw in it a high throne, and its
appearance (was) like ice and its surrounds like the shining sun and the
sound of Cherubim. 19And from underneath the high throne there
flowed out rivers of burning fire so that it was impossible to look at it.
20And He who is great in glory sat on it, and his raiment was brighter
than the sun, and whiter than any snow. 21And no angel could enter, and
at the appearance of the face of him who is honoured and praised no
(creature of) flesh could look. 22A sea of fire burnt around him, and a
great fire stood before him, and none of those around him came near to
him. Ten thousand times ten thousand (stood) before him, but he
needed no holy counsel. 23And the Holy Ones who were near to him did
not leave by night or day, and did not depart from him. 24And until then
I had a covering on my face, as I trembled. And the Lord called me with
his own mouth and said to me, Come hither, Enoch, to my holy word.

And he lifted me up and brought me near to the door. And I looked, with my face down.

15. And he answered me and said to me with his voice, Hear! Do not be afraid, Enoch, (you) righteous man and scribe of righteousness. Come hither and hear my voice. ²And go, say to the Watchers of heaven who sent you to petition on their behalf, You ought to petition on behalf of men, not men on behalf of you. ³Why have you left the high, holy and eternal heaven, and lain with the women and become unclean with the daughters of men, and taken wives for yourselves, and done as the sons of the earth and begotten giant sons? ⁴And you (were) spiritual, holy, living an eternal life, (but) you became unclean upon the women, and begat (children) through the blood of flesh, and lusted after the blood of men, and produced flesh and blood as they do who die and are destroyed. ⁵And for this reason I gave them wives, (namely) that they might sow seed in them and (that) children might be born by them, that thus deeds might be done on the earth. ⁶But you formerly were spiritual, living an eternal, immortal life for all the generations of the world. ⁷For this reason I did not arrange wives for you because the dwelling of the spiritual ones (is) in heaven. ⁸And now the giants who were born from body and flesh will be called evil spirits upon the earth, and on the earth will be their dwelling. ⁹And evil spirits came out from their flesh because from above they were created; from the holy Watchers was their origin and first foundation. Evil spirits they will be on the earth, and spirits of the evil ones they will be called. ¹⁰And the dwelling of the spirits of heaven is in heaven, but the dwelling of the spirits of earth, who were born on the earth, (is) on earth. ¹¹And the spirits of the giants the clouds (?) which do wrong and are corrupt, and attack and fight and break on the earth, and cause sorrow; and they eat no food and do not thirst, and are not observed. ¹²And these spirits will rise against the sons of men and against the women because they came out from them. In the days of slaughter and destruction

16. and the death of the giants, wherever the spirits have gone out from (their) bodies, their flesh shall be destroyed before the judgement; thus they will be destroyed until the day of the great consummation is accomplished upon the great age, upon the Watchers and the impious ones. ²And now to the Watchers who sent you to petition on their behalf, who were formerly in heaven—³and now (say), You were in heaven, but (its) secrets had not yet been revealed to you and a worthless mystery you knew. This you made known to the women in the hardness of your hearts, and through this mystery the women and the men cause evil to increase on the earth. 4Say to them therefore, You will not have peace.

17. And they took me to a place where they were like burning fire, and, when they wished, they made themselves look like men. 2And they led me to a place of storm, and to a mountain the tip of whose summit reached to heaven. 3And I saw lighted places and thunder in the outermost ends, in its depths, a bow of fire and arrows and their quivers, and a sword of fire, and all the flashes of lightning. 4And they took me to the water of life, as it is called, and to the fire of the west which receives every setting of the sun. 5And I came to a river of fire whose fire flows like water and pours out into the great sea which (is) towards the west. 6And I saw all the great rivers, and I reached the great darkness and went where all flesh walks. 7And I saw the mountains of the darkness of winter and the place where the water of all the deep pours out. 8And I saw the mouths of all the rivers of the earth and the mouth of the deep.

18. And I saw the storehouses of all the winds, and I saw how with them he has adorned all creation, and (I saw) the foundations of the earth. 2And I saw the cornerstone of the earth, and I saw the four winds which support the earth and the firmament of heaven. 3And I saw how the winds stretch out the height of heaven and (how) they position themselves between heaven and earth; they are the pillars of heaven. 4And I saw the winds which turn heaven and cause the disk of the sun and all the stars to set. 5And I saw the winds on the earth which support the clouds, and I saw the paths of the angels. I saw at the end of the earth the firmament of heaven above. 6And I went towards the south—and it was burning day and night—where (there were) seven mountains of precious stones, three towards the east and three towards the south. 7And (those) towards the east (were) of coloured stone, and one (was) of pearl and one of healing stone; and those towards the south (were) of red stone. 8And the middle one reached to heaven, like the throne of the Lord, of stibium, and the top of the throne (was) of sapphire. 9And I saw a burning fire and what was in all the mountains. 10And I saw there a place beyond the great earth; there the waters were gathered together. 11And I saw a deep chasm of the earth with pillars of heavenly fire, and I saw among them fiery pillars of heaven, which were falling, and as regards both height and depth they were immeasurable. 12And beyond this chasm I saw a place and (it had) neither the firmament of heaven

155

above it, nor the foundation of earth below it; there was no water on it, and no birds, but it was a desert place. [13]And a terrible thing I saw there—seven stars like great burning mountains. And like a spirit questioning me [14]the angel said, This is the place of the end of heaven and earth; this is the prison for the stars of heaven and the host of heaven. [15]And the stars which roll over the fire, these are the ones which transgressed the command of the Lord from the beginning of their rising because they did not come out at their proper times. [16]And he was angry with them and bound them until the time of the consummation of their sin in the year of mystery.

19. And Uriel said to me, The spirits of the angels who were promiscuous with the women will stand here; and they, assuming many forms, made men unclean and will lead men astray so that they sacrifice to demons as gods—(that is,) until the great judgement day on which they will be judged so that an end will be made of them. [2]And their wives, having led astray the angels of heaven, will become peaceful. [3]And I, Enoch, alone saw the sight, the ends of everything; and no man has seen what I have seen.

20. And these are the names of the holy angels who keep watch. [2]Uriel, one of the holy angels, namely (the angel) of thunder and of tremors. [3]Raphael, one of the holy angels, (the angel) of the spirits of men. [4]Raguel, one of the holy angels, who takes vengeance on the world and on the lights. [5]Michael, one of the holy angels, namely the one put in charge of the best part of mankind, in charge of the nation. [6]Saraqael, one of the holy angels, who (is) in charge of the spirits of men who cause the spirits to sin. [7]Gabriel, one of the holy angels, who (is) in charge of the serpents and the Garden and the Cherubim.

21. And I went round to a place where there was nothing made. [2]And I saw there a terrible thing—neither the high heaven, nor the (firmly) founded earth, but a desert place, prepared and terrible. [3]And there I saw seven stars of heaven bound on it together, like great mountains, and burning like fire. [4]Then I said, For what sin have they been bound, and why have they been thrown here? [5]And Uriel, one of the holy angels who was with me and led me, spoke to me and said, Enoch, about whom do you ask? About whom do you inquire and ask and care? [6]These are (some) of the stars which transgressed the command of the Lord Most High, and they have been bound here until ten thousand ages are completed, the number of the days of their sin. ⁷And from there I went to another place, more terrible than this, and I saw a terrible thing: (there was) a great fire there which burnt and blazed, and the place had a cleft reaching to the abyss, full of great pillars of fire which were made to fall; neither its extent nor its size could I see, nor could I see its source. ⁸Then I said, How terrible this place (is), and (how) painful to look at! ⁹Then Uriel, one of the holy angels who was with me, answered me. He answered me and said to me, Enoch, why do you have such fear and terror because of this terrible place, and before this pain? ¹⁰And he said to me, This place (is) the prison of the angels, and there they will be held for ever.

22. And from there I went to another place, and he showed me in the west a large and high mountain, and a hard rock and four {beautiful}ᶜ places, ²and inside it was deep and wide and very smooth. How smooth {(is) that which rolls},ᵈ and deep and dark to look at! ³Then Raphael, one of the holy angels who was with me, answered me and said to me, These beautiful places (are intended for this), that the spirits, the souls of the dead, might be gathered into them; for them they were created, (that) here they might gather all the souls of the sons of men. ⁴And these places they made where they will keep them until the day of their judgement and until their appointed time—and that appointed time (will be) long—until the great judgement (comes) upon them. ⁵And I saw the spirits of the sons of men who were dead,ᵉ and theirᶠ voice reached heaven and complained. ⁶Then I asked Raphael, the angel who was with me, and said to him, Whose is this spirit whose voice thus reaches heaven and complains? ⁷And he answered me and said to me, saying, This spirit is the one which came out of Abel whom Cain, his brother, killed. And he will complain about him until his offspring is destroyed from the face of the earth, and from amongst the offspring of men his offspring perishes. ⁸Then I asked about him and about the judgement on allᵍ and I said, Why is one separated from another? ⁹And

---

ᶜSo reads the Ethiopian manuscript, but it is a misreading of the Greek word for "hollow."

ᵈSo reads the Ethiopian manuscript, but it is a mistranslation of the Greek; one Greek manuscript reads, "(are) these hollow places."

ᵉAnd I saw . . . were dead: so reads the Ethiopian manuscript, but fairly clearly only one spirit was mentioned originally (cp. verses 6ff.); the Greek manuscript is corrupt, but perhaps read, "I saw [the spirit] of a dead man complaining"; Aramaic manuscript has, "There I saw the spirit of a dead man complaining."

ᶠSome Greek manuscripts read "his" for "their." Aramaic also has "his."

ᵍabout the judgement on all: so reads the Ethiopian manuscript; perhaps corrupt for "about all the hollow places."

he answered me and said to me, These three[h] (places) were made in order that they might separate the spirits of the dead. And thus the souls of the righteous have been separated; this is the spring of water (and) on it (is) the light. [10]Likewise (a place) has been created for sinners when they die and are buried in the earth and judgement has not come upon them during their life. [11]And here their souls will be separated for this great torment, until the great day of judgement and punishment and torment for those who curse for ever, and of vengeance on their souls, and there he will bind them for ever. Verily he is from the beginning of the world. [12]And thus (a place) has been separated for the souls of those who complain and give information about (their) destruction, when they were killed in the days of the sinners. [13]Thus (a place) has been created for the souls of men who are not righteous, but sinners, accomplished in wrongdoing, and with the wrongdoers will be their lot. But their souls will not be killed on the day of judgement, nor will they rise from here. [14]Then I blessed the Lord of Glory and said, Blessed be my Lord, the Lord of Glory and Righteousness, who rules everything for ever.

23. And from there I went to another place towards the west, to the ends of the earth. [2]And I saw a fire which burnt and ran without resting or ceasing from running by day or night, but (continued) in exactly the same way. [3]And I asked saying, What is this which has no rest? [4]Then Raguel, one of the holy angels who was with me, answered me and said to me, This burning fire whose course you saw, towards the west, is (the fire of) all the lights of heaven.

24. And from there I went to another place of the earth, and he showed me a mountain of fire which blazed day and night. [2]And I went towards it and saw seven magnificent mountains, and all were different from one another, and precious and beautiful stones, and all (were) precious and their appearance glorious and their form beautiful; three (of the mountains) towards the east, one fixed firmly on another, and three towards the south, one on another, and deep and rugged valleys, no one (of which) was near another. [3]And (there was) a seventh mountain in the middle of these, and in their height they were all like the seat of a throne, and fragrant trees surrounded it. [4]And there was among them a tree such as I have never smelt, and none of them nor any

---

[h]three: So reads the Ethiopian manuscript and one Greek manuscript, but we expect "four" because four places are mentioned in verse 1 and four seem to be described in verses 9b-13.

others were like it: it smells more fragrant than any fragrance, and its leaves and its flowers and its wood never wither; its fruit (is) good, and its fruit (is) like the bunches of dates on a palm. 5 And then I said, Behold, this beautiful tree! Beautiful to look at and pleasant (are) its leaves, and its fruit very delightful in appearance. 6 And then Michael, one of the holy and honoured angels who was with me and (was) in charge of them, answered me

25. and said to me, Enoch, why do you ask me about the fragrance of this tree, and (why) do you inquire to learn? 2 Then I, Enoch, answered him, saying, I wish to learn about everything, but especially about this tree. 3 And he answered me, saying, This high mountain which you saw, whose summit is like the throne of the Lord, is the throne where the Holy and Great One, the Lord of Glory, the Eternal King, will sit when he comes down to visit the earth for good. 4 And this beautiful fragrant tree—and no (creature of) flesh has authority to touch it until the great judgement when he will take vengeance on all and will bring (everything) to a consummation for ever—this will be given to the righteous and humble. 5 From its fruit life will be given to the chosen; towards the north it will be planted, in a holy place, by the house of the Lord, the Eternal King. 6 Then they will rejoice with joy and be glad in the holy (place), they will each draw the fragrance of it into their bones, and they will live a long life on earth, as your fathers lived, and in their days sorrow and pain and toil and punishment will not touch them. 7 Then I blessed the Lord of Glory, the Eternal King, because he has prepared such things for righteous men, and has created such things and said that they are to be given to them.

26. And from there I went to the middle of the earth and saw a blessed, (well-)watered, place which had branches which remained (alive) and sprouted from a tree which had been cut down. 2 And there I saw a holy mountain, and under the mountain, to the east of it, (there was) water and it flowed towards the south. 3 And I saw towards the east another mountain which was of the same height, and between them (there was) a deep and narrow valley; and in it a stream ran by the mountain. 4 And to the west of this one (was) another mountain which was lower than it, and not high; and under it (there was) a valley between them, and (there were) other deep and dry valleys at the end of the three mountains. 5 And all the valleys (were) deep and narrow, of hard rock,

159

and trees were planted on them. 6 And I was amazed at the rock and I was amazed at the valley; I was very much amazed.

27. Then I said, What (is) the purpose of this blessed land which is completely full of trees and of this accursed valley in the middle of them? 2 Then Raphael, one the holy angels who was with me, answered me and said to me, This accursed valley is for those who are cursed for ever; here will be gathered together all who speak with their mouths against the Lord words that are not fitting and say hard things about his glory. Here they will gather them together, and here (will be) their place of judgement. 3 And in the last days there will be the spectacle of the righteous judgement upon them before the righteous for ever, for evermore; here the merciful will bless the Lord of Glory, the Eternal King. 4 And in the days of the judgement on them they will bless him on account of (his) mercy, according as he has assigned to them (their lot). 5 Then I myself blessed the Lord of Glory and I addressed him, and I remembered his majesty, as was fitting.

28. And from there I went towards the east to the middle of the mountain of the wilderness, and I saw only desert. 2 But (it was) full of trees from this seed, and water gushed out over it from above. 3 The torrent, which flowed towards the north-west, seemed copious, and from all sides there went up . . . water and dew.

29. And I went to another place (away) from the wilderness; I came near to the east of this mountain. 2 And there I saw trees of judgement,ⁱ {especially vessels of the fragrance of incense and myrrh},ʲ and the trees were not alike.

30. And above it, above these, above the mountains of the east, and not far away, I saw another place, valleys of water like that which does not fail. 2 And I saw a beautiful tree and its fragrance (was) like that of the mastic. 3 And by the banks of these valleys I saw fragrant cinnamon. And beyond those (valleys) I came near towards the east.

31. And I saw another mountain on which there were trees, and there

---

ⁱtrees of judgement: so reads the Ethiopian manuscript, but perhaps a corruption in the original Aramaic of "fragrant trees."
ʲSo reads the Ethiopian manuscript, but the text is corrupt; Greek manuscript has "which smelt of the fragrance of incense and myrrh."

flowed out water, and there flowed out from it as it were a nectar whose name is styrax and galbanum. 2And beyond this mountain I saw another mountain, and on it (there were) aloe trees, and those trees (were) full of (a fruit) which (is) like an almond and (is) hard. 3And when they {take}k this fruit, it is better than any fragrance.

32. And after these fragrances, to the north, as I looked over the mountains, I saw seven mountains full of fine hard and fragrant trees and cinnamon and pepper. 2And from there I went over the summits of those mountains, far away to the east, and I went over the Red Sea and I was far from it, and I went over the angel Zotiel. 3And I came to the Garden of Righteousness, and I saw beyond those trees many large trees growing there, sweet-smelling, large, very beautiful and glorious, and the tree of wisdom from which they eat and know great wisdom. 4And it is like the carob-tree, and its fruit (is) like the bunches of grapes on a vine, very beautiful, and the smell of this tree spreads and penetrates afar. 5And I said, This tree (is) beautiful! How beautiful and pleasing (is) its appearance! 6And the holy angel Raphael, who was with me, answered me and said to me, This is the tree of wisdom from which your old father and your aged mother, who were before you, ate and learnt wisdom; and their eyes were opened, and they knew that they were naked, and they were driven from the garden.

33. And from there I went to the ends of the earth and I saw there large animals, each different from the other, and also birds (which) differed in form, beauty and call—each different from the other. 2And to the east of these animals I saw the ends of the earth on which heaven rests, and the open gates of heaven. 3And I saw how the stars of heaven come out, and counted the gates out of which they come, and wrote down all their outlets, for each one individually according to their number and their names, according to their constellations, their positions, their times and their months, as the angel Uriel, who was with me, showed me. 4And he showed me everything and wrote it down, and also their names he wrote down for me, and their laws and their functions.

34. And from there I went towards the north to the ends of the earth, and there I saw a great and glorious wonder at the ends of the whole

kSo reads the Ethiopian manuscript, but corrupt for "crush."

earth. ²And there I saw three gates of heaven open in heaven; through each of them north winds go out; when they blow, (there is) cold, hail, hoar-frost, snow, dew and rain. ³And from one gate it blows for good; but when they blow through the other two gates, it is with force and it brings torment over the earth, and they blow with force.

35. And from there I went towards the west to the ends of the earth, and I saw there, as I saw in the east, three open gates—as many gates and as many outlets.

36. And from there I went towards the south to the ends of the earth, and there I saw three gates of heaven open; and the south wind and dew and rain and wind come out from there. ²And from there I went towards the east of the ends of heaven, and there I saw the three eastern gates of heaven open, and above them (there were) smaller gates. ³Through each of those smaller gates the stars of heaven pass and go towards the west on the path which has been shown to them. ⁴And when I saw, I blessed, and I will always bless the Lord of Glory who has made great and glorious wonders that he might show the greatness of his work to his angels and to the souls of men, that they might praise his work, and that all his creatures might see the work of his power and praise the great work of his hands and bless him for ever.

THE SIMILITUDES OF ENOCH (1 ENOCH 37–71)

Commentary

The "Similitudes of Enoch" (or the "Parables of Enoch"), contained in chapters 37–71 of *1 Enoch*, consists primarily of three "parables" told by Enoch (see the discussion of *1 Enoch* in the introduction to the "Animal Apocalypse"). These parables divide the work into three sections: chapters 38–44, 45–57, and 58–69. Chapter 37 serves as an introduction to the work, setting the parables in the context of a vision that Enoch received and stating the eschatological thrust of the revelation. Chapters 70 and 71 are two separate epilogues to the work.

The first parable tells of Enoch's journey to "the end of heaven" (39:3), where he sees the righteous and chosen dwelling in peace and safety in the presence of God. The righteous are those who "believe in the name of the Lord of Spirits for ever and ever" (43:4). God's foreknowledge of the course of world history is explicitly stated as Enoch exclaims, "He [God] knew before the world was created what the world would be, even for all the generations which are to come" (39:11). This first parable also describes various cosmological secrets that Enoch saw.

One of the major elements in the second parable is the mighty figure known variously as the Chosen One, the Chosen and Righteous One, the Son of man, and God's Messiah. This individual had already been mentioned in the first parable (38:2; 40:5). The second parable describes the eschatological role of this Son of man figure. Existing before the world was created, he remains hidden until the last days, when he will execute judgment against the kings and the powerful of the earth and against all other sinners who "denied the Lord of Spirits and his Messiah" (48:10). When the dead are raised, he will serve as judge between the sinners and the righteous. He will be enthroned with God and will be a source of wisdom and righteousness.

The Son of man figure in *1 Enoch* likely is based on the "one like a son of man" found in Daniel 7 who is given everlasting dominion over all the world. The Son of man in *1 Enoch,* however, is a more complex figure than the one in Daniel. In *1 Enoch,* the Son of man plays a more active role, serving as judge, as redeemer, as support to the righteous, and as a light to the nations. Furthermore, the Enochic Son of man is a pre-existent figure and is explicitly identified as the Messiah.

In addition to the Son of man, the second parable also describes the place of punishment that is reserved for the kings and the powerful, and for the "hosts of Azazel" (the latter group is a reference to the disobedient Watchers described in the "Book of the Watchers," *1 Enoch* 1–36).

The final parable (chaps. 58–69), like the first two, deals with cosmological secrets and eschatological events. The Son of man is prominent in this section also, where he is enthroned by God and serves as the eschatological judge. Enoch sees the place of punishment for the mighty kings and the disobedient angels and is told of the future rewards for the righteous and the chosen. Chapters 65–68, along with sections of chapter 60, appear to be fragments from an independent Noah tradition, perhaps a "Book of Noah," which the author of the "Similitudes" has incorporated into his work. In these sections, Noah, not Enoch, is addressed and responds. Chapter 69 deals primarily with the fallen angels and their sins.

Two separate epilogues have been added to the "Similitudes." Chapter 70 briefly describes Enoch's final translation into heaven. Chapter 71 also describes Enoch's removal to heaven, but elaborates on what Enoch sees there. When Enoch comes before God, Enoch's body melts, his spirit is transformed, and an angel declares him to be the Son of man. Nowhere else in the work is Enoch identified as the Son of man. In fact, a distinction between the two figures seems to be presupposed throughout the rest of the "Similitudes." Furthermore, the pre-existence of the Son of man, declared in the second and third parables, argues against Enoch's identity as the Son of man elsewhere in the "Similitudes." For this reason, along with the fact that the contents of chapter 71 are basically a reiteration of revelations contained in the three parables, many scholars would argue that chapter 71 was a later addition to the "Similitudes."

The lack of any fragments from the "Similitudes" among the Dead Sea manuscripts has led some scholars to posit a late date for the composition of this material, as late as the third century C.E. Furthermore, some scholars have argued that the "Similitudes" are Christian, and not Jewish, in origin. Scholars who argue for an earlier dating usually point to two passages in the "Similitudes" that possibly allude to historical events during the time of the author. The first passage is 56:5-7, which describes an eschatological attack upon Palestine by the Parthians and Medes. This is taken to be a reference to the invasion of Palestine by the Parthians in 40 B.C.E. The second passage is 67:5-13. These verses describe hot springs, which "the kings and the mighty and the exalted" use for bodily healing but that "will undergo a change in those days" and will become a place of punishment. Some scholars understand this to be a reference to Herod's attempt to heal himself by bathing in the warm springs at Callirrhoe shortly before his death in 4 B.C.E. Since this is the last historical event mentioned in the "Similitudes," it is possible that the work was composed shortly after this time.

Additional support for an early dating is found in the New Testament. Whereas most of the New Testament uses of the phrase "Son of man" can be explained from traditions arising out of the book of Daniel, several New Testament passages describe the Son of man in ways more similar to the Enochic Son of man than to the Danielic figure. Matthew 19:28 and 25:31 state that at the coming of the Son of man, he will sit on his "glorious throne" (compare to 1 Enoch 45:3; 55:4; 61:8; 62:5; 69:27, 29). In John 5:22, 27 the Son (of man) is granted authority by God to execute judgment. This is a role performed by the figure in the "Similitudes," but not in Daniel.

Although neither the supposed historical references nor the possible Enochic traces in the New Testament are conclusive, they do strongly suggest that the "Similitudes" were probably produced during the first half of the first century C.E. Most modern scholars would support that dating. If, indeed, the "Similitudes" were composed during the early part of the first century C.E., that would almost guarantee their Jewish, instead of Christian, authorship. Furthermore, the identification of Enoch as the Son of man (71:14) is inconceivable in a Christian work. Admittedly this chapter is likely a later addition; however, in the remainder of the work there are no specifically Christian ideas. It is hard to imagine a Christian writer describing the Son of man without including elements of the death, resurrection, and exaltation of Jesus.

The "Similitudes," then, seems to be a Jewish work composed around the early to mid first century C.E., probably originally written in Aramaic in Judea. The work offered encouragement to the "righteous" and "chosen" by assuring them that in the last days God would send the Son of man to execute judgment against the "kings and the powerful." The righteous would have a reward of eternal life with the angels, while the wicked would suffer terrible punishment. God is certainly in control, for not only has God already prepared the places for the righteous and the wicked, but also before the world was ever created God had hidden away the Son of man, to be revealed in the last days. The crisis that precipitated the writing of this work likely involved political forces, as evidenced by the repeated identification of the wicked as the "kings," the "mighty," the "powerful," and the "exalted." The identification of the crisis, however, is sufficiently vague to allow the "Similitudes" to function in various situations in which an individual or group perceived itself to be unjustly persecuted by evil forces.

The text of the "Similitudes of Enoch" given here is the translation by M. A. Knibb, contained in *The Apocryphal Old Testament*. Knibb's work is a translation of primarily one Ethiopic manuscript (Ryl. Eth. MS 23), corrected by other texts only in places where this manuscript does not appear to make sense.

1 Enoch 37–71

37. The second vision which he saw, the vision of wisdom which Enoch, the son of Jared, the son of Malalel, the son of Cainan, the son of Enosh, the son of Seth, the son of Adam, saw. ²And this (is) the beginning of the words of wisdom which I raised (my voice) to speak and say to those who dwell on the dry ground. Hear, you men of old, and see, you who come after, the words of the Holy One which I will speak before the Lord of Spirits. ³It would have been better to have said these things before, but from those who come after we will not withhold the beginning of wisdom. ⁴Until now there has not been given by the Lord of Spirits such wisdom as I have received in accordance with my insight, in accordance with the wish of the Lord of Spirits by whom the lot of eternal life has been given to me. ⁵And three parables were imparted to me, and I raised (my voice) and said to those who dwell on the dry ground,

38. The first parable. When the community of the righteous appears, and the sinners are judged for their sins and are driven from the face of the dry ground, ²and when the Righteous One appears before the chosen righteous whose works are weighed by the Lord of Spirits, and (when) light appears to the righteous and chosen who dwell on the dry ground, where (will be) the dwelling of the sinners, and where the resting-place of those who have denied the Lord of Spirits? It would have been better for them if they had not been born. ³And when the secrets of the righteous are revealed, the sinners will be judged and the impious driven from the presence of the righteous and the chosen. ⁴And from then on those who possess the earth will not be mighty and exalted, nor will they be able to look at the face of the holy ones for the light of the Lord of Spirits will have appeared on the face of the holy, the righteous and the chosen. ⁵And the mighty kings will at that time be destroyed and given into the hand of the righteous and the holy. ⁶And from then on no one will (be able to) seek mercy from the Lord of Spirits, for their life will be at an end.

39. And it will come to pass in these days that the chosen and holy children will come down from the high heavens, and their offspring will become one with the sons of men. ²In those days Enoch received books of indignation and anger, and books of tumult and confusion. And there will be no mercy for them, says the Lord of Spirits. ³And at that time clouds and a storm-wind carried me off from the face of the earth, and set me down at the end of heaven. ⁴And there I saw another vision, the dwelling of the righteous and the resting-places of the holy. ⁵There my eyes saw their dwelling with the angels and their resting-places with the holy ones, and they were petitioning and supplicating and praying on behalf of the sons of men; and righteousness like water flowed before them and mercy like dew upon the ground. Thus it is among them for ever and ever. ⁶And in those days my eyes saw the place of the chosen ones of righteousness and faith; and there will be righteousness in their days, and the righteous and chosen will be without number before him for ever and ever. ⁷And I saw their dwelling under the wings of the Lord of Spirits, and all the righteous and chosen shone before him like the light of fire; and their mouth was full of blessing, and their lips praised the name of the Lord of Spirits. And righteousness will not fail before him, and truth will not fail before him. ⁸There I wished to dwell, and my soul longed for that dwelling; there had my lot been assigned before, for thus it was decided about me before the Lord of Spirits. ⁹And in those days I praised and exalted the name of the Lord of Spirits with blessing and praise, for he has destined me for blessing and praise, in accordance with the wish of the Lord of Spirits. ¹⁰And for a long time my eyes looked at that place, and I blessed him and praised him, saying, Blessed is he, and may he be blessed from the beginning and for ever! ¹¹And in his presence there is no end. He knew before the world was created what the world would be, even for all the generations which are to come. ¹²Those who do not sleep bless you, and they stand before your glory and bless and praise and exalt, saying, Holy, holy, holy, Lord of Spirits; he fills the earth with spirits. ¹³And there my eyes saw all those who do not sleep standing before him and blessing and saying, Blessed are you, and blessed is the name of the Lord for ever and ever! ¹⁴And my face was transformed until I was unable to see.

167

40. And after this I saw a thousand thousands and ten thousand times ten thousand, (a multitude) beyond number or reckoning, who stood before the glory of the Lord of Spirits. [2] I looked, and on the four sides of the Lord of Spirits I saw four figures different from those who were standing; and I learnt their names, because the angel who went with me made known to me their names, and showed me all the secret things. [3] And I heard the voices of those four figures as they sang praises before the Lord of Glory. [4] The first voice blesses the Lord of Spirits for ever and ever. [5] And the second voice I heard blessing the Chosen One and the chosen who depend on the Lord of Spirits. [6] And the third voice I heard as they petitioned and prayed on behalf of those who dwell on the dry ground and supplicate in the name of the Lord of Spirits. [7] And the fourth voice I heard driving away the satans, and not allowing them to come before the Lord of Spirits to accuse those who dwell on the dry ground. [8] And after this I asked the angel of peace who went with me and showed me everything which is secret, Who are these four figures whom I have seen and whose words I have heard and written down? [9] And he said to me, This first one is the holy Michael, the merciful and long-suffering; and the second, who (is) in charge of all the diseases and in charge of all the wounds of the sons of men, is Raphael; and the third, who (is) in charge of all the powers, is the holy Gabriel; and the fourth, who (is) in charge of the repentance (leading) to hope of those who will inherit eternal life, is Phanuel. [10] And these (are) the four angels of the Lord Most High; and the four voices I heard in those days.

41. And after this I saw all the secrets of heaven, and how the kingdom is divided, and how the deeds of men are weighed in the balance. [2] There I saw the dwelling of the chosen and the resting-places of the holy; and my eyes saw there all the sinners who deny the name of the Lord of Spirits being driven from there, and they dragged them off, and they were not able to remain because of the punishment which went out from the Lord of Spirits. [3] And there my eyes saw the secrets of the flashes of lightning and of the thunder, and the secrets of the winds, how they are distributed in order to blow over the earth, and the secrets of the clouds and of the dew; and there I saw whence they go out in that place, and (how) from there the dust of the earth is saturated. [4] And there I saw closed storehouses from which the winds are distributed, and the storehouse of the hail, and the storehouse of the mist, and the storehouse of the clouds; and its cloud remained over the earth from the beginning of the world. [5] And I saw the chambers of the sun and the

168

moon, whence they go out and whither they return, and their glorious return, and how one is more honoured than the other, and their magnificent course, and (how) they do not leave the course, neither adding (anything) to, nor omitting (anything) from their course, and (how) they keep faith with one another, observing (their) oath. ⁶And the sun goes out first and completes its journey at the command of the Lord of Spirits—and his name endures for ever and ever. ⁷And after this (begins) the hidden and visible journey of the moon, and it travels the course of its journey in that place by day and by night. One stands opposite the other before the Lord of Spirits, and they give thanks, and sing praises, and do not rest, because their thanksgiving is rest for them. ⁸For the shining sun makes many revolutions, for a blessing and for a curse, and the path of the journey of the moon (is) for the righteous light, but for the sinners darkness, in the name of the Lord who has created (a division) between light and darkness, and has divided the spirits of men, and has established the spirits of the righteous in the name of his righteousness. ⁹For no angel hinders, and no power is able to hinder, because the Judge sees them all and judges them all before himself.

42. Wisdom found no place where she could dwell, and her dwelling was in heaven. ²Wisdom went out in order to dwell among the sons of men, but did not find a dwelling; wisdom returned to her place and took her seat in the midst of the angels. ³And iniquity came out from her chambers; those whom she did not seek she found, and dwelt among them, like rain in the desert, and like dew on parched ground.

43. And again I saw flashes of lightning and the stars of heaven, and I saw how he called them all by their names, and they obeyed him. ²And I saw the balance of righteousness, how they are weighed according to their light, according to the width of their areas and the day of their appearing, and (how) their revolutions produce lightning; and (I saw) their revolutions according to the number of the angels, and (how) they keep faith with one another. ³And I asked the angel who went with me and showed me what was secret, What (are) these? ⁴And he said to me, Their likeness has the Lord of Spirits shown to you; these are the names of the righteous who dwell on the dry ground and believe in the name of the Lord of Spirits for ever and ever.

44. And other things I saw in regard to lightning, how some of the stars rise and become lightning, but cannot loose their form.

45. And this (is) the second parable about those who deny the name of the dwelling of the holy ones and of the Lord of Spirits. ²They will not ascend into heaven, nor will they come upon earth: such will be the lot of the sinners who deny the name of the Lord of Spirits, who will thus be kept for the day of affliction and distress. ³On that day the Chosen One will sit on the throne of glory, and will chooseª their works, and their resting-places will be without number; and their spirits within them will grow strong when they see my Chosen One and those who appeal to my holy and glorious name. ⁴And on that day I will cause my Chosen One to dwell among them, and I will transform heaven and make it an eternal blessing and light. ⁵And I will transform the dry ground and make it a blessing, and I will cause my chosen ones to dwell upon it; but those who commit sin and evil will not tread upon it. ⁶For I have seen, and have satisfied with peace, my righteous ones, and have placed them before me; but for the sinners my judgement draws near before me, that I may destroy them from the face of the earth.

46. And there I saw one who had a head of days, and his head (was) white like wool; and with him (there was) another, whose face had the appearance of a man, and his face (was) full of grace, like one of the holy angels. ²And I asked one of the holy angels who went with me, and showed me all the secrets, about that Son of Man, who he was, and whence he was, (and) why he went with the Head of Days. ³And he answered me and said to me, This is the Son of Man who has righteousness, and with whom righteousness dwells; he will reveal all the treasures of that which is secret, for the Lord of Spirits has chosen him, and through uprightness his lot has surpassed all before the Lord of Spirits for ever. ⁴And this Son of Man whom you have seen will rouse the kings and the powerful from their resting-places, and the strong from their thrones, and will loose the reins of the strong, and will break the teeth of the sinners. ⁵And he will cast down the kings from their thrones and from their kingdoms, for they do not exalt him, and do not praise him, and do not humbly acknowledge whence (their) kingdom was given to them. ⁶And he will cast down the faces of the strong, and shame will fill them, and darkness will be their dwelling, and worms will be their resting-place; and they will have no hope of rising from their resting-places, for they do not exalt the name of the Lord of Spirits.

ªSo read all Ethiopian manuscripts (perhaps a mistranslation of an Aramaic word that can mean both "to choose" and "to test").

⁷And these are they who judge the stars of heaven, and raise their hands against the Most High, and trample upon the dry ground, and dwell upon it; and all their deeds show iniquity, and their power (rests) on their riches, and their faith is in the gods which they have made with their hands, and they deny the name of the Lord of Spirits. ⁸And they will be driven from the houses of his congregation, and of the faithful who depend on the name of the Lord of Spirits.

47. And in those days the prayer of the righteous and the blood of the righteous will have ascended from the earth before the Lord of Spirits. ²In these days the holy ones who dwell in the heavens above will unite with one voice, and supplicate, and pray, and praise, and give thanks, and bless in the name of the Lord of Spirits, because of the blood of the righteous which has been poured out, and (because of) the prayer of the righteous, that it may not cease before the Lord of Spirits, that justice may be done to them, and (that) their patience may not have to last for ever. ³And in those days I saw the Head of Days sit down on the throne of his glory, and the books of the living were opened before him, and all his host, which (dwells) in the heavens above, and his council were standing before him. ⁴And the hearts of the holy ones were full of joy that the number of righteousness had been reached, and the prayer of the righteous had been heard, and the blood of the righteous had been required before the Lord of Spirits.

48. And in that place I saw an inexhaustible spring of righteousness, and many springs of wisdom surrounded it, and all the thirsty drank from them and were filled with wisdom, and their dwelling (was) with the righteous and the holy and the chosen. ²And at that hour that Son of Man was named in the presence of the Lord of Spirits, and his name (was named) before the Head of Days. ³Even before the sun and the constellations were created, before the stars of heaven were made, his name was named before the Lord of Spirits. ⁴He will be a staff to the righteous and the holy, that they may lean on him and not fall, and he (will be) the light of the nations, and he will be the hope of those who grieve in their hearts. ⁵All those who dwell upon the dry ground will fall down and worship before him, and they will bless, and praise, and celebrate with psalms the name of the Lord of Spirits. ⁶And because of this he was chosen and hidden before him before the world was created, and for ever. ⁷But the wisdom of the Lord of Spirits has revealed him to the holy and the righteous, for he has kept safe the lot of the righteous, for they have hated and rejected this world of iniquity, and all its works and its ways they have hated in the name of the Lord of Spirits; for in his name they are saved, and he is the one who will require their lives. 8 And in those days the kings of the earth and the strong who possess the dry ground will have downcast faces because of the work of their hands, for on the day of their distress and trouble they will not save themselves. 9 And I will give them into the hands of my chosen ones; like straw in the fire, and like lead in water, so they will burn before the righteous, and sink before the holy, and no trace will be found of them. 10 And on the day of their trouble there will be rest on the earth, and they will fall down before him and will not rise; and there will be no one who will take them with his hands and raise them, for they denied the Lord of Spirits and his Messiah. May the name of the Lord of Spirits be blessed!

49. For wisdom has been poured out like water, and glory will not fail before him for ever and ever. 2 For he (is) powerful in all the secrets of righteousness, and iniquity will pass away like a shadow, and will have no existence; for the Chosen One stands before the Lord of Spirits, and his glory (is) for ever and ever, and his power for all generations. 3 And in him dwells the spirit of wisdom, and the spirit which gives understanding, and the spirit of knowledge and of power, and the spirit of those who sleep in righteousness. 4 And he will judge the things that are secret, and no one will be able to say an idle word before him, for he (has been) chosen before the Lord of Spirits, in accordance with his wish.

50. And in those days a change will occur for the holy and the chosen; the light of days will rest upon them, and glory and honour will return to the holy. 2 And on the day of trouble calamity will be heaped up over the sinners, but the righteous will conquer in the name of the Lord of Spirits; and he will show (this) to others that they may repent and abandon the works of their hands. 3 And they will have no honour before the Lord of Spirits, but in his name they will be saved; and the Lord of Spirits will have mercy on them, for his mercy (is) great. 4 And he (is) righteous in his judgement, and before his glory iniquity will not (be able to) stand at his judgement: he who does not repent before him will be destroyed. 5 And from then on I will not have mercy on them, says the Lord of Spirits.

51. And in those days the earth will return that which has been entrusted to it, and Sheol will return that which has been entrusted to it, that which it has received, and destruction will return what it owes. 2And he will choose the righteous and holy from among them, for the day has come near that they must be saved. 3And in those days the Chosen One will sit on his throne, and all the secrets of wisdom will flow out from the counsel of his mouth, for the Lord of Spirits has appointed him and glorified him. 4And in those days the mountains will leap like rams, and the hills will skip like lambs satisfied with milk, and all will become angels in heaven. 5Their faces will shine with joy, for in those days the Chosen One will have risen; and the earth will rejoice, and the righteous will dwell upon it, and the chosen will go and walk upon it.

52. And after those days, in that place where I had seen all the visions of that which is secret—for I had been carried off by a whirlwind, and they had brought me to the west—2there my eyes saw the secrets of heaven, everything that will occur on earth: a mountain of iron, and a mountain of copper, and a mountain of silver, and a mountain of gold, and a mountain of soft metal, and a mountain of lead. 3And I asked the angel who went with me, saying, What are these (things) which I have seen in secret? 4And he said to me, All these (things) which you have seen serve the authority of his Messiah, that he may be strong and powerful on the earth. 5And that angel of peace answered me, saying, Wait a little, and you will see, and everything which is secret, which the Lord of Spirits has established, will be revealed to you. 6And these mountains which you have seen, the mountain of iron, and the mountain of copper, and the mountain of silver, and the mountain of gold, and the mountain of soft metal, and the mountain of lead—all these before the Chosen One will be like wax before fire, and like the water which comes down from above on these mountains, and they will become weak under his feet. 7And it will come to pass in those days that neither by gold, nor by silver, will men save themselves; they will be unable to save themselves or to flee. 8And there will be neither iron for war, nor material for a breast-plate; bronze will be of no use, and tin will be of no use and will count for nothing, and lead will not be wanted. 9All these will be wiped out and destroyed from the face of the earth, when the Chosen One appears before the Lord of Spirits.

53. And there my eyes saw a deep valley, and its mouth (was) open; and all those who dwell upon the dry ground and the sea and the islands will bring gifts and presents and offerings to him, but that deep valley will not become full. 2And their hands commit evil, and everything at which (the righteous) toil, the sinners evilly devour; and (so) the sinners will be destroyed from before the Lord of Spirits, and will be banished from the face of his earth, unceasingly, for ever and ever. 3For I saw the angels of punishment going and preparing all the instruments of Satan. 4And I asked the angel of peace who went with me, and I said to him, These instruments—for whom are they preparing them? 5And he said to me, They are preparing these for the kings and the powerful of this earth, that by means of them they may be destroyed. 6And after this the Righteous and Chosen One will cause the house of his congregation to appear; from then on, in the name of the Lord of Spirits, they will not be hindered. 7And before him these mountains will not be (firm) like the earth, and the hills will be like a spring of water; and the righteous will have rest from the ill-treatment of the sinners.

54. And I looked and turned to another part of the earth, and I saw there a deep valley with burning fire. 2And they brought the kings and the powerful and threw them into that valley. 3And there my eyes saw how they made instruments for them—iron chains of immeasurable weight. 4And I asked the angel of peace who went with me, saying, These chain-instruments—for whom are they being prepared? 5And he said to me, These are being prepared for the hosts of Azazel, that they may take them and throw them into the lowest part of Hell; and they will cover their jaws with rough stones, as the Lord of Spirits commanded. 6And Michael and Gabriel, Raphael and Phanuel—these will take hold of them on that great day, and throw them on that day into the furnace of burning fire, that the Lord of Spirits may take vengeance on them for their iniquity, in that they became servants of Satan and led astray those who dwell upon the dry ground. 7And in those days the punishment of the Lord of Spirits will go out, and all the storehouses of the waters which (are) above the heavens . . . and under the earth will be opened, 8and all the waters will be joined with the waters which (are) above the heavens. The water which (is) above heaven is male, and the water which (is) under the earth is female. 9And all those who dwell upon the dry ground and those who dwell under the ends of heaven will be wiped out. 10And because of this they will acknowledge their iniquity which they have committed on the earth, and through this they will be destroyed.

55. And after this the Head of Days repented and said, I have destroyed to no purpose all those who dwell upon the dry ground. 2And he swore by his great Name, From now on I will not act like this towards all those who dwell upon the dry ground; and I will put a sign in heaven, and it will be a pledge of faith between me and them for ever, so long as heaven (is) above the earth. 3And this will be in accordance with my command; when I want to take hold of them by the hand of the angels on the day of distress and pain in the face of this my anger and my wrath, my wrath and my anger will remain upon them, says the Lord, the Lord of Spirits. 4You powerful kings, who dwell upon the dry ground, will be obliged to watch my Chosen One sit down on the throne of my glory, and judge, in the name of the Lord of Spirits, Azazel and all his associates and all his hosts.

56. And I saw there the hosts of the angels of punishment as they went, and they were holding chains of iron and bronze. 2And I asked the angel of peace who went with me, saying, To whom are those who are holding (the chains) going? 3And he said to me, Each to his own chosen ones and to his own beloved ones, that they may be thrown into the chasm in the depths of the valley. 4And then that valley will be filled with their chosen and beloved ones, and the days of their life will be at an end, and the days of their leading astray will no longer be counted. 5And in those days the angels will gather together, and will throw themselves towards the east upon the Parthians and Medes; they will stir up the kings, so that a disturbing spirit will come upon them, and they will drive them from their thrones; and they will come out like lions from their lairs, and like hungry wolves in the middle of their flocks. 6And they will go up and trample upon the land of my chosen ones, and the land of my chosen ones will become before them a tramping-ground and a beaten track. 7But the city of my righteous ones will be a hindrance to their horses, and they will stir up slaughter amongst themselves, and their (own) right hand will be strong against them; and a man will not admit to knowing his neighbour or his brother, nor a son his father or his mother, until through their death there are corpses enough, and their punishment—it will not be in vain. 8And in those days Sheol will open its mouth, and they will sink into it; and their destruction—Sheol will swallow up the sinners before the face of the chosen.

57. And it came to pass after this that I saw another host of chariots, with men riding on them, and they came upon the wind from the east and from the west to the south. 2And the sound of the noise of their chariots was heard, and when this commotion occurred, the holy ones observed (it) from heaven, and the pillars of the earth were shaken from their foundations, and (the sound) was heard from the ends of earth to the ends of heaven throughout one day. ³And all will fall down and worship the Lord of Spirits. And this is the end of the second parable.

58. And I began to speak the third parable about the righteous and about the chosen. ²Blessed (are) you, the righteous and chosen, for your lot (will be) glorious! ³And the righteous will be in the light of the sun, and the chosen in the light of eternal life; and there will be no end to the days of their life, and the days of the holy will be without number. ⁴And they will seek the light, and will find righteousness with the Lord of Spirits. Peace (be) to the righteous with the Lord of the world! ⁵And after this it will be said to the holy that they should seek in heaven the secrets of righteousness, the lot of faith; for it has become bright as the sun upon the dry ground, and darkness has passed away. ⁶And there will be ceaseless light, and to a limit of days they will not come, for darkness will have been destroyed previously; and the light will endure before the Lord of Spirits, and the light of uprightness will endure before the Lord of Spirits for ever.

59. And in those days my eyes saw the secrets of the flashes of lightning, and the lights, and the regulations governing them; and they flash for a blessing or for a curse, as the Lord of Spirits wishes. ²And there I saw the secrets of the thunder, and (how) when it crashes in heaven above, the sound of it is heard; and they showed me the dwellings of the dry ground,ᵇ and the sound of the thunder for peace and for blessing, or for a curse, according to the word of the Lord of Spirits. ³And after this all the secrets of the lights and of the flashes of lightning were shown to me; they flash to bring blessing and satisfaction.

60. In the five hundredth year, in the seventh month, on the fourteenth (day) of the month in the life of Enoch. In that parable I saw how the heaven of heavens was shaken violently, and the host of the Most High and the angels, a thousand thousands and ten thousand times ten thousand, were extremely disturbed. ²And then I saw the Head of Days sitting on the throne of his glory, and the angels and the righteous were standing around him. ³And a great trembling seized me, and fear took hold of me, and my loins collapsed and gave way, and my

---

ᵇand they . . . ground; the text makes no sense and is probably an interpolation (although it is just possible that an original Aramaic "and they showed me the dwellings of the lightning" was misread by the translator).

whole being melted, and I fell upon my face. 4And the holy Michael sent another holy angel, one of the holy angels, and he raised me; and when he raised me, my spirit returned, for I had been unable to endure the sight of that host, and the disturbance, and the shaking of heaven. 5And the holy Michael said to me, What sight has disturbed you like this? Until today has the day of his mercy lasted, and he has been merciful and long suffering towards those who dwell upon the dry ground. 6And when the day, and the power, and the punishment and the judgement come, which the Lord of Spirits has prepared for those who worship the righteous judgement,^c and for those who deny the righteous judgement, and for those who take his name in vain—and that day has been prepared, for the chosen a covenant, but for the sinners a visitation. 7And on that day two monsters will be separated from one another; a female monster, whose name (is) Leviathan, to dwell in the depths of the sea above the springs of the waters; 8and the name of the male (is) Behemoth, who occupies with his breast an immense desert named Dendayn, on the east of the garden where the chosen and righteous dwell, where my great-grandfather was received, who was the seventh from Adam, the first man whom the Lord of Spirits made. 9And I asked that other angel to show me the power of those monsters, how they were separated on one day and thrown, one into the depths of the sea, and the other onto the dry ground of the desert. 10And he said to me, Son of Man, you here wish to know what is secret. 11And the other angel spoke to me, (the one) who went with me and showed me what (is) secret, what (is) first and last in heaven, in the heights, and under the dry ground, in the depths, and at the ends of heaven, and at the foundations of heaven, and in the storehouses of the winds;^d 12and how the spirits^e are distributed, and how they are weighed, and how the springs and the winds are counted according to the power of (their) spirit;^f and the power of the light of the moon . . . and the divisions of the stars according to their names, and (how) all the divisions are made, 13and the thunder according to the places where it falls; and all the divisions that are made in lightning that it may flash, and its hosts, how they quickly obey; 14for the thunder has fixed intervals (which) have been given to its sound for waiting; and the thunder and the lightning are not separate,

---

^cSo read all Ethiopian manuscripts, but possibly a mistranslation of an original "judge."
^dSome manuscripts read "of the spirits" (but here and in the next verse it is possible that the common word "spirit" has the meaning "wind").
^eOr "the winds."
^fOr "according to the power of the wind."

and (although) not one, through a spirit the two of them move inseparably; 15for when the lightning flashes, the thunder utters its voice, and the spirit at the proper time causes (it) to rest, and divides equally between them; for the storehouse of the times for their occurrence is (like) that of the sand, and each of them at the proper time is held by a rein, and turned back by the power of the spirit, and likewise driven forward, according to the number of the regions of the earth. 16And the spirit of the sea is male and strong, and according to the power of its strength (the spirit) turns it back with a rein, and likewise it is driven forward and scattered amongst all the mountains of the earth. 17And the spirit of the hoar-frost is its (own) angel; and the spirit of the hail is a good angel. 18And the spirit of the snow has withdrawn because of its power, and it has a special spirit; and that which rises from it is like smoke, and its name (is) frost. 19And the spirit of the mist is not associated with them in their storehouses, but has a special storehouse; for its course (is) glorious both in light and in darkness, and in winter and in summer, and in its storehouse is an angel. 20The spirit of the dew (has) its dwelling at the ends of heaven, and it is connected with the storehouses of the rain; and its course (is) in winter and in summer, and its clouds and the clouds of the mist are associated, and one gives to the other. 21And when the spirit of the rain moves from its storehouse, the angels come and open the storehouse, and bring it out; and when it is scattered over all the dry ground, it joins with all the water that (is) on the dry ground; and whenever it joins with the water that (is) on the dry ground, 22 . . . for the waters are for those who dwell upon the dry ground, for (they are) nourishment for the dry ground from the Most High who is in heaven; therefore there is a fixed measure for the rain, and the angels comprehend it. 23All these things I saw towards the Garden of Righteousness. 24And the angel of peace who was with me said to me, These two monsters, prepared in accordance with the greatness of the Lord, will be fed that the punishment of the Lord . . . in vain. And children will be killed with their mothers, and sons with their fathers. 25When the punishment of the Lord of Spirits rests upon them, it will remain resting that the punishment of the Lord of Spirits may not come in vain upon these. Afterwards the judgement will be according to his mercy and his patience.

61. And in those days I saw long cords given to those angels, and they acquired wings for themselves, and flew, and went towards the north. 2And I asked the angel, saying Why did these take the long cords and go?

And he said to me, They went that they may measure. ³And the angel who went with me said to me, These will bring the measurements of the righteous and the ropes of the righteous to the righteous, that they may rely on the name of the Lord of Spirits for ever and ever. ⁴The chosen will begin to dwell with the chosen, and these measurements will be given to faith, and will strengthen righteousness. ⁵And these measurements will reveal all the secrets of the depths of the earth, and those who were destroyed by the desert, and those who were devoured by the fish of the sea and by animals, that they may return and rely on the day of the Chosen One; for no one will be destroyed before the Lord of Spirits, and no one can be destroyed. ⁶And all those in the heavens above received a command, and power and one voice and one light like fire were given to them. ⁷And him, before everything, they blessed and exalted and praised in wisdom; and they showed themselves wise in speech and in the spirit of life. ⁸And the Lord of Spirits set the Chosen One on the throne of his glory, and he will judge all the works of the holy ones in heaven above, and in the balance he will weigh their deeds. ⁹And when he lifts his face to judge their secret ways according to the word of the name of the Lord of Spirits, and their path according to the way of the righteous judgement of the Lord Most High, they will all speak with one voice, and bless, and praise, and exalt and glorify the name of the Lord of Spirits. ¹⁰And he will call all the host of the heavens, and all the holy ones above, and the host of the Lord, the Cherubim, and the Seraphim and the Ophannim, and all the angels of power, and all the angels of the principalities, and the Chosen One, and the other host which is upon the dry ground and over the water, on that day, ¹¹and they will raise one voice, and will bless, and praise, and glorify and exalt (him), in the spirit of faith, and in the spirit of wisdom and of patience, and in the spirit of mercy, and in the spirit of justice and of peace, and in the spirit of goodness; and they will all say with one voice, Blessed is he, and blessed be the name of the Lord of Spirits for ever and ever. ¹²All those who do not sleep in heaven above will bless him; all his holy ones who (are) in heaven will bless him, and all the chosen ones who dwell in the Garden of Life, and every spirit of light which is able to bless, and praise, and exalt and hallow your holy name, and all flesh which beyond (its) power will praise and bless your name for ever and ever. ¹³For great (is) the mercy of the Lord of Spirits, and (he is) long-suffering; and all his works and all his forces, as many as he has made, he has revealed to the righteous and the chosen in the name of the Lord of Spirits.

62. And thus the Lord commanded the kings and the mighty and the exalted, and those who dwell upon the earth, and said, Open your eyes, and raise your horns, if you are able to acknowledge the Chosen One. [2]And the Lord of Spirits sat[g] on the throne of his glory, and the spirit of righteousness was poured out on him, and the word of his mouth kills all the sinners and all the lawless, and they are destroyed before him. [3]And on that day all the kings and the mighty and the exalted, and those who possess the earth, will stand up; and they will see and recognize how he sits on the throne of his glory, and the righteous are judged in righteousness before him, and no idle word is spoken before him. [4]And pain will come upon them as (upon) a woman in labour for whom giving birth is difficult, when her child enters the mouth of the womb, and she has difficulty in giving birth. [5]And one half of them will look at the other, and they will be terrified, and will cast down their faces, and pain will take hold of them, when they see that Son of a Woman sitting on the throne of his glory. [6]And the mighty kings, and all those who possess the earth, will praise and bless and exalt him who rules everything which is hidden. [7]For from the beginning the Son of Man was hidden, and the Most High kept him in the presence of his power, and revealed him (only) to the chosen; [8]and the community of the holy and the chosen will be sown, and all the chosen will stand before him on that day. [9]And all the mighty kings, and the exalted, and those who rule the dry ground, will fall down before him on their faces and worship; and they will set their hope upon that Son of Man, and will entreat him, and will petition for mercy from him. [10]But that Lord of Spirits will then so press them that they will hasten to go out from before him, and their faces will be filled with shame, and the darkness will grow deeper on their faces. [11]And the angels of punishment will take them, that they may repay them for the wrong which they did to his children and to his chosen that Son of Man they will dwell, and eat, and lie down, and rise up for ever and ever. [15]And the righteous and chosen will have risen from the earth, and will have ceased to cast down their faces, and will have put on the garment of life. [16]And this will be a garment of life from the Lord of Spirits; and your garments will not wear out, and your glory will not fail before the Lord of Spirits.

---

[g]All manuscripts have "sat," but the text is often emended to "set him."

63. In those days the mighty kings who possess the dry ground will entreat the angels of his punishment to whom they have been handed over that they might give them a little respite, and that they might fall down and worship before the Lord of Spirits, and confess their sin before him. ²And they will bless and praise the Lord of Spirits, and say, Blessed be the Lord of Spirits and the Lord of kings, the Lord of the mighty and the Lord of the rich, and the Lord of glory and the Lord of wisdom! ³And everything secret is clear before you, and your power (is) for all generations, and your glory for ever and ever; deep, and without number, are all your secrets, and your righteousness is beyond reckoning. ⁴Now we realise that we ought to praise and bless the Lord of kings and the one who is king over all kings. ⁵And they will say, Would that we might be given a respite, that we might praise and thank and bless him, and make our confession before his glory. ⁶And now we long for a little respite, but do not find (it); we are driven off, and do not obtain (it); and the light has passed away from before us, and darkness (will be) our dwelling for ever and ever. ⁷For we have not made our confession before him, and we have not praised the name of the Lord of kings, and we have not praised the Lord for all his works, but our hope has been on the sceptre of our kingdom and of our glory. ⁸And on the day of our affliction and distress he does not save us, and we find no respite to make our confession that our Lord is faithful in all his doings, and in all his judgements and his justice, and (that) his judgements show no respect for persons. ⁹And we pass away from before him because of our works, and all our sins have been counted exactly. ¹⁰Then they will say to them, Our souls are sated with possessions gained through iniquity, but they do not prevent our going down into the flames of the torment of Sheol. ¹¹And after this their faces will be filled with darkness and shame before that Son of Man, and they will be driven from before him, and the sword will dwell among them before him. ¹²And thus says the Lord of Spirits, This is the law and the judgement for the mighty and the kings and the exalted, and for those who possess the dry ground, before the Lord of Spirits.

64. And I saw other figures hidden in that place. ²I heard the voice of the angel saying, These are the angels who came down from heaven onto the earth, and revealed what is secret to the sons of men, and led astray the sons of men so that they committed sin.

65. And in those days Noah saw that the earth had tilted, and that its

181

destruction was near. ²And he set off from there, and went to the ends of the earth, and cried out to his great-grandfather Enoch; and Noah said three times in a bitter voice, Hear me, hear me, hear me! ³And he said to him, Tell me what it is that is being done on the earth that the earth is so afflicted and shaken, lest I be destroyed with it. ⁴And immediately there was a great disturbance on the earth, and a voice was heard from heaven, and I fell upon my face. ⁵And my great-grandfather Enoch came and stood by me, and said to me, Why did you cry out to me with such bitter crying and weeping? ⁶And a command has gone out from before the Lord against those who dwell upon the dry ground that this must be their end, for they have learnt all the secrets of the angels, and all the wrongdoing of the satans, and all their secret power, and all the power of those who practise magic arts, and the power of enchantments, and the power of those who cast molten images for all the earth; ⁷and further how silver is produced from the dust of the earth, and how soft metal occurs on the earth; ⁸for lead and tin are not produced from the earth like the former; there is a spring which produces them, and an angel who stands in it, and that angel distributes (them). ⁹And after this my great-grandfather Enoch took hold of me with his hand, and raised me, and said to me, Go, for I have asked the Lord of Spirits about this disturbance on the earth. ¹⁰And he said to me, Because of their iniquity their judgement has been completed, and they will no longer be counted before me; because of the ⟨sorceries⟩ which they have searched out and learnt, the earth and those who dwell upon it will be destroyed. ¹¹And for these there will be no place of refuge for ever, for they showed to them what is secret, and they have been condemned; but not so for you, my son; the Lord of Spirits knows that you (are) pure and innocent of this reproach concerning the secrets. ¹²And he has established your name among the holy, and will keep you from amongst those who dwell upon the dry ground; and he has destined your offspring in righteousness to be kings and for great honours, and from your offspring will flow out a spring of the righteous and holy without number for ever.

66. And after this he showed me the angels of punishment who were ready to come and release all the forces of the water which is under the earth in order to bring judgement and destruction on all those who reside and dwell upon the dry ground. ²And the Lord of Spirits commanded the angels who were (then) coming out not to raise (their) hands, but to keep watch; for those angels were in charge of the forces of the waters. ³And I came out from before Enoch.

67. And in those days the word of the Lord came to me, and he said to me, Noah, behold your lot has come up before me, a lot without reproach, a lot of love and of uprightness. ²And now the angels are making a wooden (structure), and when the angels come out for that (task), I will put my hand on it, and keep it safe, and from it will come the seed of life, and a change shall take place that the dry ground may not remain empty. ³And I will establish your offspring before me for ever and ever, and I will scatter those who dwell with you over the face of the dry ground; I will not (again) put (them) to the test on the face of the earth, but they will be blessed and will increase on the dry ground in the name of the Lord. ⁴And they will shut up those angels who showed iniquity in that burning valley which my great-grandfather Enoch had shown to me previously, in the west, near the mountains of gold and silver and iron and soft-metal and tin. ⁵And I saw that valley in which (there was) a great disturbance, and a heaving of the waters. ⁶And when all this happened, from that fiery molten metal and the disturbance which disturbed (the waters) in that place a smell of sulphur was produced, and it was associated with those waters. And that valley of the angels who led (men) astray burns under the ground; ⁷and through the valleys of that same (area) flow out rivers of fire where those angels will be punished who led astray those who dwell upon the dry ground. ⁸And in those days those waters will serve the kings and the mighty and the exalted, and those who dwell upon the dry ground, for the healing of soul and body, but (also) for the punishment of the spirit. And their spirits are (so) full of lust that they will be punished in their bodies, for they denied the Lord of Spirits. And they see their punishment every day, yet they do not believe in his name. ⁹And the more their bodies are burnt, the more a change will come over their spirits for ever and ever; for no one can speak an idle word before the Lord of Spirits. ¹⁰For judgement will come upon them, for they believe in the lust of their bodies, but deny the spirit of the Lord. ¹¹And those same waters will undergo a change in those days; for when those angels are punished in those days, the temperature of those springs of water will change, and when the angels come up (from the water), that water of the springs will change and will become cold. ¹²And I heard the holy Michael answering and saying, This judgement with which the angels are judged is a testimony for the kings and the mighty who possess the dry ground.

¹³For these waters of judgement (serve) for the healing of the bodies of the ⟨kings⟩, and for the lust of their bodies; but they do not see and do not believe that these waters will change, and will become a fire which burns for ever.

68. And after this my great-grandfather Enoch gave me the explanation of all the secrets in a book and the parables which had been given to him; and he put them together for me in the words of the Book of the Parables. ²And on that day the holy Michael answered Raphael, saying, The power of the spirit seizes me ⟨and makes me tremble⟩ because of the harshness of the judgement of the secrets, the judgement of the angels. Who can endure the harshness of the judgement which has been executed, and before which they melt (with fear)? ³And the holy Michael answered Raphael again, and said to him, Who would not soften his heart over it, and (whose) mind would not be disturbed by this word? Judgement has gone out against them, upon those whom they have led out like this. ⁴But it came to pass, when he stood before the Lord of Spirits, that the holy Michael spoke as follows to Raphael, I will not take their part under the eye of the Lord, for the Lord of Spirits is angry with them, for they act as if they were the Lord. ⁵Because of this the hidden judgement will come upon them for ever and ever; for neither any (other) angel, nor any man, will receive their lot, but they alone have received their judgement for ever and ever.

69. And after this judgement they will terrify them and make them tremble, for they have shown this to those who dwell upon the dry ground. ²And behold the names of those angels. And these are their names: the first of them (is) Semyaza, and the second Artaqifa, and the third Armen, and the fourth Kokabiel, and the fifth Turiel, and the sixth Ramiel, and the seventh Daniel, and the eighth Nuqael, and the ninth Baraqiel, and the tenth Azazel, the eleventh Armaros, the twelfth Batriel, the thirteenth Basasael, the fourteenth Ananel, the fifteenth Turiel, the sixteenth Samsiel, the seventeenth Yetarel, the eighteenth Tumiel, the nineteenth Turiel, the twentieth Rumiel, the twenty-first Azazel. ³And these are the chiefs of their angels, and the names of their leaders of hundreds, and their leaders of fifties and their leaders of tens. ⁴The name of the first (is) Yequn, and this (is) the one who led astray all the children of the holy angels; and he brought them down onto the dry ground, and led them astray through the daughters of men. ⁵And the name of the second (is) Asbeel: this one suggested an evil plan to the children of the holy angels, and led them astray, so that they corrupted their bodies with the daughters of men. 6And the name of the third (is) Gadreel: this is the one who showed all the deadly blows to the sons of men; and he led astray Eve, and he showed the weapons of death to the children of men, the shield and the breastplate and the sword for slaughter, and all the weapons of death to the sons of men. 7And from his hand they have gone out against those who dwell upon the dry ground, from that time and for ever and ever. 8And the name of the fourth (is) Penemue: this one showed the sons of men the bitter and the sweet, and showed them all the secrets of their wisdom.9He taught men the art of writing with ink and paper, and through this many have gone astray from eternity to eternity, and to this day. 10For men were not created for this, that they should confirm their faith like this with pen and ink. 11For men were created no differently from the angels, that they might remain righteous and pure, and death, which destroys everything, would not have touched them; but through this knowledge of theirs they are being destroyed, and through this power it is consuming me. 12And the name of the fifth (is) Kasdeyae: this one showed the sons of men all the evil blows of the spirits and of the demons, and the blows (which attack) the embryo in the womb so that it miscarries, and the blows (which attack) the soul, the bite of the serpent and the blows which occur at midday, the son of the serpent who is . . . strong. 13And this is the ⟨task⟩ of Kesbeel, the chief of the oath, who showed (the oath) to the holy ones when he dwelt on high in glory, and its name (is) Beqa. 14And this one told the holy Michael that he should show him the secret name, that they might mention it in the oath, so that those who showed the sons of men everything which is secret trembled before that name and oath. 15And this (is) the power of this oath, for it is powerful and strong; and he placed this oath Akae in the charge of the holy Michael. 16And these are the secrets of this oath . . . and they are strong through his oath, and heaven was suspended before the world was created and for ever. 17And through it the earth was founded upon the water, and from the hidden (recesses) of the mountains come beautiful waters from the creation of the world and for ever. 18And through that oath the sea was created, and as its foundation, for the time of anger, he placed for it the sand, and it does not go beyond (it) from the creation of the world and for ever. 19And through that oath the deeps were made firm, and they stand and do not move from their place from (the creation of) the world and for ever. 20And through that oath the sun and the moon complete their course and do not transgress their command from (the creation of) the world and for ever. ²¹And through that oath the stars complete their course, and he calls their names, and they answer him from (the creation of) the world and for ever; ²²and likewise the spirits of the water, of the winds, and of all the breezes, and their paths, according to all the groups of the spirits. ²³And there are kept the storehouses of the sound of the thunder and of the light of the lightning; and there are kept the storehouses of the hail and the hoar-frost, and the storehouses of the mist, and the storehouses of the rain and dew. ²⁴And all these make their confession and give thanks before the Lord of Spirits and sing praises with all their power; and their food consists of all their thanksgiving, and they give thanks and praise and exalt in the name of the Lord of Spirits for ever and ever. ²⁵And this oath is strong over them, and through it they are kept safe, and their paths are kept safe, and their courses are not disturbed. ²⁶And they had great joy, and they blessed and praised and exalted because the name of that Son of Man had been revealed to them. ²⁷And he sat on the throne of his glory, and the whole judgement was given to the Son of Man, and he will cause the sinners to pass away and be destroyed from the face of the earth. ²⁸And those who led astray the world will be bound in chains, and will be shut up in the assembly-place of their destruction, and all their works will pass away from the face of the earth. ²⁹And from then on there will be nothing corruptible, for that Son of Man has appeared and has sat on the throne of his glory, and everything evil will pass away and go from before him; and the word of that Son of Man will be strong before the Lord of Spirits. This is the third parable of Enoch.

70. And it came to pass after this (that), while he was living, his name was lifted from those who dwell upon the dry ground to the presence of that Son of Man and to the presence of the Lord of Spirits. ²And he was lifted on the chariots of the spirit, and his name vanished among them. ³And from that day I was not counted among them, and he placed me between two winds, between the north and the west, where the angels took the cords to measure for me the place for the chosen and the righteous. ⁴And there I saw the first fathers and the righteous who from (the beginning of) the world dwelt in that place.

71. And it came to pass after this that my spirit was carried off, and it went up into the heavens. I saw the sons of the holy angelsʰ treading

---

ʰthe sons of the holy angels: Possibly a false translation of "the holy sons of God."

upon flames of fire, and their garments (were) white, and their clothing, and the light of their face (was) like snow. 2And I saw two rivers of fire, and the light of that fire shone like hyacinth, and I fell upon my face before the Lord of Spirits. 3And the angel Michael, one of the archangels, took hold of me by my right hand, and raised me, and led me out to all the secrets of mercy and the secrets of righteousness. 4And he showed me all the secrets of the ends of heaven and all the storehouses of all the stars and the lights, from where they come out before the holy ones. 5And the spirit carried Enoch off to the highest heaven, and I saw there in the middle of that light something built of crystal stones, and in the middle of those stones tongues of living fire. 6And my spirit saw a circle of fire which surrounded that house; from its four sides (came) rivers full of living fire, and they surrounded that house. 7And round about (were) the Seraphim, and the Cherubim and the Ophannim; these are they who do not sleep, but keep watch over the throne of his glory. 8And I saw angels who could not be counted, a thousand thousands and ten thousand times ten thousand, surrounding that house; 9and Michael and Raphael and Gabriel and Phanuel, and the holy angels who (are) in the heavens above, went in and out of that house. And Michael and Raphael and Gabriel and Phanuel, and many holy angels without number, came out from that house; 10and with them the Head of Days, his head white and pure like wool, and his garments indescribable. 11And I fell upon my face, and my whole body melted, and my spirit was transformed; and I cried out in a loud voice in the spirit of power, and I blessed and praised and exalted. 12And these blessings which came out from my mouth were pleasing before that Head of Days. 13And that Head of Days came with Michael and Gabriel, Raphael and Phanuel, and thousands and tens of thousands of angels without number. 14And that angel came to me, and greeted me with his voice, and said to me, You are the Son of Man who was born to righteousness, and righteousness remains over you, and the righteousness of the Head of Days will not leave you. 15And he said to me, He proclaims peace to you in the name of the world which is to come, for from there peace has come out from the creation of the world; and so you will have it for ever and for ever and ever. 16And all will walk according to your way, inasmuch as righteousness will never leave you; with you will be their dwelling, and with you their lot, and they will not be separated from you, for ever and ever and ever. 17And so there will be length of days with that Son of Man, and the righteous will have peace, and the righteous will have an upright way in the name of the Lord of Spirits for ever and ever.

THE TESTAMENT OF LEVI 2–5

Commentary

The *Testament of Levi* is one of the sections of the *Testaments of the Twelve Patriarchs,* which in its present form is a Christian work probably dating to the late second century c.e. The *Testaments* consists of twelve writings, all in the form of a testament, a farewell speech of a dying individual. The origin of the *Testaments* is a strongly debated issue among scholars. Some have argued that the work is basically Jewish, later revised by a Christian editor. Others have argued that the *Testaments* was a Christian composition, although based on earlier Jewish traditions. The *Testament of Levi* 2–5 is included here as an example of a Jewish apocalypse because its contents are basically consistent with Jewish thought, and the extent of Christian editing, though debated, seems to be minimal. (Passages that are often suspected of being Christian alterations are 2:10, "the one who is to come to set Israel free"; all of 2:11; 4:1, "through the suffering of the Most High"; 4:4, "of his son" and "Nevertheless, your sons will lay hands on him to get him out of their way"; 4:5, "about him"; and 4:6, "him" in place of "you.")

The *Testament of Levi* claims to be the farewell instructions of Levi, one of the sons of Jacob, to his sons. Chapters 2–5 of this work are a small apocalypse in which Levi saw the heavens opened and an angel inviting him to come up. Other Jewish apocalypses that contain ascent-visions in which the recipient of the revelation is taken up through the various levels of heaven include *2 Enoch* and *3 Baruch*; Christian examples are the *Apocalypse of Paul* and the *Ascension of Isaiah* 6–11. Similarities between the *Testament of Levi* 2–5 and the ascent of Enoch to the throne room of God (*1 Enoch* 14–16) have often been noted. One major difference, however, is that in *1 Enoch* the various heavens are not enumerated.

In his vision, Levi journeys through the seven heavens, guided by an angel. Variant traditions have apparently been combined rather awkwardly in these verses. The descriptions in chapter 2 and in the opening verses of chapter 3 pertain to the bottom three heavens, listing them in ascending order. Suddenly at 3:4 the highest heaven is described, and the three below it are given in descending order.

Levi's descriptions of the heavens contain both cosmological and eschatological elements. Cosmological elements dominate, although, compared with other apocalypses, cosmological speculation is minimal.

Levi reports that the first heaven is the darkest or gloomiest because it observes the unrighteous deeds of people. The second heaven holds fire, snow, and ice that will be used in God's judgment and also contains the spirits that will punish the wicked. The third heaven contains "the warrior hosts appointed to wreak vengeance on the spirits of error and of Beliar at the day of judgement" (3:3). The fourth heaven contains thrones and powers, which offer praise to God continually. In the fifth and sixth heavens are angels. The seventh, and highest, heaven is the dwelling place of God (3:5).

Chapter 4 describes the cosmic disturbances on the day of judgment. God will punish the wicked but will protect Levi and make him God's "son and servant and a minister of his presence" (4:2). In the fifth chapter the angel opens the gates of heaven, and Levi sees the heavenly temple and God enthroned in glory. God tells Levi that he has been given the office of priest to exercise until God comes to dwell in Israel. After this commissioning, Levi is returned to earth by the angel, who gives him a sword and shield and sends him out to exact vengeance on Shechem for the rape of Dinah, Levi's sister (see the story in Gen. 34:1-31).

The identification of the angel in this vision as the intercessory angel for the nation of Israel (5:6) is similar to portions of the book of Daniel, in which Michael plays the role of the guardian, or patron, angel of the Jewish people (chaps. 10–12). In Daniel, other nations also have patron angels. See also *1 Enoch* 89–90, where the seventy shepherds represent patron angels. This idea of guardian angels is a part of the notion, common in apocalyptic literature, that events on earth are paralleled and even controlled by events in heaven.

The purpose, setting, and date of composition of the *Testament of Levi* 2–5 are almost impossible to determine on the basis of currently available evidence. The traditional answers to the questions have been that the work was produced in Palestine during the end of the rule of John Hyrcanus (134–104 B.C.E.), one of the Hasmonean rulers of Judea, as pro-Hasmonean propaganda. This understanding has been seriously questioned recently, however, partially due to the discovery of manuscripts at Qumran containing material very similar to the *Testament of Levi*. The Qumran community was anti-Hasmonean, not pro-Hasmonean. If, as is likely, the work was originally Jewish, it probably arose during the first or second centuries B.C.E. A clue to its purpose is perhaps found in the commissioning of Levi to the priesthood: the journey to God's throne and subsequent commissioning serves to make legitimate the levitical priesthood. If, on the other hand, the work is Christian in origin, as some scholars claim, its composition may be as late as the end of the second century C.E.

Two New Testament passages share some similarities with ideas in the *Testament of Levi*. In 2 Corinthians 12:2, Paul refers to an earlier experience of being caught up to the third heaven, although he does not elaborate on his experience or describe the contents of the heavens. John of Patmos, in Revelation 4–5, tells of seeing an open door in heaven and being invited to "Come up hither." This is similar to the experience of Levi, who claims that he saw "the heavens opened, and an angel of the Lord said to me 'Levi, come in' " (2:6). Like Levi, John also sees God seated in the heavenly throne room.

The translation given here is by M. de Jonge from *The Apocryphal Old Testament*.

The Testament of Levi 2–5

2. I, Levi, was conceived in Haran and born there; and after that I came with my father to Shechem. 2 And I was a young man, about twenty, when, with Simeon, I took vengeance on Hamor (because) of (what he had done to) our sister Dinah. 3 And when we were feeding the flocks in Abel-meholah a spirit of understanding from the Lord came upon me, and I observed all men's evil ways, and that unrighteousness had built itself walls, and iniquity had entrenched itself behind ramparts. 4 And I was grieved on man's behalf; and I prayed to the Lord that I might be saved. 5 Then sleep fell upon me, and I saw a high mountain—that is mount Aspis in Abel-meholah. 6 And behold, the heavens opened, and an angel of the Lord said to me, Levi, come in. 7 And I went from the first heaven into the second; and I saw there water hanging between the two. 8 And I saw a third heaven, far brighter and more brilliant than these two, and infinite in height. 9 And I said to the angel, Why is this? And the angel said to me, Do not stay wondering at these, for when you have gone up there, you will see four other heavens even more brilliant and beyond comparison (with them); 10 for you will stand close to the Lord and be his minister, and you will declare his mysteries to men and be the herald (of the good news) about the one who is to come to set Israel free. 11 And through you and Judah will the Lord appear among men and bring salvation through them to all mankind. 12 And the Lord's portion will provide your livelihood; and he will be your field (and) vineyard, (your) fruits, (and your) gold (and) silver.

3. Hear, then, about the seven heavens. The lowest is the gloomiest because it witnesses all the unrighteous deeds of men. 2 The second holds fire, snow, ice, ready for the day which the Lord has decreed in the righteous judgement of God: in it are all the spirits of retribution for vengeance on the wicked. 3 In the third are the warrior hosts appointed to wreak vengeance on the spirits of error and of Beliar at the day of judgement. But the (heavens down) to the fourth above these are holy. 4 For in the highest of all the Great Glory dwells, in the holy of holies, far above all holiness. 5 And in the (heaven) next to it are the angels of the Lord's presence, who minister and make expiation to the Lord for all the sins committed unwittingly by the righteous; 6 and they offer to the Lord a soothing odour, a spiritual and bloodless offering. 7 And in the (heaven) below (it) are the angels who bear the answers to the angels of the Lord's presence. 8 And in the (heaven) next to it are thrones (and) powers, in which praises, are offered to God continually. 9 And when the Lord looks upon us, all of us are shaken; and the heavens and the earth and the abysses are shaken at the presence of his majesty. 10 Yet men do not perceive these things, and they sin and provoke the Most High.

4. But know that the Lord will execute judgement on men, because when the rocks are being rent, and (the light of) the sun extinguished, and the waters dried up, and fire losing its power, and all creation in confusion, and the unseen spirits wasting away, and Hades despoiled through the suffering of the Most High, men will be unbelieving and persist in their iniquities; (and) on this account will they be judged and punished. 2 But the Most High has heard your prayer: he will separate you from iniquity and make you his son and servant and a minister of his presence.

> 3A bright light of knowledge will make you to shine in Jacob,
> And like the sun will you be to the whole race of Israel.
> 4And a blessing shall be given to you and to all your sons,
> Until the Lord looks upon all the Gentiles with the affection
> of his son for ever.

Nevertheless, your sons will lay hands on him to get him out of their way. 5 And this is why wisdom and understanding have been given you, that you may instruct your sons about him. 6 For blessed shall he be who blesses him, and they who curse him shall perish.

5. And the angel opened to me the gates of heaven, and I saw the holy temple, and the Most High (sitting) on a throne of glory. 2 And he said to me, Levi, To you have I given the blessings of the priesthood until I come and dwell in the midst of Israel. 3 Then the angel brought me down to earth; and he gave me a shield and a sword and said, Take vengeance on Shechem because of Dinah, and I will be with you, for the Lord has sent me. 4 And it was at that time that I killed the sons of Hamor, as it is written in the heavenly tablets. 5 And I said to him, Please, sir, tell me your name, so that I can call on you in time of trouble. 6 And he said, I am the angel that intercedes for the nation of Israel, so that no one may destroy them completely, for every evil spirit is ranged against them. 7 And afterwards I woke up, and I blessed the Most High and the angel that intercedes for the nation of Israel and all the righteous.

THE TESTAMENT OF ABRAHAM

Commentary

In spite of its title, the *Testament of Abraham* is not a testament. Abraham explicitly fails to give final advice and instructions, even when repeatedly warned of his impending death. Furthermore, testaments are normally first-person accounts, whereas the *Testament of Abraham* is a third-person account of the events leading up to the patriarch's death. Although some scholars disagree, the *Testament of Abraham* is usually classified as an apocalypse. The revelation that comes to Abraham consists of knowledge of his impending death and information about the judgment of humanity. The archangel Michael mediates the revelation to Abraham through dialogue and a heavenly journey. The figure of Death also serves as an otherworldly mediator, as it, too, tells Abraham that he is about to die.

The scenes describing the judgment of souls after death reveal the eschatological interests of the *Testament of Abraham*. Three stages of judgment are outlined: each person must be judged by Abel, by the twelve tribes of Israel, and by God. The souls who are found guilty—that is, whose evil deeds outweigh their good deeds—are carried off to "a most disagreeable place of punishment" (13:18). The righteous, on the other hand, enter paradise. In addition, those who suffer premature death thereby atone for their sins and escape eschatological punishment (14:18-19).

The *Testament of Abraham* falls readily into two parts. The first section begins with a visit by the archangel Michael to inform Abraham that his time to die has come. Abraham refuses to die until he has seen "the whole earth and all created things" (9:9). After being instructed by God to fulfill Abraham's wish, Michael takes Abraham in a chariot into the heavens, where he observes all that takes place on earth. The righteous Abraham, incensed at the wickedness he sees, requests (and receives) the destruction of several sinners.

Concerned that the overzealous and merciless Abraham will destroy everyone on earth, God commands Michael to take Abraham to the first gate of heaven, where Abraham watches the judgment of individuals after death (compare the scene of the two gates in chap. 11 with similar imagery in Matt. 7:13-14). The climax of this judgment scene occurs when a soul is brought forward whose good deeds and sins are equal. Sent neither to paradise nor to destruction, this soul is placed "in the

193

middle." Abraham has compassion for the soul and asks Michael to join him in interceding on the soul's behalf. Their efforts are successful, and the soul is taken to paradise. Abraham then pleads for the souls of those persons whom he had earlier caused to be destroyed. This scene is pivotal to the story because Abraham learns to be merciful and realizes that his own self-righteous attitude was sinful. After asking and receiving forgiveness from God, Abraham is taken back to earth.

The otherworldly journey that is integrated into this part of the story differs considerably from the journeys found in many other apocalypses. In the present work, there is no interest in the details of heaven or hell, no journeys through the various levels or regions of heaven, and no elaboration of the punishment of the wicked or the reward for the righteous. The major emphasis in the *Testament of Abraham* is on the heavenly judgment scene and the lesson Abraham learns about the mercy of God toward sinners.

In the second part of the work, God sends the figure of Death to Abraham to accomplish what Michael was unable to accomplish: the procurement of the soul of Abraham. At first, Death is as unsuccessful as Michael was in persuading Abraham that his time to die has come. Finally, only through trickery does Death succeed in bringing about Abraham's death. Immediately, Abraham's soul is taken by Michael and a host of angels, who prepare it for its journey to heaven.

Some scholars have stated that the purpose of the *Testament of Abraham* was simply to present an inspiring and moving story about the venerable patriarch. Others have understood the work to be primarily an exhortation about the dangers of self-righteousness. The suggestion has been made, however, that, like most apocalypses, the *Testament of Abraham* was a response to a crisis situation. The crisis here, though, is not a political or historical crisis but the universal crisis of death. The heavenly journey provides a partial resolution of the crisis by showing Abraham (and the readers of the work) that God has no desire to punish anyone and is merciful to sinners who repent. Likewise, the closing scene, which shows Abraham's soul being tenderly cared for by the host of angels, helps to lessen the fear of death.

The date of the writing of the *Testament of Abraham* is uncertain. Estimates by scholars usually range from the first century B.C.E. to the second century C.E. With regard to the place of its writing, similarities in vocabulary and motifs between the *Testament of Abraham* and other Jewish writings produced in Egypt point to Egypt as the most likely location.

194

This work exists in two editions, or recensions: Recension A, the longer edition; and Recension B, the shorter edition. Most scholars have concluded that neither recension is directly dependent on the other; both go back to a common original, probably written in Greek. Although some scholars have argued that Recension B is truer to the original version of the *Testament of Abraham,* the general consensus of present scholarship seems to be that Recension A better preserves the content and arrangement of the original version, whereas Recension B may at times be closer to the precise wording of the original version.

The version of the Testament of Abraham included here basically follows Recension A, supplemented in a few places by Recension B. The supplements are marked by a solid black line in the margin of the text.

The translation is by Nigel Turner from *The Apocryphal Old Testament.*

The Testament of Abraham

1. Now Abraham had lived out his life's span of nine hundred and ninety-five years. ²All the years of his life he had lived in peace, gentleness, and righteousness. ³He was, moreover, very hospitable; for he pitched his tent at the crossroads by the oak of Mamre and welcomed everyone, rich and poor, kings and rulers, the maimed and the weak, friends and strangers, neighbours and travellers. ⁴And the pious, all-holy, righteous, and hospitable Abraham made them (all) welcome without distinction. ⁵But the bitter cup of death, which is universal and inevitable, and life's uncertain end, overtook even him. ⁶So it came about that the Lord God summoned his archangel Michael and said to him, Prince Michael! ⁷Go down to Abraham and tell him about his death, so that he can set his affairs in order. ⁸For I have blessed him as the stars of heaven and as the sand of the sea shore: throughout his life and in his many business concerns he has prospered exceedingly; and he is very rich indeed. ⁹He has been righteous beyond all men in every good deed, hospitable and loving to the end of his days. ¹⁰Go, archangel Michael, to Abraham, my well-loved friend, and inform him about his death. ¹¹Give him this assurance, You are going now to leave this vain world: you are going to forsake (your) body, and amid blessings come to your Lord.

2. The Prince left God's presence and went down to Abraham at the oak of Mamre. ²And he found the righteous Abraham in the field nearby, assisting with the yokes of oxen that did the ploughing, together with the sons of Masek, and with others of his servants, twelve in number. ³The Prince Michael was approaching, when lo, Abraham saw him in the distance looking like a most handsome soldier. ⁴So Abraham got up and went to meet him, as it was his custom to go out and welcome every stranger. ⁵But the Prince welcomed him first and said, Greetings, most honourable father, God's righteous chosen one, the Heavenly One's true friend! ⁶Abraham said to the Prince, Greetings, most honourable soldier, (whose face) shines like the sun and (whose form is) more handsome than any of the sons of men: you are welcome indeed! ⁷But I must ask your Presence, what is the secret of your youthful bloom? ⁸Tell me, I beg you, where (do you come) from, what army (do you belong to), and what is the purpose of your Grace's journey that you have come here? ⁹And the Prince replied, I come, righteous Abraham, from a great city. ¹⁰I have been sent by the great king (of that city) to arrange for the departure of a true friend of his; for the king is calling for him. ¹¹And Abraham said, Come sir! Come with me to my field. ¹²The Prince replied, I (will) come. ¹³They went to the field where the ploughing was going on and sat down to talk. ¹⁴And Abraham said to his servants, the sons of Masek, Go to the stable. ¹⁵And fetch two good-natured and gentle horses, that have been broken in, for me and this (our) guest to ride on. ¹⁶But the Prince said, No, my lord Abraham: let them not fetch horses, for I never ride on a four-footed beast. ¹⁷My king is indeed rich, with great commercial interests; and he has every kind of man and animal at his command. ¹⁸But I myself never ride on a four-footed beast. ¹⁹So, righteous one, let us make our way to your house, without fuss, on foot. ²⁰And Abraham said, Very well: so let it be!

3. And as they were going from the field towards his house, a cypress tree by the roadside cried out with a human voice at God's bidding and said, Holy, Holy, Holy, is the Lord God who calls to himself those who love him. ²Abraham said nothing, supposing the Prince had not heard the tree's voice. ³And when they came to the house they sat down in the court. ⁴And Isaac saw the angel's face and said to Sarah his mother, My lady mother, the man sitting with my father Abraham is no member of the race that dwells on earth. ⁵And Isaac ran out and welcomed him respectfully, falling at the spirit's feet. ⁶The spirit blessed him and said, The Lord God will graciously grant you his promise which he made to your father Abraham and his descendants, and he will also graciously grant you your father's and mother's dear prayer. ⁷And Abraham said to his son Isaac, Isaac, my child, draw some water from the well and bring it to me in a basin, so that we can wash (our) guest's feet; for he has come to us after a long journey and is tired. [8]So Isaac ran to the well, drew water in the basin, and brought it to them. [9]Abraham got up and washed the Prince Michael's feet; and he was much moved and wept over the stranger. [10]Isaac saw his father weeping, and he wept too. [11]And the Prince saw them weeping, and he also wept with them. [12]And the Prince's tears fell onto the basin, into the water of the bowl, and became precious stones. [13]When Abraham saw the wonder he was astonished, and he took the stones surreptitiously and said nothing and kept the matter to himself.

4. Then Abraham said to his son Isaac, Go, my beloved son, to the dining-room and make it festive. [2]Make up two couches for us there, one for me and one for this man, who is our guest to-day; and see that there is there a seat for two, a lamp-stand, and a table full of good things. [3]Make the room festive, my son: lay out the napkins and the purple cloths and the silk. [4]Burn every (kind of) costly and precious incense; and bring in sweet-smelling plants from the garden and fill our house with them. [5]Light seven oil lamps, so that we may make merry, because this guest of ours to-day deserves more honour than kings and governors: his very appearance is superior to that of all other men. [6]So Isaac set everything in excellent order. [7]And Abraham took the Prince Michael and went up to the dining-room. [8]Both of them took their seats on the couches, and Isaac brought forward (the) table full of good things (and put it) between them. [9]Then the Prince got up and went outside, as if wanting to relieve himself; and he went up to heaven in the twinkling of an eye. [10]He stood before God and said to him, Sovereign Lord, thy Majesty must know that I cannot make mention of (his) death to that righteous man. [11]For I have never seen upon earth a man like him—merciful, hospitable, righteous, trusty, religious, (and) incapable of doing anything that is evil. [12]So now thou knowest, Lord, that I cannot make mention of (his) death. [13]But the Lord replied, Go down, Prince Michael, to my friend Abraham; and whatever he tells you, do it. [14]Whatever he eats, eat (it) also with him. [15]I will send forth my Holy Spirit upon his son Isaac, and I will put into Isaac's mind the thought of his death, so that he sees his father's death in a dream. [16]Isaac will recount what he has seen and you shall interpret (it). [17]And (then Abraham) himself will recognize that his end (is near). [18]The Prince said, Lord, all heavenly spirits are without bodies and neither eat nor drink, but this man has laid a table for me with an abundance of every kind of earthly and perishable dainty. [19]What now, Lord, am I to do? How am I

197

to see he does not notice when I am sitting at the same table with him? [20]The Lord said, Go down to him, and have no anxiety on this score. [21]For while you are sitting with him I will send upon you an all-devouring spirit, and it will consume from your hands and through your mouth everything that is on the table; (and) make merry with him in every way. [22]Only you must interpret properly the meaning of the vision, so that Abraham can recognize Death's reaping-hook and life's uncertain end, and so make a settlement of all his goods. [23]For I have blessed him above the sand of the sea and as the stars of heaven.

5. The Prince then went down to Abrahams's house and took his seat with him at the table; and Isaac waited on them. [2]When the meal was over Abraham said his customary prayer, and the archangel prayed with him. [3]Each was resting upon his couch, and Isaac said to his father, Father, I would like to stay with you in this room, to listen to your talk; for I think I should gain much profit from what this excellent man has to say. [4]But Abraham said, No, my son: go to your (own) room and rest on your (own) bed: we do not want to be a burden to this man. [5]Then Isaac, after being blessed by them and having blessed them, went off to his own room and lay down upon his bed. [6]And God put the thought of death into Isaac's mind by means of dreams; and about the third hour of the night Isaac woke up. [7]He got up from his bed and went in great haste to the room where his father and the archangel were sleeping. [8]When he got to the door he cried out, saying, Father Abraham, get up and open (the door) for me quickly, so that I can come in and put my arms round you and kiss you before they take you away from me. [9]So Abraham got up and opened (the door) for him. [10]Isaac went in and put his arms round him and began to weep loudly. [11]Abraham was in consequence much moved and wept loudly himself in sympathy. [12]When the Prince saw them weeping, he wept also. [13]Now Sarah was in her tent, and when she heard them weeping, she came running to them and found them weeping in one another's arms. [14]And Sarah said with tears, My lord Abraham, what does this weeping mean? Tell me, my lord: this brother, who is our guest to-day, has he brought you news about your nephew Lot, that he is dead, and is that why you are making this lamentation? [15]The Prince replied and said to her, No, sister Sarah, it is not as you say. Your son Isaac, I think, had a dream, and he came to us weeping; and when we saw him, we were much moved, and we wept too.

6. And Sarah recognized something in the way the Prince spoke and realized immediately that the speaker was an angel of the Lord. [2]So

Sarah made signs to Abraham to go outside the door; and she said to him, My lord Abraham, do you know who this man is? ³Abraham said, I do not. ⁴And Sarah said, My lord, you remember the three heavenly beings who were our guests in our tent by the oak of Mamre, when you killed the calf without blemish and prepared a meal for them? ⁵When the meat had been eaten, the calf rose up again and joyfully sucked from its mother. You remember, my lord Abraham, do you not, that they gave us the promise of a child, Isaac? This is one of those three holy men. ⁶And Abraham said, What you say, Sarah, is true. Praise and glory be to God the Father. ⁷Indeed, when I was washing his feet in the bowl of the washing-basin late this evening, I said to myself, These are the feet of (one of) the three men that I washed then. ⁸And later on his tears fell into the basin and turned into precious stones. ⁹And Abraham took the stones from the fold of his cloak and gave them to Sarah saying, If you do not believe me, now look at these. ¹⁰And Sarah took them and kissed (them) and fondled (them), saying, Glory be to God who shows his wonders to us. ¹¹You may be certain, my lord Abraham, that we are to receive a revelation about something, whether for evil or for good.

7. And Abraham left Sarah and went back inside the room, and he said to Isaac, Come, dear son: tell me the truth. ²What was it that you saw, and what happened to you that you came to us in such a hurry? ³And Isaac made answer and began, (In my sleep) to-night, my lord, I saw the sun and moon over my head. ⁴(The sun) encircled me with its rays and gave me light. ⁵And while I was looking on at this and rejoicing at it, I saw heaven wide open; and I saw a brilliant man coming down out of heaven, who shone more brightly than seven suns. ⁶And that man, who was like the sun, came and took the sun away from my head, and he went back into the heavens, where he had come from; and I was very upset, because he had taken the sun from me. ⁷And after a little, while I was still upset and ill at ease, I saw that man leave heaven a second time; and he took away the moon from my head as well. ⁸And I wept bitterly. ⁹And I implored that brilliant man and said, No, my lord, please do not take my glory from me: have pity on me and hear me! Even if you must take the sun from me, at least leave me the moon. ¹⁰And he said, You must let them be taken up to the King above, for he wills (to have) them there. ¹¹And he took them from me; but the rays he left upon me.

¹²The sun and the moon and the stars mourned, saying, Do not take away our glorious might. ¹³And that radiant man

199

answered and said to me, Do not weep because I have taken the light of your house; for he has been removed from toils to rest, and from a humble state to an exalted one. [14]He is being lifted from adversity into prosperity: he is being lifted from darkness into light. [15]And I said to him, I beg you sir, take the rays with him as well. [16]And he said to me, There are twelve hours in the day, and then (will) I take all the rays. [17]And while the radiant man was speaking I saw the sun of my house going up into heaven; but I saw that crown no more. And that sun was like you, father.

[18]And the Prince said, Listen, righteous Abraham. The sun your boy has seen is you, his father; and the moon, similarly, is his mother Sarah. The brilliant man, who came down out of heaven, he is a man sent from God, and he is about to take your righteous soul away from you. [19]For you must realize, most honoured Abraham, that you are now about to leave your earthly life behind (you) and depart to God. [20]Then said Abraham to the Prince, This is the most astonishing thing I have ever heard! So it is you, is it, who are to take my soul away from me? [21]The Prince said to him, I am Michael, the Prince, who stands in the presence of God, [22]I have been sent to you in order to put into your mind the thought of death. [23]After that I shall go back to him, as we were commanded. [24]And Abraham said, Now I know that you are an angel of the Lord and you have been sent to take away my soul: yet I will not follow you. [25]But do whatever he commands.

8. And when he heard what Abraham said, the Prince at once disappeared. [2]And he went up to heaven and stood before God and gave an account of everything he had seen in Abraham's house. [3]Furthermore, the Prince also told (his) Lord, Thy friend Abraham also says this, I will not follow you; but do whatever he commands. [4]Is there then anything, Almighty Lord, that thy Glory and immortal Majesty now commands? [5]And God said to the Prince Michael, Go down to my friend Abraham once again and tell him, [6]Thus says the Lord your God, who has brought you into the land of promise, who has blessed you above the sand of the sea and above the stars of heaven, and who granted you the child Isaac, born of the barren Sarah, in your old age: [7]I promise you I will bless you in every way and make your descendants too many to be counted. [8]I will give you everything you can ask of me; for I am the Lord your God and there is none other but me. [9]But why are you resisting me, and why are you distressed? Tell me. [10]And why are you resisting my archangel Michael? [11]Do you not know that all (men who are descended) from Adam and Eve have died? [12]Not one of the prophets has escaped death: no ruler has ever been immortal: none of your ancestors has escaped death's mystery. [13]All have died: all have been received in Hades: all have been gathered by the reaping-hook of Death. [14]But to you I did not send Death. [15]I did not allow any deadly disease to come near you: I did not agree that Death's reaping-hook should visit you; nor did I permit the nets of Hades to enfold you. [16]I willed that no evil should befall you at any time. [17]Instead, I have sent you my Prince Michael for (your) good comfort, to inform you of your departure from the world, so that you can make arrangements about your house and all your goods, and so that you can pronounce a blessing over your dear son Isaac. [18]And you must know that I have done this out of no desire to cause you pain. [19]Why, then, did you say to my Prince, I will not follow you? [20]Why did you say this? [21]Are you not aware that if I were to allow Death to come to you, then I could indeed see whether you would come or not?

9. After receiving the Lord's instructions the Prince went down to Abraham. [2]And when the righteous (man) saw him, he fell on his face to the ground as (if he were) dead; and the Prince told him everything he had heard from the Most High. [3]Then the pious and righteous Abraham got up and threw himself at the spirit's feet and with many tears made supplication to him, saying, [4]I implore you, Prince of the powers on high, since you yourself have deigned to come to me, your sinful and unworthy servant, I beg you now to take a message for me yet once more to the Most High. [5]Tell him, Abraham thy slave has this to say, Lord, Lord, in every deed and word when I besought thee, thou hast heard me and hast brought to completion everything I planned. [6]And now, O Lord, I would not resist thy might, for I know indeed that I am not immortal but must die. [7]And so, just as all things yield to thine ordinance, and shudder and tremble in the presence of thy power, I also am full of fear. [8]Yet one request I would make of thee; and now, O Sovereign Lord, listen to my prayer. [9]I would, while yet in this body, see the whole earth and all created things, which thou didst establish by a single word. [10]When I have seen these, then will I depart from life without regret.

[11]So the Prince went away again and stood before God. [12]And he told him everything, saying, Thy friend Abraham has this to say, I would

behold the whole earth in my life (here) before I die. [13]And when the Most High heard this he gave instructions to the Prince Michael once again. [14]And he said to him, Take a cloud of light and the angels who are in command of the chariots. [15]Then go down and take the righteous Abraham (and set him) on the cherubim-chariot and lift him up to the heights of heaven, so that he may see the whole earth.

10. And the archangel Michael went down and took Abraham (and set him) on the cherubim-chariot and lifted him up to the heights of heaven and acted as his guide on the cloud together with sixty angels. [2]And Abraham went up on the chariot over the entire earth; and Abraham looked out on the world just as it was that day. [3](He saw) some men ploughing, others driving wagons: in one place they were looking after their sheep, elsewhere they were out in the fields, dancing and making merry and playing the kithara: here they were in conflict and going to law with one another, there they were weeping and then burying (their) dead. [4]He saw too the newly-married being escorted home. [5]In a word, he saw everything that was happening in the world, both good and evil. [6]So, as Abraham journeyed, he saw (a group of) swordsmen brandishing (their) sharpened swords in their hands. [7]And Abraham asked the Prince, Who are these? [8]And the Prince said, These are thieves, whose intention it is to commit murder and steal and kill and destroy. [9]And Abraham said, Sir, could you not bid wild beasts come out of the wood and eat them up? [10]And immediately, as he spoke, wild beasts came out of the wood and ate them up. [11]And in another place he saw a man and a woman in fornication together; and he said, Sir, bid the earth open and swallow them. [12]And the earth was split in two at once and swallowed them. [13]In another place he saw men breaking into a house and carrying off another man's property; and he said, Sir, bid fire descend from heaven and consume them. [14]And immediately, as he spoke, fire descended from heaven and consumed them. [15]And there came at once a voice from heaven to the Prince, saying, Prince Michael, bid the chariot stand still and stop Abraham from seeing the whole of the earth. [16]For if he sees all those who are engaged in sin, he will destroy every living thing. [17]For lo, Abraham has not sinned, and he has no pity for sinners. [18]But I have made the world, and I have no wish to destroy any of the men I have created; but I put off the sinner's death until he turns again and lives. [19]Take Abraham up to the first gate of heaven, so that he may view the judgements and the retributions there, and repent for the sinners' souls he has destroyed.

11. Michael turned the chariot and brought Abraham eastwards to the first gate of heaven. ²And Abraham saw two ways: the first way was narrow and restricted and the second broad and spacious. ³[And he saw there two gates: one broad gate] across the broad way, and one narrow gate across the narrow way. ⁴And outside the two gates there, they saw a man seated on a golden throne. ⁵And the man's appearance was terrifying, like (that) of the Sovereign (Lord himself). ⁶And they saw many souls being driven along by angels and herded through the broad gate; and they saw a few other souls being taken by angels through the narrow gate. ⁷And whenever the wondrous being who was seated on the golden throne saw a few going in through the narrow gate and many through the broad one, he at once tore the hair of his head and his beard, and hurled himself from his throne to the ground, weeping and wailing. ⁸But whenever he saw many souls going in through the narrow gate, then he got up from the ground and he took his seat on his throne rejoicing and exulting with great gladness. ⁹And Abraham asked the Prince, My lord Prince, who is this most wondrous man, who is decked out with so great a glory, and who at one moment weeps and wails, and at the next rejoices and exults? ¹⁰The spirit made answer, This is Adam, the first man to be made, who is in so great a glory. ¹¹He surveys the world, inasmuch as all men owe their origin to him. ¹²Whenever he sees many souls going in through the narrow gate, then he gets up and sits on his throne, rejoicing and exulting with gladness. ¹³For this narrow gate is (the gate) of the righteous, which leads to life, and those who go in by it go to Paradise. ¹⁴That is why the first man Adam rejoices, because he sees souls being saved. ¹⁵And when he sees many souls going in through the broad gate, then he plucks at the hair of his head and hurls himself to the ground, weeping and wailing bitterly. ¹⁶(It is) because the broad gate is the gate of sinners, and it leads to destruction and eternal punishment. ¹⁷That is why the first man Adam throws himself from his throne and weeps and wails at the sinners' destruction, because those who are perishing are many, whereas those who are being saved are few. ¹⁸For in seven thousand there is scarcely to be found a single soul who is being saved, (who is) righteous and undefiled.

¹⁹And Abraham said, He that cannot enter through the narrow gate, can he not enter into life? ²⁰Then Abraham wept and said, Ah me! What shall I do? I am a big man, and how can I enter through the narrow gate, when a youth of fifteen could not get through it? ²¹And Michael answered

and said to Abraham, Do not be afraid, father, and do not worry; for you will go through it without hindrance, and so will all who are like you.

12. While he was still speaking, lo, two angels (came), fiery in appearance, merciless in purpose, and relentless in expression, and they were driving ten thousand souls along, beating them mercilessly with fiery thongs; and one soul the angel seized (?). ²And they directed all the souls through the broad gate for destruction. ³So we also followed the angels and came inside that broad gate. ⁴Now between the two gates stood a fearsome throne, flashing like fire. ⁵On it sat a wondrous man, bright as the sun, like a son of God; and before him stood a table, all of gold and (covered with) the finest linen, (which shone) like crystal. ⁶On the table lay a book, six cubits thick and ten cubits broad, and on its right and on its left were standing two angels holding paper and pen and ink. ⁷In front of the table sat a brilliant angel holding in his hand a pair of scales. ⁸On his left sat a fiery angel, entirely without mercy and relentless, and in his hand he held a trumpet that contained all-devouring fire inside it, as a means of testing sinners. ⁹And while the wondrous man who sat on the throne was giving his judgements and sentencing the souls, the two angels on his right and on his left were recording. ¹⁰The (angel) on the right recorded the good deeds, the one on the left the sins. ¹¹And the angel in front of the table, who held the pair of scales, weighed the souls, and the fiery angel, who held the fire, put the souls to the test. ¹²And Abraham asked the Prince Michael, What is it we are looking at? ¹³And the Prince replied, What you are seeing, holy Abraham, is the judgement and retribution. ¹⁴And lo, the angel who held the soul in his hand (appeared), and he brought it before the judge. ¹⁵And the judge said to one of the angels that were waiting on him, Open this book for me and find me the sins of this soul. ¹⁶And when he had opened the book he found that its sins and its good deeds balanced evenly. ¹⁷So he neither gave it over to the torturers, nor (did he assign it a place among) those who were being saved, but set it in the middle.

¹⁸And Abraham said to Michael, Sir, is this the angel that takes souls out of their bodies, or is it not? ¹⁹Michael answered and said, This is Death; and he takes them away to the judgement-place for the judge to pass judgement on them. ²⁰And Abraham said, My Lord, I beg you to take me up to the

judgement-place, so that I can see for myself how they are judged. 21Then Michael took Abraham on a cloud and brought him to Paradise. 22And as he came near the place where the judge was, the angel appeared and presented a soul to the judge; and the soul was saying, Have mercy on me, lord. 23And the judge said, Why should I have mercy on you, when you yourself had no mercy on your daughter that you had, your own child? Why did you murder her? 24And (the soul) made answer, No lord! I am no murderer: my daughter has told lies about me. 25The judge then ordered the writer of the records to come. 26And lo, cherubim (came) carrying two books, and with them was a man of immense size. 27And he had on his head three crowns: one crown was higher than the other two; and they were called Crowns of Witness. 28In his hand the man had a pen of gold; and the judge said to him, Let us have the details of the sin of this soul. 29And the man opened one of the books belonging to the cherubim, and he searched for the sin of the woman's soul and found (it). 30And the judge said, Wretched soul! How (can) you say that you have done no murder? Did you not after your husband's death, go and commit adultery with your daughter's husband and kill your daughter? 31And he convicted her of other sins as well, all that she had committed since she was a child. 32When the woman heard this she cried out, saying, Alas! (While I was) in the world I forgot all the sins that I committed, but here they are not forgotten. 33Then they took her and handed her over to the torturers.

13. And Abraham said, My lord Prince, who is this wondrous judge, and who are these recording angels? 2And who is the angel like the sun, who holds the scales, and who is the fiery angel who holds the fire? 3And the Prince said, Most holy Abraham, do you see the terrifying man who is sitting on the throne? 4He is the son of the first man Adam, and is called Abel, and he was killed by the wicked Cain. 5He sits here to judge every creature, examining both righteous and sinners, because God has said, It is not I who judge you, but by man shall every man be judged. 6For this reason he has committed judgement to him, to judge the world until his (own) great and glorious Coming. 7And then, righteous Abraham, will follow the final judgement and retribution, eternal and unchangeable, which no one will be able to dispute. 8For all men have their origin from the first man; and so by his son they are first judged here. 9At the second coming they and every spirit and every creature will be judged by the twelve tribes of Israel. 10At the third stage they will be judged by the Sovereign God of all; and then at last will the whole process reach its end. 11The sentences will strike terror; and (there will be) no one to rescind (them). 12And so through three tribunals the judgement of the world will be accomplished and (its) retribution. 13And that is why a matter cannot finally be settled on the evidence of one or two witnesses but 'on the evidence of three witnesses every fact must be established'. 14The two angels, one on the right and one on the left, these record the sins and the good deeds. 15The one on the right records the good deeds, the one on the left the sins. 16The angel who is like the sun, who holds the scales in his hand, he is the archangel Dokiel: he preserves an honest balance and weighs the good deeds and the sins with the justice of God. 17The fiery and merciless angel, who holds the fire in his hand, he is the archangel Pyruel, who has power over fire, and he tests men's deeds by fire. 18If the fire burns up a man's deed, the angel of judgement takes him at once and carries him off to the sinners' place—a most disagreeable place of punishment. 19If the fire tests a man's deed and does not touch it, he is accounted righteous and the angel of righteousness takes him and carries him up to be saved among the number of the righteous. 20And so, most righteous Abraham, all things in all men are tested by fire and scales.

21This one, who presents the souls is the teacher of heaven and earth, the scribe of righteousness, Enoch. 22For the Lord sent them here that the sins and the good deeds of each might be recorded. 23And Abraham said, But how can Enoch take responsibility for the souls, since he has not (himself) experienced death? How can he pronounce sentence on all the souls? 24And Michael said, If he were to pronounce sentence on them, (his sentence) would not stand. It is not Enoch's function to sentence: it is the Lord who sentences; and (Enoch's) only function is to write. 25For Enoch prayed to the Lord, saying, Lord, I have no wish to sentence souls; in case I might be harsh to any of them. 26Then said the Lord to Enoch, I shall bid you write the sins of the soul that makes atonement, and it shall enter into life. 27But if a soul makes no atonement and does not repent, you will find its sins in writing, and (that soul) will be sent off to punishment.

14. And Abraham said to the Prince, My lord Prince, the soul that the angel was holding in his hand, how (is it that) it was condemned to (be set in) the middle? ²And the Prince said, Listen, righteous Abraham: (it was) because the judge found its sins and (its) good deeds equal. ³So he consigned it neither to judgement nor to salvation, until the Judge of all shall come. ⁴Abraham said to the Prince, What more does the soul require to be saved? ⁵The Prince answered, If it can come by one good deed more than its sins, it attains salvation. ⁶And Abraham said to the Prince, Come, Prince Michael and let us make intercession on this soul's behalf, and let us see whether God will hear us. ⁷And the Prince said, Amen: so let it be! ⁸And they made supplication and intercession on the soul's behalf, and God heard them; and when they got up from their prayer, they did not see the soul standing there. ⁹And Abraham said to the angel, Where is the soul you were keeping in the middle? ¹⁰And the angel said, It has been saved by your righteous intercession; and lo, the brilliant angel has taken it and carried it up into Paradise. ¹¹And Abraham said, I will glorify the name of God Most High and his mercy that is without measure. ¹²And Abraham said to the Prince, I beg you, archangel, grant me my request, and let us beseech the Lord once more and throw ourselves on his compassion. ¹³And let us entreat his mercy for the souls of the sinners I once cursed in malice and sent to their destruction—(those) that the earth swallowed up, and the wild beasts tore to pieces, and the fire consumed, because of what I said. ¹⁴Now I realize that I sinned before the Lord our God. ¹⁵Come, Michael, Prince of the powers on high: come, let us with tears beseech God to forgive me (my) sin and grant them to me. ¹⁶And the Prince listened to him, and they made supplication before God. ¹⁷When they had been praying for a long time, there came a voice from heaven, saying, Abraham, Abraham, I have heard your voice and your supplication; and I forgive you (your) sin. ¹⁸And those, whom you imagine I destroyed, I have recalled and in my mercy brought them (back) to life; because for a time I have requited them in judgement. ¹⁹But those whom I destroy while they are alive on earth, I will not requite in death.

15. The voice of the Lord said also to the Prince, Michael, Michael, my minister, return Abraham to his house. ²For lo, his end is near and the span of his life complete. ³He will thus be able to set everything in order; and after that, take him and bring him up to me. ⁴And the Prince turned the chariot and the cloud and brought Abraham to his house. ⁵And (Abraham) went into his dining-room and sat upon his couch.

⁶And Sarah his wife came and flung her arms round the spirit's feet, as if she were a suppliant, and said, I thank you, sir, for bringing back my lord Abraham; for lo, we thought he had been taken up from us. ⁷And his son Isaac also came and put his arms round his neck. ⁸And so too all his male and female slaves assembled about Abraham and embraced him, praising God. ⁹And the spirit said to him, Listen, righteous Abraham, behold, your wife Sarah; and behold, your beloved son Isaac; and behold, your men-servants and maid-servants all around you. ¹⁰Set everything you have in order, because the day is at hand when you are to leave (your) body and go once again to the Lord. ¹¹And Abraham said, Has the Lord said (this), or are you saying it yourself? ¹²And the Prince said, Listen, righteous Abraham: the Sovereign (Lord) has commanded (it), and I am telling you (so). ¹³And Abraham said, I will not follow you. ¹⁴And when the Prince heard that answer he left Abraham immediately and went up into the heavens and stood before God Most High. ¹⁵And he said, Lord Almighty, behold, I have listened to everything thy friend Abraham has said to thee, and I have granted his request. ¹⁶I have shown him (the extent of) thy dominion, and all the land and sea that is under heaven. ¹⁷Judgement and retribution have I shown him by means of cloud and chariot. ¹⁸And yet again he says, I will not follow you. ¹⁹And the Most High said to the angel, Does my friend Abraham really say again, I will not follow you? ²⁰And the archangel said, Lord Almighty, this is what he says. ²¹And I would not touch him because he has been thy friend from the beginning and has done everything that is pleasing in thy sight, and there is no man like him on earth, not even Job, that wondrous man; and that is why I would not touch him. ²²So may I have instructions, Immortal King, about what should now be done?

16. Then the Most High said, Call Death here to me—(the one) who is called The Shameless Face and the Pitiless Look. ²And Michael the spirit went away and said to Death, Come: the Sovereign of creation, the Immortal King is calling for you. ³When Death heard (this) he was much alarmed and shivered and shook; and he came with great trepidation and stood before the invisible Father, shivering, groaning, and trembling, as he awaited his Sovereign's bidding. ⁴And the invisible God said to Death, Come, you (most) bitter and savage name in (all) the world! ⁵Hide your ferocity, cover up your corruption, put off your asperity from you, and put on your beauty and all your glory, and go down to my friend Abraham. ⁶Take him and bring him to me. ⁷Yet I tell you now not to frighten him, but win him with gentle guile, for he is my own true friend. [8]Death listened and went out from the presence of the Most High; and he put on a most brilliant robe and made his face shine like the sun. [9]He appeared more handsome and beautiful than any human, having assumed an archangel's form, and his cheeks flashed with fire. [10]And so he went off to Abraham. [11]Now the righteous Abraham had left his room and was sitting under the trees of Mamre, his chin on his hand, waiting for the archangel Michael to come (back), when lo, there came in his direction a pleasant smell and a flashing light. [12]And Abraham turned round and saw Death coming towards him in great glory and beauty. [13]And Abraham got up to meet him, for he thought he was God's Prince. [14]And when Death saw him, he bowed to him and said, Greetings, honoured Abraham, righteous soul, true friend of God Most High, and companion of the holy angels. [15]And Abraham said to Death, Greetings to you. [16]You are like the sun, and you shine as does the sun: most glorious helper, brilliant, wondrous man! [17]Whence comes your Splendour to us? Who are you? And whence come you? [18]Death said, Most righteous Abraham, lo, I tell you the truth: I am the bitter cup of death. [19]Abraham said to him, No: you are the world's paragon of loveliness: you are the glory and the beauty of angels and of men: you are more nobly formed than any form there is; and (yet) you say you are the bitter cup of death. [20]Should you not rather say, I am more nobly formed than nobility itself? [21]And Death said, No: I am telling you the truth: (it is) that very name which God has given me that I am telling you. [22]And Abraham said, Why have you come here? [23]And Death said, I have come for your holy soul. [24]So Abraham said, I understand what you are saying; but I will not follow you. [25]And Death was silent and answered him not a word.

17. Then Abraham got up and went into his house. [2]But Death followed him all the way. [3]And Abraham went up to his room; but Death also went up with him. [4]And Abraham lay down on his couch; and Death came and sat at his feet. [5]And Abraham said, Go away, go away from me; for I want to rest on my couch. [6]Death said, I will not go away until I take your spirit from you. [7]Abraham said to him, By God, who is immortal, I bid you tell me the truth: are you Death? [8]Death said to him, I am Death: I am the one who destroys the world. [9]And Abraham said, Since you are Death, I pray you, tell me whether you come to all men in this way, in fine form and glory and beauty like this? [10]And Death said, No, my lord Abraham: your righteous deeds and the boundless ocean of your hospitality and the immensity of your love of God have become a crown upon my head. [11]I approach the righteous in beauty, and very quietly, and with gentle guile; but sinners I approach, stinking of corruption, with the greatest possible ferocity and asperity, and an expression that is both savage and without mercy. [12]And Abraham said, I pray you, listen to me, and show me your ferocity, and all (your) corruption and asperity. [13]And Death said, You could not see my ferocity, most righteous Abraham. [14]And Abraham said, Yes: I could scc all your ferocity, because of the name of the living God; for the power of my God who is in heaven is with me. [15]Then Death stripped himself of all his radiance and beauty, and all the glory and sun-like appearance he had assumed, and he put on a tyrant's robe. [16]And he gave himself a threatening look, more savage than any kind of wild beast and fouler than any foul thing known to man. [17]He displayed to Abraham seven fiery dragons' heads and fourteen faces of blazing fire and great ferocity—[18]one dark-looking face, one viper-like of the blackest kind, one a most horrible cliff, one fiercer than an asp, one of a fearsome lion, and one of a horned viper and a basilisk. [19]And he displayed also the face of a fiery sword, a face bearing a sword, a face of dreadful flashing lightning, and a sound of fearful thunder. [20]Moreover, he displayed another face of a ferocious raging sea, and a fiercely boiling river, and a terrifying three-headed dragon, and a cup of poisons mixed together. [21]In short, he displayed to him ferocity in plenty, asperity beyond endurance, and every kind of deadly disease—the smell of death hung about it all. [22]And so great was the asperity and ferocity displayed that (the) men-servants and maid-servants died, in number about seven thousand. [23]And even the righteous Abraham (himself) came to the brink of death, and his spirit failed him.

18. And when the all-holy Abraham had seen all this in this way, he said to Death, I beg you, all-destructive Death, hide your ferocity, and put on the beauty and the form you had before. [2]Thereupon Death hid his ferocity and put on his beauty he had had before. [3]And Abraham said to Death, Why have you done this? You have killed all my men-servants and maid-servants: did God send you here to-day for this? [4]And Death said, No, my lord Abraham, it is not as you suggest: it was because of you I was sent here. [5]And Abraham said to Death, And how then was it that these (servants) died, if the Lord had not given word? [6]And Death said, Believe (me), most righteous Abraham, the marvel is that you too were not taken off along with them. [7]I am only telling you the truth when I say that if the right hand of God had not been with you in that hour, you too would have had to depart this life. [8]And righteous Abraham said, I realize now that I have come to the brink of death, and my spirit fails me. [9]Nevertheless, I beg you, all-destructive Death, since my servants have died before their time, come, let us beseech the Lord our God to hear us and raise up those who perished before their time through your ferocity. [10]And Death said, Amen: so let it be! [11]So Abraham got up and fell upon his face on the earth in prayer, and Death with him; and God sent (the) spirit of life upon those who had died, and they were restored to life. [12]So then the righteous Abraham ascribed glory to God.

19. And (Abraham) went up to his room and lay down to rest; but Death came and stood before him. [2]And Abraham said to him, Go away from me: I want to rest; for I am exhausted. [3]And Death said, I will not leave you until I take your soul. [4]And Abraham, with a sullen face and angry look, said to Death, Who has ordered you to say this? [5]You are bluffing and saying this on your own; and I will not follow you until the Prince Michael comes to me, and (then) I will go with him. [6]And further, if you want me to follow you, explain to me all your changes of appearance—[7]the seven fiery dragons' heads, and what the face of the cliff (means), and the ruthless sword, and the great boiling river, and the turbid sea raging furiously. [8]Explain to me also the insufferable thunder and the terrifying lightning, and what the stinking cup of poisons mixed together (means): explain them all to me. [9]And Death said, Listen righteous Abraham, for seven ages I create havoc in the world and bring all (men) down to Hades: kings and rulers, rich and poor, slaves and free men, I escort to the depths of Hades; and that is why I showed you the seven dragons' heads. [10]The face of fire I showed you because many are burned to death by fire, and (so it is) through the face of fire (that) they see death. [11]The face of the cliff I showed you because many men fall from the top of trees or fearful cliffs and disappear and perish; and (so it is) in the form of a fearful cliff (that) they see death. [12]The face of the sword I showed you because many are killed by the sword in wars; and they see death in (the form of) a sword. [13]The face of the great boiling river I showed you because many are carried off by inundations and swept away by mighty rivers and die by drowning; and they see death before their time. [14]The face of the ferocious raging sea I showed you because many encounter violent storms at sea, are shipwrecked, and sink beneath the waves; and they see death as the sea. [15]The insufferable thunder and the fearful lightning I showed you because many men come to a time of wrath, with insufferable thunder and fearful lightning, and perish suddenly; [16]and that is the way they see death. I showed you also poisonous creatures, asps and basilisks, and leopards, and lions, and cubs, and bears, and vipers, and, in short, the face of every beast did I show you, most righteous one, because many men are killed by beasts, and others die after being bitten by poisonous snakes, [dragons, asps, horned vipers, basilisks], and the viper. [17]I showed you also deadly cups of poisons mixed together, because many men are given poisons to drink by other men and without (apparent) cause are carried off at once.

20. And Abraham said, Tell me, I pray you, is (the kind of) death (that comes to a man) incalculable? [2]Death said, I tell you truly, by God's truth, there are seventy-two deaths. [3]One (of these) is the righteous death which has its appointed hour; and many men arrive at death and burial within a single hour. [4]Lo, I have told you everything you asked. [5]Now I tell you, most righteous Abraham, have done with all this discussing, and once and for all stop questioning me. [6]Come, follow me, even as God, the Judge of all has directed me. [7]But Abraham said to Death, Leave me yet a little longer to rest on my couch, for I am very feeble. [8]From the moment I set eyes upon you my strength failed: all my limbs seem like lumps of lead; and I am very short of breath. [9]Go away for a little while, for I must confess I cannot bear the sight of you. [10]And his son Isaac came and fell upon his breast, weeping. [11]And his wife Sarah came too, and she flung her arms round his feet, wailing bitterly. [12]And all his male and female slaves came as well, and they gathered round his couch; and Abraham came to the brink of death. [13]And Death said to Abraham, Come, kiss my right hand; and may joy and life and power come to you—for Death was deceiving Abraham. [14]And (Abraham) kissed his hand, and immediately his soul stuck fast to Death's hand. [15]And at once the archangel Michael was at his side, with a host of angels, and they took his precious soul in their hands, in a sheet divinely woven. [16]And with divinely-scented myrrh and spices they tended righteous Abraham's body until the third day after his death; and they buried him in the land of promise, at the oak of Mamre. [17]And the angels escorted his precious soul and went up into heaven, chanting the Trisagion hymn to God, the Sovereign of all; and they placed it where it could worship God the Father. [18]And when the great hymn of praise and doxology to the Lord was ended, and when Abraham had worshipped, there came the clear voice of God the Father, saying, Take my friend Abraham to Paradise, where are the tents of my righteous ones and the resting-places of my saints{, Isaac and Jacob in his bosom}. [19]There is no toil there, no grief, no sighing, but peace and rejoicing and endless life.

CHAPTER THREE

RELATED WORKS

THE TESTAMENT OF MOSES

Commentary

The *Testament of Moses* is not an apocalypse; it belongs to a related genre of literature labeled testaments. A testament is a farewell speech of an aged or dying person in which instructions, advice, and often predictions of the future are given. Both apocalypses and testaments are often pseudonymous. In testaments, however, the fictional author (in this case Moses) is the giver of a revelation, whereas in apocalypses the fictional author is the recipient of a revelation that is often mediated by an otherworldly being.

The *Testament of Moses* is preserved today in only one manuscript, an incomplete Latin text published in 1861 by Antonio Ceriani. The first three lines of text are missing, and the end of the work stops abruptly in mid-sentence. The Latin text was translated from Greek, but the original language of the work was probably Hebrew or Aramaic.

In the Latin manuscript, this work is untitled. Ceriani labeled it the *Assumption of Moses* based on a quotation of verse 14 of chapter 1 by Gelasius of Cyzicus, a fifth-century church historian who attributed the quoted words to a work called the *Assumption of Moses*. Two other quotations that Gelasius attributed to the *Assumption of Moses,* both dealing with a dispute between the archangel Michael and the devil, are not found in the existing text. (Verse 9 of the book of Jude in the New Testament mentions a dispute between Michael and the devil over the body of Moses, but does not attribute the incident to any source.) Other early church writers also mention a document known as the *Assumption of Moses*, and ancient lists of apocryphal books mention an Assumption of Moses as well as a separate work called the *Testament of Moses*.

Since the preserved text contains neither the story of Moses' death or assumption nor the disputes between the devil and Michael, which Gelasius cited from the *Assumption of Moses*, most modern scholars consider the present work to be the *Testament of Moses* mentioned by ancient writers. Whether Gelasius's attribution of 1:14 to the *Assumption of Moses* was due to confusion on his part or whether the two works, the *Testament* and the *Assumption*, were combined at an early date is unknown.

Historical references in the text are used to date the composition of the work. By means of *ex eventu* prophecies, an overview of Israel's history is presented, beginning with the possession of the land of Canaan in chapter 2 and ending in chapters 8 and 9 with the period of Antiochus Epiphanes (ca. 167 B.C.E.). A chronological problem arises, however, with chapters 6 and 7, which are out of place. In chapter 6 the "insolent king" who will rule for thirty-four years is clearly a reference to Herod the Great, who ruled from 37 to 4 B.C.E.; and the "powerful king of the west" who will conquer the Jews and burn a part of the Temple is a reference to Varus, governor of Syria, who squelched a Jewish uprising in 4 B.C.E. Both of these events should be placed after chapter 9 since they occurred after the period of Antiochus Epiphanes, described in chapters 8 and 9.

The best solution to this problem is to see chapters 6 and 7 as a later interpolation into the work. Chapters 1–5 and 8–12 represent basically the original form of the work, composed during the time of the persecution of the Jews by Antiochus Epiphanes around 167 B.C.E. The story of Taxo in chapter 9 has much in common with the stories of the Jewish martyrs during the time of Antiochus Epiphanes, contained in 1 and 2 Maccabees. The purpose of the original form of the *Testament of Moses* was to provide hope and assurance to the faithful who were facing persecution and death during the fourth decade of the second century B.C.E. The earliest version of this work would have been contemporaneous with the book of Daniel, a response to the same historical crisis.

Later, during the time of the sons of Herod, the work was updated by the insertion of chapters 6 and 7. No exact date can be established for the revised version of the work. Nevertheless, the date for this revision could not be later than 30 C.E. due to its prediction that Herod's sons would rule for shorter periods than he did (6:7). Herod's reign lasted thirty-four years. At his death in 4 B.C.E. his sons took over. By 30 B.C.E., both Philip and Herod Antipas had ruled for thirty-four years. If chapter 6 had been written after 30 C.E., the prediction about Herod's sons would already have been false.

The updated version of the *Testament of Moses* served a purpose similar to that of the initial version: to encourage and exhort the faithful in a time of crisis. The new crisis that the revision addressed was the unrest and turmoil in the years following the death of Herod.

In both the original and the revised versions of the *Testament of Moses*, the message to the faithful is the same: they are to rely on God for help, because at the right time God will intervene to destroy the wicked and exalt the righteous, who will go to dwell with God. There is no call for armed resistance; rather, the faithful are to remain obedient to God at all costs. The heroic Taxo tells his sons: "Let us die rather than transgress the commandments of the Lord of lords, the God of our fathers. For if we do this and die, our blood will be avenged before the Lord" (9:6-7).

The framework for the *Testament of Moses* is Deuteronomy 31–34, Moses' farewell address to the people of Israel. Although most of the Deuteronomy speech is directed to all the people, the speech in the *Testament of Moses* is given to Joshua alone. At the end of this work, Joshua complains to Moses that after Moses dies the people of Israel will have no one to intercede with God on their behalf and that he is not capable of leading them as Moses did. In a highly deterministic message, similar to that of most apocalypses, Moses assures Joshua that everything that has happened and will happen has already been foreseen by God and will be brought about by God. The people need only to keep God's commandments, and God will bless them.

Although the *Testament of Moses* is not an apocalypse, it does contain apocalyptic eschatology: the final days will be filled with cosmic catastrophes (10:4-6); the devil will meet his end (10:1); the enemies of God will be punished (10:2, 7-8); and the righteous will be rewarded with a heavenly home where they will rejoice (10:9-10).

The translation used here is a revision of the translation of R. H. Charles, made by J. P. M. Sweet in *The Apocryphal Old Testament*.

216

The Testament of Moses

1. [The Testament of Moses—the instructions he gave in the one hundred and twentieth year of his life,] [2]that is the two thousand five hundredth year from the creation of the world— [3]or according to oriental reckoning [the two thousand seven hundredth—and the four hundredth] after the departure from Phoenicia, [4]when the people had gone out after the Exodus, under the leadership of Moses, to Amman beyond the Jordan {, [5]in the prophecy that was made by Moses in the book Deuteronomy}. [6]Moses called to him Joshua the son of Nun, a man approved by the Lord [7]to be the minister of the people and of the Tabernacle of the Testimony with all its holy things, [8]and to bring the people into the land given ⟨to their fathers⟩, [9]so that it might be given them in accordance with the covenant and the oath, (by) which he had declared in the Tabernacle that he would give (it them) by Joshua. [10]And Moses said to Joshua, Promise to do with all diligence everything you have been commanded, so that ⟨you may be⟩ blameless ⟨before⟩ God. [11]So says the Lord of the world. [12]For he created the world for his people's sake. [13]But he did not reveal this purpose in creation at the world's foundation, so that the Gentiles might thereby be convicted, and might by their arguments with one another, to their own humiliation, convict themselves. [14]Accordingly, he chose and appointed me, and prepared me from the foundation of the world, to be the mediator of his covenant. [15]And ⟨now⟩ I warn you that my span of life is near its end and that I am about to pass on to sleep with my fathers, even in the presence of all the people. [16]So study this writing carefully, so that you may know how to preserve the books that I entrust you with. [17]Set them in order and anoint them with cedar-oil and store them away in jars of earthenware in the place the Lord intended from the beginning of the creation of the world (as the place where) [18]men should invoke his name till the Day of Repentance, when he will look on them with favour at the final consummation.

2. [And now] under your leadership they shall enter the land which he determined to give (them) and promised to their fathers. [2]You shall bless (them) and give to each one of them (a portion) in it, and confirm their inheritance ⟨in it⟩, and establish for them a kingdom; and you shall ⟨appoint⟩ local magistrates for them, in accordance with their Lord's design, in justice and in righteousness. . . . [3]But after they enter their land . . . years; and afterwards they shall be ruled by chiefs and kings for eighteen years, and (for) nineteen years. . . . [4]For two tribes will go

217

down and transfer the ⟨Tabernacle of the Testimony⟩. 5Then the God of heaven ⟨will⟩ make (there) the court of his tabernacle and the ⟨tower⟩ of his sanctuary, and the two holy tribes shall be established (there)—but the ten tribes will establish kingdoms for themselves according to their own arrangements. 6And they will offer sacrifices for twenty years. 7And seven will surround (the place) with walls, and I will protect nine, and [four] shall ⟨transgress⟩ the Lord's covenant and profane the ⟨oath⟩ the Lord made with them. 8And they will sacrifice their sons to foreign gods, and they will set up idols in the sanctuary and serve them. 9And in the Lord's house they will commit all kinds of abominations and carve (representations of) every kind of animal (all round the walls).

3. [And] in those days a king from the east will come against them and his cavalry will cover their land. 2And he will burn their city with fire, together with the Lord's holy temple, and he will carry off all the holy vessels. 3And he will drive out the whole population and take them to his own country; and the two tribes he will take along with him. 4Then will the two tribes call ⟨indignantly⟩ on the ten tribes, like a lioness on the dusty plains, hungry and thirsty. 5And they will cry out aloud, Righteous and holy is the Lord, for because you have sinned, we too, in just the same way, have been carried ⟨off⟩ with you, together with our children. 6Then the ten tribes will mourn, when they hear the reproaches of the two tribes, 7and they will say, What can we do for you, brothers: has not this misery come to all the house of Israel? 8And all the tribes will mourn and cry to heaven saying, 9God of Abraham, and God of Isaac, and God of Jacob, remember thy covenant which thou didst make with them, and the oath which thou didst swear to them by thyself, that they should never lack descendants in the land which thou didst give them. 10Then will they remember me in that day, tribe saying to tribe, and (one) man (saying) to another, 11Is not this what Moses said would happen to us in his prophecies—(Moses) who suffered much in Egypt and in the Red Sea and in the wilderness for forty years? 12He warned us—and summoned heaven and earth to witness against us—not to transgress God's commandments, of which he was (himself) the mediator to us. 13These things have happened to us after his death, just as he said they would and as he warned us at the time; and his prophecies have been fulfilled, even to our being carried off as captives into eastern lands. 14And they will be kept in slavery for some seventy-seven years.

4. Then one of those (set) over them will go into (his house) and spread out his hands and fall on his knees and pray for them, saying, [2]Lord of all, king (who sittest) on the lofty throne, who rulest the world, and dost will that this people should be thy chosen people: then didst thou will that thou shouldest be called their God, according to the covenant thou didst make with their fathers. [3]And they have gone as captives into another land with their wives and their children, and (they are living) among foreign peoples and where there is much ⟨idolatry⟩. [4]Look upon (them) and have pity on them, O Lord of heaven. [5]Then will God remember them because of the covenant that he made with their fathers, and he will show his pity at that time also. [6]And he will put it into the mind of a king to pity them; and he will send them back to their (own) land and country. [7]Then some from the tribes will go up and come to their appointed place and once again surround the place (with walls). [8]And the two tribes will continue in the faith appointed for them, in sadness and lamentation because they will be unable to offer sacrifices to the Lord of their fathers. [9]And the ten tribes will be fruitful and ⟨increase⟩ among the ⟨Gentiles⟩ during the time of their ⟨captivity⟩.

5. And when the day of reckoning draws near and retribution comes through kings who share their guilt and punish them, [2]they themselves also will be divided as to truth—[3]hence ⟨the sayings⟩, They will abandon righteousness and turn to iniquity, and, They will defile with (their) ⟨pollutions⟩ the house of their worship, and, They will turn wantonly to foreign gods. [4]For they will not follow the truth of God; but some (of them) will pollute the altar with the [very] gifts they offer to the Lord, who are not priests but slaves (and) sons of slaves. [5]And those who are (their) masters, (that is) their teachers at that time, will show favour to ⟨the rich⟩ and ⟨take⟩ bribes and sell judgements in return for ⟨presents⟩. [6]And so (their) city and their whole land will be filled with acts of lawlessness and deeds of evil; and their judges will be ungodly men, ⟨men have turned their backs⟩ on the Lord, and are ready to give judgements ⟨for money⟩ as each man wants.

6. Then shall arise kings to rule over them, and they shall be called priests of the Most High God—they will be responsible for much ungodliness in the holy of holies. [2]And an insolent king will succeed them, who will not be of priestly stock, an arrogant and a shameless man; and he will judge them as they deserve. [3]And he will put their leaders to death with the sword, and ⟨bury⟩ them secretly so that no one should know where their bodies are. [4]He will kill (both) old and young and spare no (one). [5]He will be the object of universal dread and detestation. [6]And he will treat them ruthlessly, as the Egyptians treated them, for thirty-four years, and make their lives unbearable. [7]And he will produce children, who will succeed him and ⟨rule⟩ for shorter periods. [8]Into their ⟨parts⟩ will come ⟨the cohorts⟩ and a powerful king of the west, ⟨who⟩ will conquer them, [9]and take them captive, and burn a part of their temple with fire, (and) crucify some (of them) round their city.

7. And after this the times shall come to an end, ⟨in a moment⟩ the . . . course shall [come to an end]: the four hours shall come. [2]They will be forced . . . [3]And in their time pestilential and impious men will bear rule, alleging that they are righteous. [4]And these will stir up their minds to anger, for they will be crafty men, self-indulgent, hypocritical, ready for a party at any hour of the day, gluttons, guzzlers, [5]. . . , [6]who devour the goods of the [poor] on the pretext of ⟨justice, [7]but⟩ (in reality) ⟨to destroy them⟩, grumblers, deceitful (people) who hide themselves away in case they should be recognized, impious, full of (every) vice and villany, who say from sunrise to sunset, [8]Let us have feasts and revels, eating and drinking; and let us behave like princes. [9]And although their hands and minds are occupied with things unclean, they will make a fine show in words, even saying, [10]Do not touch [me], lest you pollute me in the place where. . . .

8. . . . And there shall come upon them [a second] retribution and wrath, such as has not befallen them from the beginning until that time, when he will stir up against them the king of the kings of the earth, ⟨a man who rules⟩ with great power, who will crucify those who confess their circumcision. [2]And those who ⟨deny⟩ (it) he will torture and put in chains and imprison. [3]And their wives will be given to the gods among the Gentiles, and their young sons will be operated on by the doctors ⟨to look as though they had not been circumcised⟩. [4]And others among them will suffer punishment by torture and fire and sword; and they will be forced to carry round their idols publicly, polluted things, just like (the shrines) that house them. [5]And in the same way they will be forced by those who torture them to enter their inmost sanctuary and forced with goads to blaspheme and insult ⟨the Name⟩, and, as if that were not enough, the laws as well by having ⟨a pig⟩ upon the altar.

9. Then in that ⟨day there will be⟩ a man of the tribe of Levi, whose name will be Taxo, and he will have seven sons. [2]And he will ask them, saying, See, (my) sons, a second cruel and unclean retribution has come upon the people and a punishment without mercy and ⟨far worse than⟩ the first. ³For what nation or what region or what people among those who do not worship ⟨the Lord⟩, who have done many atrocious things, have suffered as great calamities as have befallen us? ⁴So now, (my) sons, listen to me: you know well enough that neither the fathers nor their forefathers provoked God by transgressing his commandments. ⁵For you know that our strength lies here, and let us act accordingly. ⁶Let us fast for three days; and on the fourth day let us go out to a cave in the country, and let us die rather than transgress the commandments of the Lord of lords, the God of our fathers. ⁷For if we do this and die, our blood will be avenged before the Lord.

10. And then shall his kingdom appear throughout all his creation;
   And then shall the Devil meet his end,
   And sorrow shall depart with him.
² Then shall be consecrated the angel who has been appointed chief,
   Who will immediately avenge them of their enemies.
³ For the Heavenly One will [arise] from his royal throne,
   And go forth from his holy dwelling-place
   With wrath and anger because of his sons.
⁴ And the earth will tremble:
   It will be shaken to its farthest bounds;
   And high mountains will collapse
   And ⟨hills⟩ be shaken and fall.
⁵ And the sun will not give (its) light;
   And the horns of the moon will be turned into darkness,
   And they will be broken,
   And it will be turned wholly into blood;
   And the orbit of the stars will be disturbed.
⁶ And the sea will retire into the abyss,
   ⟨And⟩ the fountains of waters will fail,
   And the rivers ⟨dry up⟩.
⁷ For the Most High will arise, the Eternal God alone,
   And he will appear to punish the Gentiles,
   And he will destroy all their idols.
⁸ Then happy will you be, Israel;
   And you will trample upon (their) necks {and the wings of an
      eagle},
   For the time allotted them will have run its course.

⁹ And God will exalt you,
   And set you in heaven above the stars,
   In the place where ⟨he⟩ dwells ⟨himself⟩.
¹⁰ And you ⟨will look⟩ from on high and see your enemies on earth,
   And you will recognize them and rejoice,
   And give thanks and confess your Creator.

¹¹And as for you, Joshua, (son of) Nun, take heed of what is written in this book. ¹²For from (my) death{, (that is my) assumption,} until his advent there shall be two hundred and fifty times. ¹³And this is the course of these [times], which they will pursue until they are complete. ¹⁴But I am about to depart to sleep with my fathers. ¹⁵So then, Joshua, (son of) Nun, ⟨Be strong⟩: God has chosen you to be the minister in my place of the same covenant.

11. And when Joshua had heard what Moses had written in his writing and all he had foretold, he rent his clothes and threw himself at the feet of Moses. ²And Moses comforted him and wept with him. ³And Joshua answered him and said, ⁴What kind of ⟨consolation⟩ is it that you give me, (my) lord Moses, and how can I be ⟨consoled⟩ when ⟨you⟩ tell me something so distressing? When you say that you are about to leave this people, tears and laments are bound to be. ⁵[But now], where will you be buried? ⁶Or what shall be the sign that marks (your) burial place? ⁷Or who shall dare to move your body ⟨from it⟩ as (if it were that of an ordinary) man from place to place? ⁸For all men when they die have their burial-places corresponding to the age (in which they live) on earth, but your burial-place is from the rising to the setting sun, and from the south to the confines of the north: the whole world is your burial-place. ⁹(My) lord, ⟨you are about to go away⟩; and who shall feed this people? ¹⁰Or who is there to pity them, and who shall guide them on the way? ¹¹Or who shall pray for them day by day, so that I may be able to lead them into the land of (their) ⟨forefathers⟩? ¹²How, then, am I to ⟨look after⟩ this people as a father (looks after his) only son, or as a mother (her) virgin daughter, who is being brought up ⟨to be given⟩ the husband she will revere—(for the mother) will shield her body from the sun and (take care) she does not run about without her shoes? ¹³[And how] shall I supply them with food and drink according to their needs? ¹⁴For they number some ⟨six⟩ hundred thousand [men], and they have become so many through your prayers, lord Moses. ¹⁵And what wisdom or understanding have I that I should either give judgement or answer by word in the house [of the Lord]? [16]And the kings of the Amorites also, when they hear we are attacking (them, and) believing that there is no longer ⟨among them⟩ (that) sacred spirit worthy of the Lord, made up of many parts and beyond all understanding, the lord of the word, faithful in all things, the divine prophet throughout the earth, the most perfect teacher in the world—(believing) that he is no longer among them, ⟨they will⟩ say, Let us go against them. [17]If only once (our) enemies have done what is wrong against the Lord, they have no advocate to offer prayers for them to the Lord, as did Moses the great messenger, who hour by hour, day and night, prayed without ceasing (for them), looking to him who rules the ⟨whole⟩ world with mercy and justice, (and) reminding (him) of the covenant (made with their) fathers and propitiating the Lord with an oath. [18]For they will say, He is not with them: so let us go and wipe them off the face of the earth. [19]What then shall become of this people, (my) lord Moses?

12. And when Joshua had finished speaking, he threw himself to the ground again at the feet of Moses. [2]And Moses took his hand and lifted him up into the seat in front of him. [3]And he answered and said to him, Joshua, do not belittle ⟨yourself⟩, but take courage and listen to me, [4]God has created all the nations on the earth, and (he has created) us: he has foreseen (what will happen to both) them and us from the beginning of the creation of the earth to the end of the age; and nothing has been overlooked by him, not even the smallest detail, but he has foreseen everything and ⟨brought everything about⟩. [5][And] everything that is to be on this earth the Lord has foreseen, and lo, it is ⟨brought⟩ [into the light. . . . [6]The Lord] has appointed me [to pray] for them and for their sins and [to make intercession] for them. [7]For it was not because of any virtue or ⟨steadfastness⟩ on my part, but because he willed it so, that his pity and patience took hold of me. [8]And I tell you, Joshua, it is not because of this people's godliness that you are to destroy the nations. [9]All the pillars of the heaven (and) the earth have been made ⟨and⟩ approved by God and are under ⟨the signet ring⟩ of his right hand. [10]Thus, those who keep and observe ⟨God's⟩ commandments will increase and prosper. [11]But those who sin and ignore the commandments will be denied the blessings that have been mentioned, and they will be punished with many torments by the nations. [12]Yet it is impossible that he should wholly destroy them and forsake them. [13]For God has gone forth, he who has foreseen everything to the end, and his covenant has been established; and by the oath which . . . *(the manuscript breaks off in mid-sentence.)*

THE COMMUNITY RULE (1QS) 3–4

Commentary

Since the initial discovery in 1947 of some Jewish writings in the caves around Qumran, at the northwestern end of the Dead Sea, several hundred manuscripts have been found in the area. These manuscripts, referred to as the Dead Sea Scrolls, belonged to the Jewish community that lived near the Dead Sea from the mid-second century B.C.E. to 68 C.E., when the community was destroyed by the Romans. The community was formed when a group of Jewish people, disturbed about the current Jewish High Priest and certain practices in Jerusalem, moved to Qumran to practice what they considered to be the pure form of Judaism. The leader of these people, usually considered to have been Essenes, was an individual known as the Teacher of Righteousness.

The Dead Sea Scrolls contained almost all the writings now in the Hebrew Bible as well as other Jewish religious literature and works produced by the Qumran community itself. The last category would include biblical commentaries, hymns, and rules for the organization and operation of the group. The group at Qumran is often described as an apocalyptic community because apocalyptic ideas are part of several of the Qumran writings. Although all the manuscripts discovered around the Dead Sea have not been published, no complete apocalypse has yet been found. Three examples are included here of writings from Qumran that contain apocalyptic elements.

The *Community Rule* (also known as the *Manual of Discipline*) is a collection of rules and ordinances for the regulation of the community life of the people at Qumran. The topics that are covered in the document include entrance into the community, the stages of initiation, the organization of the community, rules for individual behavior, punishments for various violations, instructions for the Master of the community, and a closing thanksgiving hymn. These regulations were to remain in effect "until there shall come the Prophet and the Messiahs of Aaron and Israel" (9:11). (This expectation of the coming of an eschatological prophet and two messiahs is contained in other Qumran writings and in other Jewish apocalyptic works.)

Columns 3 and 4 of the *Community Rule* include a section sometimes referred to as the "Instruction on the Two Spirits." This section, 3:13–4:26, contains two elements that are important components of apocalyptic thought: a dualistic understanding of the universe and a predestined view of history. Two spirits are said to exist in the world, the spirit of light or truth and the spirit of darkness or falsehood. A great struggle rages between these two spirits, both in the world at large and within the hearts of individuals, because God "has set everlasting hatred between their divisions" (4:17). This cosmic conflict between good and evil is reflected in the moral struggles that each person encounters. Individual ethical dilemmas are not trivial matters, but are part of the grand cosmic struggle between good and evil. This understanding of moral struggle heightens the human predicament and places it in a larger perspective.

The leader of the forces of light and truth is the Angel of Truth (or Prince of Light). The leader of the forces of evil is the Angel of Darkness. Those who walk in the way of light are helped in their struggle by the Angel of Truth. The ones who walk in darkness are led astray by the Angel of Darkness.

The struggle between the two spirits will not last forever. God has predetermined the outcome of the struggle and "has ordained an end for falsehood, and at the time of the visitation He will destroy it for ever" (4:18-19). At the eschatological visitation of God upon the earth, the righteous will be rewarded with "healing, great peace in a long life, and fruitfulness, together with every everlasting blessing and eternal joy in life without end, a crown of glory and a garment of majesty in unending light" (4:7-8). On this day of judgment the righteous will be purified by the "spirit of holiness" (4:21). The wicked, on the other hand, will experience "a multitude of plagues by the hand of all the destroying angels, everlasting damnation by the avenging wrath of the fury of God, eternal torment and endless disgrace together with shameful extinction in the fire of the dark regions" (4:12-13).

The dualistic thought of the *Community Rule* has close affinities with ideas in the New Testament, especially in Johannine and Pauline literature. In the Gospel of John and the Johannine letters, the dualities of light/darkness and truth/falsehood (John 1:4-9; 1 John 4:1-6) are reminiscent of similar concepts in the Qumran literature. The promise in the Gospel of John of the Spirit of truth or Counselor who will come to guide and support the believers (14:16-17; 15:26; 16:7-14) is similar to the description of the Angel of Truth in the *Community Rule*, who will aid all the "Sons of Light" (3:25). Paul's contrast in 2 Corinthians 6:14-15 between light and darkness and between Christ and Beliar (another name for Satan) is very close to the dualistic ideas of Qumran.

The *Community Rule* is considered to be one of the oldest writings of

225

the Qumran community, dating perhaps from the latter part of the second century B.C.E. Like many of the other Qumran texts, the *Community Rule* underwent several revisions during its use at Qumran. The best preserved manuscript of the *Community Rule* is designated as 1QS. Eleven other manuscripts of the *Community Rule* have also been found.

The selection given here from the *Community Rule* is the "Instruction on the Two Spirits" (3:13–4:26). The translation of the text is by Geza Vermes from *The Dead Sea Scrolls in English*. The numbers in the text indicate column and line locations in 1QS. Line numbers (according to the divisions indicated in *The Essene Writings from Qumran* by A. Dupont-Sommer) have been added to the translation made by Vermes.

The Community Rule (1QS) 3–4

3. [13]The Master shall instruct all the sons of light and shall teach them the nature of all the children of men [14]according to the kind of spirit which they possess, the signs identifying their works during their lifetime, their visitation for chastisement, and [15]the time of their reward.

From the God of Knowledge comes all that is and shall be. Before ever they existed He established their whole design, [16]and when, as ordained for them, they come into being, it is in accord with His glorious design that they accomplish their task without change. [17]The laws of all things are in His hand and He provides them with all their needs.

He has created man to govern [18]the world, and has appointed for him two spirits in which to walk until the time of His visitation: the spirits [19]of truth and falsehood. Those born of truth spring from a fountain of light, but those born of falsehood spring from a source of darkness. [20]All the children of righteousness are ruled by the Prince of Light and walk in the ways of light, but all the children of falsehood are ruled by the Angel of [21]Darkness and walk in the ways of darkness.

The Angel of Darkness [22]leads all the children of righteousness astray, and until his end, all their sin, iniquities, wickedness, and all their unlawful deeds are caused by his dominion [23]in accordance with the mysteries of God. Every one of their chastisements, and every one of the seasons of their distress, shall be brought about by the rule of his persecution; [24]for all his allotted spirits seek the overthrow of the sons of light.

But the God of Israel and His Angel of Truth will succour all [25]the sons of light. For it is He who created the spirits of Light and Darkness and founded every action ²⁶upon them and established every deed [upon] their [ways]. And He loves the one **4.** everlastingly and delights in its works for ever; but the counsel of the other He loathes and for ever hates its ways.

²These are their ways in the world for the enlightenment of the heart of man, and that all the paths of true righteousness may be made straight before him, and that the fear of the laws of God may be instilled in his heart: ³a spirit of humility, patience, abundant charity, unending goodness, understanding, and intelligence; (a spirit of) mighty wisdom which trusts in all ⁴the deeds of God and leans on His great lovingkindness; a spirit of discernment in every purpose, of zeal for just laws, of holy intent ⁵with steadfastness of heart, of great charity towards all the sons of truth, of admirable purity which detests all unclean idols, of humble conduct ⁶sprung from an understanding of all things, and of faithful concealment of the mysteries of truth. These are the counsels of the spirit to the sons of truth in this world.

And as for the visitation of all who walk in this spirit, it shall be healing, ⁷great peace in a long life, and fruitfulness, together with every everlasting blessing and eternal joy in life without end, a crown of glory ⁸and a garment of majesty in unending light.

⁹But the ways of the spirit of falsehood are these: greed, and slackness in the search for righteousness, wickedness and lies, haughtiness and pride, falseness and deceit, cruelty ¹⁰and abundant evil, ill-temper and much folly and brazen insolence, abominable deeds (committed) in a spirit of lust, and ways of lewdness in the service of uncleanness, ¹¹a blaspheming tongue, blindness of eye and dullness of ear, stiffness of neck and heaviness of heart, so that man walks in all the ways of darkness and guile.

And the visitation ¹²of all who walk in this spirit shall be a multitude of plagues by the hand of all the destroying angels, everlasting damnation by the avenging wrath of the fury of God, eternal torment and endless disgrace ¹³together with shameful extinction in the fire of the dark regions. The times of all their generations shall be spent in sorrowful mourning and in bitter misery and in calamities of darkness until ¹⁴they are destroyed without remnant or survivor.

¹⁵The nature of all the children of the men is ruled by these (two spirits), and during their life all the hosts of men have a portion of their divisions and walk in (both) their ways. And the whole reward ¹⁶for their deeds shall be, for everlasting ages, according to whether each man's portion in their two divisions is great or small. For God has established

the spirits in equal measure until the [17]final age, and has set everlasting hatred between their divisions. Truth abhors the works of falsehood, and falsehood hates all the ways of truth. And their struggle [18]is fierce in all their arguments for they do not walk together.

But in the mysteries of His understanding, and in His glorious wisdom, God has ordained an end for falsehood, and at the time [19]of the visitation He will destroy it for ever. Then truth, which has wallowed in the ways of wickedness during the dominion of falsehood until [20]the appointed time of judgement, shall arise in the world for ever. God will then purify every deed of man with his truth; He will refine for Himself the human frame by rooting out all spirit of falsehood from [21]the bounds of his flesh. He will cleanse him of all wicked deeds with the spirit of holiness; like purifying waters He will shed upon him the spirit of truth (to cleanse him) of all abomination and falsehood. [22]And he shall be plunged into the spirit of purification that he may instruct the upright in the knowledge of the Most High and teach the wisdom of the sons of heaven to the perfect of way. For God has chosen them for an everlasting Covenant [23]and all the glory of Adam shall be theirs. There shall be no more lies and all the works of falsehood shall be put to shame.

Until now the spirits of truth and falsehood struggle in the hearts of men [24]and they walk in both wisdom and folly. According to his portion of truth so does a man hate falsehood, and according to his inheritance in the realm of falsehood so is he wicked and so [25]hates truth. For God has established the two spirits in equal measure until the determined end, and until the Renewal, and He knows the reward of their deeds from all [26]eternity. He has allotted them to the children of men that they may know good [and evil, and] that the destiny of all the living may be according to the spirit within [them at the time] of the visitation.

THE WAR SCROLL (1QM) 1, 15–19

Commentary

The *War Scroll* (also known as the *War Rule* or the *War of the Sons of Light Against the Sons of Darkness*) describes the final eschatological battle between the Sons of Light and the Sons of Darkness. The Sons of Light, described in the text as "the sons of Levi, Judah, and Benjamin, the exiles in the desert" (1:2), are the faithful Israelites, primarily the members of the Qumran community. They will be joined in the battle by a host of angels and will be led by the archangel Michael. The Sons of Darkness, on the other hand, are described as the army of Belial (or Satan, according to the translation given below), composed of the traditional enemies of the Israelite people (the Edomites, Moabites, Ammonites, Philistines, the "sons of the East," and the "Kittim of Assyria") along with "the ungodly of the Covenant," the unfaithful Jews (1:1-2). They are assisted in the struggle by the angels of Belial. (Compare the conflict between the Prince of Light and the Angel of Darkness, which are variant titles for Michael and Belial, in the *Community Rule* 3–4.)

The first column of the *War Scroll* describes the battle that will take place and how God will triumph over Belial and his forces. Columns 2-9 contain various regulations and descriptions: arrangements for Temple worship; a description of a forty-year war against various nations; rules and inscriptions for battle trumpets and standards; descriptions of weapons and battle formations; purity regulations for the army; and directives for the priests and Levites who will be leaders in the final war. Columns 10-14 are a collection of various prayers and hymns related to the struggle, including a hymn of thanksgiving that the victorious Sons of Light shall sing.

The material in columns 15-19 is a further description of the eschatological battle, similar to the material contained in column 1. In both descriptions of this battle, the major earthly enemy of the Sons of Light is the "Kittim," widely understood by scholars as a reference to the Romans. (The name *Kittim* is derived from Citium, an ancient city-state on the island of Cyprus. The word came to be used by people in Palestine generally for any peoples or lands beyond the seas.) The author of Daniel used the term *Kittim* in a similar way, telling of the "ships of Kittim," meaning Roman forces, which would confront Antiochus Epiphanes in Egypt (11:30). In the *War Scroll*, however, the Kittim, while

229

including the Romans who had subjugated Palestine, has a wider referent. It seems to function as a term inclusive of all the powers that will be aligned against the Jews in the last days.

The apocalyptic nature of this final battle is seen in the supernatural dimension of the struggle. On the one hand, the enemies of the Sons of Light are definitely human enemies—the Romans, other nations, and apostate Jews. On the other hand, their enemies also include the "angels of Belial" and the "wicked spirits." Furthermore, the Sons of Light are aided by an army of angels. This is not simply an earthly struggle in which they are engaged, but it is a cosmic struggle—good versus evil, light versus darkness, God versus Satan.

The description of Michael as the leader of the Sons of Light at war against Belial (the leader of the Sons of Darkness) is similar to the description in Daniel 10–12 of the eschatological battle in which Michael serves as the patron angel of Israel, fighting against the patron angels of Persia and Greece. In Daniel and in the *War Scroll,* the earthly conflict is only part of a larger cosmic conflict. In fact, the outcome of the struggle does not depend on human might, for God through Michael and the heavenly army will triumph. As in other apocalyptic writings, the future course of the world is already determined; history is not left to chance. The day of the defeat of the Kittim is described as "the day appointed from ancient times for the battle of destruction of the sons of darkness" (1:10).

Although the *War Scroll* may have had no direct influence on the New Testament writers, some similarities in apocalyptic thought can be seen. The final eschatological battle involving the forces of God and the forces of evil as portrayed in the *War Scroll* is similar to the final struggle depicted in the book of Revelation (see 16:1-16; 19:11–20:10). In both of these writings, the struggles have both earthly and heavenly dimensions. Michael and Satan play important roles in both works (see especially Rev. 12). In addition, in 2 Corinthians 6:15, Paul uses the name *Beliar* for Satan. Beliar is a variant of Belial, which is a popular name for Satan in the Qumran literature, including the *War Scroll.*

Dating the *War Scroll* is difficult because it appears to be a composite work with sections added at different times. The final form of the text is usually dated to the closing decades of the first century B.C.E. The text is best preserved in one manuscript (known as 1QM), which contains most of the work. Six fragments of the text have also been discovered.

The selections given below are columns 1 and 15-19 of the *War Scroll* as translated by Geza Vermes in *The Dead Sea Scrolls in English.* The numbers in the text indicate column and line locations in 1QM. Line numbers (according to the divisions indicated in *The Scroll of the War of the Sons of Light Against the Sons of Darkness* by Yigael Yadin) have been added to the translation made by Vermes.

The War Scroll

1. For the M[aster. The Rule of] War on the unleashing of the attack of the sons of light against the company of the sons of darkness, the army of Satan: against the band of Edom, Moab, and the sons of Ammon, [2]and [against the army of the sons of the East and] the Philistines, and against the bands of the Kittim of Assyria and their allies the ungodly of the Covenant.

The sons of Levi, Judah, and Benjamin, the exiles in the desert, shall battle against them [3]in . . . all their bands when the exiled sons of light return from the Desert of the Peoples to camp in the Desert of Jerusalem; and after the battle they shall go up from there [4](to Jerusalem?).

[The king] of the Kittim [shall enter] into Egypt, and in his time he shall set out in great wrath to wage war against the kings of the north, that his fury may destroy and cut off the horn [5]of [Israel].

This shall be a time of salvation for the people of God, an age of dominion for all the members of His company, and of everlasting destruction for all the company of Satan. [6]The confusion of the sons of Japheth shall be [great] and Assyria shall fall unsuccoured. The dominion of the Kittim shall come to an end and iniquity shall be vanquished, leaving no remnant; [7][for the sons] of darkness there shall be no escape. [8][The sons of righteous]ness shall shine over all the ends of the earth; they shall go on shining until all the seasons of darkness are consumed and, at the season appointed by God, His exalted greatness shall shine [9]eternally to the peace, blessing, glory, joy, and long life of all the sons of light.

On the day when the Kittim fall, there shall be battle and terrible carnage before the God of [10]Israel, for that shall be the day appointed from ancient times for the battle of destruction of the sons of darkness. At that time, the assembly of gods and the hosts of [11]men shall battle, causing great carnage; on the day of calamity, the sons of light shall battle with the company of darkness amid the shouts of a mighty multitude and the clamour of gods and men to (make manifest) the might of God. And it shall be a time of [12][great] tribulation for the people which God shall redeem; of all its afflictions none shall be as this, from its sudden beginning until its end in eternal redemption.

On the day of their battle against the Kittim 13[they shall set out for] carnage. In three lots shall the sons of light brace themselves in battle to strike down iniquity, and in three lots shall Satan's host gird itself to thrust back the company 14[of God. And when the hearts of the detach]ments of foot-soldiers faint, then shall the might of God fortify [the hearts of the sons of light]. And with the seventh lot, the mighty hand of God shall bring down [the army of Satan, and all] the angels of his kingdom, and all the members [of his company in everlasting destruction] . . .

15. For this shall be a time of distress for Israel, [and of the summons] to war against all the nations. There shall be eternal deliverance for the company of God, 2but destruction for all the nations of wickedness.

All those [who are ready] for battle shall march out and shall pitch their camp before the king of the Kittim and before all the host 3of Satan gathered about him for the Day [of Revenge] by the Sword of God.

4Then the High Priest shall rise, with the [Priests], his brethren, and the Levites, and all the men of the army, and he shall recite aloud 5the Prayer in Time of War [written in the book] of the Rule concerning this time, and also all their Hymns. He shall marshal 6all the formations there, as is [written in the Book of War], and the priest appointed for the Day of Revenge by the voice 7of all his brethren shall go forward to strengthen the [hearts of the fighting men]. Speaking, he shall say:

Be strong and valiant; be warriors! 8Fear not! Do not be [confused and do not let your hearts be afraid!] Do not be fearful; fear them not! Do not 9fall back . . . for they are a congregation of wickedness and all their works are in Darkness; 10they tend toward Darkness. [They make for themselves] a refuge [in falsehood] and their power shall vanish like smoke. All the multitudes 11of their community . . . shall not be found. Damned as they are, all the substance of their wickedness shall quickly fade, 12like a flower in [the summer-time].

[Be brave and] strong for the battle of God! For this day is [the time of the battle of] 13God against all the host of Satan, [and of the judgement of] all flesh. The God of Israel lifts His hand in His marvellous [might] 14against all the spirits of wickedness. [The hosts of] the warrior 'gods' gird themselves for battle, [and the] formations of the Holy Ones 15[prepare themselves] for the Day [of Revenge] . . . **16** . . . . For the

God of Israel has called out the sword against all the nations, and He will do mighty deeds by the saints of His people.

[2]And they shall obey all this Rule [on] the [day] when they stand before the camps of the Kittim.

The Priests shall afterwards sound for them the trumpets [3]of the Reminder, and the gates of war shall open; the foot-soldiers shall advance and the columns shall station themselves between the formations. The Priests shall sound for them [4]the signal, 'Battle Array,' and at the sound of the trumpets the columns [shall deploy] until every man is in his place. The Priests shall then sound [5]a second signal [for them to advance], and when they are within throwing distance of the formation of the Kittim, each man shall seize his [6]weapon of war. Then the six [Priests shall blow on] the trumpets of Massacre a shrill staccato blast to direct the battle, and the Levites and all the blowers [7]of rams' horns shall sound [a battle alarm], a mighty clamour; and with this clamour they shall begin to bring down the slain from among the Kittim. All [8]the people shall cease their clamour, [but the Priests shall continue to] sound the trumpets of Massacre, and battle shall be fought against the Kittim. [9]And when [Satan] girds himself to come to the aid of the sons of darkness, and when the slain among the foot-soldiers begin to fall by the mysteries of God, and when all the men appointed for battle are put to ordeal by them, [10]the Priests shall sound the trumpets of Summons for another formation of the reserve to advance into battle; and they shall take up their stand between the formations. [11]And for those engaged [in battle] they shall sound the 'Retreat.'

Then the High Priest shall draw near, and standing before the formation, he shall strengthen by the power of God [12]their hearts [and hands] in His battle. [13]Speaking he shall say: . . .

17. He will pay their reward with burning [fire by the hand of] those tested in the crucible. He will sharpen His weapons and will not tire until all the wicked nations are destroyed. [2]Remember the judgement [of Nadab and Ab]ihu, sons of Aaron, by whose judgement God showed Himself holy in the eyes [of Israel. But Eleazar] [3]and Ithamar He confirmed in an everlasting [priestly] Covenant.

[4]Be strong and fear not; [for they tend] towards chaos and confusion, and they lean on that which is not and [shall not be. To the God] [5]of Israel belongs all that is and shall be; [He knows] all the happenings of eternity. This is the day appointed by Him for the defeat and overthrow

of the Prince of the kingdom 6of wickedness, and He will send eternal succour to the company of His redeemed by the might of the princely Angel of the kingdom of Michael. With everlasting light He will 7enlighten with joy [the children] of Israel; peace and blessing shall be with the company of God. He will raise up the kingdom of Michael in the midst of the gods, and the realm 8of Israel in the midst of all flesh. Righteousness shall rejoice on high, and all the children of His truth shall jubilate in eternal knowledge.

And you, the sons of His Covenant, 9be strong in the ordeal of God! His mysteries shall uphold you until He moves His hand for His trials to come to an end.

10After these words, the Priests shall sound to marshal them into the divisions of the formation; and at the sound of the trumpets the columns shall deploy 11until [every man is] in his place. Then the Priests shall sound a second signal on the trumpets for them to advance, and when 12the [foot-]soldiers approach throwing distance of the formation of the Kittim, every man shall seize his weapon of war. The Priests shall blow the trumpets 13of Massacre, [and the Levites and all] the blowers of rams' horns shall sound a battle alarm, and the foot-soldiers shall stretch out their hands against the host 14of the Kittim; [and at the sound of the alarm] they shall begin to bring down the slain. All the people shall cease their clamour, but the Priests 15shall continue to blow [the trumpets of Massacre and battle shall be fought against the Kittim.]

. . . 16and in the third lot . . . that the slain may fall 17by the mysteries of God . . .

18. [In the seventh lot] when the great hand of God is raised in an everlasting blow against Satan and all the hosts of his kingdom, 2and when Assyria is pursued [amidst the shouts of Angels] and the clamour of the Holy Ones, the sons of Japheth shall fall to rise no more. The Kittim shall be crushed without 3[remnant, and no man shall be saved from among them].

[At that time, on the day] when the hand of the God of Israel is raised against all the multitude of Satan, the Priests shall blow 4[the six trumpets] of the Reminder and all the battle formations shall rally to them and shall divide against all the [camps of the] Kittim 5to destroy them utterly. [And as] the sun speeds to its setting on that day, the High priest shall stand, together [with the Levites] who are 6with him and the [tribal] chiefs [and the elders] of the army, and they shall bless the God of Israel there. Speaking they shall say:

234

Blessed be Thy Name, O God [of gods], for [7]Thou hast worked great marvels [with Thy people]! Thou hast kept Thy Covenant with us from of old, and hast opened to us the gates of salvation many times. [8]For the [sake of Thy Covenant Thou hast removed our misery, in accordance with] Thy [goodness] towards us. Thou hast acted for the sake of Thy Name, O God of righteousness [9] . . . [Thou hast worked a marvellous] miracle [for us], and from ancient times there never was anything like it. For Thou didst know the time appointed for us and it has appeared [before us] this day [10] . . . [Thou hast shown] us [Thy merciful hand] in everlasting redemption by causing [the dominion of] the enemy to fall back for ever. (Thou hast shown us) Thy mighty hand [11]in [a stroke of destruction in the war against all] our enemies.

And now the day speeds us to the pursuit of their multitude [12] . . . Thou hast delivered up the hearts of the brave so that they stand no more.

For Thine is the power, and the battle is in Thy hands! [13] . . .

19. For our Sovereign is holy and the King of Glory is with us; the [host of his spirits is with our foot-soldiers and horsemen. They are as clouds, [2]as clouds of dew] covering the earth, and as a shower of rain shedding righteousness on [all that grows there].

> [Rise up, O Hero!
> Lead off Thy captives, [3]O Glorious One!
> Gather up] Thy spoils, O Author of mighty deeds!
> Lay Thy hand on the neck of Thine enemies
>   and Thy feet [on the pile of the slain!
> Smite [4]the nations, Thine adversaries],
>   and devour flesh with Thy sword!
> Fill Thy land with glory
>   and Thine inheritance with blessing!
> [Let there be a multitude of cattle in Thy fields,
>   and in] Thy palaces
> [5][silver and gold and precious stones]!
>
> O Zion, rejoice greatly!
>   Rejoice all you cities of Judah!
> [Keep your gates [6]ever open
>   that the] hosts of the nations
>   [may be brought in]!

235

    Their kings shall serve you
      and all your oppressors shall bow down before you;
      [they shall lick the dust of your feet.
7 Shout for joy, O daughters of] my people!
    Deck yourselves with glorious jewels
      [and rule over the kingdom 8of the nations!
    Sovereignty shall be to the Lord]
      and everlasting dominion to Israel.

9Then they shall gather in the camp that night to rest until the morning. And in the morning [they shall go to the place 10where the formation stood before the] warriors of the Kittim fell, and the multitudes of Assyria, and the hosts of all the nations [assembled] (to discover whether) the multitude of the stricken are dead 11(with none to bury them), those who fell there under the Sword of God. And the High Priest shall draw near, [with his vicar, and the chief Priests and the Levites] 12with the Prince of the battle, and all the chiefs of the formations and their numbered men; [they shall return to the positions 13which they held before the] slain [began to fall] from among the Kittim, and there they shall praise the God [of Israel] . . .

THE NEW JERUSALEM (5Q15)

Commentary

Several Aramaic fragments have been discovered in the Dead Sea area that contain descriptions of an idealized Jerusalem and Temple. These fragments represent several copies of a work referred to by scholars as the *New Jerusalem*. The largest fragment that has been published so far is 5Q15, published by J. T. Milik. By consulting some yet unpublished fragments, Milik has been able to provide a plausible reconstruction of much of the *New Jerusalem*. The contents of the work seem to be modeled after Ezekiel 40–48, which gives a vision of the new Jerusalem and the new Temple in the restored land of Israel.

According to Milik, the author of the *New Jerusalem* is led on a tour of the new Jerusalem of the eschatological age by an angelic surveyor who measures all the contents of the city. After noting the walls of the city, which contain twelve gates, the visionary and his angelic guide enter the city. Manuscript 5Q15 describes the angel measuring the blocks of houses; the avenues and streets running through the city; and the doors, entrances, and towers of the city. The detailed dimensions of one of the houses in the city are given, including the length and width of the house and the measurements of the rooms. The blocks of houses also contain dining halls, each with twenty-two couches and eleven windows. After listing the measurements of the windows, 5Q15 breaks off.

In addition to being similar to Ezekiel's description of the new Jerusalem, the city in 5Q15 bears some similarities to the future Jerusalem described in Isaiah 54:11-12 and Tobit 13:16-17. In 5Q15 the streets of the city are "paved with white stone . . . marble and jasper" (1:6-7); in Isaiah and Tobit the streets and foundations, as well as the rest of the city, are built of precious stones and metals.

Although the currently available texts of the *New Jerusalem* do not provide a complete picture, the description of the journey through the city is reminiscent of the otherworldly journeys found in several apocalyptic writings. As in many otherworldly journeys, an angel serves as a guide for the recipient of the revelation. The eschatological nature of the Qumran text is implicit in the idea of the new Jerusalem. The belief in a new Jerusalem of the last days is found in several Jewish apocalyptic writings (*1 Enoch* 90:29; *2 Baruch* 4:4-5, which mentions that Abraham and Moses had been shown the new Jerusalem that is preserved, along with paradise, with God; and 2 Esdras 7:26; 8:52; 10:44-59; 13:36).

In the book of Revelation in the New Testament, the description of the new Jerusalem "coming down out of heaven from God" (chap. 21) has some parallels with the description of the city in 5Q15. In both writings, an angel leads the visionary through the city and measures the contents of the city. Both works describe the city, or at least its streets, as being constructed of precious stones or metals. A major difference exists, however, in the two conceptions of the new Jerusalem. In the Qumran document, as in Ezekiel, the Temple is a part of the new Jerusalem; in Revelation, on the other hand, the city contains no Temple, for "its temple is the Lord God the Almighty and the Lamb" (21:22).

The translation of the *New Jerusalem* (5Q15) given here is by Geza Vermes from *The Dead Sea Scrolls in English*. The numbers in the text indicate column and line locations in 5Q15. Line numbers (according to the divisions indicated in *Discoveries in the Judean Desert,* vol. 3, by J. T. Milik) have been added to the translation made by Vermes.

The New Jerusalem

1. And he led me into the city, and he measured each block of houses for its length and width, fifty-one reeds by fifty-one, in a square a[ll round] = 357 cubits to each side. A passage surrounds the block of houses, a street gallery, three reeds, = 21 ²cubits, (wide).

[He] then [showed me the di]mensions of [all] the blo[cks of houses. Between each block there is a street], six reeds, = 42 cubits, wide. ³And the width of the avenues running from east to west: two of them are ten reeds, = 70 cubits, wide. And the third, ⁴that to the [lef]t (i.e. north) of the Temple, measures eighteen reeds, = 126 cubits in width. And the wid[th of the streets] running from south ⁵[to north: t]wo of [them] have nine reeds and four cubits, = 67 cubits, each street.

[And the] mid[dle street passing through the mid]dle of the city, ⁶its [width measures] thirt[een] ree[ds] and one cubit, = 92 cubits. And all [the streets of the city] are paved with white stone ⁷ . . . marble and jasper.

⁸[And he showed me the dimensions of the ei]ghty [side-doors]. The wid[th of the] side-doors is two reeds, [= 14 cubits, . . . ⁹Each door has tw]o wings of stone. The width of the w[ing] is [one] reed, [= 7 cubits.]

¹⁰And he showed me [the dimensions] of the twelve [entranc]es. The

width of their doors are three reeds, [= 21] cubits. [Each [11]door has tw]o [wings]. The width of the wing is one reed and a half, = 10 1/2 cubits . . . [12][And beside each door there are two tow]ers, one to [the r]ight and one to the l[ef]t. Its width [is of the same dimension as] its length, [five reeds by five, [13] = 35 cubits. The stairs beside] the inside door, on the [righ]t side of the towers, [rise] to the top of the to[wers. Their width is five cubits. The towers [14]and the stairs are five reeds by five and] five cubits, = 40 [cubits], on each side of the door.

[15][And he showed me the dimensions of the doors of the blocks of houses. Their width] is two reeds, = 14 cub[its. And the wi]d[th] . . . [16][And he measured] the wid[th of each th]reshold: two reeds, = 14 cubits, [and the lintel: one cubit. [17]And he measured above each] threshold i[ts win]gs. And he measured beyond the threshold. Its length is [thirteen] cubits [and its width ten cubits.]

[18][And he] le[d m]e [be]yond the threshold. [And behold] another threshold, and a door next to the inner wall [on the right side, of the same dimensions as the outer door. [19]Its width] is four [cu]bits, [its] height seven [cubits], and it has two wings. And in front of this door there is [an entrance threshold. Its width is one reed] **2.** 7 [cubits]. And the l[eng]th of the entrance is two reeds, = 14 cubits, and its height is two reeds, = 14 cubits. [And the door] [2]fa[cing the other do]or opening into the block of houses has the same dimensions as the outer door. On the left of this entrance, he showed [me] a round [stair-case]. [3]Its length is of the same dimension as its width: two reeds by two, = 14 cubits. The do[ors (of the stair-case) facing] [4]the other doors are of the same dimensions. And a pillar is inside the stair-case around which the stairs ri[se]; its width and d[epth are six cubits by six], [5]square. And the stairs which rise beside it, their width is four cubits, and they rise in a spiral [to] a height of [two] r[eeds] to [the roof].

[6]And he led me [into] the block of houses, and he showed me the houses there. From one door to the oth[er, there are fifteen: eigh]t on one side as far as the corner, [7]and sev]en from the corner to the other door. The length of the house[s is three reed]s, = 2[1 cubits, and their width], [8]two [reed]s, = 14 cubits. Likewise, for all the chambers; [and their height is t]wo [reeds], = 1[4] cu[bit]s, [and their doors are [9]in the middle.] (Their) width is t[w]o reeds, = 1[4] cubits. [And he measured the width (of the rooms) in the middle of the house, and inside the upper floor: four [10][cubits]. Length and height: one reed, = 7 cubits.

[And he showed me the dimensions of the dining-[halls]. Each has [a length] of ninete[en] cubits [11][and a width] of twelve [cubits]. Each contains twenty-two couche[s and ele]ven windows of lattice-work (?) above [the couches]. [12]And next to the hall is an outer conduit. [And he measured] the . . . of the window: its height, two cubits; [its width: . . . cubits;] and its depth is that of the width of the wall. [The height of the inner (aspect of the window) [13]is . . . cubits, and that of the outer (aspect), . . . cubits.]

[And he measured the l]im[it]s of the . . . [Their length] is nineteen [cubits] and [their] width, [twelve cubits] . . .

PART TWO

Early Christian Apocalyptic Literature

CHAPTER FOUR

APOCALYPSES THAT CONTAIN NO OTHERWORLDLY JOURNEYS

THE APOCALYPSE OF PETER

Commentary

One of the earliest and most influential Christian apocalypses, the *Apocalypse of Peter* dates from the first half of the second century. Clement of Alexandria (a leader in the church who lived approximately 150–215 C.E.) quoted from the work on several occasions, attributing it to the Apostle Peter. Its citation by Clement and other early Christian leaders, its being mentioned in several documents (*Muratorian Canon*, Codex Claromontanus, the *Stichometry* of Nicephorus), and its use in later Christian writings give evidence of the popularity of this apocalypse in the early centuries of the church.

Dating of the work is based primarily on two factors. First, Clement's knowledge of the document limits its writing to no later than the middle of the second century, since sufficient time must be allowed for the writing to have been circulated and become established. Second, the description of the false Christ who will put to death many of the faithful who reject him (chap. 2) is generally accepted as a reference to Bar Kokhba, the Jewish messianic pretender who in 132 C.E. led a revolt to free the Jewish people from Roman rule. Initially successful, Kokhba

243

was eventually killed by the Romans. During the war, Kokhba acted harshly against those who did not support his revolt, and Jewish Christians who refused to follow this messianic pretender likely fell victim to persecution and martyrdom. Early church writings claim that such persecutions did indeed occur. If Bar Kokhba was this false Christ, then the *Apocalypse of Peter* was probably written between 132 and 135 (the work indicates no knowledge of Bar Kokhba's death in 135). The pseudonymous author likely interpreted the events of the Bar Kokhba revolt as the eschatological crisis that would bring about the end of this age.

Egypt and Palestine are the two most probable places for the origin of the *Apocalypse of Peter*. Support for Egypt comes from Clement's early knowledge of the writing and from the condemnation of the worship of animal idols (chap. 10), a practice prevalent in Egypt. If, however, as seems likely, the writing is a response to persecution from Bar Kokhba, then Palestine is a more probable location.

The work falls into two parts. The first section, chapters 1–14, is set on the Mount of Olives as Jesus delivers an eschatological discourse to his disciples. The author has expanded and embellished the material found in Matthew 24 and parallels. After warning the disciples about the false Christ who will come, Jesus reveals to Peter a vision, seen in the palm of his right hand, of the events of the last days. The most memorable portion of this section is the gruesome depiction of the torments reserved for the wicked in the afterlife. Their punishments are often measure-for-measure punishments that are chosen to match their sins: blasphemers are hung by their tongues; men guilty of fornication are hung up by their thighs; women who have committed abortion (or infanticide) are tortured by beasts formed from congealed milk flowing from the mothers' breasts; liars have their lips cut off. The purpose of these vivid descriptions of punishment is to promise vindication to the righteous who are being persecuted in the present world; in the next life the wicked will not escape the wrath of God. Those who violate the will of God, especially those who persecute God's people, will receive the punishment due them.

This section closes with two rewards for the righteous: they will be able to watch the torment of those who persecuted them, and they will share in Christ's eternal kingdom in the field Acherusia, or Elysium.

The second part of the *Apocalypse of Peter* (chaps. 15–17) is a reworking of the Transfiguration scene from the Gospels (Mark 9:2-8 and parallels). While Jesus is praying with his disciples on "the holy mountain," Moses and Elijah appear to them. When asked by Peter where the righteous fathers are, Jesus shows the disciples a beautiful garden, which is the dwelling place of the righteous of the past and will be the abode for the faithful who suffer persecution. Since the writing also speaks of a general resurrection of the dead for judgment at the end of time, this garden is probably paradise, the temporary home for the righteous dead. As the disciples watch, Jesus, Moses, and Elijah are then taken away into the second heaven.

Spatial and temporal elements are both very strong in the *Apocalypse of Peter*. Otherworldly places (hell, paradise, heaven) and beings (the angel Uriel, the punishing angels, Jesus, Moses, Elijah) dominate the work, whereas the major events are eschatological events (resurrection of the dead, last judgment, punishment of the wicked, rewards of the righteous). In this apocalypse, revelation is mediated not by other-worldly journeys, but through visions and speeches. The mediator of the revelation, Jesus Christ, qualifies as an otherworldly mediator because this Jesus is apparently the risen Christ, not the earthly Jesus of the Gospels. Instead of descending the mountain with his disciples as Jesus does in the Gospel narratives, the Christ of the *Apocalypse of Peter* ascends to the second heaven.

The *Apocalypse of Peter* is extant in two major forms: an Ethiopic translation and a Greek fragment discovered at Akhmim in Egypt. Most scholars have concluded that the Ethiopic translation is closer to the original than is the Akhmim text. For that reason, the Ethiopic text is given below.

The translation is by Hugo Duensing from *New Testament Apocrypha*, volume 2.

The Apocalypse of Peter

1. And when he was seated on the Mount of Olives, his own came unto him, and we entreated and implored him severally and besought him, saying unto him, "Make known unto us what are the signs of thy Parousia and of the end of the world, that we may perceive and mark the time of thy Parousia and instruct those who come after us, to whom we preach the word of thy Gospel and whom we install in thy Church, in order that they, when they hear it, may take heed to themselves that they mark the time of thy coming." And our Lord answered and said unto us, "Take heed that men deceive you not and that ye do not become doubters and serve other gods. Many will come in my name saying 'I am

245

Christ.' Believe them not and draw not near unto them. For the coming of the Son of God will not be manifest, but like the lightning which shineth from the east to the west, so shall I come on the clouds of heaven with a great host in my glory; with my cross going before my face will I come in my glory, shining seven times as bright as the sun will I come in my glory, with all my saints, my angels, when my Father will place a crown upon my head, that I may judge the living and the dead and recompense every man according to his work.

2. And ye, receive ye the parable of the fig-tree thereon: as soon as its shoots have gone forth and its boughs have sprouted, the end of the world will come." And I, Peter, answered and said unto him, "Explain to me concerning the fig-tree, {and} how we shall perceive it, for throughout all its days does the fig-tree sprout and every year it brings forth its fruit {and} for its master. What (then) meaneth the parable of the fig-tree? We know it not."—And the Master answered and said unto me, "Dost thou not understand that the fig-tree is the house of Israel? Even as a man hath planted a fig-tree in his garden and it brought forth no fruit, and he sought its fruit for many years. When he found it not, he said to the keeper of his garden, 'Uproot the fig-tree that our land may not be unfruitful for us.' And the gardener said to God, 'We thy servants (?) wish to clear it (of weeds) and to dig the ground around it and to water it. If it does not then bear fruit, we will immediately remove its roots from the garden and plant another one in its place.' Hast thou not grasped that the fig-tree is the house of Israel? Verily, I say to you, when its boughs have sprouted at the end, then shall deceiving Christs come, and awaken hope (with the words): 'I am the Christ, who am (now) come into the world.' And when they shall see the wickedness of their deeds (even of the false Christs), they shall turn away after them and deny him to whom our fathers gave praise (?), the first Christ whom they crucified and thereby sinned exceedingly. But this deceiver is not the Christ. And when they reject him, he will kill with the sword (dagger) and there shall be many martyrs. Then shall the boughs of the fig-tree, i.e. the house of Israel, sprout, and there shall be many martyrs by his hand: they shall be killed and become martyrs. Enoch and Elias will be sent to instruct them that this is the deceiver who must come into the world and do signs and wonders in order to deceive. And therefore shall they that are slain by his hand be martyrs and shall be reckoned among the good and righteous martyrs who have pleased God in their life."

3. And he showed me in his right hand the souls of all (men) and on the palm of his right hand the image of that which shall be fulfilled at the last day; and how the righteous and the sinners shall be separated and how those will do (?) who are upright in heart, and how the evil-doers will be rooted out for all eternity. We saw how the sinners wept in great distress and sorrow, until all who saw it with their eyes wept, whether righteous, or angels or himself also. And I asked him and said, "Lord, allow me to speak thy word concerning these sinners: 'It were better for them that they had not been created.' " And the Saviour answered and said "O Peter, why speakest thou thus, 'that not to have been created were better for them'? Thou resistest God. Thou wouldest not have more compassion than he for his image, for he has created them and has brought them forth when they were not (perhaps = and has brought them forth from not-being into being). And since thou hast seen the lamentation which sinners shall encounter in the last days, therefore thy heart is saddened; but I will show thee their works in which they have sinned against the Most High.

4. Behold now what they shall experience in the last days, when the day of God comes. On the day of the decision of the judgment of God, all the children of men from the east unto the west shall be gathered before my Father who ever liveth, and he will command hell to open its bars of steel and to give up all that is in it. And the beasts and the fowls shall he command to give back all flesh that they have devoured, since he desires that men should appear (again); for nothing perishes for God, and nothing is impossible with him, since all things are his. For all things (come to pass) on the day of decision, on the day of judgment, at the word of God, and as all things came to pass when he created the world and commanded all that is therein, and it was all done—so shall it be in the last days; for everything is possible with God and he says in the Scripture: 'Son of man, prophesy upon the several bones, and say to the bones—bone unto bone in joints, sinews, nerves, flesh and skin and hair thereon.' And soul and spirit shall the great Uriel give at the command of God. For him God has appointed over the resurrection of the dead on the day of judgment. Behold and consider the corns of wheat which are sown in the earth. As something dry and without a soul does a man sow (them) in the earth; and they live again, bear fruit, and the earth gives (them) back again as a pledge entrusted to it. And this which dies, which is sown as seed in the earth and shall become alive and be restored to life, is man. How much more shall God raise up on the day of decision those who believe in him and are chosen by him and for whom he made (the earth); and all this shall the earth give back on the day of decision, since it shall also be judged with them, and the heaven with it.

5. And these things shall come to pass in the day of judgment of those who have fallen away from faith in God and have committed sin: cataracts of fire shall be let loose; and obscurity and darkness shall come up and cover and veil the entire world, and the waters shall be changed and transformed into coals of fire, and all that is in it (the earth?) shall burn and the sea shall become fire; under the heaven there shall be a fierce fire that shall not be put out and it flows for the judgment of wrath. And the stars shall be melted by flames of fire, as if they had not been created, and the fastnesses of heaven shall pass away for want of water and become as though they had not been created. And the lightnings of heaven shall be no (?) more and, by their enchantment, they shall alarm the world (perhaps = the heaven will turn to lightning and the lightnings will alarm the world). And the spirits of the dead bodies shall be like to them and at the command of God will become fire. And as soon as the whole creation is dissolved, the men who are in the east shall flee to the west ⟨and those in the west⟩ to the east; those that are in the south shall flee to the north and those in the ⟨north to the⟩ south, and everywhere will the wrath of the fearful fire overtake them; and an unquenchable flame shall drive them and bring them to the judgment of wrath in the stream of unquenchable fire which flows, flaming with fire, and when its waves separate one from another, seething, there shall be much gnashing of teeth among the children of men.

6. And all will see how I come upon an eternal shining cloud, and the angels of God who will sit with me on the throne of my glory at the right hand of my heavenly Father. He will set a crown upon my head. As soon as the nations see it, they will weep, each nation for itself. And he shall command them to go into the river of fire, while the deeds of each individual one of them stand before them. [Recompense shall be given] to each according to his work. As for the elect who have done good, they will come to me and will not see (?) death by devouring fire. But the evil creatures, the sinners and the hypocrites will stand in the depths of the darkness that passes not away, and their punishment is the fire, and angels bring forward their sins and prepare for them a place wherein they shall be punished for ever, each according to his offence. The angel of God, Uriel, brings the souls of those sinners who perished in the flood, and of all who dwell in all idols, in every molten image, in every love and in paintings, and of them that dwell on all hills and in stones and by the wayside, (whom) men call gods: they shall be burned with them (i.e. the objects in which they lodge) in eternal fire. After all of them, with their dwelling places, have been destroyed, they will be punished eternally.

7. Then will men and women come to the place prepared for them. By their tongues with which they have blasphemed the way of righteousness will they be hung up. There is spread out for them unquenchable fire. . . .

And behold again another place: this is a great pit filled, in which are those who have denied righteousness; and angels of punishment visit (them) and here do they kindle upon them the fire of their punishment. And again two women: they are hung up by their neck and by their hair and are cast into the pit. These are they who plaited their hair, not to create beauty, but to turn to fornication, and that they might ensnare the souls of men to destruction. And the men who lay with them in fornication are hung by their thighs in that burning place, and they say to one another, "We did not know that we would come into everlasting torture."

And the murderers and those who have made common cause with them are cast into the fire, in a place full of venomous beasts, and they are tormented without rest, as they feel their pains, and their worms are as numerous as a dark cloud. And the angel Ezrael will bring forth the souls of them that have been killed and they shall see the torment ⟨of those who⟩ killed ⟨them⟩ and shall say to one another, "Righteousness and justice is the judgment of God." For we have indeed heard, but did not believe that we would come to this place of eternal judgment."

8. And near this flame there is a great and very deep pit and into it there flow all kinds of things from everywhere: judgment (?), horrifying things and excretions. And the women (are) swallowed up (by this) up to their necks and are punished with great pain. These are they who have procured abortions and have ruined the work of God which he has created. Opposite them is another place where the children sit, but both alive, and they cry to God. And lightnings go forth from those children which pierce the eyes of those who, by fornication, have brought about their destruction. Other men and women stand above them naked. And their children stand opposite to them in a place of delight. And they sigh and cry to God because of their parents, "These are they who neglected and cursed and transgressed thy commandment. They killed us and cursed the angel who created (us) and hung us up. And they withheld from us the light which thou hast appointed for all." And the milk of the mothers flows from their breasts and congeals and smells foul, and from it come forth beasts that devour flesh, which turn and torture them for ever with their husbands, because they forsook the commandment of God and killed their children. And the children shall be given to the angel Temlakos. And those who slew them will be tortured for ever, for God wills it to be so.

9. Ezrael, the angel of wrath, brings men and women with the half of their bodies burning and casts them into a place of darkness, the hell of men; and a spirit of wrath chastises them with all manner of chastisement, and a worm that never sleeps consumes their entrails. These are the persecutors and betrayers of my righteous ones. And near to those who live thus were other men and women who chew their tongues, and they are tormented with red-hot irons and have their eyes burned. These are the slanderers and those who doubt my righteousness.

Other men and women—whose deeds (were done) in deception—have their lips cut off and fire enters into their mouths and into their entrails. ⟨These are those⟩ who slew the martyrs by their lying.

In another place situated near them, on the stone a pillar of fire (?), and the pillar is sharper than swords—men and women who are clad in rags and filthy garments, and they are cast upon it, to suffer the judgment of unceasing torture. These are they which trusted in their riches and despised widows and the woman (with) orphans . . . in the sight of God.

10. And into another place near by, saturated with filth, they throw men and women up to their knees. These are they who lent money and took usury.

And other men and women thrust themselves down from a high place and return again and run, and demons drive them. These are the worshippers of idols, and they drive them to the end of their wits (slope?) and they plunge down from there. And this they do continually and are tormented for ever. These are they who have cut their flesh as apostles of a man, and the women who were with them . . . and thus are the men who defiled themselves with one another in the fashion of women.

And beside them . . . (*an untranslatable word*), and beneath them the angel Ezrael prepares a place of much fire, and all the golden and silver idols, all idols, the works of men's hands, and what resembles the images of cats and lions, of reptiles and wild beasts, and the men and women who manufactured the images, shall be in chains of fire; they shall be chastised because of their error before them (the images) and this is their judgment for ever. And near them other men and women who burn in the flame of the judgment, whose torture is for ever. These are they who have forsaken the commandment of God and followed . . . (*unknown word*) of the devils.

11. And another very high place . . . (*some unintelligible words*), the men and women who make a false step go rolling down to where the fear is. And again, while the (fire) that is prepared floweth, they mount up and fall down again and continue their rolling. They shall be punished thus for ever. These are they who have not honoured their father and mother, and of their own accord withdrew themselves from them. Therefore shall they be punished eternally. Furthermore the angel Ezrael brings children and maidens to show to them those who are punished. They will be punished with pain, with hanging up (?) and with many wounds which flesh-eating birds inflict. These are they that have confidence in their sins, are not obedient to their parents, and do not follow the instruction of their fathers and do not honour those who are older than they. Beside them, maidens clad in darkness for raiment, and they shall be seriously punished and their flesh will be torn in pieces. These are they who retained not their virginity till they were given in marriage; they shall be punished with these tortures, while they feel them.

And again other men and women who ceaselessly chew their tongues and are tormented with eternal fire. These are the slaves who were not obedient to their masters. This then is their judgment for ever.

12. And near to this torment are blind and dumb men and women whose raiment is white. They are packed closely together and fall on coals of unquenchable fire. These are they who give alms and say, "We are righteous before God," while they yet have not striven for righteousness. The angel of God Ezrael allows them to come forth out of this fire and sets forth a judgment of decision (?). This then is their judgment. (And) a stream of fire flows and all judgment (=all those judged) are drawn into the midst of the stream. And Uriel sets them

251

down (there). And there are wheels of fire, and men and women hung thereon by the power of their whirling. Those in the pit burn. Now these are the sorcerers and sorceresses. These wheels (are) in all decision by fire without number (?).

13. The angels will bring my elect and righteous which are perfect in all righteousness, and shall bear them in their hands and clothe them with the garments of eternal life. They shall see (their desire) on those who hated them, when he punishes them. Torment for every one (is) for ever according to his deeds. And all those who are in torment will say with one voice, "Have mercy upon us, for now we know the judgment of God, which he declared to us beforehand, and we did not believe." And the angel Tatirokos (= Tartarouchos) will come and chasten them with even greater torment and will say unto them, "Now do ye repent when there is no more time for repentance, and nothing of life remains." And all shall say, "Righteous is the judgment of God: for we have heard and perceived that his judgment is good, since we are punished according to our deeds."

14. Then will I give to my elect and righteous the baptism and the salvation for which they have besought me, in the field Akrōsjā (= Acherusia) which is called Anēslaslejā (= Elysium). They shall adorn with flowers the portion of the righteous and I will go. . . . I will rejoice with them. I will cause the nations to enter into my eternal kingdom and show to them that eternal thing to which I have directed their hope, I and my heavenly Father. I have spoken it to thee, Peter, and make it known to thee. Go forth then and journey to the city in the west in the vineyard which I will tell thee of . . . by the hand of my Son who is without sin, that his work . . . of destruction may be sanctified. But thou art chosen in the hope which I have given to thee. Spread thou my gospel throughout the whole world in peace! For there will be rejoicing (?) at the source of my word, the hope of life, and suddenly the world will be carried off.

15. And my Lord Jesus Christ, our King, said to me, "Let us go into the holy mountain." And his disciples went with him, praying.

And behold, there were two men, and we could not look on their faces, for a light came from them which shone more than the sun, and their raiment also was glistening and cannot be described, and there is nothing sufficient to be compared to them in this world. And its gentleness . . . that no mouth is able to express the beauty of their form. For their aspect was astonishing and wonderful. And the other, great, I say, shines in his appearance more than hail (crystal). Flowers of roses is the likeness of the colour of his appearance and his body . . . his head. And upon his shoulders and on their foreheads was a crown of nard, a work woven from beautiful flowers; like the rainbow in water was his hair. This was the comeliness of his countenance, and he was adorned with all kinds of ornament. And when we suddenly saw them, we marvelled.

16. And I approached God Jesus Christ and said to him, "My Lord who is this?" And he said to me, "These are Moses and Elias." And I said to him, "(Where then are) Abraham, Isaac, Jacob and the other righteous fathers?"

And he showed us a great open garden. (It was) full of fair trees and blessed fruits, full of the fragrance of perfume. Its fragrance was beautiful and that fragrance reached to us. And of it . . . I saw many fruits.

And my Lord and God Jesus Christ said unto me, "Hast thou seen the companies of the fathers? As is their rest, so also is the honour and glory of those who will be persecuted for my righteousness' sake."

⟨And I was joyful and believed⟩ and understood that which is written in the book of my Lord Jesus Christ. And I said to him, "My Lord, wilt thou that I make here three tabernacles, one for thee, one for Moses and one for Elias?" And he said to me in wrath, "Satan maketh war against thee, and has veiled thine understanding, and the good things of this world conquer thee. Thine eyes must be opened and thine ears unstopped that . . . a tabernacle, which the hand of man has not made, but which my heavenly Father has made for me and for the elect." And we saw (it) full of joy.

17. And behold there came suddenly a voice from heaven saying, "This is my Son, whom I love and in whom I have pleasure, and my commandments. . . . And there came a great and exceeding white cloud over our heads and bore away our Lord and Moses and Elias. And I trembled and was afraid, and we looked up and the heavens opened and we saw men in the flesh, and they came and greeted our Lord and Moses and Elias, and went into the second heaven. And the word of Scripture was fulfilled: This generation seeketh him and seeketh the face of the God of Jacob. And great fear and great amazement took

253

place in heaven; the angels flocked together that the word of Scripture might be fulfilled which saith: Open the gates, ye princes! After that the heaven was shut, that had been opened. And we prayed and went down from the mountain, and we praised God who hath written the names of the righteous in heaven in the book of life.

THE SHEPHERD OF HERMAS

Commentary

The *Shepherd of Hermas,* one of the writings of the Apostolic Fathers, was highly esteemed among certain early Christians, particularly in the eastern churches. Some early church leaders (Irenaeus, Clement of Alexandria, Origen, Athanasius) referred to the *Shepherd* as "scripture" or cited it as authoritative teaching. Codex Sinaiticus, a fourth-century Greek manuscript of the Bible and one of the most important copies of the Bible, includes the *Shepherd of Hermas,* along with the *Epistle of Barnabas,* after the books of the New Testament. On the other hand, the *Muratorian Canon,* a second- or third-century list of canonical New Testament writings, sees value in the *Shepherd of Hermas,* but denies it authoritative status. This latter viewpoint eventually prevailed.

The work claims to have been written by a man named Hermas, who had apparently been born a slave and later was sold to Rhoda, a woman who lived in Rome (*Vis.* 1.1.1). Eventually he gained his freedom and lived in Rome with his wife and children. Although it is possible that this autobiographical information is fictitious, there is little reason to doubt its authenticity. The author claims to write during the time of Clement (*Vis.* 2.4.3), often understood as a reference to Clement, bishop of Rome around 96 C.E. The *Muratorian Canon,* however, identifies Hermas as the brother of Pius, bishop of Rome around 140–154 C.E. On the basis of these claims, along with other evidence, many scholars view the *Shepherd of Hermas* as resulting from multiple authorship. Portions of the work may indeed derive from Hermas around the end of the first century; portions may have been added later by the brother of Pius; and other material may have been written by an unknown author or authors. The completed work probably should be dated around the middle of the second century. The place of composition of the *Shepherd of Hermas* likely was Rome. This location is cited in the work itself and is also supported by the *Muratorian Canon.*

The *Shepherd of Hermas* is divided into three sections: the *Visions,* the *Mandates,* and the *Similitudes* (or *Parables*). The work is a series of revelations given to Hermas, which he was commanded to write in a book. The *Shepherd of Hermas* derives its name from one of the revelatory figures who appears to Hermas as a shepherd (*Vis.* 5).

In the five *Visions,* Hermas is visited by a figure who reveals special information to him. The revealer in the first four visions is an old woman who becomes increasingly younger in each vision. This "ancient lady" is identified for Hermas as the church. (At first Hermas believes that she is a Sibyl, one of the women in the ancient world who uttered ecstatic prophecies. See the introduction to *Sibylline Oracles* 2.) The woman gives Hermas a book containing a message to "God's elect ones" (*Vis.* 2.1.3-4). After Hermas copies the book, it is taken from him. He is later told to add the revelations from the woman to the book and to send copies to two individuals in the church, Clement and Grapte, who will make the contents of the book known (*Vis.* 2.4.2-3). The thrust of the revelation given by the lady is a call to repentance and an ethical life-style in the light of the impending "great persecution" or tribulation (*Vis.* 2.2.7.). Christians will have one final opportunity to repent of their post-baptismal sins.

In *Vision* 4, Hermas sees a great, terrifying beast whose head is composed of four colors. The woman appears to Hermas again and interprets the beast as a sign of the coming persecution (*Vis.* 4.2.5). The four colors of the beast represent the present world, the coming destruction of the world, the faithful, and the world to come. Hermas is instructed to warn others of this impending persecution and to advise them to repent and be prepared. The fifth vision introduces the man dressed as a shepherd (also called the angel of repentance), who appears to Hermas to bring him new revelations. The shepherd tells Hermas to write down the commandments and parables (that is, the remainder of the *Shepherd of Hermas*) that the shepherd will give him. The fifth vision, then, serves as a preface to the remainder of the book.

The second major section of the book, the *Mandates,* is a collection of religious and ethical exhortations on a variety of topics. The contents of this section are similar to ideas contained in Hellenistic Jewish moral teaching and are also similar to material in the New Testament book of James. *Mandates* 5 and 6 teach that two angels or spirits, a righteous one and a wicked one, vie for control of people. This idea is reminiscent of the doctrine of the two spirits contained in the *Community Rule,* found at Qumran (1QS 3:13–4:26).

The final section of the *Shepherd of Hermas* contains ten similitudes, or parables, told to Hermas by the shepherd-revealer. The message of the *Similitudes,* similar to the first two sections of the book, deals mainly with the themes of repentance and morality.

Some scholars have questioned the classification of the *Shepherd of Hermas* as an apocalypse because of its overwhelming emphasis on repentance and ethics. A close examination of the work, however, gives evidence that it fits the definition of an apocalypse well enough to justify its classification as such. First, the work is revelatory literature. The entire work consists of a series of revelations mediated to Hermas and interpreted for him by otherworldly figures—the ancient lady, the shepherd, and various angels. Second, the work is set within a narrative context, as Hermas relates the circumstances surrounding the reception and interpretation of the revelations. Third, its contents reflect a belief in a transcendent reality that is both spatially and temporally beyond the present world. The spatial dimension is evidenced by the presence in the book of various otherworldly figures—the ancient lady, the shepherd (angel of repentance), the angels of punishment (*Sim.* 6.2-3; 7.1-7), the righteous and wicked angels (or spirits) who compete for control over human lives (*Man.* 5.1-2; 6.2), and the devil (*Man.* 7.1-5; 12.4.6-7; 12.5-6). The eschatological aspects of the work demonstrate its temporal orientation. The eschatology of the *Shepherd of Hermas* is apocalyptic— ultimate rewards and punishments lie beyond history. The wicked will be burned (*Sim.* 4.4) and will suffer eternal destruction (*Sim.* 6.2.3-4; 8.6-8). The righteous, on the other hand, will receive eternal life (*Vis.* 2.3.2-3; 4.3.5), will be with God (*Vis.* 3.2.1), and will dwell in the world to come (*Vis.* 4.3.5). Furthermore, the present world will not endure forever but will be destroyed by blood and fire (*Vis.* 4.3.3). The end will come when the "building" of the church is completed, a process that will occur quickly (*Vis.* 3.8.9).

The selections from the *Shepherd of Hermas* given here include the initial vision in which the shepherd appears to Hermas (*Vis.* 5), the vision of the beast symbolizing the coming persecution and eschatological events (*Vis.* 4), and three parables (*Sim.* 3, 4, and 6) that contain eschatological elements. The translation of these selections is by Kirsopp Lake from volume 2 of *The Apostolic Fathers,* in the Loeb Classical Library series.

The Shepherd

Vision 4

I

1. The fourth vision which I saw, brethren, twenty days after the former vision, was a type of the persecution which is to come. **2.** I was going into the country by the Via Campana. The place is about ten furlongs from the public road, and is easily reached. **3.** As I walked by

257

myself I besought the Lord to complete the revelations and visions which he had shown me by his holy Church, to make me strong and give repentance to his servants who had been offended, 'to glorify his' great and glorious 'name' because he had thought me worthy to show me his wonders. **4.** And while I was glorifying him and giving him thanks an answer came to me as an echo of my voice, "Do not be double-minded, Hermas." I began to reason in myself, and to say, "In what ways can I be double-minded after being given such a foundation by the Lord, and having seen his glorious deeds?" **5.** And I approached a little further, brethren, and behold, I saw dust reaching as it were up to heaven, and I began to say to myself, Are cattle coming and raising dust? and it was about a furlong away from me. **6.** When the dust grew greater and greater I supposed that it was some portent. The sun shone out a little, and lo! I saw a great beast like some Leviathan, and fiery locusts were going out of his mouth. The beast was in size about a hundred feet and its head was like a piece of pottery. **7.** And I began to weep and to pray the Lord to rescue me from it, and I remembered the word which I had heard, "Do not be double-minded, Hermas." **8.** Thus, brethren, being clothed in the faith of the Lord and remembering the great things which he had taught me, I took courage and faced the beast. And as the beast came on with a rush it was as though it could destroy a city. **9.** I came near to it, and the Leviathan for all its size stretched itself out on the ground, and put forth nothing except its tongue, and did not move at all until I had passed it by. **10.** And the beast had on its head four colours, black, then the colour of flame and blood, then golden, then white.

II

1. After I had passed the beast by and had gone about thirty feet further, lo! a maiden met me, 'adorned as if coming forth from the bridal chamber,' all in white and with white sandals, veiled to the forehead, and a turban for a head-dress, but her hair was white. **2.** I recognised from the former visions that it was the Church, and I rejoiced the more. She greeted me saying, "Hail, O man," and I greeted her in return, "Hail, Lady." **3.** She answered me and said, "Did nothing meet you?" I said to her, "Yes, Lady, such a beast as could destroy nations, but by the power of the Lord, and by his great mercy, I escaped it." **4.** "You did well to escape it," she said, "because you cast your care upon God, and opened your heart to the Lord, believing that salvation can be found through nothing save through the great and glorious name. Therefore the Lord sent his angel, whose name is Thegri, who is over the beast, 'and shut his mouth that he should not hurt you.' You have escaped great tribulation through your faith, and because you were not double-minded when you saw so great a beast. **5.** Go then and tell the Lord's elect ones of his great deeds, and tell them that this beast is a type of the great persecution which is to come. If then you are prepared beforehand, and repent with all your hearts towards the Lord, you will be able to escape it, if your heart be made pure and blameless, and you serve the Lord blamelessly for the rest of the days of your life. 'Cast your cares upon the Lord' and he will put them straight. **6.** Believe on the Lord, you who are double-minded, that he can do all things, and turns his wrath away from you, and sends scourges on you who are double-minded. Woe to those who hear these words and disobey; it were better for them not to have been born.

III

1. I asked her concerning the four colours which the beast had on its head. She answered and said to me, "Are you again curious about such matters?" "Yes," I said, "Lady, let me know what they are." **2.** "Listen," she said, "the black is this world, in which you are living; **3.** the colour of fire and blood means that this world must be destroyed by blood and fire. **4.** The golden part is you, who have fled from this world, for even as gold is 'tried in the fire' and becomes valuable, so also you who live among them, are being tried. Those then who remain and pass through the flames shall be purified by them. Even as the gold puts away its dross, so also you will put away all sorrow and tribulation, and will be made pure and become useful for the building of the tower. **5.** But the white part is the world to come, in which the elect of God shall dwell, for those who have been chosen by God for eternal life will be without spot and pure. **6.** Therefore do not cease to speak to the ears of the saints. You have also the type of the great persecution to come, but if you will it shall be nothing. Remember what was written before." **7.** When she had said this she went away, and I did not see to what place she departed, for there was a cloud, and I turned backwards in fear, thinking that the beast was coming.

The Fifth Revelation

1. While I was praying at home and sitting on my bed, there entered a man glorious to look on, in the dress of a shepherd, covered with a white goatskin, with a bag on his shoulders and a staff in his hand. And he greeted me, and I greeted him back. **2.** And at once he sat down by me, and said to me, "I have been sent by the most reverend angel to dwell with you the rest of the days of your life." **3.** I thought he was come tempting me, and said to him, "Yes, but who are you? for," I said, "I know to whom I was handed over." He said to me, "Do you not recognise me?" "No," I said. "I," said he, "am the shepherd to whom you were handed over." **4.** While he was still speaking, his appearance changed, and I recognised him, that it was he to whom I was handed over; and at once I was confounded, and fear seized me, and I was quite overcome with sorrow that I had answered him so basely and foolishly. **5.** But he answered me and said, "Be not confounded, but be strong in my commandments which I am going to command you. For I was sent," said he, "to show you again all the things which you saw before, for they are the main points which are helpful to you. First of all write my commandments and the parables; but the rest you shall write as I shall show you. This is the reason," said he, "that I command you to write first the commandments and parables, that you may read them out at once, and be able to keep them." **6.** So I wrote the commandments and parables as he commanded me. **7.** If then you hear and keep them, and walk in them, and do them with a pure heart, you shall receive from the Lord all that he promised you, but if you hear them and do not repent, but continue to add to your sins, you shall receive the contrary from the Lord. All these things the shepherd commanded me to write thus, for he was the angel of repentance.

Another Parable (3)

1. He showed me many trees, without leaves, which appeared to me to be as if dry, for they were all alike. And he said to me: "Do you see these trees?" "Yes, sir," said I, "and I see that they are all alike and dry." And he answered me and said: "These trees which you see are they who dwell in this world." **2.** "Why, then," said I, "sir, are they as it were dry and all alike?" "Because," said he, "in this world, neither righteous nor sinners are apparent, but are all alike. For this world is winter for the righteous and they are not apparent, though they are living with sinners. **3.** For just as in the winter the trees which have shed their leaves are alike, and it is not apparent which are dry and which are alive, so in this world neither the righteous nor the sinners are apparent, but all are alike."

Another Parable (4)

1. He showed me again many trees, some budding and some withered, and said to me, "Do you see," said he, "these trees." "I see them, sir," said I, "some budding and some withered." **2.** "These trees," said he, "which are budding are the righteous, who are destined to live in the world to come; for the world to come is summer for the righteous, but winter for the sinners. When therefore the mercy of the Lord shall shine, then the servants of God shall be made plain and all men shall be made apparent. **3.** For, just as in the summer the fruit of each individual tree is made plain, and they are recognised for what they are, so also the fruit of the righteous will be plain, and they will all be known, by blossoming in that world. **4.** But the heathen and the sinners—the withered trees which you saw—will be found to be such, dried and fruitless in that world, and they shall be burnt up like wood and shall be made manifest, because their conduct was wicked in their lives. For the sinners shall be burnt, because they sinned and did not repent, and the heathen shall be burnt, because they did not know their Creator. **5.** Be therefore fruitful, that your fruit may be known in that summer. But abstain from much business, and you will do no sin. For those who do much business also sin much, being engrossed in their business, and serving their Lord in nothing. **6.** How then," said he, "can such a one pray for anything from the Lord and receive it, when he does not serve the Lord?" They who serve him,—they shall receive their requests. But they who do not serve the Lord,—they shall receive nothing. **7.** But if anyone be occupied with but one business, he can serve the Lord also. For his understanding is not corrupted away from the Lord, but he will serve him with a pure mind. **8.** If, therefore, you do this, you can bear fruit for the world to come. And whoever does this shall bear fruit."

Parable 6

I

1. While I was seated in my house, and was glorifying the Lord for all that I had seen, and enquiring about the commandments because they were beautiful and joyful and glorious, and 'able to save the soul' of man, I said in myself: I shall be blessed if I 'walk in these commandments,' and whoever shall walk in them shall be blessed. **2.** While I said this in myself I suddenly saw him seated by me, and saying this: "Why are you double-minded concerning the commandments which I commanded you? They are beautiful. Be not double-minded at all, but put on the faith of the Lord, and you shall walk in them, for I will strengthen you in them. **3.** These commandments are helpful to those who are going to repent, for if they do not walk in them their repentance is in vain. **4.** Do you, therefore, who repent, put away the wickednesses of this world which lead you astray, but if you put on all the virtue of righteousness, you shall be able to keep these commandments, and no longer add to your sins. Therefore walk in these commandments of mine, and you shall live to God. All these things have been spoken to you by me." **5.** And after he spoke these things with me, he said to me: "Let us go into the country, and I will show you the shepherds of the sheep." "Let us go, sir," said I. And we came into a plain, and he showed me a young shepherd, clothed with a suit of garments of yellow colour. **6.** And he was feeding very many sheep, and these sheep were well fed and very frisky, and were glad as they skipped here and there. And the shepherd himself was very joyful over his flock, and the face of the shepherd was very joyful, and he ran about among the sheep.

II

1. And he said to me: "Do you see this shepherd?" "Yes, sir," said I, "I see him." "This," said he, "is the angel of luxury and deceit. He wears out the souls of the servants of God, and perverts them from the truth, deceiving them with evil desires in which they perish. **2.** For they forget the commandments of the Living God, and walk in deceit and vain luxury, and are destroyed by this angel, some to death, and some to corruption." **3.** I said to him: "Sir, I do not know what is 'to death,' and what is 'to corruption.' " "Listen," he said, "the sheep which you see joyful and skipping, these are those which have been torn away from God completely, and have given themselves up to the lusts of this world. For these, then, there is no repentance of life, because they added to their sins and blasphemed against the name of God. Such men incur death. **4.** But the sheep which you see not skipping, but feeding in one place, these are they who have given themselves up to luxury and deceit, but have uttered no blasphemy against the Lord. These then have been corrupted from the truth; in them there is hope of repentance, in which they can live. Corruption, then, has hope of some renewing, but death has eternal destruction." **5.** Again I went on a little, and he showed me a great shepherd, as it were savage in appearance, clothed in a white goat-skin, and he had a bag on his shoulders, with a great staff, very hard and with knots, and a great whip. And he looked very bitter so that I was afraid of him, such a look had he. **6.** This shepherd then was receiving the sheep from the young shepherd; that is to say, those who were frisky and well-fed but not skipping, and put them in a certain place precipitous and thorny and full of thistles, so that the sheep could not disentangle themselves from the thorns and thistles, but were caught in the thorns and thistles. **7.** These then were being pastured all entangled in the thorns and thistles, and they were very wretched, being beaten by him, and he was driving them about here and there, and gave them no rest, and those sheep had no happy time at all.

III

1. When therefore I saw them thus beaten and miserable I grieved for them that they were being so tormented, and had no rest at all. **2.** I said to the shepherd who was speaking with me: "Sir, who is this shepherd who is so pitiless and bitter, and has no compassion at all on these sheep?" "This," said he, "is the angel of punishment. He is one of the righteous angels, but is set over punishment. **3.** Therefore he receives those who have wandered away from God, and walked in the lusts and deceits of this world, and punishes them, as they deserve, with various terrible punishments." **4.** "I should like, sir," said I, "to know these different punishments, of what kind they are." "Hear," said he, "the different tortures and punishments. The tortures befall them in this life, for some are punished with loss, others with deprivations, others with divers illnesses, others with all unsettlement, and others are insulted by the unworthy, and suffer many other things. **5.** For many have been unsettled in their counsels and try many things, and nothing goes well for them at all. And they say that they do not prosper in their undertaking, and it does not enter into their hearts that they have done wicked deeds, but they blame the Lord. **6.** When, therefore, they have been afflicted with every affliction, then they are handed over to me, for good instruction, and are made strong in the faith of the Lord, and they serve the Lord the rest of the days of their life 'with a pure heart.' And if they repent, then it enters into their hearts, that the deeds which they did were evil, and then they glorify God saying that he is 'a righteous judge,' and that they suffered righteously, 'each according to his deeds,' and for the future they serve the Lord with a pure heart, and they prosper in all their deeds, 'receiving from the Lord all things, whatever they ask'; and then they glorify the Lord that they were handed over to me, and they no longer suffer any of the evils."

IV

1. I said to him: "Sir, tell me this also." "What more," said he, "do you ask?" "Whether, Sir," said I, "those who live in luxury and are deceived are punished for the same time as they live in luxury and deceit?" And he said to me: "Yes, they are punished the same time." **2.** "Sir," said I, "they are punished a very short time, for those who live in such luxury and forget God, ought to be punished sevenfold." **3.** He said to me: "You are foolish, and do not understand the power of punishment." "No," said I, "Sir, for if I had understood it, I should not have asked you to tell me." "Listen," said he, "to the power of both. **4.** The time of luxury and deceit is one hour, but the hour of punishment has the power of thirty days. If, therefore, any man live in luxury and deceit for one day, and be punished one day, the day of punishment has the power of a whole year, for a man is punished as many years as he has lived days in luxury. You see, therefore," said he, "that the time of luxury and deceit is very short, but the time of punishment is long."

V

1. "Sir," said I, "I still do not at all understand about the time of deceit and luxury and torture; explain it to me more clearly." **2.** He answered and said to me: "Your foolishness is lasting, and you do not wish to purify your heart and to serve God. See to it," said he, "lest the time be fulfilled, and you be found still foolish. Listen, then," said he, "that you may understand it as you wish. **3.** He who lives in luxury and deceit for a single day, and does what he likes, is clothed with great foolishness, and does not understand the deed which he is doing. For he forgets to-morrow what he did yesterday. For luxury and deceit have no memory, because of the foolishness which they have put on. But when punishment and torture cleave to a man for a single day, he is punished and tortured for a year, for punishment and torture have long memories. **4.** Therefore, being tortured and punished for a whole year, he then remembers his luxury and deceit, and knows that he is suffering evil because of them. Therefore, all men who live in luxury and deceit are thus tortured, because though they have life, they have given themselves over to death." **5.** "What sort of luxuries, Sir," said I, "are harmful?" "Every act which a man does with pleasure," said he, "is luxury, for even the ill-tempered man, by giving satisfaction to his own temper, lives luxuriously. And the adulterer and drunkard and evil-speaker and liar, and the covetous and the robber, and he who does such things as these gives satisfaction to his own disease; therefore he lives in luxury from his own acts. **6.** All these luxuries are harmful to the servants of God. Those, therefore, who are punished and tortured suffer, because of these deceits. **7.** But there are also luxuries which bring men salvation, for many who do good luxuriate and are carried away with their own pleasure. This luxury therefore is profitable to the servants of God, and brings life to such a man. But the harmful luxuries spoken of already bring them torture and punishment. But if they continue in them and do not repent, they procure death for themselves."

5 EZRA 2:42-48 (2 Esdras 2:42-48)

Commentary

The title 5 Ezra is applied by modern scholars to the first two chapters of 2 Esdras. (Chaps. 3–14 of 2 Esdras are known also as 4 Ezra. See the discussion on 4 Ezra). This addition to 4 Ezra, a Jewish apocalypse, was made by a Christian writer, likely during the second century.

The purpose of 5 Ezra is to validate God's turning from the Jewish people to the Gentiles. After an initial section describing Ezra's genealogy and prophetic call, 5 Ezra recounts God's dealings with Israel, declaring that Israel had been unfaithful to its covenant with God. God will therefore reject the Jews and offer their former promises and blessings to the Gentiles—that is, the Christians. When the people of Israel refuse to heed the words from Ezra, he delivers his message to the Gentiles.

The final section of 5 Ezra (2:42-48) contains an apocalyptic vision revealed to the prophet. Ezra sees on Mount Zion an innumerable crowd of people, praising God and being given crowns and palms by another individual, "a young man of great stature." Perplexed, Ezra asks an angel to explain these sights to him. The angel replies that the multitude of people are those who "have put off mortal clothing and have put on the immortal, and they have confessed the name of God" (2:45). Ezra describes them as "those who had stood valiantly for the name of the Lord" (2:47). These are the Christian faithful, perhaps martyrs (compare this scene with Rev. 7:9-17 and 14:1-5). The young man of great stature is identified by the angel as "the Son of God, whom they confessed in the world" (2:47).

Although brief, this final section (2:42-48) fits the formal characteristics of an apocalypse. It is revelatory literature set within a narrative framework in which a human recipient (Ezra) is granted a vision interpreted by an angel. The vision of the redeemed receiving crowns and palm branches contains both spatial and temporal elements. The spatial aspect of this vision is seen in otherworldly beings (the angel mediator and the Son of God who rewards the righteous) and in otherworldly places (Mount Zion, which is not the earthly Mount Zion). The temporal aspect is evident in the eschatological rewards for the righteous. This material deserves to be classified as a small, Christian apocalypse. The remainder of 5 Ezra is not apocalyptic literature, although it does contain elements of apocalyptic eschatology.

266

The apocalypse in 2:42-48 shows striking parallels with passages in the book of Revelation. In 5 Ezra the author sees "a great multitude, which I could not number," praising God (2:42). These people, who have "put off mortal clothing and have put on the immortal" are given palm branches and crowns (2:43-46). In Revelation 7:9-10, John of Patmos sees "a great multitude which no man could number," dressed in white robes, holding palm branches in their hands, and offering praise to God. Elsewhere in Revelation (2:10; 3:11; 4:4, 10) crowns are rewards given to the righteous. Furthermore, in 5 Ezra the great multitude is gathered on Mount Zion. In Revelation 14:1-5, John sees a group (144,000) gathered on Mount Zion, singing a new song before the throne of God. (Compare also with 4 Ezra 13:33-36, where the innumerable multitude that gathers on Mount Zion are the people opposed to the Son of God.)

The dating of 5 Ezra is uncertain. It definitely originates after the first century because of its dependence upon certain New Testament writings. Allusions to passages from the Gospels and Revelation are evident in several places, especially in chapter 2. Furthermore, the description of the Son of God as a man of great stature has parallels in the *Gospel of Peter,* the *Acts of Perpetua and Felicitas,* and the *Shepherd of Hermas,* all second-century writings. Finally, the harsh polemic of 5 Ezra against Judaism probably reflects a relatively early period in the life of the Christian church, when Jewish-Christian conflicts were still volatile. For these reasons, most scholars date 5 Ezra during the second century.

Although some sections of 5 Ezra may contain reworked Jewish material, its present contents are certainly from a Christian writer. The anti-Jewish sentiment of the work and the use of the New Testament by the author demand this conclusion.

None of the oriental manuscripts of 2 Esdras contain 5 Ezra. These chapters are found only in the Latin versions. On the basis of linguistics, most scholars conclude that behind these Latin versions was a Greek manuscript, likely the original version of 5 Ezra.

The text that follows comes from the Revised Standard Version of the Bible.

5 Ezra 2:42-48

2. [42] I, Ezra, saw on Mount Zion a great multitude, which I could not number, and they all were praising the Lord with songs. [43] In their midst was a young man of great stature, taller than any of the others, and on the head of each of them he placed a crown, but he was more exalted than they. And I was held spellbound. 44 Then I asked an angel, "Who are these, my lord?" 45 He answered and said to me, "These are they who have put off mortal clothing and have put on the immortal, and they have confessed the name of God; now they are being crowned, and receive palms." 46 Then I said to the angel, "Who is that young man who places crowns on them and puts palms in their hands?" 47 He answered and said to me, "He is the Son of God, whom they confessed in the world." So I began to praise those who had stood valiantly for the name of the Lord. 48 Then the angel said to me, "Go, tell my people how great and many are the wonders of the Lord God which you have seen."

THE (FIRST) APOCALYPSE OF JAMES (V, 3)

Commentary

The *(First) Apocalypse of James* is one of the writings discovered in 1945 in Nag Hammadi, Egypt, which collectively are known as the Nag Hammadi library. The Nag Hammadi library consists of fifty-two different works, bound into thirteen books, or codices. These materials, probably originally written between the first and fourth centuries c.e., were collected and translated from Greek into Coptic by Christians. The present manuscripts date from around 400 c.e. These works reflect the teachings and beliefs of Gnosticism (from the Greek word *gnosis*, meaning "knowledge"), a complex and diverse religious system characterized by the beliefs that the physical world is evil and that salvation consists of escape from this world and a return to one's heavenly origin by means of special, revealed knowledge. Christian Gnosticism was declared heretical and was vigorously attacked by several church leaders in the second through the fourth centuries.

Two different Nag Hammadi works are entitled the *Apocalypse of James*. To differentiate them, modern scholars usually refer to them as the *(First) Apocalypse of James* and the *(Second) Apocalypse of James*. The *(First) Apocalypse of James* is pseudonymous. No clues concerning authorship are given, thus the author remains unknown. Due to supposed Valentinian influence (Valentinus was a second-century Christian Gnostic), the composition of the work is sometimes dated around 200 c.e. The place of its composition is unknown, although the references to Addai (36.15-24) suggest contact with, if not location in or near, northern Mesopotamia or northern Syria. (Addai is the traditional founder of the Syriac-speaking church at Edessa in northern Mesopotamia.)

The *(First) Apocalypse of James* consists of two revelations supposedly given to James the Just, the brother of Jesus. Unlike the revelations usually found in apocalyptic writings, which occur through visions, the revelations in this work are given by means of dialogues between Jesus and James. The otherworldly mediator is Jesus, who has come to earth to reveal the "mystery" of humanity's place in the universe and to provide the necessary knowledge for people to journey successfully to Him-who-is, the Pre-existent Father.

The first revelation is given prior to Jesus' death. In the dialogue with James, Jesus reveals that there are seventy-two heavens, controlled by

269

the twelve archons. These heavens and archons, together with their angels and "unnumbered hosts," constitute the evil powers that are armed against Jesus and those aligned with him (26.14–28.4). James is told to leave Jerusalem because it is the residence of a large number of archons (25.15-19). The deaths of both Jesus and James are foretold (25.7-14; 29.9-19). Jesus tells James, who is worried that he will not be able to escape the evil powers, that his redemption is secure (25.10-21; 28.29–29.13).

The second dialogue occurs after Jesus' death, when he appears to James on the mountain Gaugelan. After James expresses concern over the suffering that Jesus endured, Jesus assures him that he did not suffer at his death. Jesus further reveals to James what he needs to say to the hostile powers who will attempt to prevent the ascent of his soul after death. These powers not only "demand toll, but they also take away souls by theft" (33.9-11). By making the correct response to their inquiries, James will be able to escape these powers and to complete his ascent to the Pre-existent One (34.19-20). After receiving these instructions, James is told to keep them secret, revealing them only to Addai, who after ten years is to write them down.

The final part of the dialogue of Jesus with James concerns the value of the women disciples of Jesus and the high esteem in which they are held. The work then concludes with James' rebuke of the twelve disciples and probably an account of his martyrdom (the manuscript is badly damaged in this section).

The eschatology of the *(First) Apocalypse of James* is personal eschatology. Its primary concern is the ascent of James' soul after death. In keeping with Gnostic belief that the physical world is evil, there is no interest in cosmic eschatology, the creation of a new heaven and earth.

The text given here, taken from *The Nag Hammadi Library,* has been translated by William R. Schoedel and edited by Douglas M. Parrott. Page and line divisions are indicated in the text. Page numbers are given in bold type. Double lines (∥) in the text indicate line divisions. Every fifth line (or occasionally more often) the double lines are replaced by a small number indicating the line number.

The (First) Apocalypse of James (V 24, 10-44, 10)

The Apocalypse of James ∥

It is the Lord who spoke with me: ∥ "See now the completion of my redemption. ∥ I have given you a sign of these things, James, ∥ my brother.

For not without reason have I called [15] you my brother, although you are not my brother | materially. And I am not ignorant | concerning you; so that | when I give you a sign—know and | hear.

"Nothing existed except [20] Him-who-is. He is unnameable | and ineffable. | I myself also am unnameable, | from Him-who-is, just as I have been | [given a] number of names—two [25] from Him-who-is. And I, | [I] am before you. Since you have | [asked] concerning femaleness, femaleness existed, | but femaleness was | not [first]. And [30] [it] prepared for itself powers and gods. | But [it did] not exist [when] I came forth, **25** since I am an image of Him-who-is. | But I have brought forth the image of [him] | so that the sons of Him-who-is | might know what things are theirs [5] and what things are alien (to them). Behold, | I shall reveal to you everything | of this mystery. For they will seize | me the day after tomorrow. But my | redemption will be near." [10]

James said, "Rabbi, you have said, | 'They will seize me.' But I, | what can I do?" He said to me, | "Fear not, James. | You too will they seize. [15] But leave Jerusalem. | For it is she who always gives the cup of bitterness | to the sons | of light. She is a dwelling place | of a great number of archons. [20] But your redemption will be preserved | from them. So that | you may understand who they are [and] | what kinds they are, you will [. . .]. | And listen. They [are] not [. . .] [25] but [archons . . .]. | These twelve | [. . .] down [. . .] [29] archons [. . .] **26** upon his own hebdomad." |

James said, "Rabbi, are there then | twelve hebdomads | and not seven as [5] there are in the scriptures?" | The Lord said, "James, he who spoke | concerning this scripture had a limited understanding. | I, however, shall reveal to you | what has come forth from him [10] who has no number. I shall give a sign concerning their | number. As for what has come forth from him | who has no measure, I shall give a sign concerning their | measure."

James said, | "Rabbi, behold then, I have received [15] their number. There are seventy-two measures!" | The Lord said, "These | are the seventy-two heavens, which | are their subordinates. These are the powers of | all their might; and they were [20] established by them; | and these are they who were distributed | everywhere, existing under the [authority] | of the twelve archons. | The inferior power among them [25] [brought forth] for itself angels | [and] unnumbered hosts. | Him-who-is, however, has been given | [. . .] on account of | [. . .] Him-who-is [30] [. . .] they are unnumbered. **27** If you want | to give them a number now, you [will] | not be able to (do so) until you cast away | from yourself

271

blind thought, 5 this bond of flesh which encircles you. | And then you will reach | Him-who-is. | And you will no longer be | James; rather you are 10 the One-who-is. And all those who are | unnumbered will | all have been named."|

⟨James said, "Then,⟩ | Rabbi, in what way shall I reach 15 Him-who-is, since | all these powers and these | hosts are armed against me?" | He said to me, "These powers | are not armed against you specifically, 20 but are armed against another. | It is against me that they are armed. | And they are armed with other [powers]. | But they are armed against me [in] | judgment. They did not give [. . .] 25 to me in it [. . .] | through them [. . .]. | In this place [. . .] | suffering, I shall [. . .]. | He will [. . .] 28 and I shall not rebuke them. But there shall | be within me a silence and | a hidden mystery. But I | am fainthearted before their anger." 5

James said, "Rabbi, | if they arm themselves against you, then | is there no blame?

> You have come with knowledge,
> that | you might rebuke their forgetfulness.
> You have come with | recollection,
> that you might rebuke their 10 ignorance.

But I was concerned | because of you.

> For you descended into a | great ignorance,
> but | you have not been defiled by anything in it. |
> For you descended into a great mindlessness, 15
> and your recollection remained. |

> You walked in mud, |
> and your garments were not soiled, |
> and you have not been buried | in their filth,
> and 20 you have not been caught.

And I was | not like them, but I clothed myself with everything | of theirs.

> There is in me | forgetfulness,
> yet I | remember things that are not theirs. 25
> There is in me [. . .], |
> and I am in their | [. . .].

[. . .] knowledge | [. . .] not in their sufferings | [. . .]. But I have

272

become afraid 30 [before them], since they rule. For what **29** will they do? What will I be able | to say? Or what word will I be able | to say that I may escape them?" |

The Lord said, "James, I praise 5 your understanding and your fear. | If you continue to be distressed, | do not be concerned for anything else | except your redemption. | For behold, I shall complete this destiny 10 upon this earth as | I have said from the heavens. | And I shall reveal to you | your redemption."

James said, | "Rabbi, how, after these things, 15 will you appear to us again? | After they seize you, | and you complete this destiny, | you will go up to Him- | who-is." The Lord said, "James, 20 after these things I shall reveal to you | everything, not for your sake | alone but for the sake of [the] | unbelief of men, | so that [faith] may 25 exist in them. | For [a] multitude will [attain] | to faith [and] | they will increase [in . . .]. **30** And after this I shall appear | for a reproof to the archons. And I shall | reveal to them that | he cannot be seized. If they 5 seize him, then | he will overpower each of them. | But now I shall go. Remember | the things I have spoken and let them | go up before you." 10 James said, "Lord, I shall hasten | as you have said." | The Lord said farewell to him and fulfilled | what was fitting.

When James | heard of his sufferings 15 and was much distressed, | they awaited the sign | of his coming. And he came after | several days. And James | was walking upon the mountain, 20 which is called "Gaugelan," | with his disciples, | who listened to him | [because they had been distressed], and he was | [. . .] a comforter, 25 [saying], "This is | [. . .] the (or: a) second [. . . . " | Then the] crowd dispersed, | but James remained | [. . .] prayer 30 [. . .], as **31** was his custom. |

And the Lord appeared to him. | Then he stopped (his) prayer | and embraced him. He kissed 5 him, saying, "Rabbi, | I have found you! I have heard of your | sufferings, which you endured. And | I have been much distressed. My | compassion you know. 10 Therefore, on reflection, I was wishing | that I would not see this people. They must | be judged for these things that they have done. | For these things that they have done are contrary to | what is fitting."

The Lord said, 15 "James, do not be concerned | for me or for | this people. I am he who | was within me. Never | have I suffered in any way, 20 nor have I been distressed. | And this people has done | me no harm. | But this (people) existed [as] | a type of the archons, 25 and it deserved to be [destroyed] | through them. But [. . .] | the archons, [. . .] | who (or: which) has [. . .] | but since it (fem.) [. . .] 30 angry with [. . . . | The]

273

just [. . .] **32** is his servant. Therefore | your name is 'James | the Just.'
is You see | how you will become sober when you see ⁵ me. And you
stopped this prayer. | Now since you are a just | man of God, you have |
embraced me and kissed me. | Truly I say to you that ¹⁰ you have stirred
up great anger and | wrath against yourself. But | (this has happened) so
that these others might come to be." |

But James was timid | (and) wept. And he was very distressed. ¹⁵ And
they both sat down | upon a rock. The Lord said | to him, "James, thus |
you will undergo these sufferings. But do not | be sad. For the flesh is ²⁰
weak. It will receive what has been | ordained for it. But as for you, do not
| be [timid] or afraid." | The Lord [ceased].

[Now] when James | heard these things, he ²⁵ wiped away [the] tears in
| [his eyes] and very bitter (?) | [. . .] which is | [. . .]. The Lord [said] to
[him, | "James], behold, I shall **33** reveal to you your redemption. | When
[you] are seized, | and you undergo these sufferings, | a multitude will
arm themselves against you ⁵ that ⟨they⟩ may seize you. And in particular
| three of them | will seize you—they who | sit (there) as toll collectors. Not
| only do they demand toll, but ¹⁰ they also take away souls | by theft.
When | you come into their power, | one of them who is their guard will
say | to you, ¹⁵ 'Who are you or where are you from?' | You are to say to
him, 'I am | a son, and I am from | the Father.' He will say to you, | 'What
sort of son are you, and ²⁰ to what father do you belong?' You are to | say
to him, 'I am from | the Pre-existent Father, | and a son in the |
Pre-existent One.' [When he says] ²⁵ to you, [. . .], | you are to [say to
him, . . .] | in the [. . .] | that I might [. . .].

"[. . . **34** of] alien things?" You are to say to him, | 'They are not
entirely alien, | but they are from Achamoth, | who is the female. And
these ⁵ she produced as she brought down the race | from the |
Pre-existent One. So then | they are not alien, but they are ours. | They
are indeed ours because she who ¹⁰ is mistress of them is from | the
Pre-existent One. | At the same time they are alien because | the
Pre-existent One did not | have intercourse with her, when she ¹⁵
produced them.' When he also says to you, | "Where will you go?,' you
are to | say to him, 'To the place from which I have come, | there shall I
return.' | And if you say these things, you will ²⁰ escape their attacks.

"But when | you come to | [these] three detainers | [who] take away
souls by | theft in that place ²⁵ [. . .] these. You | [. . .] a vessel | [. . .]
much more than [. . .] **35** of the one (fem.) whom | you [. . .] for [. . .]
| her root. You | too will ⁵ be sober [. . .]. But I shall call | [upon] the
imperishable knowledge, | which is Sophia who | is in the Father (and)

who is the mother | of Achamoth. [10] Achamoth had no father nor | male consort, but | she is female from a | female. She produced you (pl.) | without a male, since she was alone [15] (and) in ignorance as to what | [lives through] her mother because she thought | that she alone existed. | But [I] shall cry out | to her mother. And then [20] they will fall into confusion (and) will | blame their | root and the race [of] | their mother. [But] you | will go up to [what is] [25] yours [. . .] | you will [. . .] **36** the [Pre-existent One].

"[They are | a] type [of the] twelve | disciples and [the] twelve | pairs, [. . .] [5] Achamoth, which is | translated 'Sophia.' | And who I myself am, | and (who) the imperishable Sophia (is) | through whom you will be redeemed, [10] and (who are) all the sons of Him-who- | is—these things they have known | and have hidden within | them. You are to hide ⟨these things⟩ within you, | and you are to keep silence. [15] But you are to reveal them to | Addai. When you [depart], | immediately war will be [made] | with this land. [Weep], | then, for him who dwells in Jerusalem. [20] But let Addai take these things | to heart. In the tenth | year let Addai sit | and write them down. | And when he writes them down [25] [. . .] and they are to give them | [. . .] he has the [. . .] **37**[6] he is [called] | Levi. Then he is to bring | [. . .] word | [. . .] from [10] [what I] said earlier | [. . .] a woman | [. . .] Jerusalem in her | [. . . and] he begets | [two] sons through her. [15] [They are to] inherit these things | [and] the understanding of him who | [. . .] exalts. And they are to receive | [. . .] through him from his | intellect. Now, the younger of them [20] is greater. And | may these things remain | hidden in him until [he] | comes to the age of | seventeen years [. . .] **38**[3] beginning [. . .] [5] through [them]. They will pursue | him exceedingly, since [they are] from | his [. . .] companions. He will be | proclaimed [through] them, | and [they will] proclaim this word. [10] [Then he will become] | a seed of [. . .]." |

James said, "[I am] | satisfied [. . .] | and they are [. . .] [15] my soul. Yet [another thing] | I ask of you: who are the [seven] | women who have [been] your disciples? | And behold, | all women bless you. [20] I also am amazed | how [powerless] vessels | have become strong by a perception | which is in them." | [The] Lord [said], "You [. . .] well [. . .] **39**[3] a spirit [of . . .]. | a [spirit] of thought, [a spirit] [5] of counsel of [a . . .], | a spirit [. . . , a] spirit | of knowledge [. . .] of their | fear. [. . .] when we had passed | through [the breath] of [10] [this] archon who | is [named] Adonaios | [. . .] him and | [. . .] he was ignorant | [. . .] when I came forth from him, [15] [he] remembered that I | am [a] son of his. He was gracious | [to me] at that time as | his son. And then, | before ⟨I⟩ [20]

appeared here, ⟨he⟩ | cast them among [this] | people. And from the [place] | of heaven the prophets [. . .]." **40**[4]

James [said], "Rabbi, [. . .] [6] I [. . .] all together | [. . .] in them | especially [. . .]." | The Lord said, "[James], I [10] praise [you . . .] | walk upon the earth [. . .] | the words while he [. . .] | on the [. . .]. | For cast away from [you the] [15] cup, which is bitterness. | For some from [. . .] | set themselves against you. For [you have begun] | to understand [their roots] | from beginning to end. Cast [20] away from yourself all lawlessness. | And beware lest | they envy you. When you | speak these words of this | [perception], encourage these [25] [four]: Salome and Mariam | [and Martha and Arsinoe . . .] **41**[6] since he takes | some [. . .] to me | he is [. . .] burnt offerings | and [. . .]. But I [10] [. . .] not in this way; but | [. . .] first-fruits of the | [. . .] upward | [. . .] so that | the power [of God might] appear. [15] The perishable has [gone | up] to the imperishable and | the female element has | attained to this male element." |

James said, [20] "Rabbi, into these three (things), then, | has their [. . .] been cast. | For they have been reviled, [and they have been] | persecuted [. . .]. **42**[5] Behold | [. . .] everything | [. . .] from | anyone [. . .]. | For you have received [. . .] of [10] knowledge. [And . . .] | that what is the [. . .] | go [. . .] | you will [find . . .]. | But I shall go [forth] [15] and shall reveal | that they believed in you [that they may] | be content with their [blessing] | and salvation, and | this revelation may come to pass." [20] And he went at that time | [immediately] and rebuked the | twelve, and cast | [out] of them contentment | [concerning the] way of knowledge [. . .].

[. . .]. **43**[7] And the majority | of [them . . .] when they | [saw, the] messenger took in [10] [. . .]. The others [. . .] [12] said, "[. . .] [14] him from this earth. | For [he is] not [worthy] of life." | These, then, [were] afraid. They arose, | saying, "We | have no part in this blood, | for a just man [20] will perish through | injustice." James departed | so that [. . .] **44**[6] look | [. . .] for | we (?) [. . .] him. |

The Apocalypse [10] of James

CHAPTER FIVE

APOCALYPSES THAT CONTAIN OTHERWORLDLY JOURNEYS

THE ASCENSION OF ISAIAH 6–11

Commentary

The *Ascension of Isaiah* is composed of two works that probably originated and circulated independently. The first work (chaps. 1–5), known as the *Martyrdom of Isaiah,* tells of the martyrdom of the prophet Isaiah by the Judean king, Manasseh. The narrative of the martyrdom of Isaiah was likely a Jewish writing, later revised by a Christian editor who was responsible for various Christian interpolations in the text. The major Christian alteration of the story was the addition of the material in 3:13–4:22. The second work (chaps. 6–11) describes a vision that Isaiah had in which he ascended into the seven heavens. This latter narrative, sometimes called the *Vision of Isaiah,* is a Christian apocalypse, probably written at the end of the first century or during the first half of the second century c.e. No clues concerning place of composition or the identity of the author are given in the text. The final editing and composition of the entire *Ascension of Isaiah* were apparently accomplished during the third or fourth century c.e.

The story in chapters 6–11 is set during the reign of Hezekiah, king of Judah and father of Manasseh. Isaiah and his son Josab come into the court of Hezekiah, in which are gathered "all the princes of

277

Israel . . . and the eunuchs and the king's counselors," along with forty prophets (6:3). In the midst of his speech to the king, Isaiah suddenly becomes silent, and "his mind was taken up from him" (6:10) as he experiences a vision in which an angel appears to him and takes him on a journey through the seven heavens.

In the firmament, located between earth and the first heaven, Isaiah sees Sammael (Satan) and his forces engaged in a struggle, which is reflected in the strife and dissension on earth. The angel guide then takes Isaiah up through the seven heavens. In the middle of each of the first five heavens, Isaiah sees a throne with angels on each side, offering up praise to "[the One who sits in] the seventh heaven . . . and to his Beloved" (7:17). As he ascends, Isaiah notices not only that the glory of each heaven surpasses that of the preceding heaven, but also that his own glory is being transformed as he travels from heaven to heaven (7:25).

The sixth heaven is different from those below it. In addition to being more glorious than the preceding heavens, the sixth heaven contains no throne in the middle or division of angels on the left and right. Here all angels are equal in appearance and praise; their voices also are different from those in the lower heavens. Furthermore, the light of the sixth heaven is so bright that in comparison the lower heavens appear to be in darkness. Isaiah is so overwhelmed by the sixth heaven that he does not wish to return to earth.

The seventh and highest heaven contains, in addition to an innumerable host of angels, all the righteous from the beginning of humanity, dressed in their heavenly robes. Isaiah also sees there the robes to be worn by future recipients, those who will believe in and obey the words of Christ, and the thrones and crowns that will be given to all the righteous at the time of Christ's ascension. The major portion of the seventh heaven material is a description, cast in the form of an *ex eventu* prophecy to Isaiah, of the descent of Christ through the heavens to earth, his miraculous birth, his death, his resurrection, and finally his ascension through the lower heavens back to the seventh heaven, where he sits "at the right hand of that Great Glory" (11:32). Isaiah is returned to earth, and his vision ends. After describing the contents of his vision for Hezekiah and for those who are with him, Isaiah makes the king swear that he will not reveal the vision to anyone or allow anyone to write what Isaiah had said. This command to secrecy is a technique common in apocalyptic literature and is used to explain why supposedly ancient documents had only recently become known (see Dan. 12:4; 4 Ezra 14:46).

The eschatological interest of the *Ascension of Isaiah* 6–11 is twofold: personal eschatology and the role of Christ. Aside from the statement that Christ will "judge and destroy the princes and the angels and the gods of that world, and the world which is ruled by them" (10:12), and the claim that the end of this world will occur in the last generation (11:37-38), this apocalypse contains no reference to cosmic destruction. Its focus, rather, is on the eschatological hope of the righteous. Individual judgment on the basis of one's deeds is implied in the description of the heavenly books that contain "the deeds of the children of Israel" (9:22; compare Dan. 7:10; Rev. 20:12; 4 Ezra 6:20; *1 Enoch* 89:61-64; 98:6-8). The righteous, like Isaiah, will be transformed (symbolized by the heavenly robes that they receive), will share in Christ's reign (symbolized by the thrones), and will be rewarded with heavenly crowns (9:9-18, 24-26). These rewards for the righteous (robes, thrones, and crowns) are similar to the promises given to the righteous, especially the martyrs, in the New Testament book of Revelation (see 3:5, 11, 21; 6:11; 7:9, 14; 20:4-6). The righteous in heaven seem to be accorded a status higher than that of even the angels in heaven. The righteous are the first, followed by the angels, to worship the Lord, the Holy Spirit, and the Great Glory (9:28-29, 33-34, 41-42).

Christ, God's Beloved, is the divine eschatological agent of judgment and destruction. The events on earth are a reflection of the violence, jealousy, and strife among Sammael and his hosts in the firmament (7:9-12; 10:29-31). The "god of that world" (apparently Sammael) is responsible for the crucifixion of Christ. Yet, God will ultimately triumph over evil through Christ, who will plunder the angel of death (9:16) and destroy the wicked and their world (10:12-13). When he ascends from earth to heaven, even Sammael and his forces will join in the worship of Christ (11:23). In the end, however, Sammael, too, will be destroyed (7:12).

The strong eschatological orientation of the work implies that one of the purposes of the *Ascension of Isaiah* 6–11 was to encourage and to reassure Christians of the heavenly blessings that awaited them. Nothing, not even Sammael or the guardians of the heavens, would prevent Christ from carrying out his mission and returning triumphantly to God's side. The writing gives no indication of any persecution or threat that the readers were facing (unless one sees the linking of Isaiah's martyrdom with the crucifixion of Christ in 8:12 as a veiled identification of the reader's sufferings with those of Christ; this understanding seems too subtle, however). If a crisis had precipitated the writing of this apocalypse, perhaps it was a theological crisis—namely, a loss of confidence in the fulfillment of eschatological hopes.

The *Ascension of Isaiah* 6–11 exhibits several characteristics that are similar to ideas found in some Gnostic writings. One of the most obvious parallels is the idea that the various heavens are guarded by powers or beings who control passage through the heavens. A special password is needed to pass through the gates. Christ, the heavenly redeemer, must disguise himself from the evil powers in order to journey from heaven to earth. This characteristic, along with several others (the belief that Christ stayed on earth for 545 days after his resurrection [9:16], the descent of Christ through the heavens [10:17-31], the ascent motif), suggests that the *Ascension of Isaiah* 6–11, while not necessarily itself of Gnostic origin, was influenced by Christian Gnosticism.

The translation of the text of the *Ascension of Isaiah* 6–11 included here is by M. A. Knibb from *The Old Testament Pseudepigrapha*, volume 2.

The Ascension of Isaiah 6–11

6. In the twentieth year of the reign of Hezekiah, king of Judah, Isaiah the son of Amoz and Josab the son of Isaiah came to Hezekiah in Jerusalem from Gilgal. ²And he sat on the couch of the king, and they brought a seat for him, but he would not sit (on it). ³And when Isaiah began to speak with Hezekiah the king the words of faith and righteousness, all the princes of Israel were sitting (there), and the eunuchs and the king's counselors. And there were there forty prophets and sons of the prophets; they had come from the neighboring districts, and from the mountains, and from the country, when they had heard that Isaiah was coming from Gilgal to Hezekiah. ⁴They came that they might greet him, and that they might hear his words, ⁵and that he might lay his hand on them, and that they might prophesy, and that he might hear their prophecy; and they were all in the presence of Isaiah. ⁶And when Isaiah spoke with Hezekiah the words of righteousness and faith, they all heard a door being opened and the voice of the Spirit. ⁷And the king summoned all the prophets and all the people who were to be found there, and they came. And Micah, and the aged Ananias, and Joel, and Josab were sitting on his right. ⁸And when they all heard the voice of the Holy Spirit, they all worshiped on their knees, and they praised the God of righteousness, the Most High, the One who (dwells) in the upper world and who sits on high, the Holy One, the One who rests among the holy ones, ⁹and they ascribed glory to the One who had thus graciously given a door in an alien world, had graciously given it to a man. ¹⁰And while he was speaking with the Holy Spirit in the hearing of them all, he became silent, and his mind was taken up from him, and he did not see the men who were standing before him. ¹¹His eyes indeed were open, but his mouth was silent, and the mind in his body was taken up from him. ¹²But his breath was (still) in him, for he was seeing a vision. ¹³And the angel who was sent to show him (the vision) was not of this firmament, nor was he from the angels of glory of this world, but he came from the seventh heaven. ¹⁴And the people who were standing by, apart from the circle of prophets, did [not] think that the holy Isaiah had been taken up. ¹⁵And the vision which he saw was not from this world, but from the world which is hidden from the flesh. ¹⁶And after Isaiah had seen this vision he recounted it to Hezekiah, and to Josab his son, and to the other prophets who had come. ¹⁷But the officials, and the eunuchs, and the people did not hear, apart from Samnas the secretary, and Jehoiakim, and Asaph the recorder, for they (were) doers of righteousness, and the fragrance of the Spirit was in them; but the people did not hear, for Micah and Josab his son had sent them out when the wisdom of this world was taken from him as if he were dead.

7. The vision which Isaiah saw he told to Hezekiah, and to Josab his son, and to Micah, and to the other prophets; ²it was as follows. When I prophesied in accordance with the message which you have heard, I saw a glorious angel; his glory was not like the glory of the angels which I always used to see, but he had great glory, and an office, such that I cannot describe the glory of this angel. ³And I saw when he took hold of me by my hand, and I said to him, "Who are you? And what is your name? And where are you taking me up?" For strength had been given to me that I might speak with him. ⁴And he said to me, "When I have taken you up through (all) the stages and have shown you the vision on account of which I was sent, then you will understand who I am; but my name you will not know, ⁵for you have to return into this body. But where I take you up, you will see, because for this purpose I was sent." ⁶And I rejoiced because he spoke to me with kindness. ⁷And he said to me, "Do you rejoice because I have spoken kindly to you?" And he said, "You will see one greater than me, how he will speak kindly and gently with you; ⁸and the Father of the one who is greater you will also see, because for this purpose I was sent from the seventh heaven, that I

281

might make all this clear to you." [9]And we went up into the firmament, I and he, and there I saw Sammael and his hosts; and there was a great struggle in it, {and the words of Satan, and they were envying one another}.[a] [10]And as above, so also on earth, for the likeness of what (is) in the firmament is here on earth. [11]And I said to the angel, "What is this envying?" [12]And he said to me, "So it has been ever since this world existed until now, and this struggle (will last) until the one comes whom you are to see, and he will destroy him." [13]And after this he took me up above the firmament; this is the [first] heaven. [14]There I saw a throne in the middle, and on the right and on the left of it there were angels. [15]And [the angels on the left] were not like the angels who stood on the right, but those who stood on the right had more glory, and they all sang praises with one voice. And the throne was in the middle, and it they praised, and those on the left after them; but their voice was not like the voice of those on the right, nor their praise like the praise of those (on the right). [16]And I asked the angel who led me and said to him, "To whom is this praise directed?" [17]And he said to me, "To the praise of [the One who sits in] the seventh heaven, the One who rests in the holy world, and to his Beloved, from where I was sent to you. To there it is directed." [18]And again, he took me up into the second heaven, and the height of that heaven is like that from heaven to earth and to the firmament. [19]And [I saw there, as] in the first heaven, angels on the right and on the left, and a throne in the middle, and the praise of the angels who (were) in the second heaven; and the one who sat on the throne in the second heaven had more glory than all (the rest). [20]And there was great glory in the second heaven, and their praise was not like the praise of those who (were) in the first heaven. [21]And I fell on my face to worship him, and the angel who led me would not let me, but said to me, "Worship neither throne, nor angel from the six heavens, from where I was sent to lead you, before I tell you in the seventh heaven. [22]For above all the heavens and their angels is placed your throne, and also your robes and your crown which you are to see." [23]And I rejoiced very much that those who love the Most High and his Beloved will at their end go up there through the angel of the Holy Spirit. [24]And he took me up into the third heaven, and in the same way I saw those who (were) on the right and on the left, and there also (there was) a throne in the middle and one who sat (on it), but no mention of this world was made there. [25]And I said to the angel

---

[a]So reads the Ethiopian manuscript, but it is corrupt. It should read, as found in certain Latin manuscripts, "and the angels of Satan were envying one another."

who (was) with me, for the glory of my face was being transformed as I went up from heaven to heaven, "Nothing of the vanity of that world is named here." 26And he answered me, saying, "Nothing is named because of its weakness, but nothing is hidden which is done there." 27And I wished to find out how it is known; and he answered me, saying, "When I have taken you up into the seventh heaven, from where I was sent, to the One which (is) above these, then you will know that nothing is hidden from the thrones and those who dwell in the heavens, nor from the angels." And the praises which they sang and the glory of the one who sat on the throne were great, and the angels who (were) on the right and on the left had more glory than (those in) the heaven which (was) below them. 28And again he took me up into the fourth heaven, and the height from the third to the fourth heaven was greater than (from) earth to the firmament. 29And there I again saw those who (were) on the right and those who (were) on the left, and the one who sat on the throne was in the middle, and there also they were singing praises. 30And the praise and glory of the angels on the right was greater than that of those on the left. 31And again the glory of the one who sat on the throne was greater than that of the angels who (were) on the right, but their glory (was) greater than that of those below. 32And he took me up into the fifth heaven. 33And again I saw those who (were) on the right and the left, and the one who sat on the throne had more glory than those of the fourth heaven. 34And the glory of those who (were) on the right was greater than that of those who (were) on the left . . . 35The glory of the one on the throne was greater than that of the angels who (were) on the right, 36but their praise was more glorious than that of the fourth heaven. 37And I praised the One who is not named and is unique, who dwells in the heavens, whose name is unknown to all flesh, the One who has given such glory to the different heavens, who makes the glory of the angels great and the glory of the one who sits on the throne (even) greater.

8. And again, he took me up into the air of the sixth heaven, and I saw a splendor such as I had not seen in the five heavens as I went up; 2the angels possessed great glory, 3and the praise there was holy and wonderful. 4And I said to the angel who led me, "What (is) this which I see, my lord?" 5And he said to me, "I am not your lord, but your companion." 6And again I asked him, and I said to him, "Why (are there) not corresponding groups of angels?" 7And he said to me, "From the sixth heaven and upwards there are no longer those on the left, nor is there a throne placed in the middle, but [they are directed] by the power of the seventh heaven, where the One who is not named dwells, and his Chosen One, whose name is unknown, and no heaven can learn his name; ⁸for he is alone, (he) whose voice all the heavens and thrones answer. I, therefore, have been empowered and sent to bring you up here that you may see this glory, ⁹and (that) you may see the LORD of all these heavens and of these thrones ¹⁰being transformed until he resembles your appearance and your likeness. ¹¹But I say to you, Isaiah, that no man who has to return into a body of that world [has come up, or seen], or understood what you have seen ¹²and what you are to see, for you are destined in the lot of the LORD, the lot of the tree, to come here, and from there is the power of the sixth heaven and of the air." ¹³And I proclaimed the greatness of my LORD with praise, that through his lot I should come here. ¹⁴And he said to me, "Hear then this also from your companion: [when from the body by the will of God you have come up here], then you will receive the robe which you will see, and also other numbered robes placed (there) you will see, ¹⁵and then you will be equal to the angels who (are) in the seventh heaven." ¹⁶And he took me up into the sixth heaven, and there were none on the left, nor a throne in the middle, but all (were) of one appearance, and their praise (was) equal. ¹⁷And (strength) was given to me, and I also sang praises with them, and that angel also, and our praise was like theirs. ¹⁸And there they all named the primal Father and his Beloved, Christ, and the Holy Spirit, all with one voice, ¹⁹but it was not like the voice of the angels who (were) in the five heavens, ²⁰nor (was it) like their speech, but there was a different voice there, and there was much light there. ²¹And then, when I was in the sixth heaven, I thought that light which I had seen in the five heavens darkness. ²²And I rejoiced and praised the One who has graciously given such light to those who await his promise. ²³And I entreated the angel who led me that from then on I should not return to the world of flesh. ²⁴Indeed I say to you, Hezekiah and Josab, my son, and Micah, that there is much darkness here. ²⁵And the angel who led me knew what I thought and said to me, "If you rejoice over this light, how much more (will you rejoice) in the seventh heaven when you see the light where the LORD is and his Beloved—from where I was sent—who is to be called in the world the Son! ²⁶He who is to be in the corruptible world has not (yet) been revealed, nor the robes, nor the thrones, nor the crowns which are placed (there) for the righteous, for those who believe in that LORD who will descend in your form. For the light which (is) there (is) great and wonderful. ²⁷But as regards your not returning into the body, your days are not yet complete for coming here." 28 And when I heard (this), I was sad; and he said to me, "Do not be sad."

9. And he led me into the air of the seventh heaven, and moreover I heard a voice saying, "How far is he who dwells among aliens to go up?" And I was afraid and was trembling. 2 And he said to me when I was trembling, "Behold! From there another voice which was sent out has come, and it says,ᵇ 'The holy Isaiah is permitted to come up here, for his robe is here.' " 3 And I asked the angel who (was) with me and said, "Who is the one who prevented me, and who is this one {who turned to me that I might go up}?"ᶜ 4 And he said to me, "The one who prevented you, this is the one [who (is) in charge of] the praise of the sixth heaven. 5 And the one {who turned to you},ᵈ this is your LORD, the LORD, the LORD Christ, who is to be called in the world Jesus, but you cannot hear his name until you have come up from this body. 6 And he took me up into the seventh heaven, and there I saw a wonderful light, and also angels without number. 7 And there I saw all the righteous from the time of Adam onwards. 8 And there I saw the holy Abel and all the righteous. 9 And there I saw Enoch and all who (were) with him, stripped of (their) robes of the flesh; and I saw them in their robes of above, and they were like the angels who stand there in great glory. 10 But they were not sitting on their thrones, nor were their crowns of glory on them. 11 And I asked the angel who (was) with me, "How is it that they have received these robes, but are not on (their) thrones nor in (their) crowns?" 12 And he said to me, "They do not receive the crowns and thrones of glory—nevertheless, they do see and know whose (will be) the thrones and whose the crowns—until the Beloved descends in the form in which you will see him descend. 13 The LORD will indeed descend into the world in the last days, (he) who is to be called Christ after he has descended and become like you in form, and they will think that he is flesh and a man. 14 And the god of that world will stretch out [his hand against the Son], and they will lay their hands upon him and hang him upon a tree, not knowing who he is. 15 And thus his descent, as you will see, will be concealed even from the heavens so that it will not be known who he is. 16 And when he has

---

ᵇThe Ethiopian text probably originally read, "And when I was trembling, behold from there another voice which was sent out came, and it said."
ᶜSo reads the Ethiopian manuscript, but this is a misunderstanding of the underlying Greek, which ought to have been rendered "who permitted me to go up."
ᵈSee note c on verse 3.

plundered the angel of death, he will rise on the third day and will remain in that world for five hundred and forty-five days. [17] And then many of the righteous will ascend with him, whose spirits do not receive (their) robes until the LORD Christ ascends and they ascend with him. [18] Then indeed they will receive their robes and their thrones and their crowns, when he has ascended into the seventh heaven." [19] And I said to him what I had asked him in the third heaven, [20] ["Show me how everything] which is done in that world is known here." [21] And while I was still speaking to him, behold one of the angels who were standing by, more glorious than that angel who had brought me up from the world, [22] showed me (some) books, {but not like the books of this world};[e] and he opened them, and the books had writing in them, but not like the books of this world. And they were given to me, and I read them, and behold the deeds of the children of Israel were written there, their deeds which you know, my son Josab. [23] And I said, "Truly, nothing which is done in this world is hidden in the seventh heaven." [24] And I saw many robes placed there, and many thrones and many crowns, [25] and I said to the angel who led me, "Whose (are) these robes and thrones and crowns?" [26] And he said to me, "As for these robes, there are many from that world who will receive (them) through believing in the words of that one who will be named as I have told you, and they will keep them, and believe in them, and believe in his cross; [for them (are) these] placed (here)." [27] And I saw one standing (there) whose glory surpassed that of all, and his glory was great and wonderful. [28] And when they saw him, all the righteous whom I had seen and the angels came to him. And Adam and Abel and Seth and all the righteous approached first and worshiped him, and they all praised him with one voice, and I also was singing praises with them, and my praise was like theirs. [29] And then all the angels approached, and worshiped, and sang praises. [30] And he was transformed and became like an angel.[f] [31] And then the angel who led me said to me, "Worship this one," and I worshiped and sang praises. [32] And the angel said to me, "This is the LORD of all the praise which you have seen." [33] And while I was still speaking, I saw another glorious (person) who was like him, and the righteous approached him, and worshiped, and sang praises, and I also sang praises with them; but his

---

[e] Lacking in some manuscripts and probably a doublet.

[f] The meaning seems to be that the appearance of Jesus was transformed for the sake of Isaiah. Some manuscripts (preferred by some commentators) read, "And I was transformed and became like an angel." But the transformation of Isaiah took place progressively as he ascended from heaven to heaven (7:25), and mention of it here comes too late. In any case, the easier reading "I" is unlikely to be original.

glory was not transformed to accord with their form. [34]And then the angels approached and worshiped him. [35]And I saw the LORD and the second angel, and they were standing, [36]and the second one whom I saw (was) on the left of my LORD. And I asked the angel who led me and I said to him, "Who is this one?" And he said to me, "Worship him, for this is the angel of the Holy Spirit who has spoken in you and also in the other righteous." [37]And I saw the Great Glory while the eyes of my spirit were open, but I could not thereafter see, nor the angel who (was) with me, nor any of the angels whom I had seen worship my LORD. [38]But I saw the righteous as they beheld with great power the glory of that one. [39]And my LORD approached me, and the angel of the Spirit, and said, "See how it has been given to you to see the LORD, and (how) because of you power has been given to the angel who (is) with you." [40]And I saw how my LORD and the angel of the Holy Spirit worshiped and both together praised the LORD. [41]And then all the righteous approached and worshiped, [42]and the angels approached and worshiped, and all the angels sang praises.

10. And then I heard the voices and the hymns of praise which I had heard in each of the six heavens—which I had heard as I ascended there; [2]and all (the voices and hymns of praise) were directed to that Glorious One whose glory I could not see. [3]And I also heard and saw the praise (which was directed to) him, [4]and the LORD and the angel of the Spirit heard everything and saw everything. [5]And all the praise which was sent (up) from the six heavens was not only heard, but seen. [6]And I heard the angel who led me, and he said to me, "This is the Most High of the high ones, who dwells in the holy world, who rests among the holy ones, who will be called by the Holy Spirit in the mouth of the righteous the Father of the LORD." [7]And I heard the voice of the Most High, the Father of my LORD, as he said to my LORD Christ, who will be called Jesus, [8]"Go out and descend through all the heavens. You shall descend through the firmament and through that world as far as the angel who (is) in Sheol, but you shall not go as far as Perdition. [9]And you shall make your likeness like that of all who (are) in the five heavens, [10]and you shall take care to make your form like that of the angels of the firmament and also (like that) of the angels who (are) in Sheol. [11]And none of the angels of that world shall know that you (are) LORD with me of the seven heavens and of their angels. And they shall not know that you (are) with me [12]when with the voice of the heavens I summon you, and their angels and their lights, and when I lift up (my voice) to the sixth heaven, that

287

you may judge and destroy the princes and the angels and the gods of that world, and the world which is ruled by them, 13for they have denied me and said, 'We alone are, and there is no one besides us.' 14And afterwards you shall ascend from the gods of death to your place, and you shall not be transformed in each of the heavens, but in glory you shall ascend and sit at my right hand, 15and then the princes and the powers of that world will worship you." 16This command I heard the Great Glory giving to my LORD. 17And thus I saw when my LORD went out from the seventh heaven into the sixth heaven. 18And the angel who had led me from this world was with me, and he said to me, "Understand, Isaiah, and look, that you may see the transformation and descent of the LORD." 19And I looked, and when the angels who (were) in the sixth heaven saw him, they praised him and glorified him, for he had not been transformed into the form of the angels there; and they praised him, and I also sang praises with them. 20And I saw when he descended into the fifth heaven, that in the fifth heaven he made his form like that of the angels there, and they did not praise him, for his form was like theirs. 21And then he descended into the fourth heaven and made his form like that of the angels there, 22and when they saw him, they did not praise him or glorify him, for his form (was) like their form. 23And again I saw when he descended into the third heaven, that he made his form like that of the angels who (were) in the third heaven. 24And those who kept the gate of the (third) heaven demanded the password, and the LORD gave (it) to them in order that he should not be recognized; and when they saw him, they did not praise him or glorify him, for his form (was) like their form. 25And again I saw when he descended into the second heaven, that there again he gave the password, for those who kept the gates demanded (it), and the LORD gave (it). 26And I saw when he made his form like that of the angels who (were) in the second heaven, that they saw him, but did not praise him, for his form (was) like their form. 27And again I saw when he descended into the first heaven, that there he gave the password to those who kept the gates. And he made his form like that of the angels who (were) on the left of that throne, and they did not praise him or glorify him, for his form (was) like their form. 28And as for me, no one questioned me because of the angel who led me. 29And again he descended into the firmament where the prince of this world dwells, and he gave the password to those who (were) on the left, and his form (was) like theirs, and they did not praise him there; but in envy they were fighting one another, for there is there a power of evil and envying about trifles. 30And I saw when he descended and made himself like the angels of the air, that he was like one of them. [31]And he did not give the password, for they were plundering and doing violence to one another.

11. And after this I looked, and the angel who spoke to me and led me said to me, "Understand, Isaiah son of Amoz, because for this purpose I was sent from the LORD." [2]And I saw a woman of the family of David the prophet whose name (was) Mary, and she (was) a virgin and was betrothed to a man whose name (was) Joseph, a carpenter, and he also (was) of the seed and family of the righteous David of Bethlehem in Judah. [3]And he came into his lot. And when she was betrothed, she was found to be pregnant, and Joseph the carpenter wished to divorce her. [4]But the angel of the Spirit appeared in this world, and after this Joseph did not divorce Mary; but he did not reveal this matter to anyone. [5]And he did not approach Mary, but kept her as a holy virgin, although she was pregnant. [6]And he did not live with her for two months. [7]And after two months of days, while Joseph was in his house, and Mary his wife, but both alone, [8]it came about, when they were alone, that Mary then looked with her eyes and saw a small infant, and she was astounded. [9]And after her astonishment had worn off, her womb was found as (it was) at first, before she had conceived. [10]And when her husband, Joseph, said to her, "What has made you astounded?" his eyes were opened, and he saw the infant and praised the LORD, because the LORD had come in his lot. [11]And a voice came to them, "Do not tell this vision to anyone." [12]But the story about the infant was spread abroad in Bethlehem. [13]Some said, "The virgin Mary has given birth before she has been married two months." [14]But many said, "She did not give birth; the midwife did not go up (to her), and we did not hear (any) cries of pain." And they were all blinded concerning him; they all knew about him, but they did not know from where he was. [15]And they took him and went to Nazareth in Galilee. [16]And I saw, O Hezekiah and Josab my son, and say to the other prophets also who are standing by, that it was hidden from all the heavens and all the princes and every god of this world. [17]And I saw (that) in Nazareth he sucked the breast like an infant, as was customary, that he might not be recognized. [18]And when he had grown up, he performed great signs and miracles in the land of Israel and (in) Jerusalem. [19]And after this the adversary envied him and roused the children of Israel, who did not know who he was, against him. And they handed him to the ruler, and crucified him, and he descended to the angel who (is) in Sheol. [20]In Jerusalem, indeed, I saw how they crucified him on a tree, [21]and likewise (how) after the third day he rose and remained (many) days. 22And the angel who led me said to me, "Understand, Isaiah." And I saw when he sent out the twelve disciples and ascended. 23And I saw him, and he was in the firmament, but was not transformed into their form. And all the angels of the firmament, and Satan, saw him and worshiped. 24And there was much sorrow there as they said, "How did our LORD descend upon us, and we did not notice the glory which was upon him, which we (now) see was upon him from the sixth heaven?" 25And he ascended into the second heaven, and he was not transformed, but all the angels who (were) on the right and on the left, and the throne in the middle, 26worshiped him, and praised him, and said, "How did our LORD remain hidden from us as he descended, and we did not notice?" 27And in the same way he ascended into the third (heaven), and in the same way they praised him and spoke. 28And in the fourth heaven and also in the fifth they spoke in exactly the same way. 29But there was one glory, and from it he was not transformed. 30And I saw when he ascended into the sixth heaven, that they worshiped him and praised him; 31but in all the heavens the praise grew louder. 32And I saw how he ascended into the seventh heaven, and all the righteous and all the angels praised him. And then I saw that he sat down at the right hand of that Great Glory, whose glory I told you I could not behold. 33And also I saw that the angel of the Holy Spirit sat on the left. 34This angel said to me, "Isaiah, son of Amoz, [it is enough for you], for these (are) great things, for you have observed what no one born of flesh has observed. 35And you shall return into your robe until your days are complete; then you shall come here." These things I saw. 36And Isaiah told (them) to all those who were standing before him, and they sang praises. And he spoke to Hezekiah the king and said, "These things I have spoken. 37And the end of this world 38and all this vision will be brought about in the last generation." 39And Isaiah made him swear that he would not tell this to the people of Israel, and that he would not allow any man to copy these words. 40And then they shall read them. But as for you, be in the Holy Spirit that you may receive your robes, and the thrones and crowns of glory, which are placed in the seventh heaven. 41Because of these visions and prophecies Sammael Satan sawed Isaiah the son of Amoz, the prophet, in half by the hand of Manasseh. 42And Hezekiah gave all these things to Manasseh in the twenty-sixth year of his reign. 43But Manasseh did not remember these things, nor place them in his heart, but he became the servant of Satan and was destroyed.

Here ends (the book) of Isaiah the prophet with his ascension.

THE APOCALYPSE OF PAUL

Commentary

The *Apocalypse of Paul* was one of the most popular apocalypses in the early church, as evidenced by the variety of manuscripts of this text that were produced. Copies of the *Apocalypse of Paul* have been found in Greek, Latin, Syriac, Slavonic, Armenian, and Coptic. Some of these versions contain an account of the supposed discovery of the work (which had been buried under Paul's house in Tarsus) around 388 C.E. Most scholars accept that date as the approximate date for the composition of the *Apocalypse of Paul* in its completed form.

Origen, a prominent church leader who died around 254 C.E., seems to have known an earlier version of the *Apocalypse of Paul*. If that is indeed the case, then obviously the Tarsus account is a later addition. The body of the work, then, could have been composed in the early third century, with the Tarsus tradition being added around the end of the fourth century. The later addition of this material would explain its absence from some of the versions.

In 2 Corinthians 12:2-4, Paul mentions the experience of a certain man, usually understood as a reference to Paul himself, who was caught up to the third heaven, into paradise. The present work is supposedly Paul's account of what he saw and heard while on that journey.

Chapters 1 and 2 contain the story of the discovery of Paul's written record of these revelations. (In the Syriac versions, this Tarsus story is placed at the end of the work.) Following this introduction, chapters 3–10 portray various elements of the natural world (sun, moon, stars, sea, the earth) complaining about the wickedness that is rampant on the earth. God replies to their complaints, assuring them that ultimately God will judge humanity. Next, Paul sees two groups of angels appearing before God to give reports about everyone on earth. One group is composed of angels who have been assigned to the righteous; the other group consists of those assigned to sinners. These angels report to God every day and every night on the status of humanity.

The remainder of the work, chapters 11–51, describes Paul's otherworldly journeys. After being taken up to the third heaven, Paul watches the departure of the souls from a righteous person and from a wicked person, the righteous soul being led into paradise, the wicked soul being led to the underworld. Paul then visits paradise, located in the third heaven, where he meets Enoch and Elijah. Chapters 21–22 describe Paul's visit to "the land of promise," the place to be inhabited by the righteous during Christ's millennial reign. Afterwards, Paul is taken to the city of Christ, located next to Lake Acherusia, which is inhabited by the righteous, including many figures from the Hebrew Bible (chaps. 23–30).

Following the visit to the city of Christ, the angel guide takes Paul to the place of punishment of the wicked (chaps. 31–44). As in the *Apocalypse of Peter*, many of the punishments described in the *Apocalypse of Paul* are measure-for-measure punishments. When implored by the suffering wicked, Paul and the archangel Michael intercede for the sufferers and ask God to have mercy on them. The Son of God then grants to the sufferers a respite from their torments. Every week for one day and night their torments will cease.

The angel then leads Paul back to paradise, where he meets the Virgin Mary, the patriarchs, Moses, the prophets, and other righteous individuals. At this point in chapter 51, the text breaks off in the Latin, the Syriac, and the Greek texts. The Coptic continues with Paul being caught up again into the third heaven, visiting paradise and then being returned to the Mount of Olives, where he meets the apostles. The Syriac text adds a description of Paul hiding the manuscript under his house and then revealing its location after his death.

The *Apocalypse of Paul* certainly meets the criteria of an apocalypse. A guiding and interpreting angel serves as the mediator of the revelation, which is primarily spatial, concerned with places beyond this world. The work also exhibits a special interest in otherworldly beings. In addition to the angel who serves as a guide and interpreter for Paul, various otherworldly beings appear: the archangel Michael; the individuals seen in paradise, in the city of Christ, and in the underworld; the angels who are assigned to every person on earth and who make twice daily reports to God; the angels, the twenty-four elders, and the four beasts who worship God in heaven; and the good angels and evil angels (or powers) who do battle over the souls of each person at death. The temporal dimension also is present as the work looks to the general resurrection and "the great day of judgment" (chap. 16) for the final solution to the wickedness of the world.

The oldest and most complete text of the *Apocalypse of Paul* is a Latin translation published by M. R. James in 1893. This text is believed to be a translation of a Greek version (the original language of the *Apocalypse of Paul*), made between the end of the fourth century and the beginning of the sixth century. Other Latin versions also exist, along with an abridged

Greek manuscript and several Syriac, Slavonic, Armenian, and Coptic texts. The translation given below basically follows the Latin text published by James, corrected or supplemented in places by readings from the other versions. Abbreviations used in the translation to indicate these versions are:

L—Latin;
L¹—Latin text published by James;
Gr.—Greek;
St.G.—the St. Gall Latin text;
C—Coptic;
S—Syriac;
A—Armenian.

The translation is by Hugo Duensing from *New Testament Apocrypha*, volume 2.

The Apocalypse of Paul

The revelation of the holy apostle Paul: the things which were revealed to him when he went up even to the third heaven and was caught up into Paradise and heard unspeakable words.

1. In the consulate of Theodosius Augustus the Younger and of Cynegius a certain respected man was living in Tarsus in the house which had once belonged to St. Paul; during the night an angel appeared to him and gave him a revelation telling him to break up the foundations of the house and to make public what he found. But he thought this was a delusion.

2. However the angel came the third time and scourged him and compelled him to break up the foundations. And when he had dug he discovered a marble box which was inscribed on the sides; in it was the revelation of Saint Paul and the shoes in which he used to walk when he was teaching the word of God. But he was afraid to open the box (itself?) and brought it to a judge; the judge accepted it and sent it as it was, sealed with lead, to the emperor Theodosius; for he was afraid it might be something else. And when the emperor received it he opened it and found the revelation of Saint Paul. After a copy had been made he sent the original manuscript to Jerusalem. And it was written in it as follows:

3. The word of the Lord came to me thus: Say to this people: "How long will you transgress and add sin to sin and tempt the Lord who made you, saying that you are Abraham's children but doing the works of the devil? Walking in confidence towards God (L[1]: Christus), boasting only because of your name, but poor because of the substance of sin? Remember therefore and understand, children of men, that the whole creation is subject to God but that mankind alone sins. It rules over every creature and sins more than all nature.

4. For often the sun, the great light, has protested to the Lord, saying: O Lord God Almighty, I watch the ungodliness and unrighteousness of men; permit me to deal with them according to my powers so that they may know that thou alone art God. And a voice came to it, saying: I know all these things; for my eye sees and my ear hears, but my patience bears with them until they are converted and repent. But if they do not return to me I will judge them all.

5. Sometimes indeed the moon and the stars have protested to the Lord, saying: O Lord God Almighty, thou hast given us power over the night; how long shall we watch the ungodliness and fornications and murders which the children of men commit? permit us to deal with them according to our powers so that they may know that thou alone art God. And a voice came to them, saying: I know all these things and my eye sees and my ear hears, but my patience bears with them until they are converted and repent. But if they do not return to me, I will judge them.

6. And the sea has frequently cried out, saying: O Lord God Almighty, men have defiled thy holy name in me; permit me to rise up and cover every wood and thicket and all the world that I may blot out all the children of men from before thy face, so that they may know that thou art God alone. And a voice came again and said: I know everything; for my eye sees everything and my ear hears, but my patience bears with them until they are converted and repent. But if they do not return, I will judge them. Sometimes the waters have also protested against the sons of men, saying: O Lord God Almighty, all the children of men have polluted thy holy name. And a voice came saying: I know everything before it happens for my eye sees and my ear hears everything, but my patience bears with them until they are converted. And if not, I will judge. Often the earth has also cried out to the Lord against the children of men, saying: O Lord God Almighty I suffer more harm than all thy creatures for I (must) bear the fornications, adulteries, murders, robberies, false oaths, sorceries and evil enchantments of men, and every evil which they commit, so that the father rises up against the son and the son against the father, and stranger against stranger, each to defile his neighbour's wife. The father mounts up on the bed of his son and the son likewise mounts up on the couch of his father; and those who offer a sacrifice to thy name have defiled thy holy place with all these evil deeds. Therefore I suffer more harm than every creature and although I do not wish to, I give to the children of men my wealth and fruit. Permit me to destroy the strength of my fruit. And a voice came and said: I know everything and there is no one who can hide himself from his sin. And I know their ungodliness, but my holiness endures them until they are converted and repent. But if they do not return to me, I will judge them.

7. Behold, children of men, creation is subject to God; but mankind alone sins. Therefore, children of men, bless the Lord God unceasingly every hour and every day; but especially at sunset. For at that hour all the angels go to the Lord to worship him and bring before him all the deeds of men, whether good or evil, which each of them does from morning until evening. And one angel goes forth rejoicing from the man he indwells but another goes with sad face. When then the sun has set at the first hour of the night, in the same hour (come) the angel of each people and the angel of each man and woman, (the angels) which protect and preserve them, because man is the image of God: and similarly at the hour of morning which is the twelfth hour of the night all the angels of men and women meet God to worship him and to bring before him every deed which each man has done, whether good or evil. Every day and (every) night the angels present to God an account of all the actions of mankind. Therefore I tell you, children of men, bless the Lord continually every day of your life.

8. Therefore at the appointed hour all the angels, every one rejoicing, go forth together before God that they may meet to worship at the hour arranged. And, behold, suddenly at the time there was a meeting (?), and the angels came to worship before God, and the Spirit went to meet them; and a voice came forth and said, Whence have you come, our angels, bringing burdens of news?

9. They answered and said: We have come from those who have renounced this world on account of thy holy name; they wander as strangers and live in a (the) cave(s) of the rocks; they weep every hour they dwell on earth, and they are hungry and thirst for the sake of thy name; their loins girt, they hold in their hands the incense of their hearts; they pray and bless at every hour; they are distressed and subdue themselves. More than all others who live on earth they are weeping and mourning. And we, their angels, mourn with them; wherever then it may please thee, command us to go and serve. Command them, Lord, to abide even to the end in righteousness. And the voice of God came to them saying: Know that to you here my grace is established now, and my help, who is my dearly beloved Son, will be with them and guide them every hour; he will also serve them and never forsake them because their place is his dwelling. (*In Gr the Divine voice speaks briefly at the end of ch. 8*: I have kept them and shall keep them void of offence in my Kingdom.)

10. When these angels had retired, behold, other angels who were weeping came into the meeting to worship in the presence of the Majesty. And the Spirit of God went forth to meet them; and the voice of God came, saying: Whence have you come, our angels, bearing burdens as servants of the world's news? And they answered and said in the presence of God: We have come from those who have called on thy name, whom the difficulties of the world have made miserable; for every hour they devise many opportunities, not making one pure prayer, not even with the whole heart, all the time they live; why therefore must we be present with men who are sinners? And the voice of God came to them: You must serve them until they are converted and repent: but if they do not return to me, I shall judge them. Understand then, children of men, that whatever you do, whether it is good or evil, these angels report (it) to God.

11. And after that I saw one of the spiritual beings beside me and he caught me up in the Holy Spirit and carried me up to the third part of Heaven, which is the third heaven. And the angel answered and said to me: Follow me and I shall show you the place of the righteous where they are brought when they are dead; and after that I shall take you to the abyss and I shall show you the souls of sinners and the kind of place to which they are brought when they are dead. And I went behind the angel and he led me to heaven and I saw the firmament and I saw there the Power, and the forgetfulness which deceives and seduces to itself the hearts of men, and the spirit of slander and the spirit of fornication and the spirit of wrath and the spirit of presumption were there, and the princes of wickedness were there. These I saw under the firmament of heaven. And again I looked and I saw angels who were pitiless, who had no compassion; their faces were full of wrath and their teeth projected from their mouths; their eyes flashed like the morning star in the east, and from the hairs of their head and out of their mouth went forth sparks of fire. And I asked the angel, saying: Who are these, sir? And the angel answered and said to me: These are those who are appointed for the souls of the wicked in the hour of need, for those who did not believe that they had the Lord for their helper and did not hope in him.

12. And I looked into the height and I saw other angels with faces shining like the sun; their loins were girt with golden girdles and they had palms in their hands, and the sign of God; and they were clothed in raiment on which was written the name of the Son of God; and they were filled with all gentleness and pity. And I asked the angel and said: Who are these, sir, who have so much beauty and pity? And the angel answered and said to me: These are the angels of righteousness; they are sent to lead in the hour of their need the souls of the righteous who believed God was their helper. And I said to him: Must the righteous and the sinners meet the witnesses when they are dead? And the angel answered and said to me: There is one way by which all pass over to God, but the righteous, because they have a holy helper with them, are not troubled when they go to appear before God.

13. And I said to the angel: I wish to see the souls of the righteous and of sinners as they leave the world. And the angel answered and said to me: Look down at the earth. And from heaven I looked down on earth, and I saw the whole world and it was as nothing in my sight. And I saw the children of men as if they were nothing and growing weaker; and I was amazed and I said to the angel: Is this the size of men? And the angel answered and said to me: It is, and these are those who do harm (*Syr.*: sin) from morning to evening. And I looked and I saw a great cloud of fire spread out over the whole world, and I said to the angel: What is this, sir? And he said to me: This is the unrighteousness which is mixed by the princes of sinners (?) (*Gr.*: with the destruction of sinners. *Syr.*: with the prayer of men.)

14. And when I heard this, I sighed and wept; and I said to the angel: I wish to wait for the souls of the righteous and of sinners and observe in what way they go out of the body. And the angel answered and said to me: Look down again at the earth. And I looked and I saw the whole world, and men were as nothing and growing weaker; and I looked and saw a man at the point of death. And the angel said to me: This man whom you see is righteous. And again I looked and I saw all his deeds which he had done for the sake of the name of God; and all his desires, which he remembered and which he did not remember, all of them stood before him in the hour of need. And I saw that the righteous man had progressed and found refreshing and confidence; and before he left the world holy and wicked angels stood together by him; and I saw them all; however the wicked found no dwelling in him, but the holy had power over his soul, directing it until it left the body. And they roused the soul, saying: Soul, take knowledge of your body which you have left, for in the day of resurrection you must return to that same body to receive what is promised to all the righteous. They received therefore the soul from the body and at once kissed it just as if they had known it every day, and said to it: Be of good heart, for you did the will of God while you were on the earth. And the angel that watched over it day by day came to meet it and said to it: Be of good heart, soul; for I rejoice over you because you did the will of God on earth; for I have reported to God of what kind all your deeds were. In the same way also the spirit advanced to meet it and said: Soul, neither be afraid nor troubled until you come to a place which you never knew; I however will be your helper, for I found in you a place of refreshing during the time I dwelt in you while I (?) was on earth. And its spirit strengthened it and its angel took it up and led it into heaven. {And the angel said}: And there went to meet it the evil powers who are under heaven, and the spirit of error came to it and said (to it; L[1]: Whither, soul, do you hasten and dare to enter heaven? Wait and let us see if there is anything of ours in you.) (S alone continues as follows:) And the soul was bound there. And there was a fight between the good angels and the evil angels. And when that spirit of error saw (it), he wailed with a (loud) voice and said: Alas for you, because we have found nothing of ours in you. And behold! every angel and spirit helps you against me, and behold, all these are with you and you have passed over from us. And there came forth another spirit, a slandering spirit, and a spirit of fornication, and they came to meet it. But when they saw it, they wept over it and said: How did this soul escape us? It did the will of God on earth. And, behold, the angels indeed helped it and allowed it to pass over from us.—And all the powers and evil spirits came to meet it, even up to it. But they did not find anything of their own in it. And they were not able to do anything for themselves. And they gnashed their tooth (teeth) against this soul and said: How did it escape us? And the angel which led it answered and said to them: Be turned to confusion. There is no way for you to it. Indeed you were very cunning; you flattered it while it was on earth, but it paid no heed to you.

And then I heard the voice of myriad upon myriad of holy angels as they said: Rejoice and exult, O soul, be strong and do not tremble!—And they were greatly amazed at that soul because it had held fast by the sign of the living God. And so they encouraged it and called it happy and said: We all rejoice over you because you have done the will of your Lord.—And they led it until it worshipped in the presence of God. And when it had ceased, at once Michael and all the host of angels fell down and worshipped the footstool of his feet and displayed the soul, saying: This is the God of all who made you in his image and likeness. However an angel ran on ahead of it and declared, saying: Lord, remember its works; for this is the soul on whose deeds I reported to thee daily, acting according to thy judgment. And in the same way the spirit said: I am the spirit of quickening, breathing on it and dwelling in it. For I was refreshed in it during the time I dwelt in it. It behaved according to thy judgment. And the voice of God came and said: As this soul has not grieved me, so I shall not grieve it; as it has had compassion, so I shall have compassion on it. Let it therefore be handed over to Michael, the angel of the covenant, and let him lead it into the paradise of jubilation, that it may be there until the day of resurrection and become also a fellow-heir with all the saints. And after that I heard the voices of a thousand times a thousand angels and archangels and the cherubim and the twenty-four elders who sang hymns and glorified God and cried: Righteous art thou, O Lord, and righteous are thy judgments; there is no respect of persons with thee and thou dost requite every man according to thy judgment. And the angel answered and said to me: Have you believed and understood that whatever each of you has done, he sees it in the hour of his need? And I said: Yes, sir.

15. And he said to me: Look down again at the earth and wait for that other soul of an ungodly man as it comes forth from the body, a soul which has provoked the Lord day and night by saying: I know nothing other than this world; I eat and drink and enjoy what is in the world. For who has gone down into the underworld and coming up has told us that there is a judgment there? And I looked and saw all the scorn of the sinner and all that he had done and that stood before him in the hour of his need. And I saw that that hour was more bitter to him than the future judgment. And that man said: O that I had not been born nor been in the world! And then holy and wicked angels came together and the soul of the sinner saw both, and the holy angels found no place in it. The wicked angels had power over it; and when they led it out from the body, the angels admonished it three times, saying: O unfortunate soul, look at your flesh, which you have left. For on the day of resurrection you will have to return into your flesh to receive what is fitting to your sins and your ungodliness.

16. And when they led it out, its familiar angel went before it and said to it: O unfortunate soul, I am the angel who clung to you and reported daily to the Lord the evil deeds which you did night and day. And if it had been in my power I would not have served you one single day, but I was not able to do that (anything of those things). For God is merciful and a righteous judge and he has ordered us not to cease to serve a soul until you repent. But you have wasted the time for repentance. And today I am become a stranger to you, and you to me. Let us then go to the righteous judge; I will not discharge you before I know that from the present day I am become a stranger to you. And the spirit afflicted it and the angel troubled it. However when it had reached the powers, as already it went to enter heaven, there was laid on it one evil burden after another. For error and forgetfulness and tale-bearing met it and the spirit of fornication and the rest of the powers and they said to it: Where are you going, unfortunate soul? do you dare to rush on into heaven? Stop and let us see if we have any of our possessions in you, for we do not see any holy helper with you.

(S:) And when they had inspected it, they rejoiced and said: Yes, indeed, there is in you and you belong wholly to us; now we know that even your angel cannot help you and wrest you from us.—But the angel answered and said: Understand that it is a soul of the Lord, and he does not leave it and I also do not leave the image of God in the hands of the evil. For he who supported me all the days of the life of this soul can support and help me and it. And I shall not leave it until it goes up to the throne of God on high. And when he sees it he will have power over it and send it wherever he wishes.

And after that I heard voices in the height of heaven which said: Present the unfortunate soul to God that it may know there is a God whom it has despised. Therefore when it had entered heaven, all the angels, thousands of thousands of them, saw it (and) they all cried with one voice saying: Woe to you, unfortunate soul, for the deeds which you did on earth; what answer will you give God when you approach to worship him? And the angel which was with it answered and said: Weep with me, my beloved ones, for I found no rest in this soul. And the angels answered him and said: Let such a soul be sent away from our midst; for since it came in, its foul stench has gone through to all the angels. And then it was taken away to worship in the presence of God, and the angel showed to it the Lord God who had made it after his own image and likeness. But its angel ran on ahead and said: Lord God Almighty, I am the angel of that soul on whose deeds I reported to thee day and night (not behaving according to thy judgment). Deal with it according to thy judgment. And in the same way the spirit said: I am the spirit which dwelt in it from the time when it was made in the world, and it did not follow my will. Judge it, Lord, according to thy judgment. And the voice of God came forth to it and said: Where is your fruit which you have brought forth corresponding to the good things you received? Did I set even the difference of one day between you and the righteous? Did I not make the sun to rise over you just as over the righteous? It however kept silent because it had nothing to say. And again a voice came saying: God's judgment is righteous and there is no respect of persons with him. For whoever has shown mercy, to him will mercy be shown, and whoever has not been merciful, God will not have mercy on him. Let him therefore be handed over to the angel Tartaruchus, who is appointed over punishments, and let him send him into outer darkness where there is wailing and gnashing of teeth, and let him remain there until the great day of judgment. After that I heard the voice of the angels and archangels who said: Righteous art thou, O Lord, and righteous is thy judgment.

17. I looked again and behold two angels were leading a soul which was weeping and saying: Have mercy on me, O God, righteous judge. For it is seven days today since I came out of my body and was handed over to these two angels and they have led me to places which I had never seen. And God the righteous judge said to it: What have you done? You never showed mercy, and for that reason you have been handed over to such angels as have no mercy; and because you did not do what was right they have not treated you compassionately in the hour of your need. Confess therefore the sins which you committed while you were set in the world. And it answered and said: Lord, I have not sinned. And the Lord God, the righteous judge, burned with anger when it said, "I have not sinned," because it was lying; and God said: Do you think that you are still living in the world, where each of you sins and conceals it and hides it from his neighbour? Here, however, nothing is hidden. For if souls have come to worship in the presence of the throne then the good works of each and his sins are revealed. And when the soul heard this, it kept quiet, for it had no answer. And I heard the Lord God, the righteous judge, speaking again: Come, angel of this soul, and stand in the middle. And the angel of the sinful soul came and he had a document in his hands and he said: This, Lord, in my hands is (the account of) all the sins of this soul from its youth up to the present day, from the day of its birth onward; and if thou order (it), Lord, I shall recount its deeds from when it was fifteen years old. And the Lord God, the righteous judge, said: I tell you, angel, that I do not expect from you an account from the time when it was fifteen years old, but set forth its sins for the five years before it died and came here. And again, God, the righteous judge, said: I swear by myself and by my holy angels and my power, that if it had repented five years before it died, because of a conversion one year old the evils which it had formerly done would now be forgotten and it would have remission and pardon of sins; now however let it perish. And the angel of the sinful soul answered and said: Command, Lord, that angel to bring forth those souls.

18. And in that same hour the souls were brought out into the middle and the soul of the sinner recognized them. And the Lord said to the soul of the sinner: I say to you, soul, confess the deeds which you committed against these souls which you see, when they were in the world. And it answered and said: Lord, it is not a full year since I slew this soul and shed its blood on the ground, and with (that) other I committed fornication; but that is not all, for I also injured it greatly by taking away its property. And the Lord God, the righteous judge said: Or did you not know that whoever has done violence to another, if the person who has suffered violence should die first, he is kept in this place until the one who has committed the offence dies and then both stand before the judge, and now each has received (*St. G. and L.*: 'will receive') according to what he did? And I heard the voice of one who said: Let that soul be handed over into the hands of Tartarus, and it must be led down to the underworld. Let it be led into the prison of the underworld and be cast into torments and be left there until the great day of judgment. And again I heard thousands of thousands of angels who were singing a hymn to the Lord and crying: Righteous art thou, Lord, and righteous are thy judgments.

19. The angel answered and said to me: Have you understood all this? And I said: Yes, sir. And he said to me: Follow me again, and I will take you and show you the places of the righteous. And I followed the angel and he lifted me up to the third heaven and he set me at the door of a gate. And I looked at it and saw that it was a golden gate and that there were two golden pillars before it and two golden tables above the pillars full of letters. And again the angel turned to me and said: Blessed are you if you enter in by these gates, because only those are allowed to enter who have goodness and purity of body. And I asked the angel and said: Sir, tell me, for what reason are these letters set on those tables? The angel answered and said to me: These are the names of the righteous who while they dwell on earth serve God with a whole heart. And again I said: Are then their names written in heaven while they are still on earth? And he said: Not only their names but also their faces are written, and the likeness of those who serve God is in heaven, and the servants of God, who serve him with a whole heart, are known to the angels before they leave the world.

20. And when I had entered within the gates of Paradise there came to meet me an old man whose face shone as the sun. And he embraced me and said: Hail, Paul, dearly beloved of God. And with joyful face he kissed me. And then he began to weep. And I said to him: Father, why are you weeping? And he sighed and wept again, and said: Because we are injured by men and they trouble us much; for there are many good things which the Lord has prepared and his promise is great, but many do not accept them. And I asked the angel and said: Who is this, sir? And he said to me: This is Enoch, the scribe of righteousness. And I entered within that place and immediately I saw Elijah and he came and greeted me with gladness and joy. And when he had seen (me), he turned away and wept and said to me: Paul, may you receive the reward for the work which you have accomplished among mankind. As for me, I have seen the great and numerous good things which God has prepared for all the righteous, and the promises of God are great, but the majority do not accept them; but even with difficulty through many labours do a few (one and another) enter into these places.

21. And the angel answered and said to me: Whatever I now show you here and whatever you will hear, do not make it known to anyone on earth. And he brought me and showed me and I heard there words which it is not lawful for a man to speak. And again he said: Follow me further and I shall show you what you ought to tell openly and report.

And he brought me down from the third heaven and he led me into the second heaven and he led me again to the firmament, and from the firmament he led me to the gates of heaven. And he opened an aperture and there was the beginning of its foundation over a river which watered the whole earth. And I asked the angel and said: Sir, what is this river of water? And he said to me: This is the Ocean. And suddenly I came out of heaven and perceived that it is the light of heaven which gives light to the whole land there. That land, however, was seven times brighter than silver. And I said: Sir, what is this place? And he said to me: This is the land of promise. Have you not yet heard what is written, "Blessed are the meek, for they will inherit the earth"? The souls of the righteous, however, when they have come out of the body are sent for a while to this place. And I said to the angel: Will then this land come to be seen after a time? The angel answered and said to me: When Christ whom you preach comes to reign, then by the fiat of God the first earth will be dissolved and this land of promise will then be shown and it will be like dew or a cloud; and then the Lord Jesus Christ, the eternal king, will be revealed and he will come with all his saints to dwell in it and he will reign over them for a thousand years and they will eat of the good things which I shall now show you.

22. And I looked round that land and I saw a river flowing with milk and honey; and at the edge of the river were planted trees full of fruit. And each tree was bearing twelve times twelve fruits in the year, various and different. And I saw the creation of that place and all the work of God. And I saw there palm trees, some of twenty cubits and others of ten cubits. Now that land was seven times brighter than silver. And the trees were full of fruit from root (up) to tree-top. (L¹ is incomprehensible here and we replace with C:) From the root of each tree up to its heart there were ten thousand branches with tens of thousands of clusters {and there were ten thousand clusters on each branch} and there were ten thousand dates in each cluster. And it was the same with the vines. Each vine had ten thousand branches, and each branch had on it ten thousand bunches of grapes, and each bunch had ten thousand grapes. And there were other trees there, myriads of myriads of them, and their fruit was in the same proportion. (L:) And I said to the angel: Why does each single tree yield thousands of fruits? And the angel answered and said to me: Because the Lord God of his abundance gives gifts profusely to the worthy, for they, while they were in the world, afflicted themselves of their own will and did everything for his holy name's sake.

And again I said to the angel: Sir, are these the only promises which the Lord God has promised to his saints? And the angel replied and said: No! for there are those which are seven times greater.

I tell you however that when the righteous have come forth from the body and see the promises and good things which God has prepared for them, they will sigh and weep yet again, saying: Why did we utter a word from our mouth to irritate our neighbour even for a single day? I however asked and said again: Are these the only promises of God? And the angel answered and said to me: What you now see is for the married who have kept the purity of their marriages in acting chastely. But to virgins and to those who hunger and thirst after righteousness and afflict themselves for the name of the Lord, God will give things seven times greater than what I shall now show you.

And after that he took me up away from that place where I had seen these things and, behold, a river whose waters were very white, whiter than milk. And I said to the angel: What is this? And he said to me: This is Lake Acherusia where the city of Christ is, but not every man is allowed to enter into that city. For this is the way which leads to God; and if there is anyone who is a fornicator and ungodly and who turns and repents and brings forth fruit worthy of repentance, first when he has come forth from the body he is brought and worships God and (he) is handed over from there at the command of God to the angel Michael and he baptizes him in Lake Acherusia. Thus he leads him into the city of Christ with those who have not sinned. And I marvelled and blessed the Lord God because of all I had seen.

23. And the angel answered and said to me: Follow me and I shall lead you into the city of Christ. And he stood by Lake Acherusia and put me in a golden boat and about three thousand angels were singing a hymn before me until I reached the city of Christ. Now the inhabitants of the city of Christ rejoiced greatly over me as I came to them, and I entered and saw the city of Christ; and it was completely golden and there were twelve walls around it and twelve towers in it (C: a tower on each wall; S: and twelve thousand fortified towers are in its midst), and the individual walls as they encircled were distant from one another a stadium. And I said to the angel: Sir, how much is one stadium? The angel answered and said to me: It is as great as between the Lord God and men on earth, for indeed the city of Christ is uniquely great. And in the circuit of the city there were twelve gates of great beauty, and four rivers which encircled it. Now there was a river of honey and a river of milk and a river of wine and a river of oil. And I said to the angel: What are these rivers which encircle this city? And he said to me: These are the four rivers which flow abundantly for those who are in this land of promise; as for their names: the river of honey is called Phison, and the river of milk Euphrates, and the river of oil Gihon and the river of wine Tigris. As therefore the righteous when they were in the world did not use their power over these things but went hungry without them and afflicted themselves for the name of the Lord God, therefore when they enter into this city the Lord will give them these above number or measure.

24. And when I entered in through the gate I saw before the doors of the city trees which were big and very high and which had no fruit (but) only leaves. And I saw a few men scattered about among the trees and they wept greatly when they saw anyone enter into the city. And the trees did penance for them by abasing themselves and bowing down and by raising themselves up again. And I saw it and wept with them and asked the angel and said: Sir, who are these who are not allowed to enter into the city of Christ? And he said to me: These are those who fasting day and night have zealously practiced renunciation, but they have had a heart proud beyond that of other men in that they have glorified and praised themselves and done nothing for their neighbours. For some they greeted in a friendly way, but to others they did not even say "Greetings": and to whom they wished they opened the doors of the monastery, and if they did some small good to their neighbour they became puffed up. And I said: What then, sir? Has their pride prevented them from entering into the city of Christ? And the angel answered and said to me: Pride is the root of all wickedness. Are they better than the Son of God who came to the Jews in great humility? And I asked him and said: Why is it then that the trees abase themselves and raise themselves up again? And the angel answered and said to me: All the time these spent on earth serving God they humbled themselves shamefacedly during that time because men confounded and re-proached them, but they were not sorry nor did they repent in order to desist from the pride which was in them. This is why the trees abase themselves and rise up again. And I asked and said: For what reason are they allowed into the gates of the city? The angel answered and said to me: Because of the great goodness of God and because the entrance of all his saints who enter into this city is here. Therefore they have been left in this place so that when Christ the eternal king enters with all his saints, all the righteous at his entry may pray for them; and then they will enter with them into the city; yet none of them can have the same confidence as those who humbled themselves by serving the Lord God all their life.

25. And with the angel leading me I went on, and he brought me to the river of honey; and I saw there Isaiah and Jeremiah and Ezekiel and Amos and Micah and Zechariah, the major and minor prophets, and they greeted me in the city. I said to the angel: What is this way? And he said to me: This is the way of the prophets. Everyone who has grieved his own soul and on account of God has not done his own will, when he has come forth from the world and been led to the Lord God and has worshipped him, then at God's command he is handed over to Michael who leads him into the city to this place of the prophets; and they greet him as their friend and neighbour because he did the will of God.

26. Again he led me where the river of milk was; and there I saw in that place all the infants whom king Herod had slain for the name of Christ, and they greeted me. And the angel said to me: All who preserve their chastity and purity, when they come forth from their bodies, are handed over to Michael after they have worshipped the Lord God, and they are brought to the children and they greet them saying, "You are our brothers and friends and associates (members)". Among them they will inherit the promises of God.

27. Again he took me up and brought me to the north of the city and he led me where the river of wine was, and I saw there Abraham, Isaac and Jacob, Lot and Job and other saints; and they greeted me. And I asked and said: What is this place, sir? The angel answered and said to me: All those who have given hospitality to strangers, when they come forth from the world, first worship the Lord God and are handed over to Michael and by this route are led into the city, and all the righteous greet them as sons and brothers and say to them, "Because you have kept humanity and hospitality for strangers, come, receive an inheritance in the city of our God." And each righteous man will receive the good gifts of God in the city in accordance with his own behaviour.

307

28. And again he brought me to the river of oil to the east of the city. And I saw there men who rejoiced and sang psalms, and I said: Who are these, sir? And the angel said to me: These are those who dedicated themselves to God with the whole heart and had no pride in themselves. For all who rejoice in the Lord God and sing praises to him with the whole heart are brought here into this city.

29. And he brought me into the middle of the city close to the twelfth wall. Now at this place it was higher than the others. And I asked and said: Is there a wall in the city of Christ surpassing this spot in honour? And the angel answered and said to me: The second is better than the first and similarly the third than the second because each one surpasses the other right up to the twelfth wall. And I said: Why, sir, does one surpass another in glory? Explain to me. And the angel answered and said to me: From all who in themselves have only a little slander or envy or pride something is taken away from their glory, although they appear to be in the city of Christ. Look behind you.

And I turned and saw golden thrones which were set at the several gates, with men on them who had golden diadems and gems. And I looked and saw within, between the twelve men, thrones set in another rank which appeared (to be) of greater glory, so that no one was able to declare their praise. And I asked the angel and said: Sir, who are those who shall sit on the thrones? And the angel answered and said to me: These are the thrones of those who had goodness and understanding of heart and (yet) made themselves fools for the Lord God's sake in that they neither knew the Scriptures nor many Psalms but paid heed to one chapter concerning the commandments of God and hearing them acted with great carefulness in conformity to these (commandments) and have (thereby) shown a true zealousness before the Lord God. And admiration of these lays hold on all the saints before the Lord God, for they discuss with one another and say: Wait and see these unlearned men who understand nothing more, how they have merited such a great and beautiful robe and such glory because of their innocence.

And I saw in the midst of the city a great and very high altar; and there was standing alongside the altar one whose face shone like the sun and who held in his hands a psaltery and a harp and who sang saying, "Hallelujah!" And his voice filled all the city. And as soon as all who were on the towers and at the gates heard him they replied, "Hallelujah!", so that the foundations of the city were shaken. And I asked the angel and said: Who, sir, is this here with such great power? And the angel said to me: This is David; this is the city of Jerusalem. But when Christ, the king of eternity, shall have come with the confidence (?) of his kingdom, then he will again step forward to sing and all the righteous will sing in reply at the same time, "Hallelujah". And I said: Sir, why is it that David alone begins the singing before all the other saints? And the angel answered and said to me: Because (?) Christ, the Son of God, sits at the right hand of his Father, this David will sing psalms before him in the seventh heaven; and just as it is done in the heavens, so it is done below, because it is not permitted to offer to God a sacrifice without David, but it is necessary for David to sing psalms at the time of the offering of the body and blood of Christ; as it is carried out in the heavens, so also on earth.

30. And I said to the angel: Sir, what is "Hallelujah"? And he answered and said to me: You search and inquire into everything. And he said to me: Hallelujah is a word in Hebrew, the language of God and angels. And the meaning of Hallelujah is this: tecel. cat. marith. macha. And I said: Sir, what is tecel. cat. marith. macha? And the angel answered and said to me: Tecel. cat. marith. macha is this: Let us bless him all together. I asked the angel and said: Sir, do all who say "Hallelujah" bless the Lord? And the angel answered and said to me: That is so; and again, if anyone should sing Hallelujah and there are some present who do not sing (it) at the same time, they commit sin because they do not join in the singing. And I said: Sir, does someone who is doting or very old sin in the same way? And the angel answered and said to me: No, but whoever is able, and does not join in the singing, you know that he is a despiser of the word. And it would be proud and discreditable that he should not bless the Lord God his maker.

31. And when he had ceased speaking to me, he led me forth out of the city through the midst of the trees and back from the sites of the land of good things, and he set me above the river of milk and honey. And then he led me to the ocean that bears the foundations of the heavens. And the angel answered and said to me: Do you understand that you are going away from here? And I said: Yes, sir. And he said to me: Come, follow me, and I shall show you the souls of the godless and sinners that you may know what the place is like. And I set out with the angel and he brought me towards the setting of the sun, and I saw the beginning of heaven, founded on a great river of water, and I asked: What is this river of water: And he said to me: This is the ocean which encircles the whole earth. And when I was beyond the ocean I looked and there was no light in that place, but darkness and sorrow and distress; and I sighed.

And there I saw a river boiling with fire, and in it was a multitude of men and women immersed up to their knees, and other men up to the navel, others up to the lips, and others up to the hair. And I asked the angel and said: Sir, who are these in the river of fire? And the angel answered and said to me: They are those who are neither hot nor cold because they were found neither among the number of the righteous nor among the number of the godless. For these spent the period of their life on earth in passing some days in prayers but other days in sins and fornications right up to their death. And I asked and said: Who are these, sir, who are immersed up to the knees in fire: And he answered and said to me: These are those who when they have come out of church occupy themselves in discussing (in) strange discourses. Those, however, who are immersed up to the navel are those who when they have received the body and blood of Christ go away and fornicate and do not cease from their sins until they die. And those who are immersed up to the lips are those who when they meet in the church of God slander one another. Those immersed up to the eyebrows are those who give the nod to one another and (in that way) secretly prepare evil against their neighbour.

32. And I saw to the north a place of varied and different punishments which was full of men and women, and a river of fire poured over them. And I looked and saw very deep pits and in them there were very many souls together; and the depth of that place was about 3,000 cubits, and I saw them sighing and weeping and saying: Lord, have mercy on us. But no one had mercy on them. And I asked the angel and said: Who are these, sir? And the angel answered and said to me: These are those who did not hope in the Lord that they would be able to have him for a helper. And I asked and said: Sir, if these souls remain through thirty or forty generations thus one above another, I believe the pits will not hold them unless they are made to go deeper. And he said to me: The abyss has no measure; moreover there also follows on it the (gulf, void?) which is below it. And it is as if perhaps someone takes a stone and throws it into a very deep well and after many hours it reaches the ground; so is the abyss. For when these souls are thrown in they have scarcely reached the bottom after five hundred years.

33. Now when I had heard that, I wept and sighed for the race of men. The angel answered and said to me: Why do you weep? Are you more compassionate than God? For since God is good and knows that there are punishments, he bears patiently the race of men, permitting each one to do his own will for the time that he lives on earth.

34. And I looked yet again at the river of fire and I saw there a man being strangled by angels, the guardians of Tartarus, who had in their hands an iron instrument with three prongs with which they pierced the intestines of that old man. And I asked the angel and said: Sir, who is that old man on whom such torments are inflicted? And the angel answered and said to me: He whom you see was a presbyter who did not execute his ministry properly. While he ate and drank and fornicated he offered to the Lord the sacrifice on his holy altar.

35. And not far away I saw another old man whom four evil angels brought running in haste and they immersed him up to his knees in the river of fire and they struck him with stones and they wounded his face like a storm and they did not allow him to say: Have mercy on me. And I asked the angel and he said to me: He whom you see was a bishop but he did not execute his episcopal office properly; he did indeed receive a great name but he did not enter into the holiness of him who gave to him that name all his life, for he did not give righteous judgments and he had no compassion on the widows and orphans. But now he is being requited according to his iniquity and his deeds.

36. And I saw another man up to his knees in the river of fire. And his hands were stretched out and bloody, and worms came out of his mouth and from his nostrils and he was groaning and weeping and crying, and he said: Have mercy on me, for I suffer more than the rest who are in this punishment. And I asked: Who is this, sir? And he said to me: He whom you see was a deacon who ate up the offerings and committed fornication and did not do right in the sight of God. Therefore unceasingly he pays this penalty.

And I looked and saw at his side another man who was brought with haste and thrown into the river of fire, and he was (in it) up to the knees. And the angel came who was (appointed) over the punishments and he had a great blazing razor with which he lacerated the lips of that man and in the same way his tongue. And sighing I wept and asked: Who is that, sir? And he said to me: He whom you see was a reader (lector) and he read to the people; but he himself did not keep the commandments of God. Now he also pays his own penalty.

37. And in that place I saw another set of pits and in the middle of it a river full of a multitude of men and women whom worms were devouring. I then wept, and with a sigh I asked the angel and said: Sir, who are these? And he said to me: They are those who exacted usury at compound interest and trusted in their riches and did not hope in God that he would be a helper to them.

And then I looked and I saw another place which was very confined, and there was as it were a wall and fire in its bounds. And in it I saw men and women chewing at their tongues. And I asked: Who are these, sir? And he said to me: They are those who reviled the Word of God in church, paying no attention to it, but counting God and his angels as nothing. Therefore in the same way they now pay their own special penalty.

38. And I looked and I saw another hole below in the pit, and it had the appearance of blood. And I asked and said: Sir, what is this place? And he said to me: All (the) punishments flow together into this pit. And I saw men and women submerged up to their lips and I asked: Who are these, sir? And he said to me: These are magicians who dispensed magical charms to men and women and made it impossible for them to find peace until they died. And again I saw men and women with very black faces in the pit of fire; and sighing and weeping I asked: Who are these, sir? And he said to me: These are fornicators and adulterers who although they had their own wives committed adultery; and similarly the women committed adultery in the same way, though they had their own husbands. Therefore unceasingly they pay the penalty.

39. And there I saw girls wearing black clothing and four dreadful angels who had blazing chains in their hands. And they set them (the chains) on their necks and led them into darkness. And again weeping I asked the angel: Who are these, sir? And he said to me: They are those who although they were appointed as virgins defiled their virginity unknown to their parents. For that reason they pay their own particular penalty unceasingly.

And again I saw there men and women set with lacerated hands and feet (*or* with hands and feet cut off) and naked in a place of ice and snow, and worms consumed them. And when I saw it I wept and asked: Who are these, sir? And he said to me: They are those who harmed orphans and widows and the poor, and did not hope in the Lord; therefore they pay their own particular penalty unceasingly.

And I looked and saw others hanging over a channel of water and their tongues were very dry and much fruit was placed within their sight and they were not allowed to take of it; and I asked: Who are these, sir? And he said to me: They are those who broke their fast before the appointed hour; therefore they pay these penalties unceasingly.

And I saw other men and women suspended by their eyebrows and hair, and a river of fire drew (?) them; and I said: Who are these, sir? And he said to me: They are those who did not give themselves to their own husbands and wives but to adulterers, and therefore they pay their own particular penalty unceasingly.

And I saw other men and women covered in dust, and their faces were like blood, and they were in a pit of tar and brimstone, and they were running in a river of fire. And I asked: Who are these, sir? And he said to me: They are those who have committed the iniquity of Sodom and Gomorrah, men with men. Therefore they pay the penalty unceasingly.

40. And I looked and saw men and women clothed in bright clothing, whose eyes were blind, and they were set in a pit of fire; and I asked: Who are these, sir? And he said to me: They are the heathen who gave alms and did not know the Lord God; therefore they pay unceasingly their own particular penalty.

And I looked and saw other men and women on a fiery pyramid and wild animals were tearing them to pieces, and they were not allowed to say: Lord have mercy on us. And I saw the angel of punishments laying punishments most vigorously on them and saying: Acknowledge the judgment of the Son of God! For you were forewarned; when the divine Scriptures were read to you, you did not pay attention; therefore God's judgment is just; for your evil deeds laid hold on you and have led you into these punishments. But I sighed and wept; and I asked and said: Who are these men and women who are strangled in the fire and pay the penalty? And he answered me: They are the women who defiled what God had fashioned in that they gave birth to children from the womb and they are the men who went to bed with them. However their children appealed to the Lord God and the angels who are (set) over the punishments, saying: Defend us from our parents, for they have defiled what is fashioned by God; they have the name of God but they do not keep his commandments, and they gave us for food to dogs and to be trampled by pigs; and they threw others into the river. But those children were handed over to the angels of Tartarus, who were over the punishments, so that they should lead them into a spacious place of mercy. However their fathers and mothers were strangled in an everlasting punishment. And after this I saw men and women clothed in rags full of tar and sulphurous fire, and dragons were wound about their necks and shoulders and feet; and angels with fiery horns confined them and struck them and closed up their nostrils, saying to them: Why did you not know the time in which it was right for you to repent and to serve God, and did not do it? And I asked: Who are these, sir? And he said to me: They are those who seemed to renounce the world by wearing our raiment, but the tribulations of the world made them miserable so that they did not arrange a single Agape and had no compassion on the widows and the orphans; they did not take in the stranger and the pilgrim nor present a gift (oblation) nor show mercy to their neighbour. Not even for one day did their prayer go up pure unto the Lord God. But the many tribulations of the world held them back and they were not able to do right in the sight of God. And angels went round with them to the place of punishments. And those who were being punished saw them and said to them: We, while we were living in the world, neglected God; why have you done the same? And they led them to another place and these also spoke in the same way to them: We, while we were in the world, knew that we were sinners; we saw you in holy clothing and we called you happy and said, "These are the righteous and the servants of God." But now we have recognized that in vain were you called by the name of God; therefore you pay the perpetual penalty.

And I sighed and wept and said: Woe to men! woe to sinners! Why were you born? And the angel answered and said to me: Why are you weeping? Are you more compassionate than the Lord God, who is blessed for ever, who has appointed judgment and allowed every man to choose good or evil and act as he wishes? Again I wept even very vehemently, and he said to me: Are you weeping, when you have not yet seen the greater punishments? Follow me and you will see those that are seven times greater than these.

41. And he brought me to the north, to the place of all punishments, and he placed me above a well and I found it sealed with seven seals. And the angel who was with me answered and spoke to the angel of that place: Open the mouth of the well that Paul, God's dearly beloved, may look in, because power has been given him to see all the punishments of the underworld. And the angel said to me: Stand at a distance, for you will not be able to bear the stench of this place. Then when the well was opened there came up immediately a disagreeable and very evil smell which surpassed all the punishments. And I looked into the well and saw fiery masses burning on all sides, and the narrowness of the well at its mouth was such that it was only able to take a single man. And the angel answered and said to me: If some one is sent into this well of the abyss and it is sealed above him, reference is never made to him before the Father and the Son and the Holy Spirit and the holy angels. And I said: Who are these, sir, who are sent into this well? And he said to me: They are those who have not confessed that Christ came in the flesh and that the Virgin Mary bore him, and who say that the bread of the Eucharist and the cup of blessing are not the body and blood of Christ.

42. And I looked from the north towards the west and I saw there the worm that never rests, and in that place there was gnashing of teeth. Now the worm was a cubit in size and it had two heads. And I saw there men and women in the cold and gnashing of teeth. And I asked and said: Sir, who are these in this place? And he said to me: They are those who say that Christ has not risen from the dead and that this flesh does not rise. And I asked and said: Sir, is there neither fire nor heat in this place? And he said to me: In this place there is nothing other than cold and snow. And again he said to me: Even if the sun were to rise over them they would not become warm because of the excessive coldness of the place and the snow.

When I heard this, I stretched out my hands and wept and with a sigh I said again: It would be better for us if we who are all sinners had not been born.

43. However when those who were in this very place saw me weeping with the angel, they cried out and themselves wept, saying: O Lord God, have mercy on us! And after that I saw heaven opened and the archangel Michael coming down from heaven, and with him the whole host of angels, and they came to those who were placed in the punishments. And seeing him they cried out again with tears, and said: Have mercy on us, archangel Michael, have mercy on us and on the human race, for because of your prayers the earth continues. We have now seen the judgment and known the Son of God. It was impossible for us to pray for this previously before we came to this place. For we did hear that there was a judgment before we came forth from the world, but tribulations and a worldly-minded life did not allow us to repent. And Michael answered and said: Listen when Michael speaks: It is I who stand in the presence of God every hour. As the Lord lives, in whose presence I stand, for one day or one night I do not cease from praying continually for the human race, and I pray for those who are (still) on earth. They, however, do not stop committing iniquity and fornication and they do not help me in what is good while they are placed on earth. And the time during which you ought to have repented you used up in vanity. But I have always thus prayed and now I beseech that God may send dew and that rain may be appointed over the earth, and I continue to pray until the earth bring forth its fruit; and I say that if anyone has done even only a little good I will strive for him and protect him until he escapes the judgment of punishments. Where are your prayers? Where is your repentance? You have squandered time contemptibly. But now weep, and I will weep with you, and the angels who are with me together with the dearly beloved Paul, if perchance the merciful God will show mercy and give you ease. And when they heard these words they cried out and wept much and said all together: Have mercy on us, Son of God. And I, Paul, sighed and said: Lord God, Have mercy on what thou hast fashioned, have mercy on the children of men, have mercy on thine own image.

44. And I looked and I saw heaven move as a tree shaken by the wind. And they suddenly threw themselves on their faces before the throne; and I saw the 24 elders and the 4 beasts worshipping God, and I saw the altar and the veil and the throne, and all were rejoicing; and the smoke of a good odour rose up beside the altar of the throne of God, and I heard the voice of one who said: For what reason do you pray, angels and ministers of ours? And they cried out and said: We pray because we see thy great goodness to the race of men. And after that I saw the Son of God coming down from heaven, and a diadem was on his head. And when those who were placed in the punishments saw him, they all cried out together: Have mercy on us, Son of the most High God; it is thou who hast granted ease to all in heaven and on earth; have mercy likewise on us; for since we have seen thee, we have had ease. And a voice went forth from the Son of God throughout all the punishments, saying: What work have you done, that you ask me for ease? My blood was poured out for your sakes and even so you did not repent. For your sakes I bore the crown of thorns on my head; for you I was slapped on the cheeks, and even so you did not repent. Hanging on the cross I begged for water, and they gave me vinegar mingled with gall; with a spear they laid open my right side. For my name's sake they killed my servants, the prophets and the righteous, and in all these things I gave you the opportunity for repentance, and you were not willing. Now, however, for the sake of Michael, the archangel of my covenant, and the angels who are with him, and for the sake of Paul, my dearly beloved, whom I would not sadden, and for the sake of your brethren who are in the world and present offerings, and for the sake of your children, because my commandments are in them, and even more for my own goodness—on the very day on which I rose from the dead I grant to you all who are being punished a day and a night of ease for ever. And they all cried out and said: We bless Thee, Son of God, because thou hast granted to us ease for a day and a night. For one day's ease is better for us than all the time of our life which we were on earth: and if we had clearly known that this (place) was appointed for those who sin we would have done no other work at all, have practised nothing, and have committed no evil. What need was there for us to be born into the world? For here is our pride comprehended, which rose up out of our mouth against our neighbours. Discomfort and our exceptionally great anguish and tears and the worms which are under us, these are worse for us than the punishments which . . . us. When they said this, the wicked angels and those in charge of the punishments were angry with them and said: How long have you wept and sighed? For you have shown no mercy. This indeed is the judgment of God on him who has shown no mercy. However you have received this great grace—ease for the day and night of the Lord's day for the sake of Paul, the dearly beloved of God, who has come down to you.

45. And after this the angel said to me: Have you seen everything? And I said: Yes, sir. And he said to me: Follow me and I will lead you into paradise, and the righteous who are there will see you: for behold, they hope to see you and are ready to come to meet you with joy and exultation. Impelled by the Holy Spirit I followed the angel and he transferred (*lit.* 'set') me to (in) Paradise, and said to me: This is Paradise where Adam and his wife sinned. And I entered into Paradise and I saw the origin of the waters; and the angel beckoned to me and said to me: See, he said, the waters; for this is the river Pison which encircles the whole land of Evila, and this other is the Gihon which encircles the whole land of Egypt and Ethiopia, and this other is the Tigris which is opposite

Assyria, and this other is the Euphrates which waters the land of Mesopotamia. And going in further I saw a tree planted out of whose roots waters flowed, and the source of the four rivers was in it. And the Spirit of God rested over that tree and when the Spirit breathed the waters flowed. And I said: Sir, is it this tree itself which makes the waters flow? And he said to me: Because in the beginning before heaven and earth appeared everything was invisible, the Spirit of God hovered over the waters; but since the commandment of God brought to light heaven and earth, the Spirit rests over this tree. Therefore when the Spirit has breathed, the waters flow from the tree. And he took me by the hand and led me to the tree of the knowledge of good and evil and said: This is the tree through which death entered into the world, and Adam receiving from his wife ate of it and death came into the world. And he showed to me another tree in the middle of paradise, and he said to me: This is the tree of life.

46. While I still considered the wood (= the tree), I saw a virgin coming from a distance, and two hundred angels singing hymns before her. And I asked and said: Sir, who is this who comes in such great glory? And he said to me: This is the Virgin Mary, the Mother of the Lord. And when she had come near, she greeted me and said: Greetings, Paul, of God and angels and men dearly beloved. For all the saints have implored my son Jesus, who is my Lord, that you might come here in the body so that they might see you before you depart out of the world; and the Lord said to them: Wait and be patient. Just a short time and you will see him and he will be with you for ever. And again all together they said to him: Do not sadden us for we wish to see him while he is in the flesh; through him thy name has been greatly glorified in the world, and we have seen that he has taken on himself all the works both of little and great. From those who come here we inquire saying: Who is it who guided you in the world? And they answer us: There is a man in the world whose name is Paul; he in his preaching proclaims Christ, and we believe that because of the power and sweetness of his speech many have entered into the Kingdom. Behold, all the righteous are behind me coming to meet you. But I say to you, Paul, that I come first to meet those who have done the will of my Son and Lord Jesus Christ, I go first to meet them and I do not leave them to be as strangers until they meet my beloved Son in peace.

47. While she was still speaking I saw coming from a distance three very beautiful men, in appearance like Christ, with shining forms, and their angels; and I asked: Who are these, sir? And he said to me: Do you not know them? And I said: I do not, sir. And he answered: These are the fathers of the people, Abraham, Isaac and Jacob. And when they had come near to me they greeted me and said: Greetings, Paul, dearly beloved of God and men; blessed is he who endured violence for the sake of the Lord. And Abraham answered me and said: This is my son Isaac, and Jacob my dearly beloved. And we knew the Lord and followed him. Blessed are all those who believed your word, that they might inherit the kingdom of God through work, renunciation and holiness and humility and love and gentleness and right faith in the Lord. And we also have devoted ourselves to the Lord whom you preach, covenanting that we will assist and serve all the souls that believe in him, just as fathers serve their sons.

While they were still speaking I saw twelve others coming in honour from a distance, and I asked: Who are these, sir? And he said: These are the patriarchs. And they stepped up and greeted me and said: Greetings, Paul, dearly beloved of God and men. The Lord has not saddened us, so that we see you while you are still in the body before you leave the world. And in accordance with their order each of them gave me his name, from Reuben to Benjamin; and Joseph said to me: I am the one who was sold; and I tell you, Paul, that for all that my brothers did against me, I have not behaved in any way badly towards them, not even in all the labour that they laid on me, nor have I hurt them in any thing for that reason from morning until evening. Blessed is he who for the Lord's sake has been injured in something and has endured, for the Lord will repay him many times when he has come forth from the world.

48. While he was still speaking I saw another beautiful one coming from a distance and his angels were singing hymns, and I asked: Who is this, sir, who is beautiful of face? And he said to me: Do you not know him? And I said: No, sir. And he said to me: This is Moses the lawgiver, to whom God gave the law. And when he had come near me he immediately began to weep, and then he greeted me. And I said to him: Why are you weeping? for I have heard that you excel all men in meekness. And he answered and said: I weep over those whom with trouble I planted, because they have borne no fruit and none of them has made progress. And I saw that all the sheep whom I pastured were scattered and become as those who had no shepherd and that all the labours which I endured for the children of Israel were considered of no value and how many mighty deeds I had done among them and they had not understood; and I am amazed that aliens and uncircumcised and

319

idol-worshippers are converted and have entered into the promises of God, but Israel has not entered. And I tell you, brother Paul, that at that hour when the people hanged Jesus, whom you preach, that the Father, the God of all, who gave me the law, and Michael and all the angels and archangels and Abraham and Isaac and Jacob and all the righteous wept for the Son of God as he hung on the cross. And all the saints turned their attention to me at that time, looking at me and saying: See, Moses, what those of your people have done to the Son of God. Therefore you are blessed, Paul, and blessed is the generation and people who have believed your word.

49. While he was still speaking twelve others came, and when they saw me they said: Are you Paul, who are extolled in heaven and on earth? And I answered and said: Who are you? The first answered and said: I am Isaiah whose head Manasseh cut off with a wooden saw. And the second likewise said: I am Jeremiah who was stoned by the children of Israel and killed. And the third said: I am Ezekiel whom the children of Israel dragged by the feet over the rocks on the mountain until they dashed out my brains. And we bore all these trials because we wished to save the children of Israel. And I tell you that after the trials which they inflicted on me, I threw myself on my face before the Lord, praying for them, bending my knees until the second hour of the Lord's Day, until Michael came and lifted me up from the earth. Blessed are you, Paul, and blessed the people who have believed through you.

When these had passed on I saw another with a beautiful face and I asked: Who is this, sir? {When he had seen me he rejoiced}[a] And he said to me: This is Lot who was found righteous in Sodom. (When he had seen me he rejoiced), and coming up to me he greeted me and said: Blessed are you, Paul, and blessed the generation which you have served. And I answered and said to him: Are you Lot, who was found righteous in Sodom? And he said: I received angels into my house as strangers, and when the men of the city wished to violate them, I offered to them my two virgin daughters who had never known men, and gave to them saying: Use them as you wish, so long as you do nothing evil to these men; for this reason they have entered under the roof of my house. We ought therefore to have confidence and understand that whatever anyone has done God will repay it to him many times over

---

[a] The words in braces have been transposed to the beginning of the following sentence, where they appear in parentheses.

when they come to him. Blessed are you, Paul, and blessed the race which has believed your word.

When then he had ceased speaking to me I saw coming from a distance another man with a very beautiful face and he was smiling, and his angels were singing hymns; and I said to the angel who was with me: Does then each of the righteous have an angel as his companion?

And he said to me: Each of the saints has his own angel who helps him and sings a hymn, and the one does not leave the other. And I said: Who is this, sir? And he said: This is Job. And he approached and greeted me and said: Brother Paul, you have great honour with God and men. For I am Job who suffered much through thirty years from the suppuration of a wound. And at the beginning the sores that came out on (from) my body were like grains of wheat; on the third day, however, they became like an ass's foot; and the worms which fell were four fingers long. And the Devil appeared to me for the third time and said to me: Speak a word against the Lord and die. I said to him: If it is the will of God that I continue in affliction all the time I live until I die, I shall not cease to praise the Lord God and shall receive greater reward. For I know that the trials of this world are nothing in comparison to the consolation that comes afterwards. Therefore, Paul, you are blessed, and blessed is the race which has believed through your agency.

50. While he was still speaking another man came from a distance crying and saying: You are blessed, Paul, and I am blessed because I have seen you, the beloved of the Lord. And I asked the angel: Who is this, sir? And he answered and said to me: This is Noah from the time of the flood. And immediately we greeted one another. And with great joy he said to me: You are Paul, the dearly beloved of God. And I asked him: Who are you? And he said: I am Noah who lived in the time of the flood. And I tell you, Paul, that I spent a hundred years making the ark when I did not take off the shirt I wore nor cut the hair of my head. Moreover I strove after continence, not coming near my wife; and in those hundred years the hair of my head did not grow in length nor were my clothes dirty. And I implored the men of that time, saying: Repent, for a flood of water will come upon you. But they ridiculed me and mocked at my words. And again they said to me: This time is rather for those who can play and would sin as they please, for him to whom it is possible to commit fornication not a little; for God does not see and does not know what is done by us all, and a flood of water will certainly not come on this world. And they did not cease from their sins until God destroyed all flesh which had the spirit of life in itself. But know, God cares more for one righteous man than for a whole generation of the ungodly. Therefore you, Paul, are blessed, and blessed is the people who believed through your agency.

51. And I turned and saw other righteous men coming from a distance and I asked the angel: Who are these, sir? And he answered me: They are Elijah and Elisha. And they greeted me. And I said to them: Who are you? And one of them answered me and said: I am Elijah, the prophet of God. I am Elijah who prayed and because of my word heaven did not rain for three years and six months on account of the unrighteousness of men. God who does the will of his servants is righteous and true. For often the angels prayed the Lord for rain, and he said: Be patient until my servant Elijah prays and begs for this, and I will send rain on the earth. . . .

The suffering which each endures for God's sake, God will repay him twofold. Blessed are you, Paul, and blessed is the people who will believe through you. And as he was speaking another, Enoch, came and greeted me and said to me: The sufferings which a man endures for the sake of God, God does not afflict him when he leaves the world.

As he was speaking to me, behold, two others came up together and another was coming after them crying out to them: Wait for me, that I may come to see Paul the beloved of God; there will be deliverance for us (?) if we see him while he is still in the body. I said to the angel: My lord, who are these? He said to me: This is Zacharias and John his son. I said to the angel: And the other who runs after them? He said: This is Abel whom Cain killed. They greeted me and said to me: Blessed are you, Paul, you who are righteous in all your works. John said: I am he whose head they took off in prison for the sake of a woman who danced at a feast. Zacharias said: I am he whom they killed while I was presenting the offering to God; and when the angels came for the offering, they carried up my body to God, and no man found where my body was taken. Abel said: I am he whom Cain killed while I was presenting a sacrifice to God. The sufferings which we endured for the sake of God are nothing; what we have done for the sake of God we have forgotten. And the righteous and all the angels surrounded me, and they rejoiced with me [because] they had seen me in the flesh.

And I looked and saw another who surpassed them all, very beautiful. And I said to the angel: Who is this, my lord? He said to me: This is Adam, the father of you all. When he came up to me, he greeted me with joy. He said to me: Courage, Paul, beloved of God, you who have brought a multitude to faith in God and to repentance, as I myself have repented and received my praise from the Compassionate and Merciful One.

[Translator's note: M. R.] James considers it possible that the Apocalypse ended here. On the other hand a real conclusion is lacking. When C continues now with a fresh visit to the third heaven with many doublets, this is secondary. However perhaps the conclusion of C with the return of the Apostle to the circle of fellow-apostles on the Mount of Olives contains the original conclusion and would lead us to assume that the rapture also took place on the Mount of Olives. In what follows we give an abstract of C, with the conclusion, however, in a full translation.

Paul is caught up in a cloud into the third heaven. There he receives the command to reveal to no one the things which he will see. Nevertheless he tells about a seal and an altar with seven angels to its right and left. Many thousands of angels sing to the Father. When Paul falls prostrate the angel who accompanies him raises him up and promises to show him his place. He is now brought into Paradise with its shining inhabitants and its glorious thrones. At his request he is shown his own throne in a tabernacle of light; before it there are two singing angels who are presented as Uriel and Suriel. He is greeted by the inhabitants; the angel explains that these are the plants which Paul planted in the world. After further information from the angel he sees Paradise. Three concentric walls surround it, two of silver and in the middle between them one of gold. In the description of Paradise a remarkable feature is its trees which praise God three times daily, morning, noon and evening. The angel argues Paul out of the idea that he might not be worthy to dwell in Paradise: he will win the victory over the Accuser in the underworld (Amente). Moreover he will have great honour on his return to the world. And whenever the whole human race hears the words of this Apocalypse then it will repent and live. Paul then gets a sight of the clothes and crowns of his fellow-apostles on thrones, and yet once more meets David who is singing with his harp. After that he sees the place of the martyrs.

The angel of the Lord took me up and brought me to the Mount of Olives. There I, Paul, found the apostles gathered together. I greeted them and made known to them everything which had happened to me and what I had seen and the honours which would be for the righteous and the ruin and destruction which would be for the ungodly. Then the apostles were glad and rejoiced and blessed God, and they commanded us together, i.e. myself, Mark and Timothy, the disciples of Saint Paul(!)

the teacher of the Church, to put in writing this holy apocalypse for the benefit and help of those who will hear it. While the apostles were talking with us the Saviour Christ appeared to us out of the chariot of the cherubim, and he said to us: Greetings, my holy disciples, whom I have chosen out of the world! Greetings, Peter, crown of the apostles! Greetings, John, my beloved! Greetings to all (you) apostles! The peace of my good Father be with you. Then he turned to our father and said to him: Greetings, Paul, honoured letter writer! Greetings, Paul, mediator of the covenant! Greetings, Paul, roof and foundation of the Church! Are you convinced by the things which you have seen? Are you fully convinced by the things which you have heard? Paul answered: Yes, my Lord. Thy grace and thy love have accomplished for me a great good. The Saviour answered and said: O beloved of the Father, Amen, Amen, I tell you that the words of this apocalypse will be preached in the whole world for the benefit of those who shall hear it. Amen, Amen, I tell you, Paul, that whoever will take care of this apocalypse, and will write it and set it down as a testimony for the generations to come, to him I shall not show the underworld with its bitter weeping, until the second generation of his seed. And whoever reads it with faith, I shall bless him and his house. Whoever scoffs at the words of this apocalypse, I will punish him. And men are not to read therein except on the holy days because I have revealed the whole mystery of my deity to you, O my holy members. Behold, I have already made known everything to you. Now go and go forth and preach the Gospel of my kingdom because indeed your course and your holy contest has drawn near. But you yourself, Paul, my chosen one, will finish your (sing.) course with Peter, my beloved, on the fifth day of the month Epeph. You (sing.) will be in my kingdom for ever. My power will be with you.—And he immediately commanded the clouds to take up the disciples and lead them to the country which he had allotted to (each of) them. And they were to preach the Gospel of the kingdom of heaven in every place for ever because of the grace and love for man of our Lord Jesus Christ, our Saviour, to whom be glory and to his gracious Father and to the Holy Spirit for ever and ever. Amen.

[Translator's note:] After the words 'And the angels have often prayed that he would give them rain' at the break in ch. 51 the Syriac continues:

until I invoked him anew, and then he gave to them. But you are blessed, Paul, that your generation and all whom you teach are children of the kingdom. And understand, Paul, that everyone who believes through you is blessed and blessedness is preserved for him.—Then he parted from me. And when he had gone away from me the angel who was with me led me out and said with great seriousness: Paul, the mystery of this revelation has been given to you; as it pleases you, make it known and reveal it to men.—I Paul, however, came to myself and I knew and understood what I had seen and I wrote it in a roll. And while I lived, I did not have rest to reveal this mystery, but I wrote it (down) and deposited it under the wall of a house of that believer with whom I was in Tarsus, a city of Cilicia. And when I was released from this temporal life (and stood) before my Lord, he spoke thus to me: Paul, have I shown everything to you so that you should put it under the wall of a house? Rather send and reveal it for its sake so that men may read it and turn to the way of truth that they may not come into these bitter torments.

And thus this revelation was discovered.

Then the account of the discovery follows.

THE (GNOSTIC) APOCALYPSE OF PAUL (V, 2)

Commentary

One of the works contained in the Nag Hammadi library (see the introduction to the *[First] Apocalypse of James*) is the *Apocalypse of Paul*. To distinguish this work from the Greek work bearing the same name, the Nag Hammadi document will be referred to as the *(Gnostic) Apocalypse of Paul*. As is the case with the other Nag Hammadi writings, authorship of this work remains unknown. Attribution of authorship to Paul is clearly an example of pseudonymity. The place of composition of the work also cannot be determined. The date for the work has been suggested as the second century C.E.

This work is an example of an apocalypse containing an otherworldly journey. Paul is traveling to Jerusalem when, on the "mountain of Jericho," he meets a small child who converses with him. The child, also called the Holy Spirit, then becomes Paul's guide on his journeys through the heavens, beginning at the third heaven and traveling to the tenth heaven. No description is given of the third heaven. At the gate of the fourth heaven, Paul sees a soul being whipped and judged for its sins. In the fifth heaven, three angels are seen whipping souls and driving them on to judgment. The sixth heaven contains a "toll-collector," one of the powers guarding the heavens. Paul commands the gate to be opened so that they might pass, whereupon the toll-collector obeys.

The seventh heaven contains an old man seated on a throne that is described as seven times brighter than the sun. The old man threatens to keep Paul from ascending any further until, at the Spirit's urging, Paul gives him "the sign." The old man then allows Paul to proceed. Paul continues his ascent through the Ogdoad (the eighth heaven) and the ninth and tenth heavens. His ascent ends in the tenth heaven, where he greets his fellow spirits.

Significantly, the journey of Paul in the *(Gnostic) Apocalypse of Paul* begins at the third heaven. This journey is intended to take Paul beyond his experience of being "caught up to the third heaven," mentioned in 2 Corinthians 12:2-4. Heavenly ascents, such as this one, accompanied by descriptions of the various heavens, are found in several Jewish or Christian apocalypses (*2 Enoch*, the *Testament of Levi* 2–5, the *Apocalypse of Isaiah* 6–11, the *Apocalypse of Paul*). Likewise, the judgment and punishment of the souls in the fourth and fifth heavens is similar to scenes described in the *Testament of Abraham* 11–13. The mediator of this

326

revelation to Paul serves only as a guide and not as an interpreter of what Paul sees on his journeys.

The intriguing figure in the seventh heaven, the old man on the throne, is possibly the creator-god of Gnostic speculation. He is described as looking down at "his creation" (23.26-27). The depiction of the creator-god as evil coheres with Gnostic thought, in which the physical world is considered to be evil and therefore not created by the good god. The description of this individual as an old man seated on a throne has affinities with the enthroned "Ancient of Days" in Daniel 7 and the "Head of Days" in the "Similitudes of Enoch" (*1 Enoch* 37–71).

The *(Gnostic) Apocalypse of Paul* is concerned only with personal, not cosmic, eschatology. Its focus is on the judgment and punishment of sinful souls and the ascent of the righteous Paul to the tenth heaven. By possessing special knowledge, "the sign" (23.23-26), Paul is able to thwart the efforts of the evil powers to impede his progress and is able to reach his goal.

The text given here, taken from *The Nag Hammadi Library,* has been translated by George W. MacRae and William R. Murdock and edited by Douglas M. Parrott. Page and line divisions are indicated in the text. Page numbers are given in bold type. Double lines in the text indicate line divisions. Every fifth line (or occasionally more often) the double lines are replaced by a small number, indicating the line number.

The (Gnostic) Apocalypse of Paul (V 17, 19-24, 9

[The Apocalypse of] Paul

[. . .] **18**³ the road. And [he spoke to him], | saying, "[By which]⁵ road [shall I go] up to [Jerusalem]?" | The little child [replied, saying], | "Say your name, so that [I may show] | you the road." [The little child] | knew [who Paul was]. 10 He wished to make conversation with | him through his words [in order that] he | might find an excuse for speaking | with him.

The little child spoke, | saying, "I know 15 who you are, Paul. | You are he who was blessed from | his mother's womb. For I have [come] | to you that you may [go up to Jerusalem] | to your fellow [apostles. And] 20 for this reason [you were called. And] | I am the [Spirit who accompanies] | you. Let [your mind awaken, | Paul], with [. . .]. **19** For [. . .] | whole which [. . .] | among the [principalities and] these authorities [and] | archangels and powers 5 and the whole race of demons, | [. . .] the one that reveals | bodies to a soul-seed." |

And after he brought that speech | to an end, he spoke, saying [10] to me, "Let your mind awaken, | Paul, and see that this mountain | upon which you are standing is the mountain | of Jericho, so that you may know the | hidden things in those that are visible. [15] Now it is to the twelve apostles | that you shall go, | for they are elect spirits, and they will | greet you." He raised | his eyes and saw them [20] greeting him.

Then the | Holy [Spirit] who was speaking | with [him] caught him up | on high to the third | heaven, and he passed [25] beyond to the fourth [heaven]. | The [Holy] Spirit spoke to him, | saying, "Look | and see your [likeness] | upon the earth." And he [looked] [30] down and saw those [who were upon] | the earth. He stared [and saw] | those who were upon the [. . . . Then **20** he] gazed [down and] saw | the [twelve] apostles | [at] his right [and] at his left | in the creation; and the Spirit was [5] going before them.

But I saw | in the fourth heaven according to class—I | saw the angels resembling | gods, the angels bringing | a soul out of the land of [10] the dead. They placed it at the gate | of the fourth heaven. And | the angels were whipping it. | The soul spoke, saying, | "What sin was it that I committed [15] in the world?" | The toll-collector who dwells in the | fourth heaven replied, saying, | "It was not right to commit all those lawless deeds | that are in the world [20] of the dead." | The soul replied, saying, | "Bring witnesses! Let them [show] you | in what body I committed lawless deeds. | [Do you wish] to bring a book [25] [to read from]?"

And | the three witnesses came. | The first spoke, saying, | "Was I [not | in] the body the second hour [30] [. . .]? I rose up against you **21** until [you fell] into anger [and | rage] and envy." And | the second spoke, saying, | "Was I not [5] in the world? And I entered at | the fifth hour, and I saw you | and desired you. And behold, | then, now I charge you with the | murders you committed." [10] The third spoke, saying, | "Did I not come to you at | the twelfth hour of the day when | the sun was about to set? I gave you darkness | until you should accomplish your sins." [15] When the soul heard these things, | it gazed downward in | sorrow. And then it gazed | upward. It was cast down. | The soul that had been cast down [20] [went] to [a] body which had been prepared | [for it. And] behold | [its] witnesses were finished.

[Then I | gazed] upward and [saw | the] Spirit saying [to me], [25] "Paul, come! [Proceed | toward] me!" Then as I [went], | the gate opened, [and] | I went up to the fifth [heaven]. | And I saw my fellow apostles [30] [going with me] **22** while the Spirit accompanied us. | And I saw a great angel | in the fifth heaven holding | an iron rod in his [5] hand. There were three other angels with | him, and I stared into | their faces. But they were rivalling | each other, with whips | in their hands, goading the [10] souls on to the judgment. | But I went with the Spirit | and the gate opened for me. |

Then we went up to the sixth heaven. | And I saw my fellow apostles [15] going with me, and the Holy Spirit | was leading me before them. | And I gazed up on high and saw a | great light shining down | on the sixth heaven. I spoke, [20] saying to the toll-collector | who was in the sixth heaven, "[Open | to me and the [Holy] Spirit [who | is] before [me]." He opened [to me].

[Then | we went] up to the seventh [heaven [25] and I saw] an old man [. . .] | light [and | whose garment] was white. [His throne], | which is in the seventh heaven, | [was] brighter than the sun [30] by [seven] times. **23** The old man spoke, saying to [me], | "Where are you going, Paul, | O blessed one and the one who was | set apart from his mother's womb?" [5] But I looked at the Spirit, | and he was nodding his head, saying | to me, "Speak with him!" | And I replied, saying | to the old man, "I am going to the place [10] from which I came." And | the old man responded to me, "Where are you from?" | But I replied, saying, | "I am going down to the world of | the dead in order to lead captive [15] the captivity | that was led captive | in the captivity of Babylon." | The old man replied to me, | saying, "How will you be [20] able to get away from me? Look | and see the principalities and | authorities." [The] | Spirit spoke, saying, "Give him [the] | sign that you have, and [he will] [25] open for you." And then I gave [him] | the sign. He turned his face | downwards to his creation | and to those who are his own authorities. |

And then the [30] ⟨seventh⟩ heaven opened and we went up to [the] **24** Ogdoad. And I saw the | twelve apostles. They | greeted me, and we went | up to the ninth heaven. I [5] greeted all those who were in the | ninth heaven, and we went up | to the tenth heaven. And I | greeted my fellow spirits. |

The Apocalypse of Paul

CHAPTER SIX

RELATED WORKS

THE APOCALYPSE OF THOMAS

Commentary

Two versions exist of the work known as the *Apocalypse of Thomas.* The shorter work (which is given here) is generally recognized to be more original. Although the longer version probably originated in the fifth century (it contains references to historical events of the early fifth century), the shorter version is likely earlier than the fifth century. How much earlier is unknown. Its latest date is set by the discovery of a fifth-century Latin manuscript containing the shorter version. Its earliest date is limited by its use of New Testament writings, including the book of Revelation. The range of dates, then, is from the second to the beginning of the fifth centuries. The original language of the work possibly was Greek.

In spite of its title, the *Apocalypse of Thomas* does not fit the definition of an apocalypse. The work lacks a narrative framework and any description of the mediation of the revelation to Thomas. Thomas is mentioned only in the opening and closing sentences of the work, in which he is identified as the recipient of the words of "the Son of God the Father," "the father of all spirits," "the Saviour." He plays no further role in the work. The work perhaps should be classified as an oracle instead of an apocalypse.

Even though in form the *Apocalypse of Thomas* is not an apocalypse, it does contain elements found in many apocalyptic writings. Other-worldly beings, specifically angels, are prominent in the work. Heaven is seen as the dwelling place of God, the place from which eschatological punishments and destruction originate, and the ultimate destiny of the righteous. The eschatology of the work is apocalyptic, involving the destruction of the world and the removal of the transformed righteous to the heavens, where they will abide with God and the holy angels.

The *Apocalypse of Thomas* contains elements of both cosmic and personal eschatology. The cosmic eschatology involves the destruction of the earth by flood, earthquakes, and fire; disturbances of the sun, moon, and stars; and warfare in heaven among the angels. There is no renewal or transformation of the world after destruction. Rather, the location of God's rewards and blessings for the righteous will be the heavens.

The personal eschatology of the work involves the salvation of the righteous. On the sixth day, the spirits of the righteous dead will leave paradise and be reunited with their bodies, which have been "changed into the image and likeness and honour of the holy angels and into the power of the image" of God. They will rejoice with the angels and enjoy eternal life with God in heaven. On the eighth day, the elect, or righteous, who are still living will be saved from the destruction of the world (see 1 Thess. 4:13-18). The fate of the wicked is destruction. They will be destroyed along with the rest of the world.

In the *Apocalypse of Thomas*, the signs of the endtime are structured according to a seven-day pattern. Seven days of destruction will be followed by the eighth day, which will be a day of joy and peace. This sevenfold pattern is reminiscent of the sevenfold judgments (seven seals, seven trumpets, and seven bowls) of the book of Revelation. In fact, this sevenfold pattern is likely borrowed from Revelation, since the *Apocalypse of Thomas* shows evidence throughout of familiarity with and borrowing from Revelation. The author of the *Apocalypse of Thomas* has drawn heavily from other apocalyptic texts in the New Testament, also, including Mark 13, Luke 21, Matthew 24, 1 Thessalonians 4:13-18, and 2 Peter 3:7.

The translation of the text given here is by Aurelio de Santos Otero, contained in *New Testament Apocrypha*, volume 2.

The Apocalypse of Thomas

Hearken, Thomas, for I am the Son of God the Father and I am the father of all spirits. Hear from me the signs which will be at the end of this world, when the end of the world will be fulfilled before my elect come forth from the world.

I tell you openly what now is about to happen to men. When these are to take place the princes of the angels do not know, for they are now hidden from them. Then the kings will divide the world among themselves; there will be great hunger, great pestilences and much distress on the earth. The sons of men will be enslaved in every nation and will perish by the sword. There will be great disorder on earth.

331

Thereafter when the hour of the end draws near there will be great signs in the sky for seven days and the powers of the heavens will be set in motion. Then at the beginning of the third hour of the first day there will be a mighty and strong voice in the firmament of the heaven; a cloud of blood will go up from the north and there will follow it great rolls of thunder and powerful flashes of lightning and it will cover the whole heaven. Then it will rain blood on all the earth. These are the signs of the first day.

And on the second day a great voice will resound in the firmament of heaven and the earth will be moved from its place. The gates of heaven will be opened in the firmament of heaven from the east. The smoke of a great fire will burst forth through the gates of heaven and will cover the whole heaven as far as the west. In that day there will be fears and great terrors in the world. These are the signs of the second day.

And on the third day at about the third hour there will be a great voice in heaven and the depths of the earth will roar out from the four corners of the world. The pinnacles of the firmament of heaven will be laid open and all the air will be filled with pillars of smoke. An exceedingly evil stench of sulphur will last until the tenth hour. Men will say: We think the end is upon us so that we perish. These are the signs of the third day.

And at the first hour of the fourth day the Abyss will melt and rumble from the land of the east; then the whole earth will shake before the force of the earthquake. In that day the idols of the heathen will fall as well as all the buildings of the earth before the force of the earthquake. These are the signs of the fourth day.

But on the fifth day at the sixth hour suddenly there will be great thunderings in the heaven and the powers of the light (will flash) and the sphere of the sun will be burst and great darkness will be in the (whole) world as far as the west. The air will be sorrowful without sun and moon. The stars will cease their work. In that day all nations will so see as (if they were enclosed) in a sack, and they will despise the life of this world. These are the signs of the fifth day.

And at the fourth hour of the sixth day there will be a great voice in heaven. The firmament of heaven will be split from east to west and the angels of the heavens will look out on the earth through the rents in the heavens and all men who are on earth will see the angelic host looking out from heaven. Then all men will flee into the tombs and hide themselves from before the righteous angels, and say, "Oh that the earth would open and swallow us". For such things will happen as never happened since this world was created. Then they will see me as I come down from above in the light of my Father with the power and honour of the holy angels. Then at my arrival the restraint on the fire of paradise will be loosed, for paradise is enclosed with fire. And this is the eternal fire which devours the earthly globe and all the elements of the world. Then the spirits and souls of the saints will come forth from paradise and come into all the earth, and each go to its own body where it is laid up; and each of them will say, "Here my body is laid up". And when the great voice of those spirits is heard there will be an earthquake everywhere in the earth and by the force of that earthquake the mountains will be shattered above and the rocks beneath. Then each spirit will return to its own vessel and the bodies of the saints who sleep will rise. Then their bodies will be changed into the image and likeness and honour of the holy angels and into the power of the image of my holy Father. Then they will put on the garment of eternal life: the garment from the cloud of light which has never been seen in this world; for this cloud comes down from the upper kingdom of the heavens by the power of my Father, and will invest with its glory every spirit that has believed in me. Then they will be clothed and, as I said to you before, borne by the hands of the holy angels. Then they will be carried off in a cloud of light into the air, and rejoicing go with me into the heavens and remain in the light and honour of my Father. Then there will be great joy for them in the presence of my Father and in the presence of the holy angels. These are the signs of the sixth day.

And at the eighth hour of the seventh day there will be voices in the four corners of heaven. All the air will be set in motion and filled with holy angels. These will make war among themselves for the whole day. In that day the elect will be delivered by the holy angels from the destruction of the world. Then all men will see that the hour of their destruction is come near. These are the signs of the seventh day.

And when the seven days are finished, on the eighth day at the sixth hour there will be a gentle and pleasant voice in heaven from the east. Then that angel who has power over the holy angels will be made manifest. And there will go forth with him all the angels sitting on my holy Father's chariots of clouds, rejoicing and flying around in the air under heaven, to deliver the elect who believed in me; and they will rejoice that the destruction of the world has come.

The words of the Saviour to Thomas about the end of this world are finished.

SIBYLLINE ORACLES 2:34-55, 149-347

Commentary

In the ancient world, a Sibyl was an elderly woman who made ecstatic prophetic utterances, usually of a negative nature. (The origin of the word *Sibyl* is unknown. It perhaps was originally the proper name of a woman prophet.) Sibyls were famous in several locations, especially Erythrea and Marpessus in Asia Minor and Cumae in Italy. Several other ancient Sibyls were known, including Persian, Libyan, Hellespontian, Phrygian, Egyptian, Babylonian, and Hebrew. Written collections of the oracles of the Sibyls were made, the most famous collection of Sibylline oracles being the one at Rome, which was consulted during times of public misfortune or crisis.

Jewish and Christian writers adopted the Sibylline oracle form of writing and produced oracles. The Jewish-Christian collection of these works, known as the *Sibylline Oracles,* consists of twelve different books. Some of these are substantially Jewish works, some are original Christian compositions, and others are Jewish works that have been heavily reworked by Christian writers.

Books 1 and 2 of the *Sibylline Oracles* are really one work, not two. They are not divided in the ancient manuscripts. This work, by a Jewish writer, originally described the course of world history from creation to the end of the world. At some point in the history of the work, however, a Christian writer reworked this material, adding some Christian interpolations. The descriptions of the events of the eighth and ninth generations, which would have been contained in the original Jewish document, are missing from the Christian redaction. The portion of the material referred to as book 1 is free from Christian influence, aside from the interpolation at the end of the work describing the manifestation and life of Christ (1:324-400). Book 2, on the other hand, was more extensively redacted by a Christian writer. The amount of Christian redaction is uncertain because much of the writing is consistent with either a Jewish or a Christian perspective. Certain passages, however, are almost certainly Christian, including 2:45-55, 179-83, 190-92, 238-51, 263, 311-12. These passages either reflect Christian ideas or are dependent on other Christian writings.

The selection included here is from book 2, lines 34-55 and 149-347, which describe the events of the tenth and final generation of humanity. The endtime will be preceded by a series of signs, similar to those described in apocalyptic writings: infants who are elderly at the time of birth, famines, pestilence, wars, false prophets, the coming of Beliar (2:154-73). Prior to the end, the Jews will enjoy universal rule (2:174-76). Elijah, "the Thesbite," will appear as an eschatological prophet to give signs that the end is near (2:187-89). Then the earth, the firmament, and Hades will be consumed by a great river of fire (2:196-205). All the dead will be raised and will appear before God to be judged (2:214-51). All people will be forced to pass through a river of fire. The righteous will not be harmed by the flames, whereas the wicked will be tortured eternally. The punishments of the wicked in the underworld inferno are described at length. The damned will long for death and will plead with God for mercy, all to no avail. The righteous, meanwhile, will be lifted out of the fiery river and taken "to light and to life without care" (2:316) on a transformed earth. A special privilege is given to the righteous by God: they can intercede with God on behalf of individuals who are suffering punishment in the underworld, and God will release them from their punishment and give them eternal life in the Elysian plain (compare with the *Apocalypse of Paul* 43–44).

This work is not an apocalypse, but an oracle. Unlike an apocalypse, in which a revelation is mediated to the recipient by an otherworldly being, an oracle is direct speech by a divinely-inspired person. The work does, however, contain elements common to apocalyptic literature. The periodization of history, although a typical feature of other *Sibylline Oracles*, is also found in several apocalypses. The "Apocalypse of Weeks" (*1 Enoch* 93:1-10; 91:11-17) exhibits this characteristic of dividing history into periods. As in *Sibylline Oracles* 1–2, the "Apocalypse of Weeks" enumerates ten periods, called "weeks" in the latter work. *Sibylline Oracles* 2 shares with apocalyptic literature an interest in otherworldly places and otherworldly beings, as evidenced by its graphic depiction of the punishment of the wicked in the underworld by the angels of God (2:283-312).

This work contains both cosmic and personal eschatology. The world will be destroyed by fire, but the earth will then be transformed into a paradise-like dwelling for the righteous. The righteous will enjoy a glorious afterlife, while the wicked will suffer in eternal torment.

Similarities with eschatological ideas in other Jewish and Christian writings are noticeable in several places in *Sibylline Oracles* 2. The description of the signs of the end (2:154-73) resembles those in 4 Ezra 5:1-13; 6:21-28; 9:3-4; *2 Baruch* 27; and Mark 13 (and parallel passages in the other Gospels). The destruction of the world by fire (2:196-213), a common motif in the writings of the Persian religion of Zoroastrianism, is also found in *2 Baruch* 27:10 and 70:8; 2 Peter 3:10-12; Revelation 8:5, 7; and the *Apocalypse of Peter* 5. The falling of the stars to earth that accompanies the destruction by fire is reminiscent of events described in 4 Ezra 5:5; Mark 13:25 (and parallels); and Revelation 6:13 and 8:10.

One of the major elements in the eschatology of *Sibylline Oracles* 2 is the torment of the damned in the fiery underworld. This idea, hinted at in Isaiah 66:24, is common in Jewish apocalyptic writings (see *1 Enoch* 21:1-10; 54:1-6; 63:10; 90:24-27; *2 Bar.* 85:13; 4 Ezra 7:[36]) and is also popular in the New Testament (see Mark 9:43, 45, 48, and parallels; Matt. 3:12; 5:22; 13:42, 50; 25:41; Jude 7; Rev. 14:10; 19:20; 20:10, 14, 15; 21:8) and other Christian writings (particularly the *Apocalypse of Peter* 7-12 and the *Apocalypse of Paul* 31-42). The description of the various underworld torments is similar to the "tours of hell" found in several apocalyptic writings (such as the *Apocalypse of Peter* and the *Apocalypse of Paul*). The underworld tour is best known to the modern reader through Dante's *Inferno,* a further development of this same motif.

Although the underlying material in 2:34-55, 149-347 is Jewish, this selection is included as an example of a Christian work because in its present form it is Christian, having been thoroughly edited by a Christian redactor. Because of the importance given to Phrygia in the work (1:196-98; 261-62), it seems likely that the Jewish original of *Sibylline Oracles* 1–2 was composed in Phrygia. The date of its composition has been variously proposed as around the time of the birth of Christ or during the third century C.E. The earlier proposal is more plausible since in the description of historical events the writer fails to mention the destruction of Jerusalem in 70 C.E. (1:387-400 is likely a part of the Christian interpolation). The work gives no clues for determining the location where the Christian redaction of the work occurred. The reference to the destruction of Jerusalem in 1:387-400 places the Christian redaction no earlier than 70 C.E.; apparent familiarity with the book of Revelation would move the earliest date to the second century. Scholarly opinion, therefore, has placed the Christian redaction in the middle of the second century or during the third century.

The translation of the text given here is by John J. Collins from *The Old Testament Pseudepigrapha,* volume 1.

Book 2:34-55, 149-347

34 And then again God will perform a great sign,

35 for a star will shine like a resplendent crown,
resplendent, gleaming from the radiant heaven
for no small number of days. For then he will show
from heaven a crown to men who strive in contest.
Then again there will be a great contest for entry
40 to the heavenly city. It will be universal for all
men, holding the glory of immortality.
Then every people will strive for the immortal prizes
of most noble victory. For no one there can shamelessly
buy a crown for silver.
45 For holy Christ will make just awards to these
and crown the worthy. But to martyrs he will give
an immortal treasure, to those who pursue the contest even to
death.
He will give an imperishable prize from the treasure
to virgins who run well and to all men
50 who perform justice and to diverse nations
who live piously and acknowledge one God,
who love marriage and refrain from adultery.
He will give rich gifts and eternal hope to these also.
For every soul of mortals is a gracious gift of God
55 and it is not lawful for men to defile it with any grievous things.

149 This is the contest, these are the prizes, these the awards.
150 This is the gate of life and entry to immortality
which the heavenly God appointed as reward of victory
for most righteous men. But they, when they receive
the crown, will pass through this in glory.
But whenever this sign appears throughout the world,
155 children born with gray temples from birth,
afflictions of men, famines, pestilence, and wars,
change of times, lamentations, many tears;
alas, how many people's children in the countries will feed
on their parents, with piteous lamentations. They will place
160 their flesh in cloaks and bury them in the ground, mother of
peoples,
defiled with blood and dust. O very wretched
dread evildoers of the last generation,
infantile, who do not understand that when the species of females
does not give birth, the harvest of articulate men has come.

337

165 The gathering together is near when some deceivers,
in place of prophets, approach, speaking on earth.
Beliar also will come and will do many signs
for men. Then indeed there will be confusion of holy
chosen and faithful men, and there will be a plundering
170 of these and of the Hebrews. A terrible wrath will come upon them
when a people of ten tribes will come from the east
to seek the people, which the shoot of Assyria destroyed,
of their fellow Hebrews. Nations will perish after these things.
Later the faithful chosen Hebrews will rule over
175 exceedingly mighty men, having subjected them
as of old, since power will never fail.
The Most High, who oversees all, living in the sky,
will spread sleep over men, having closed their eyes.
O blessed servants, as many as the master, when he comes,
180 finds awake; for they have all stayed awake
all the time looking expectantly with sleepless eyes.
For he will come, at dawn, or evening, or midday.
He will certainly come, and it will be as I say.
It will come to pass for future generations, when from the starry
heaven
185 all the stars appear in midday to all,
with the two luminaries, as time presses on.
Then the Thesbite, driving a heavenly chariot at full stretch from
heaven, will come on earth and then display three signs
to the whole world, as life perishes.
190 Alas, for as many as are found bearing in the womb
on that day, for as many as suckle
infant children, for as many as dwell upon the wave;
alas, for as many as will see that day.
For a dark mist will cover the boundless world
195 east and west and south and north.
And then a great river of blazing fire
will flow from heaven, and will consume every place,
land and great ocean and gleaming sea,
lakes and rivers, springs and implacable Hades
200 and the heavenly vault. But the heavenly luminaries
will crash together, also into an utterly desolate form.
For all the stars will fall together from heaven on the sea.
All the souls of men will gnash their teeth,

338

burning in a river, and brimstone and a rush of fire
205 in a fiery plain, and ashes will cover all.
And then all the elements of the world will be bereft—
air, land, sea, light, vault of heaven, days, nights.
No longer will innumerable birds fly in the air.
Swimming creatures will no longer swim the sea at all.
210 No laden ship will voyage on the waves.
No guiding oxen will plow the soil.
No sound of trees under the winds. But at once all
will melt into one and separate into clear air.
Then the imperishable angels of immortal God,
215 Michael, Gabriel, Raphael, and Uriel,
who know what evils anyone did previously,
lead all the souls of men from the murky dark
to judgment, to the tribunal of the great
immortal God. For one alone is imperishable,
220 the universal ruler, himself, who will be judge of mortals.
Then the heavenly one will give souls and breath and
voice to the dead and bones fastened
with all kinds of joinings . . . flesh and sinews
and veins and skin about the flesh, and the former hairs.
225 Bodies of humans, made solid in heavenly manner,
breathing and set in motion, will be raised on a single day.
Then Uriel, the great angel, will break the gigantic bolts,
of unyielding and unbreakable steel, of the gates
of Hades, not forged of metal; he will throw them wide open
230 and will lead all the mournful forms to judgment,
especially those of ancient phantoms, Titans
and the Giants and such as the Flood destroyed.
Also those whom the wave of the sea destroyed in the oceans,
and as many as wild beasts and serpents and birds
235 devoured; all these he will call to the tribunal.
Again, those whom the flesh-devouring fire destroyed by flame,
these also he will gather and set at the tribunal of God.
When Sabaoth Adonai, who thunders on high, dissolves fate
and raises the dead, and takes his seat
240 on a heavenly throne, and establishes a great pillar,
Christ, imperishable himself, will come in glory on a cloud
toward the imperishable one with the blameless angels.

339

He will sit on the right of the Great One, judging at the tribunal
the life of pious men and the way of impious men.
245 Moses, the great friend of the Most High, also will come,
having put on flesh. Great Abraham himself will come,
Isaac and Jacob, Joshua, Daniel and Elijah,
Habbakuk and Jonah, and those whom the Hebrews killed.
He will destroy all the Hebrews after Jeremiah,
250 judged on the tribunal, so that they may receive and make
appropriate retribution for as much as anyone did in mortal life.
And then all will pass through the blazing river
and the unquenchable flame. All the righteous
will be saved, but the impious will then be destroyed
255 for all ages, as many as formerly did evil
or committed murders, and as many as are accomplices,
liars, and crafty thieves, and dread destroyers of houses,
parasites, and adulterers, who pour out slander,
terrible violent men, and lawless ones, and idol worshipers;
260 as many as abandoned the great immortal God
and became blasphemers and ravagers of the pious,
breakers of faith and murderers of the righteous men,
and as many elders and reverend deacons
as, by crafty and shameless duplicity regard . . .
265 judge with respect, dealing unjustly with others,
trusting in deceitful statements . . .
More destructive than leopards and wolves, and most wicked;
or as many as are very arrogant or are usurers,
who gather interest upon interest in their homes
270 and harm in each case orphans and widows,
or as many as give to widows and orphans
what derives from unjust deeds, and as many as make reproach
when they give from the fruit of their own labors; as many as
abandoned their parents in old age, not making return at all, not
providing
275 nourishment to their parents in turn. Also as many as disobeyed
or answered back an unruly word to their parents,
or as many as denied pledges they had taken, and
such servants as turned against their masters.
Again, those who defiled the flesh by licentiousness,

280 or as many as undid the girdle of virginity
by secret intercourse, as many as aborted
what they carried in the womb, as many as cast forth their
offspring unlawfully.
These and the sorcerers and sorceresses in addition to them
will the anger of the heavenly imperishable God
285 also bring near to the pillar, around which an undying
fiery river flows in a circle. All these at once
the angels of the immortal, everlasting God will
punish terribly from above with whips of flame,
having bound them around with fiery chains
290 and unbreakable bonds. Then, in the dead of night,
they will be thrown under many terrible infernal beasts
in Gehenna, where there is immeasurable darkness.
But when they have inflicted many punishments
on all whose heart was evil, then later
295 a fiery wheel from the great river will press them hard
all around, because they were concerned with wicked deeds.
Then they will wail here and there at a distance
in most piteous fate, fathers and infant children,
mothers and weeping children at the breast.
300 They will not have their fill of tears, nor will their voice
be heard as they lament piteously here and there,
but in distress they will shout at length
below dark, dank Tartarus. In places unholy
they will repay threefold what evil deed they committed,
305 burning in much fire. They will all gnash their teeth,
wasting away with thirst and raging violence.
They will call death fair, and it will evade them.
No longer will death or night give these rest.
Often they will request God, who rules on high in vain,
310 and then he will manifestly turn away his face from them.
For he gave seven days of ages to erring men
for repentance through the intercession of the holy virgin.
But as for the others, as many as were concerned with justice and
noble deeds,
and piety and most righteous thoughts,
315 angels will lift them through the blazing river
and bring them to light and to life without care,

341

in which is the immortal path of the great God
and three springs of wine, honey, and milk.
The earth will belong equally to all, undivided by walls
320 or fences. It will then bear more abundant fruits
spontaneously. Lives will be in common and wealth will have no
division.
For there will be no poor man there, no rich, and no tyrant,
no slave. Further, no one will be either great or small anymore.
No kings, no leaders. All will be on a par together.
325 No longer will anyone say at all "night has come" or "tomorrow"
or "it happened yesterday," or worry about many days.
No spring, no summer, no winter, no autumn,
no marriage, no death, no sales, no purchases,
no sunset, no sunrise. For he will make a long day.
330 To these pious ones imperishable God, the universal ruler, will
also give
another thing. Whenever they ask the imperishable God
to save men from the raging fire and deathless gnashing
he will grant it, and he will do this.
For he will pick them out again from the undying fire
335 and set them elsewhere and send them on account of his own
people
to another eternal life with the immortals
in the Elysian plain where he has the long waves
of the deep perennial Acherusian lake.
Alas for me, wretched one. What will become of me on that day
340 in return for what I sinned, ill-minded one,
busying myself about everything but caring neither for marriage
nor for reasons?
But also in my dwelling, which was that of a very wealthy man,
I shut out those in need; and formerly I committed lawless deeds
knowingly. But you, savior, rescue me, a brazen one,
345 from my scourges, though I have done shameless deeds.
I beseech you to give me a little rest from the refrain,
holy giver of manna, king of a great kingdom.

6 EZRA (2 ESDRAS 15–16)

Commentary

The material contained in chapters 15 and 16 of 2 Esdras is sometimes called 6 Ezra (see discussion on 4 Ezra). Although some scholars have argued that the work is a Jewish composition because of its lack of any specifically Christian elements, most scholars have concluded nonetheless that the author was a Christian. Echoes of New Testament passages scattered throughout 6 Ezra support this conclusion (compare 15:15 with Mark 13:8 and parallels; 15:35 with Rev. 14:20; 16:41-42 with 1 Cor. 7:29-31; 16:73 with 1 Peter 1:7). The most interesting similarity is the portrayal of certain enemies of God's people as a drunken harlot who has killed God's chosen people (15:46-56). The book of Revelation paints a similar picture, although even more graphic, of Rome (called "Babylon") as a great harlot, arrayed in jewels and fine clothing, "drunk with the blood of the saints and the blood of the martyrs of Jesus" (17:1-6; 14:8).

Dating the writing is difficult. On the basis of events mentioned in the text that seem to refer to historical events in the third century C.E., most scholars assign 6 Ezra to the latter half of the third century. The location of the writing is also uncertain. Because the countries mentioned are all located in the Middle East, some scholars have suggested that 6 Ezra originated somewhere in the eastern part of the Roman Empire.

This writing is not an apocalypse. It contains no visions or otherworldly mediators of revelation. In form, 6 Ezra is a collection of oracles delivered by the Lord to an unnamed recipient. The recipient, presumably Ezra, is commanded to proclaim this message to the people and then to preserve it in writing.

This work is included in this collection as a related writing because of the apocalyptic elements contained in its eschatology. The writer interprets events that will occur shortly (or are already taking place) as the beginning of the end. God will take appropriate action to punish the wicked—Babylon (Rome), Asia, Egypt, Syria—and preserve the righteous. Several stock elements of apocalyptic literature appear in 6 Ezra: animal symbolism; eschatological woes of poverty, famine, war, and pestilence; description of the final disasters as birth pangs; judgment on the world and its destruction; and persecution and eventual deliverance of the righteous. As in several other Jewish and Christian works, destruction of the world will occur by fire (16:15).

Persecution is a major concern in 6 Ezra and probably was a reality for

343

the Christian community known to the author. By means of this addition to 4 Ezra, the author attempted to bring hope and encouragement to the Christians who were being persecuted and to pronounce judgment on their persecutors. The word of the Lord to the faithful was, "Behold, the days of tribulation are at hand, and I will deliver you from them. Do not fear or doubt, for God is your guide" (16:74-75). Two aspects of the writer's message would add particular comfort to the righteous who suffer. First, God's punishment of the wicked is certain. Nothing will prevent its being accomplished. The mighty powers of the earth will be no match for the instruments of God's destruction (16:1-17). Second, the destruction of the wicked will occur soon, in "just a little while" (16:52). The faithful will not have to endure persecution and oppression much longer, for already the fire of God's judgment "is kindled, and shall not be put out until it consumes the foundations of the earth" (16:15).

Chapters 15 and 16 are not contained in any of the oriental manuscripts of 2 Esdras but are found in the Latin versions only. The text is taken from the Revised Standard Version of the Bible.

6 Ezra 15-16

15. The Lord says, "Behold, speak in the ears of my people the words of the prophecy which I will put in your mouth, ²and cause them to be written on paper; for they are trustworthy and true. ³Do not fear the plots against you, and do not be troubled by the unbelief of those who oppose you. ⁴For every unbeliever shall die in his unbelief."

⁵"Behold," says the Lord, "I bring evils upon the world, the sword and famine and death and destruction. ⁶For iniquity has spread throughout every land, and their harmful deeds have reached their limit. ⁷"Therefore," says the Lord, ⁸"I will be silent no longer concerning their ungodly deeds which they impiously commit, neither will I tolerate their wicked practices. Behold, innocent and righteous blood cries out to me, and the souls of the righteous cry out continually. ⁹I will surely avenge them," says the Lord, "and will receive to myself all the innocent blood from among them. ¹⁰Behold, my people is led like a flock to the slaughter; I will not allow them to live any longer in the land of Egypt, ¹¹but I will bring them out with a mighty hand and with an uplifted arm, and will smite Egypt with plagues, as before, and will destroy all its land."

¹²Let Egypt mourn, and its foundations, for the plague of chastisement and punishment that the Lord will bring upon it. ¹³Let the

farmers that till the ground mourn, because their seed shall fail and their trees shall be ruined by blight and hail and by a terrible tempest. [14]Alas for the world and for those who live in it! [15]For the sword and misery draw near them, and nation shall rise up to fight against nation, with swords in their hands. [16]For there shall be unrest among men; growing strong against one another, they shall in their might have no respect for their king or the chief of their leaders. [17]For a man will desire to go into a city, and shall not be able. [18]For because of their pride the cities shall be in confusion, the houses shall be destroyed, and people shall be afraid. [19]A man shall have no pity upon his neighbors, but shall make an assault upon their houses with the sword, and plunder their goods, because of hunger for bread and because of great tribulation.

[20]"Behold," says God, "I call together all the kings of the earth to fear me, from the rising sun and from the south, from the east and from Lebanon; to turn and repay what they have given them. [21]Just as they have done to my elect until this day, so I will do, and will repay into their bosom." Thus says the Lord God: [22]"My right hand will not spare the sinners, and my sword will not cease from those who shed innocent blood on the earth." [23]And a fire will go forth from his wrath, and will consume the foundations of the earth, and the sinners, like straw that is kindled. [24]"Woe to those who sin and do not observe my commandments," says the Lord; [25]"I will not spare them. Depart, you faithless children! Do not pollute my sanctuary." [26]For the Lord knows all who transgress against him; therefore he will hand them over to death and slaughter. [27]For now calamities have come upon the whole earth, and you shall remain in them; for God will not deliver you, because you have sinned against him.

[28]Behold, a terrifying sight, appearing from the east! [29]The nations of the dragons of Arabia shall come out with many chariots, and from the day that they set out, their hissing shall spread over the earth, so that all who hear them fear and tremble. [30]Also the Carmonians, raging in wrath, shall go forth like wild boars of the forest, and with great power they shall come, and engage them in battle, and shall devastate a portion of the land of the Assyrians with their teeth. [31]And then the dragons, remembering their origin, shall become still stronger; and if they combine in great power and turn to pursue them, [32]then these shall be disorganized and silenced by their power, and shall turn and flee. [33]And from the land of the Assyrians an enemy in ambush shall beset them and destroy one of them, and fear and trembling shall come upon their army, and indecision upon their kings.

³⁴Behold, clouds from the east, and from the north to the south; and their appearance is very threatening, full of wrath and storm. ³⁵They shall dash against one another and shall pour out a heavy tempest upon the earth, and their own tempest; and there shall be blood from the sword as high as a horse's belly ³⁶and a man's thigh and a camel's hock. ³⁷And there shall be fear and great trembling upon the earth; and those who see that wrath shall be horror-stricken, and they shall be seized with trembling. ³⁸And, after that, heavy storm clouds shall be stirred up from the south, and from the north, and another part from the west. ³⁹And the winds from the east shall prevail over the cloud that was raised in wrath, and shall dispel it; and the tempest that was to cause destruction by the east wind shall be driven violently toward the south and west. ⁴⁰And great and mighty clouds, full of wrath and tempest, shall rise, to destroy all the earth and its inhabitants, and shall pour out upon every high and lofty place a terrible tempest, ⁴¹fire and hail and flying swords and floods of water, that all the fields and all the streams may be filled with the abundance of those waters. ⁴²And they shall destroy cities and walls, mountains and hills, trees of the forests, and grass of the meadows, and their grain. ⁴³And they shall go on steadily to Babylon, and shall destroy her. ⁴⁴They shall come to her and surround her; they shall pour out the tempest and all its wrath upon her; then the dust and smoke shall go up to heaven, and all who are about her shall wail over her. ⁴⁵And those who survive shall serve those who have destroyed her.

⁴⁶And you, Asia, who share in the glamour of Babylon and the glory of her person— ⁴⁷woe to you, miserable wretch! For you have made yourself like her; you have decked out your daughters in harlotry to please and glory in your lovers, who have always lusted after you. ⁴⁸You have imitated that hateful harlot in all her deeds and devices; therefore God says, ⁴⁹"I will send evils upon you, widowhood, poverty, famine, sword, and pestilence, to lay waste your houses and bring you to destruction and death. ⁵⁰And the glory of your power shall wither like a flower, when the heat rises that is sent upon you. ⁵¹You shall be weakened like a wretched woman who is beaten and wounded, so that you cannot receive your mighty lovers. ⁵²Would I have dealt with you so violently," says the Lord, ⁵³"if you had not always killed my chosen people, exulting and clapping your hands and talking about their death when you were drunk? ⁵⁴Trick out the beauty of your face! ⁵⁵The reward of a harlot is in your bosom, therefore you shall receive your recompense. ⁵⁶As you will do to my chosen people," says the Lord, "so God will do to you, and will hand you over to adversities. ⁵⁷Your children

shall die of hunger, and you shall fall by the sword, and your cities shall be wiped out, and all your people who are in the open country shall fall by the sword. [58]And those who are in the mountains and highlands shall perish of hunger, and they shall eat their own flesh in hunger for bread and drink their own blood in thirst for water. [59]Unhappy above all others, you shall come and suffer fresh afflictions. [60]And as they pass they shall wreck the hateful city, and shall destroy a part of your land and abolish a portion of your glory, as they return from devastated Babylon. [61]And you shall be broken down by them like stubble, and they shall be like fire to you. [62]And they shall devour you and your cities, your land and your mountains; they shall burn with fire all your forests and your fruitful trees. [63]They shall carry your children away captive, and shall plunder your wealth, and abolish the glory of your countenance."

16. Woe to you, Babylon and Asia! Woe to you, Egypt and Syria! [2]Gird yourselves with sackcloth and haircloth, and wail for your children, and lament for them; for your destruction is at hand. [3]The sword has been sent upon you, and who is there to turn it back? [4]A fire has been sent upon you, and who is there to quench it? [5]Calamities have been sent upon you, and who is there to drive them away? [6]Can one drive off a hungry lion in the forest, or quench a fire in the stubble, when once it has begun to burn? [7]Can one turn back an arrow shot by a strong archer? [8]The Lord God sends calamities, and who will drive them away? [9]Fire will go forth from his wrath, and who is there to quench it? [10]He will flash lightning, and who will not be afraid? He will thunder, and who will not be terrified? [11]The Lord will threaten, and who will not be utterly shattered at his presence? [12]The earth and its foundations quake, the sea is churned up from the depths, and its waves and the fish also shall be troubled at the presence of the Lord and before the glory of his power. [13]For his right hand that bends the bow is strong, and his arrows that he shoots are sharp and will not miss when they begin to be shot to the ends of the world. [14]Behold, calamities are sent forth and shall not return until they come over the earth. [15]The fire is kindled, and shall not be put out until it consumes the foundations of the earth. [16]Just as an arrow shot by a mighty archer does not return, so the calamities that are sent upon the earth shall not return. [17]Alas for me! Alas for me! Who will deliver me in those days?

[18]The beginning of sorrows, when there shall be much lamentation; the beginning of famine, when many shall perish; the beginning of wars, when the powers shall be terrified; the beginning of calamities, when all

shall tremble. What shall they do in these circumstances, when the calamities come? [19]Behold, famine and plague, tribulation and anguish are sent as scourges for the correction of men. [20]Yet for all this they will not turn from their iniquities, nor be always mindful of the scourges. [21]Behold, provisions will be so cheap upon earth that men will imagine that peace is assured for them, and then the calamities shall spring up on the earth—the sword, famine, and great confusion. [22]For many of those who live on the earth shall perish by famine; and those who survive the famine shall die by the sword. [23]And the dead shall be cast out like dung, and there shall be no one to console them; for the earth shall be left desolate, and its cities shall be demolished. [24]No one shall be left to cultivate the earth or to sow it. [25]The trees shall bear fruit, and who will gather it? [26]The grapes shall ripen, and who will tread them? For in all places there shall be great solitude; [27]one man will long to see another, or even to hear his voice. [28]For out of a city, ten shall be left; and out of the field, two who have hidden themselves in thick groves and clefts in the rocks. [29]As in an olive orchard three or four olives may be left on every tree, [30]or as when a vineyard is gathered some clusters may be left by those who search carefully through the vineyard, [31]so in those days three or four shall be left by those who search their houses with the sword. [32]And the earth shall be left desolate, and its fields shall be for briers, and its roads and all its paths shall bring forth thorns, because no sheep will go along them. [33]Virgins shall mourn because they have no bridegrooms; women shall mourn because they have no husbands; their daughters shall mourn, because they have no helpers. [34]Their bridegrooms shall be killed in war, and their husbands shall perish of famine.

[35]Listen now to these things, and understand them, O servants of the Lord. [36]Behold the word of the Lord, receive it; do not disbelieve what the Lord says. [37]Behold, the calamities draw near, and are not delayed. [38]Just as a woman with child, in the ninth month, when the time of her delivery draws near, has great pains about her womb for two or three hours beforehand, and when the child comes forth from the womb, there will not be a moment's delay, [39]so the calamities will not delay in coming forth upon the earth, and the world will groan, and pains will seize it on every side.

[40]"Hear my words, O my people; prepare for battle, and in the midst of the calamities be like strangers on the earth. [41]Let him that sells be like one who will flee; let him that buys be like one who will lose; [42]let him that does business be like one who will not make a profit; and let him that

builds a house be like one who will not live in it; ⁴³let him that sows be like one who will not reap; so also him that prunes the vines, like one who will not gather the grapes; ⁴⁴them that marry, like those who will have no children; and them that do not marry, like those who are widowed. ⁴⁵Because those who labor, labor in vain; ⁴⁶for strangers shall gather their fruits, and plunder their goods, and overthrow their houses, and take their children captive; for in captivity and famine they will beget their children. ⁴⁷Those who conduct business, do it only to be plundered; the more they adorn their cities, their houses and possessions, and their persons, ⁴⁸the more angry I will be with them for their sins," says the Lord. ⁴⁹Just as a respectable and virtuous woman abhors a harlot, ⁵⁰so righteousness shall abhor iniquity, when she decks herself out, and shall accuse her to her face, when he comes who will defend him who searches out every sin on earth.

⁵¹Therefore do not be like her or her works. ⁵²For behold, just a little while, and iniquity will be removed from the earth, and righteousness will reign over us. ⁵³Let no sinner say that he has not sinned; for God will burn coals of fire on the head of him who says, "I have not sinned before God and his glory." ⁵⁴Behold, the Lord knows all the works of men, their imaginations and their thoughts and their hearts. ⁵⁵He said, "Let the earth be made," and it was made; "Let the heaven be made," and it was made. ⁵⁶At his word the stars were fixed, and he knows the number of the stars. ⁵⁷It is he who searches the deep and its treasures, who has measured the sea and its contents; ⁵⁸who has enclosed the sea in the midst of the waters, and by his word has suspended the earth over the water; ⁵⁹who has spread out the heaven like an arch, and founded it upon the waters; ⁶⁰who has put springs of water in the desert, and pools on the tops of the mountains, to send rivers from the heights to water the earth; ⁶¹who formed man, and put a heart in the midst of his body, and gave him breath and life and understanding ⁶²and the spirit of Almighty God; who made all things and searches out hidden things in hidden places. ⁶³Surely he knows your imaginations and what you think in your hearts! Woe to those who sin and want to hide their sins! ⁶⁴Because the Lord will strictly examine all their works, and will make a public spectacle of all of you. ⁶⁵And when your sins come out before men, you shall be put to shame; and your own iniquities shall stand as your accusers in that day. ⁶⁶What will you do? Or how will you hide your sins before God and his angels? ⁶⁷Behold, God is the judge, fear him! Cease from your sins, and forget your iniquities, never to commit them again; so God will lead you forth and deliver you from all tribulation.

[68]For behold, the burning wrath of a great multitude is kindled over you, and they shall carry off some of you and shall feed you what was sacrificed to idols. [69]And those who consent to eat shall be held in derision and contempt, and be trodden under foot. [70]For in many places and in neighboring cities there shall be a great insurrection against those who fear the Lord. [71]They shall be like mad men, sparing no one, but plundering and destroying those who continue to fear the Lord. [72]For they shall destroy and plunder their goods, and drive them out of their houses. [73]Then the tested quality of my elect shall be manifest, as gold that is tested by fire.

[74]"Hear, my elect," says the Lord. "Behold, the days of tribulation are at hand, and I will deliver you from them. [75]Do not fear or doubt, for God is your guide. [76]You who keep my commandments and precepts," says the Lord God, "do not let your sins pull you down, or your iniquities prevail over you." [77]Woe to those who are choked by their sins and overwhelmed by their iniquities, as a field is choked with underbrush and its path overwhelmed with thorns, so that no one can pass through! [78]It is shut off and given up to be consumed by fire.

BIBLIOGRAPHY

The following works are suggested for further study of apocalyptic literature:

TEXTS (WITH INTRODUCTIONS)

Charles, R. H., ed. *The Apocrypha and Pseudepigrapha of the Old Testament*. 2 vols. Oxford: Clarendon, 1913.

Charlesworth, James H., ed. *The Old Testament Pseudepigrapha*. 2 vols. Garden City, NY: Doubleday & Co., 1983, 1985.

Robinson, James M., ed. *The Nag Hammadi Library*. 3d rev. ed. San Francisco: Harper & Row, 1988.

Schneemelcher, Wilhelm and Edgar Hennecke, eds. *New Testament Apocrypha*, vol. 2. English translation edited by R. McL. Wilson. Philadelphia: Westminster, 1966.

Sparks, H. F. D., ed. *The Apocryphal Old Testament*. Oxford: Clarendon, 1984.

Vermes, Geza. *The Dead Scrolls in English*. 3d ed. Harmondsworth, England: 1987.

STUDIES

Collins, Adela Yarbro, ed. *Early Christian Apocalypticism: Genre and Social Setting*. *Semeia* 36 Missoula, MT: Scholars Press, 1986.

Collins, John J. *The Apocalyptic Imagination: An Introduction to the Jewish Matrix of Christianity*. New York: Crossroad, 1984.

——, ed. *Apocalypse: The Morphology of a Genre*. *Semeia* 14. Missoula, MT: Scholars Press, 1979.

Hanson, Paul D. *The Dawn of Apocalyptic: The Historical and Sociological Roots of Jewish Apocalyptic Eschatology*. Rev. ed. Philadelphia: Fortress, 1979.

Hanson, Paul D., *Old Testament Apocalyptic*. Interpreting Biblical Texts. Nashville: Abingdon Press, 1987.

————, ed. *Visionaries and Their Apocalypses*. Issues in Religion and Theology 4. Philadelphia: Fortress Press, 1983; London: SPCK, 1983.

Hellholm, David, ed. *Apocalypticism in the Mediterranean World and the Near East*. Tübingen: J. C. B. Mohr (Paul Siebeck), 1983.

Himmelfarb, Martha. *Tours of Hell: An Apocalyptic Form in Jewish and Christian Literature*. Philadelphia: Fortress, 1983.

Koch, Klaus. *The Rediscovery of Apocalyptic*. London: SCM, 1972.

Minear, Paul S. *New Testament Apocalyptic*. Interpreting Biblical Texts. Nashville: Abingdon Press, 1981.

Nickelsburg, George W. E. *Jewish Literature Between the Bible and the Mishnah: A Historical and Literary Introduction*. Philadelphia: Fortress, 1981.

Rowland, Christopher. *The Open Heaven: A Study of Apocalyptic in Judaism and Early Christianity*. New York: Crossroad, 1982.

Rowley, H.H. *The Relevance of Apocalyptic*. New and rev. ed., 1963. Reprint. Greenwood, S.C.: Attic, 1980.

Russell, D. S. *The Method and Message of Jewish Apocalyptic*. Old Testament Library. Philadelphia: Westminster, 1964.

Schmithals, Walter. *The Apocalyptic Movement*. Translated by John E. Steely. Nashville: Abingdon Press, 1975.

Schürer, Emil. *The History of the Jewish People in the Age of Jesus Christ (175 B.C.–A.D. 135)*. Vol. 3 in 2 parts. English version revised and edited by Geza Vermes, Fergus Millar, and Martin Goodman. Edinburgh: T. & T. Clark, 1986 (Part 1), 1987 (Part 2).

Stone, Michael E., ed. *Jewish Writings of the Second Temple Period: Apocrypha, Pseudepigrapha, Qumran Sectarian Writings, Philo, Josephus. Compendia Rerum Iudaicarum ad Novum Testamentum*. Section Two: *The Literature of the Jewish People in the Period of the Second Temple and the Talmud*, vol. 2. Assen, the Netherlands: Van Gorcum, 1984; Philadelphia: Fortress, 1984.